_£2 99_

REVELATIONS OF A MELCHIZEDEK INITIATE

Dr. Joshua David Stone

THE EASY-TO-READ ENCYCLOPEDIA of the SPIRITUAL PATH
✦ Volume XI ✦

D1556368

Published by
Light Technology Publishing

Cover design by
Fay Richards

ISBN 1-891824-10-4

Published by
Light Technology Publishing
P.O. Box 1526
Sedona, AZ 86339
(800) 450-0985

Printed by

MI☏ION
PO☏IBLE
COMMERCIAL
PRINTING
P.O. Box 1495
Sedona, AZ 86339

Dedication

This book is dedicated to his holiness Lord Melchizedek, the Universal Logos in whose glorious radiance we all live and move and have our being. This book is also dedicated to the Order of Melchizedek. It is the destiny of every being on this planet to become fully realized Melchizedeks and priests and priestesses in this order whether conscious of it or not. This order is the essence and glue that unites all religions, all spiritual paths and all mystery schools.

This book is also dedicated to all of you, my fellow Melchizedeks, for in truth we are and have always been of the same universal family. It is my sincere hope and prayer that the story of my Melchizedek journey sheds greater light on the process of Melchizedek realization for each of you, my beloved readers. Welcome home to your true spiritual heritage, which permeates this entire universe. We are all brother and sister Melchizedeks at different stages of realizing this noble and blessed ideal. This book is dedicated to this wonderful being, this order, this family and this aim for every beloved brother and sister on this planet.

Foreword

This spiritual autobiography begins a couple of days prior to achieving my ascension and continues through the completion of my ascension levels, sharing my dreams, meditations, conversations with the masters, spiritual background, thoughts and reflections and actual ascension experiences. It traces my journey through the seven levels of initiation, through the process of anchoring and activating my fifty chakras, 99 percent light quotient, then on to anchoring and fully activating all twelve bodies, which include the five higher bodies. Detailed information is given on the workings of the inner-plane ashram under the guidance of Djwhal Khul, Lord Maitreya and Lord Melchizedek. I unfold the process of my initiations, beginning at the sixth, moving through the equivalent of the tenth initiation and into the beginning of the twelfth. This book was written as a personal log, which reveals some uncharted experiences.

Everything written in these pages is true. Much occurred on the inner planes and some experiences were actual, physical events. In truth, the inner and outer planes are reflective of the same reality, which is God. To my newly awakening readers, understand that the only difference between the physical and spiritual worlds are their varying degrees of vibrational frequencies. Matter vibrates more slowly than the energies of the various inner-plane regions. Therefore, the difference between what occurred physically and what occurred spiritually is simply the difference between rates of frequencies. If you do not already know this, I guarantee that your own spiritual path will reveal this truth to you.

The book you are about to read is faithful to its title. The pages unfold a series of revelations, each growing more and more profound as I logged my personal process of initiation. I was aided to take my initiations at an accelerated pace due in great part to the support from and interaction with a group body. It is my intent through this book to create a type of inner-plane group body with all of you, and by sharing my experiences help you accelerate your own personal path to Source.

In one sense, we each travel alone through the portal of initiation, and it is up to each of us to do the required work and maintain the level of purity necessary to become ascended masters. The responsibility rests upon each of us. On the other hand, we all in truth form one group body within the body of God. This is the ultimate paradox: We each are responsible for our own initiatory process, yet we each are linked together in the oneness that is God. In that sense we are indeed our brothers' and sisters' keepers, eternally linked in our great pilgrimage back to the Godhead.

It is in that spirit that I share my journey and revelations with you. Each one of you is part of me as I am part of you, for we are all part of God. I therefore ask that you sit back, buckle your seat belts and take with me the journey I have recorded on these pages.

Part of my joy is in sharing these revelations. I welcome you, my beloved readers, into the unfoldment of my revelation, with the heartfelt prayer that I may light your candle with the light that has graced my own and that you light your brother's and sisters' candles with the light of your own candle. The personal experiences and individual revelations of each of us serve to add more luster and brilliance to our candles.

Let us each pass the light one unto the other until our world itself is transformed into a star of light. We may then say in unison with the Christ, "It is finished. Father, into Thy hands I commend my spirit." Like the risen Christ, we will then continue to move forward into our cosmic evolution, having completed our planetary evolution, thereby transforming Earth herself.

It is both my privilege and humble honor to share with you this, my ascension story: *Revelations of a Melchizedek Initiate.*

Contents

Introduction by Melchizedek, the Universal Logos

I step forward to greet you with love. The love I give is all-embracing, for you are, one and all, part of my very being in a most unique manner. I make myself known via the channeling process, speaking in a vibration that steps down into words of holy communion.

I wish for you to know me as your very self. In holding the position of Universal Logos, know that I at once hold you all within myself as part of myself, yet span a cosmic vastness that you at your stage of evolution could not possibly comprehend. Yet within this great vastness do I embrace you, my children divine, and take voice to activate our holy communion and make myself ever available to you all.

This book you are about to read bears the title *Revelations of a Melchizedek Initiate*. Know that it is the story of one who awakens within me, and that you too are all Melchizedeks, for it is of me that you are made. You too are in the likeness of God the Absolute, unfathomable and unknowable. The universe is so vast and incomprehensible, yet it is able to be revealed by the process of stepping down into the human mind from that which exists on the higher and vaster realms. The basic axiom, "as above, so below," makes simple an otherwise complex task. In that vein shall I speak with you.

As this is the introduction of a book whose title bears my name, I wish to restate why it is so. It is so because the author, even as all of you, evolves, grows, initiates, expands and ascends within the specific vibrational tone and frequencies of who I Am. As it is literally my divine and cosmic job to oversee and embody this particular universe, so all of you bear the stamp of this particular matrix, whose purpose within which you unfold. Thus it is that the evolution of one within this universe could be nothing other than the revelation of a Melchizedek, as that is the order that pervades this universe. The love I hold for you all, my dear and blessed children, is a love so deep and refined and all-encompassing that words fail. Words must always fail, for the level of love and light with which I embrace you must be known through direct contact, through meditation, through expansion, in ever-upgraded and heightened degrees.

To say it is like unto the love that a father/mother has for the child is barely to touch the hem of the garment of this love. Know ye, I am love itself. I am the ultimate of self-love embracing and nurturing itself.

One of my more human aspects (if that term could be loosely applied for purposes of this discourse) is to be like a father to you. I nurture you, my child-selves and feed you with the love and light of my being. I am in reality self feeding self. As one who has expanded and expanded through eons of time, I have the honor to hold the office of Universal Logos and to hold you and all forms of consciousness within the sphere of my self. Some have likened me to president of the local universe, but I prefer the title of father. "Father" connotes abundant love, sacrifice, strength; one to be counted on (I might add that earthly fathers would do well to contemplate their divine heritage and ponder the fulfilling of their roles), the breadwinner, the source of what is brought into the home.

I am this while also being a balance of feminine and masculine energies alike. From my seed came ye forth and from my efforts and my sacrifice, which is a joyful song, do I hold the position of Universal Logos. I do not merely leaven the bread, but I am the bread upon your tables even as I am ye who eat of the bread and the substance of the table itself. All within my sphere holds and carries my divine imprint and my seed, which you too in your group and cosmic monads will one day carry beyond the ring-pass-not of this universe.

Although equally balanced in the masculine and feminine, I am Father and work with divine Mother. There is a purpose to the dividing of the yin and yang, even as there is purpose to the unifying of these aspects. There are cosmic divine puzzle pieces even as there are earthly, planetary, solar and so forth, up through all graded ranks of development.

Do not be discontented with your puzzle pieces, my children. The vast universe itself functions in a unity-in-diversity format and takes joy in doing so. As all is one, ever was one and ever shall be so, what matters most is that you express that oneness in the greatest and fullest aspect possible. Play your puzzle piece to the hilt, but do not seek to be all puzzle pieces. Thus you may know me and my puzzle piece divine and take sustenance and comfort in the divine Father role I hold in the universe. Take the same but slightly different comfort in the divine Mother aspect of the universe. We are who we are, and seek to be known for who we are, with no division, but simply recognition of the varying puzzle pieces.

With that said, I wish to explain a bit about cosmology. Let us begin with the process of man/woman ascending. As you are awakening as a whole to the divinity you are, so are you equally awakening to the vaster aspects of yourself. You first become soul-infused, monad-infused and then connect with group energies. As your world awakens, so I come to help move you forward. In truth, I have ever been here, as you are my seeds, my Melchizedeks awakening, and we bear the same stamp. I have from time to time and through various agents of high initiation made myself thus known, but never on so vast a scale as I am now doing. It is your awakening that has called me forth at the appointed hour, and I wish it to be known that I am here for each one of you. I am here to speak and guide you in the words most familiar to you as I operate within you individually, for we are one. In the same vein, hosts of cosmic and planetary masters are here to aid you.

I will explain, though briefly, how this is so in the light of divine unfoldment. Just as your monad has a unique imprint and individuality, which it will retain even as it (which is you) expands in ever-greater group formation, so it is true for beings at all levels of existence. All have their own divine blueprint.

He who holds the office of Planetary Logos, now beloved Lord Buddha, must as part of his work become in a sense the very essence of your planet. Earth itself has a particular stamp, code and frequency. Although these frequencies heighten, they are unique even as you are. The Planetary Logos then ensouls the planet with his uniqueness, and in him you live and move and have your being.

To step it down one step further before we again expand, this is likewise the case with each specific chohan of a ray. You who are at your monadic level will carry with you the unique ray quality to which you belong. Lord Maitreya, working in conjunction with Jesus/Sananda, was so at one with these higher and more inclusive levels that he could speak the words, "Eat of this bread, for it is my body, and drink of this wine, for it is my blood." This was and is truth.

The Solar Logos is yet another unique ensouling aspect of self. The master who holds this office functions more like the Planetary Logos, but on a higher level. I am much as they are, but on a more inclusive level still. It has been said, As above, so below, and this is true of every level of existence.

Keeping all this in mind, you can see how I, Melchizedek, hold you within the great being of my universal self and am also bound in total oneness with you. My more advanced cosmic initiates and I are lovingly here to aid, enlighten and initiate you along the pathways of your own expansion. That is why I encourage you to ask for my aid and why I am so readily available, for we are one. All God-realized cosmic masters are ever ready to be of aid to the awakening parts of themselves. So I am readily available and accessible for the asking.

Therefore, I beseech you to know me thus and meditate on the fact that you are all awakening Melchizedeks. The universe, which is ever awake, reawakens through its children aspects. The unique seeds of a particular encodement spread and ultimately bring the next cosmic revelation outward, inward, upward and throughout universe upon universe.

As you go through the various initiations and ascension processes within the planet upon which you play your part, I am here as a father to help you. The vast angelic beings (and some will carry a tone more like your own than others) and hosts of cosmic, planetary and solar beings are also here to help. In helping you we are helping ourselves. The true unity and interrelationship of everything cannot be overstated.

So one Joshua David Stone has set down in a kind of journal format of sorts the process of his personal initiations, understandings and ascensions as a Melchizedek initiate. He must be a Melchizedek initiate, for he, as you, lives, moves and has his being within my universal being.

As you read the ensuing pages, I ask that you read it by and through the light of your higher mind. This is, after all, how the process of initiation he speaks of took place. The book unfolds as the writer, the initiate, unfolds. It takes you with him on the journey of revelation.

Therefore, the words thus written by Joshua's hand reveal the light of intuition and the journey into higher realms of soul and monadic unfolding. It is not a book that is meant to be examined via the concrete or dense mind, although certain aspects of it deal directly with the day-to-day journey of this Melchizedek initiate. However, bear in mind that it comes forth on the streams of light intuition, and one should ride the beams of light as they unfold in this unique accounting of his personal journey home.

I ask that you read this with a mind and heart open to your own personal journey. You are all Melchizedeks of one degree of unfoldment or another, so much can be gained by the sharing and the hearing of the revelations of another Melchizedek, one who has traversed the realms of light at lightning speed. He and his core group have done this out of their own fiery intent for liberation and ascension, yes. But they were also advanced so quickly to be more able to share the story. And so it is that Joshua speaks, not for himself, but for the process—the process of liberation, ascension and revelation of a Melchizedek initiate. As one part of the whole speaks to the other, so I embrace you all.

Melchizedek

1

The Order of Melchizedek

I am writing this book as a Melchizedek initiate. I am doing this in order to share my experiences with you, my fellow Melchizedeks. Although there are many aspects, facets and levels of initiation within the Order of Melchizedek, we of this Earth school, galaxy and universe itself fall under the auspices of Melchizedek. The very being who ensouls our universe is called by no other name than Melchizedek. This sacred order, therefore, dates back to antiquity, and many are its mysteries.

Most of us who have been disciples of long standing can trace our roots back to ancient Egypt, and before that to Atlantis and even Lemuria. We will unveil ancient rituals and ceremonies within the Order of Melchizedek that have progressively brought us to this present moment in history, when we once again make conscious contact with this holy and sanctified order.

The bulk of this book is the story of my initiations as they were traversed in this lifetime, but in truth this is but the continuation of a journey I began ages ago. My connection with Melchizedek did not begin during this lifetime. This is equally true for almost all of you reading these pages. Some few of you are first waking up to your connection with Melchizedek, but even you have always been connected to that which holds our universe within the light and love of its being. It could not be otherwise.

I would like to begin by first making it clear to those whose vision is perhaps a bit unclear in the matter of the various beings who have been called by the name of Melchizedek. The most encompassing of these beings is the Universal Logos, who himself sets the energies, frequencies, tones, color, form and light for all that is contained within his sphere. There is then that great galactic being, also called Melchizedek, who is a member of the governing council of this sector of the galaxy. One of beloved Master Jesus/Sananda's incarnations was also under the name of Melchizedek. Some of us have officially taken certain initiations within the sacred Order of Melchizedek and are therefore initiates of that order. The point that often creates the most confusion is that we are all in fact Melchizedeks, for we are in effect sons and daughters of the universe of Melchizedek.

Let us begin by together exploring the sacred Order of Melchizedek and the process of initiation within this order. It is important to understand that one can and often does evolve along various lineages, such as various Hindu yogic lines, or follow various Buddhist or Judeo/Christian practices, and still be part of this great order. There comes a point, however, when either on the inner or outer planes one is formally ordained within the Order of Melchizedek, taking certain vows and oaths appropriate to the given level of initiation and the historical period when this rite is given. There have been and still are certain hidden physical-plane ceremonies at which all this occurs; however, it is just as binding a rite of passage if taken solely upon the inner planes.

Most of this book is devoted to the initiations taken in this present life, as my recollection of them is perfectly clear. I will, however, share with you some of the more distant memories I have regarding past-life initiations into and within this most holy order.

There was a lifetime in Egypt where I recall taking extensive training in order to further my progress upon the path of initiation. Although highly secretive and exclusive, this particular period in history very much externalized the process of initiation within this order to the few who were so called. I humbly recall being such a one in training, although there were many others, each at various stages of development and each with specific duties.

What stands out most clearly in my mind is how in that day, following the instructions of one further along the path was quite easily accepted. That was so because what I today call the negative ego was not involved in the slightest. Those who were given specific duties to carry out in order to expedite the training of younger disciples and initiates were totally worthy of their position. Some of these great ones had come from other sections of our universe and were extremely capable and honorable in the training of those seeking admittance and attainment in this order. The vortex of the Great Pyramid provided much of the training ground. Those glorious beings who were revered as gods and goddesses, such as Isis, were involved in the proceedings. To this day they play their divine part.

I see myself, along with others, taking and passing the initiations that were the order of the day. I am certain that many of the austerities and practices that come so naturally to me in this life are directly linked to that specific life and period of training. As I earlier stated, the training in this order continued in following lives while yet outwardly following various practices, traditions and lineages.

I am certain that I owe the incredible speed with which I passed my many tests and initiations in this incarnation to the direct training I received within the Order of Melchizedek. Because Melchizedek forms the order of the universe, you my beloved readers, are all Melchizedeks in the true sense of the word. What varies from individual to individual, soul to soul and indeed monad to monad is the progress made upon that path of initiation and ascension. The great news is that it lies within our own hands how much progress we make.

The thrust toward initiation and ascension is occurring on our planet as a whole in a manner never before seen. The planet, galaxy and universe are evolving and we are all part of this wondrous process. If you are determined, all the forces are here with you now to pass through the portals of the sixth and seventh initiation and gain ascension in this lifetime. In this book I have made available the key tools and experiences that have helped to catapult me through the gateway of ascension to become an initiate of the twelfth degree in the Order of Melchizedek. Although as I have stated elsewhere, no one can actually be a full-fledged initiate beyond that of the seventh degree while still in body, yet I am also here to tell you that one can indeed become the equivalent of an initiate of a much higher degree during this lifetime. This I have done. What I have done, you likewise can do.

Higher initiations beyond the seventh can be taken by completing the requirements for those initiations even though the actual rod of initiation is not officially given until one leaves the physical vehicle. The requirements I speak of are, for example, certain percentages of light and love quotient, chakra anchorings, higher-body anchoring and activations, soul-extension cleansing and integrations, transcendence of negative ego, Christ-consciousness integration, twelve-body balance and integration, and feminine/masculine balancing and service. This process should not be done in a way that simulates storming the gates of heaven. When one proceeds step by step in an integrated manner and in keeping with his/her own inner rhythm, all will be attained in divine order and in the perfect Tao.

The Order of Melchizedek and the Mahatma

Before proceeding with any further discussion regarding the Order of Melchizedek, I must present to you how the energies of the Mahatma and the Mahatma himself work in conjunction with that of Melchizedek. Although the Mahatma energies were not directly on the Earth until fairly recently, the Mahatma, also known as the Avatar of Synthesis, always played a great part in the process of initiation through the Order of Melchizedek.

The Mahatma, incorporating all 352 levels of existence within his being, likewise contains all paths, religions, disciplines and so forth. This being so, it is easy to see that the Order of Melchizedek can and does embrace all these various paths. It is this fact that allows the many and varied disciplines to bring their students into initiation within the Order of Melchizedek. Much of the training involved in all true paths of spirit is in fact the training mandated by this order.

I believe it is the truth of the perfect coming of both the Mahatma and Melchizedek energies that has led me to be a devout student of the various disciplines during this incarnation. As each path stresses one aspect of God more than the others, such as the wonderful devotion inspired by his holiness Lord Sai Baba, I have had the benefit of exploring them all to their very essences. It is the same regarding the study of various occult literature and practices. These particular studies, however, have done much to jar my memory to a full awareness of my divine plan and purpose: to focus solely on God and bring to fruition my spiritual attainments of the past. It is also to write in detail about the many paths as the one Path and to share my journey with all who are interested.

As you will see upon further reading, much of my training in this life has taken place during sleep. I am not speaking of ordinary sleep, but in sleep of the body while the soul moves about freely to continue to study, to converse with the masters and to serve. It is because of my past training and the work I have done this lifetime that I have access to many of these inner-plane experiences. Everyone has them. You too can program yourself to bring forth that awareness upon awakening. It is all a matter of practice, my friends.

The point I am getting at is simply that the Order of Melchizedek trains initiates everywhere along all the different pathways. Many of us have formally belonged to the Order of Melchizedek but have not carried that knowledge into other lifetimes. Now, with the mass ascension and acceleration of the Earth, the reality of the order is once again springing forth into humanity's awareness.

I urge you all to read the following pages with an open mind, heart and intuition. Although much of what I bring forth are new tools of access, they are written to help you reawaken ancient memories. Please bear this in mind while taking my spiritual journey of this lifetime along with me. Ask that all that I share be a prod to your own remembrance of yourself as an initiate in the Order of Melchizedek. Likewise, call forth the synthesizing energies of the Mahatma so that you may all the more clearly see how the separate incidents in your life combine to form one great portal of initiation.

Unity

Brother and sister Melchizedeks, much of my lineage is directly linked to the beloved master Djwhal Khul. Likewise am I directly linked with beloved masters Kuthumi, Lord Maitreya, the Mahatma and, of course, Melchizedek. My studies, however, have brought the divine presence of many planetary and cosmic ascended masters as well as archangels into my auric field and to my aid. You too have a direct lineage. Perhaps it is with the self-realization gurus or with his holiness the Lord Sai Baba. Perhaps it is upon a ray other than the second, where my own lineage lies. It might be upon the first ray, the line of El Morya and Lord Michael, or upon any of the seven rays. Yet we are all Melchizedeks.

I restate this here so that you who feel more of a direct bond and spiritual lineage with masters other than those focused on in this book may know that you are Melchizedeks also. In truth, all mystery schools and various spiritual paths are acting as representatives for the Order of Melchizedek. It is therefore not necessary or even desired that you leave the path you are on in order to become a full-fledged Melchizedek. A person is initiated into this order when the appropriate spiritual requirements are met and fulfilled. For many this has happened without any conscious awareness on their part.

The cosmic wheel has once more spun around to where it is again appropriate, as in the Egyptian era, for those so initiated to bring this into conscious awareness and even, for some, to enact this sacred ceremony on the Earth. For the great majority of us, the actual ceremony is yet to remain on the inner planes where it can be enacted in all its purity. This is in a transitional phase, however, and as more and more people ascend, this official ceremony will once more be reestablished on the physical plane.

The Age of Melchizedek

For a long period of our human evolution, even the very name "Melchizedek" was spoken in a hush by those who knew themselves to be initiates of this holy order. The exception to this has been in those cases where individuals such as Jesus took an incarnation under this auspicious name. There were various kings and some few others who did this as well. Their purpose was to act as a focal point via the toning and vibration of the name Melchizedek as well as through the connective link between those who bore his name and Melchizedek himself.

With the exception of those who held this holy name, the voice and energies of the Melchizedek priesthood were known primarily on the inner planes. Of course, the existence of the Order of Melchizedek was known to those blessed enough to partake of its sacred rites on the Earth plane, as well as to the advanced civilizations that have been holding his light within the hollow hallowed Earth.

Today the name of Melchizedek is spoken by many. The most esoteric fact of this great order and of the very beingness of Melchizedek is once more being brought into the light of day. In fact, Melchizedek is now anchoring and activating his divine energies upon our planet in a way never before known. This, of course, is due to the evolution of Earth herself and the taking of ascension by so many of us.

Many advanced beings are bringing through into consciousness their actual initiation into the Order of Melchizedek. Two of the most fascinating accounts I have read are those of Earlyne Chaney in *Initiation in the Great Pyramid* and Elizabeth Haich in *Initiation*. I have also noticed a number of small articles written by others who have had similar experiences. I can do nothing less than tell you that except for the limitations inherent in the human language, these accounts are quite accurate. I tell you this because they match my own personal recollections, of which I earlier wrote.

I would suggest to all of you, my beloved readers, to request conscious connection with this vast and sacred order. Speak to Melchizedek directly in your meditations and ask to be shown your own relationship to him and to your own experiences in this order. You may also request to be formally initiated into its ranks, although if you have passed certain requirements on your spiritual journey, you cannot help but already be a part of this all-pervading and all-inclusive divine order. Your formal request would therefore serve more as a bridge to conscious or superconscious remembrance.

I must clearly state here that belonging to this order is not at all predicated on your conscious recollections of the fact. It is a divine truth that not all individuals access information in the same way, nor are they meant to. If you are not particularly clairvoyant or clairaudient, do not be at all troubled if some of what is seen or heard by others is not seen or heard by you. It is not designed that all bring through past-life or inner-plane visions. If this is your case, simply make a heart-and-energy connection with Melchizedek and have faith that all is as it should be.

Just because a person has his/her psychic abilities opened, this in no way means that he is more advanced spiritually. In truth, often the opposite is the case. The memories I am seeking to awaken within you is within the cellular level and refers to a deeper consciousness beyond even the etheric, psychic, astral and mental realms.

I do urge all of you to be aware of how prevalent both the name and the once highly secret order of Melchizedek is on the Earth at this time. Be assured that one of the aspects of the new millennium is the reemergence and greater emergence of the Order of Melchizedek. Many are now acting as representatives of him and his sacred name. Use your discernment when listening to their teachings and take in only that which resonates as truth within your own soul. This should always be your practice in all situations, as it is the god, the priest and priestess within each of us that must ultimately follow our own higher selves and monads. Yet do be open, for this is indeed the age of Melchizedek revealed.

Conclusion

I close this first chapter by welcoming you to participate with me in my personal journey as a Melchizedek initiate. I have held back nothing of this life's adventure, from the taking of my sixth initiation through the taking of my twelfth. I offer you the tools I have worked with and the insights I have gained. Use any and all of the tools thus provided, for they are given from one initiate to another. On behalf of this most sacred and sanctified Order of Melchizedek, I welcome each and every one of you to share my wondrous journey with me and to take from it whatever is useful to you on your own hallowed journey as Melchizedeks.

2

My Actual Ascension

In the days leading up to my sixth initiation and ascension I knew I was getting very close. I had a great number of dreams that told me so. I had been praying very much for an acceleration of the process. The break-through came about a month prior to April 23. This was the date we had picked to ascend.

We (a small group of friends that I will refer to as the core group) picked April 23, 1994, because it was the time of the full moon in May, which is Wesak. It was also the time when a certain astrological configura-tion that happens once every 90,000 years was about to occur. Djwhal Khul confirmed to us that we were on the mark in picking this date. Our prayers and spiritual work intensified. After about a week I got a little impatient and began wondering if we could ascend even sooner. Djwhal Khul told us that this was a possibility.

Meanwhile, one of my friends was vacationing in Bali. She received a telepathic message from me (without my conscious awareness) that I had made a deal with the masters to ascend six months earlier than previously planned.

This might sound funny, but in a way this was actually the truth. I was the force working behind the scenes trying to accelerate the timing of the whole process. It was probably a character flaw on my part, although I will give myself the benefit of the doubt, taking the optimistic interpretation that ascension was the only thing on my mind twenty-four hours a day, seven days a week and 365 days a year. I was excited to achieve my completion, as I am sure the readers of this book are.

I began to realize that we did not want to wait until April 23 and were ready March 24. I began to pray, affirm and perform small ceremonies and rituals before bed each night, requesting to ascend imminently—always surrendering this to God's will, however. This went on for two nights, and then, as synchronicity would have it, my friend was stopping in Los Angeles

for two days on her return trip from Bali. We had made plans before she left
to meditate together and visit on Tuesday, March 22. She got in late, so we
got together a little later than planned. I spoke to her around 9 A.M. and we
chatted on the phone and caught up.

We had been ascension buddies during the past couple of years, so I
couldn't wait to tell her the news. I told her that the masters said that we
should be ascending about six months earlier than our previous inner guidance had told us, and she told me of the telepathic message I had sent her.
We laughed together and did a Huna prayer on the phone, requesting to ascend at any time that our monads and Sanat Kumara were ready. (The Huna
prayer is a special prayer process in which you write down what you want
and say it three times out loud. You then see and command the subconscious mind to take the prayer to the higher self and monad, with all the vital force and mana necessary to manifest and demonstrate the request. This
is explained in detail in *Hidden Mysteries* in the chapter "The Huna Teachings.")

Upon completing this prayer on the phone, my friend was then to come
over in about three hours. Meanwhile, I also did a long meditation on the
phone with my other dear friend and ascension buddy. All of us had been
ascension buddies and were working together in a group-consciousness format as a team. When any one of us meditated, we would always bring the
others in. I honestly believe that this is one of the factors that greatly accelerated all of our ascension processes. All of us were aware that our ascension was imminent.

We began to meditate and had been meditating for all of three minutes
when Lord Maitreya wanted to tell us the good news. I became electrified
inwardly with the intuitive knowing that there was only one thing this good
news could be.

There were many thoughts and feelings running through my mind. I
don't think there was anyone on planet Earth who wanted to ascend as
much as I did, and I began to realize that my prayer of prayers and desire of
desires was happening. My mind and consciousness were racing. We were
asked to stand in a certain geometrical formation with the masters Lord
Maitreya, Djwhal Khul and Sanat Kumara. There was some kind of balancing effect that was taking place.

Lord Maitreya made reference to the fact that Djwhal Khul was beaming like a proud father. He had a grin from cheek to cheek. We were the
first members of the physical-plane Djwhal Khul synthesis ashram to ascend and achieve sixth-degree status. He was extremely proud, and we all
were extremely grateful for the enormous amount of help he had given to us.

Sanat Kumara then took his rod of initiation, which looked like some
kind of spiritual sword, and made a striking diagonal slash across my body.

It didn't hurt; it was some kind of indication of completion of fifth-degree status and officially becoming a sixth-degree initiate. With one of the others in this small group, the angle was a little different, more toward her throat chakra, then he tipped her head back a little. I am not sure what this meant exactly, but that is what happened.

We all had a series of strikes on our shoulder pads. There were four strikes on each shoulder and they seemed to indicate a new level of initiation status.

There was some kind of reference made to our being like the rising sun, and the Lord Maitreya, Djwhal Khul and Sanat Kumara being like the setting sun. There was also some other reference to our being lined up to the equator both on a planetary level and also on our individual axis or equator within our own four-body system.

I might add that I felt incredibly good physically during the actual ascension process. I felt like all my energies were perfectly aligned. The others felt the same way. There was some kind of star or symbol that appeared in our heart chakras, and we were either given a new root chakra or else a special symbol was placed there.

Sanat Kumara was then channeled, and we were given a series of ten vows to say aloud. They were one-line affirmations fully claiming our ascended-master status and merging with the light. We sat silently for a while, just enjoying the tremendous influx of energy. I have to admit, however, that it didn't feel stronger than many meditations I'd had in previous months leading up to this moment. There was a part of me that was expecting the actual energetic part of the experience to be a little more dramatic.

However, we had been forewarned (as I mentioned in *The Complete Ascension Manual*) that we should take the slow path of ascension integration. Djwhal was to tell us later that 99.99 percent of the people who ascend and take their sixth initiation will be doing it by this slower method.

The experience was like an extremely profound meditation. The process of integrating the full potential of sixth-degree status and all the process of integrating the ascended-master abilities available to all sixth-degree initiates is a slow process of gradual development.

In the days that followed I felt a profound transformation in my consciousness and entire being. I felt ascended and felt the attunement, power and grace of being a sixth-degree initiate. This transformation reverberated through every level of my being. I sensed a two-year process of gradual unfolding and flowering of my ascended-master potentials. To be perfectly frank, I also felt a great relief to have completed this process.

Even though the fourth initiation is freedom from the wheel of rebirth, I knew that until I ascended and passed the sixth initiation there was still a big possibility that I was going to incarnate again. I am much more of an ethereal type of being. Although I love the Earth and am glad to be staying after my ascension, I am still cognizant of the fact that I am visiting and that this is not my ultimate home.

Vywamus told me that the action of Sanat Kumara slicing his rod of initiation or sword through me was symbolic of not being bound by the laws of the physical plane any longer. It also had to do with the concept of physical immortality. The six-pointed geometric formation also represented in part a Star of David, which is also made of two equilateral triangles.

Vywamus also told me that in my ascension process there was a greater balancing of my mental and emotional bodies in terms of the structuring process. When I spoke to him about the integration of my ascension process, he said that my monad was considering a physical trip to Arcturus in anywhere from a day to a week. This was not something I asked about; it was something he just volunteered. He had told me that in the past I had been an ambassador for extraterrestrials and would be in the future. (Out of all the extraterrestrial groups, I am most drawn to and attracted to the Arcturians.)

He told me that this was something my monad was considering on the inner plane as a two-to-five-year period. I have always been interested in the extraterrestrial movement. In *Hidden Mysteries* I took on the assignment to give a comprehensive overview of the entire subject in an easy-to-read form. This feedback from Vywamus was not something I had ever thought about, but is now something I would certainly be open to.

I was also told that there were certain energy points in the back of my neck and at the base of my spine, third eye and brain that the masters could work with to help open up my psychic faculties and spiritual senses to an even greater degree. This was something I specifically asked about.

Misconceptions about Ascension

What I have come to understand about ascension is that it is a profound transformation and completion of one's spiritual journey. However, on another level it is the same continuation of the process one has always been in except at a higher rung of the ladder. Vywamus has said that there are 352 rungs, or levels, to reach to merge completely back to Source. Realizing this, there is little reason for false pride. However, from the perspective of the Earth, it is the completion of hundreds and hundreds of incarnations and thousands of incarnations of all the soul extensions of one's soul group.

After going through the experience, I now realize that the ascension process is a gradual unfolding. In most cases it would be a mistake to think you are going to instantly walk on water, raise the dead, stop eating food, bilocate or completely stop the aging process. The main misconception about ascension is that these powers are magically or mystically bestowed on everyone upon taking this initiation. In most cases this is not so.

The same strengths and weakness in your four-body structure that you had before ascension will probably be there afterward. You will be operating, however, at a much higher octave and frequency. All these abilities will be available to you and will be developed as a sixth-degree initiate over a gradual unfoldment like the unfolding of a beautiful flower. The flower doesn't open in one second, and it is not impatient, either.

The ascension process's greatest effect on me has been in my emotional body. I feel profoundly different. I was always happy; however, I feel even happier, even blissful. I feel transformed. I very much look forward to continuing the process I have already been in, except at a higher level and octave. I also feel much more focused on service. I was always focused on service as my main purpose; however, there was a part of me that was also very focused on completing my own personal evolution so I would have more to offer humanity. I am very happy to remain on Earth and continue this process and give back what has been given to me.

3

Some Reflections on My Path of Ascension

In my first book, *The Complete Ascension Manual*, I made reference to the fact that Vywamus told me there were 800 physicalized ascended masters on the Earth plane in March 1994. In May 1994 after Wesak I explored this subject a little more. I came to realize that I had not completely understood this subject the first time I asked. The whole subject of ascension can be confusing because of definition of terms. For example, if I ask how many ascended masters are on Earth at this time, am I asking about dense, physical ascended masters or ethereal ascended masters? Am I including the ascended masters in the hollow Earth? Am I including ascended masters who have just let go of their physical bodies? Am I referring to ascended masters who have just taken their sixth initiation, or am I talking about ascended masters who have completed and fully realized their ascension?

I think you can see that if we don't define our terms, this subject can get very confusing. When I initially asked this question of Vywamus I was not considering in the slightest all these factors. As I have researched this subject more during the past couple months, I have obtained some absolutely fascinating information from him.

First off, Vywamus told me that since Wesak 1993, 400 ascended masters on Earth had left. By "ascended masters" I mean ascended masters who have actually completed and fully realized their ascension, not what I will call kindergarten ascended masters. I do not mean this as a put-down, just that every time you take any of the seven levels of initiation, you become a kindergarten initiate until you fully integrate it. It doesn't necessarily have to take very long. Djwhal Khul told me that we could realize our ascension in approximately eight months, which is extraordinarily fast to go from kindergarten to realization. It took six months to move from the kindergarten level of my fifth initiation to full realization of the fifth. This is an extremely important understanding about ascension that cannot be emphasized enough.

So the 800 ascended masters on Earth that Vywamus spoke of in March were fully realized ascended masters. As of Wesak in April there were 400,000 kindergarten sixth-degree initiates, or ascended masters who had not yet fully realized their ascension. Of the 400 ascended masters on the planet in May 1994, 300 were from the Earth's interior and 100 were on the surface. The 400 who left have gone for further training elsewhere, and it will be the job of the kindergarten ascended masters to realize their ascension and take their places. Vywamus told me, upon intensive questioning on this subject, that he was predicting that in the first wave of mass ascension 500 masters of this 400,000-master group would be completing their ascensions.

In May 1995, which is the first wave of mass ascension, there would be 200,000 people becoming kindergarten ascended masters. By May 1994 there were 300 seventh-degree initiates on the planet; approximately 210 of these have fully realized and completed the seventh initiation. The other ninety members of this group might be called seventh-degree kindergarten masters. This "kindergarten" term is not the most appropriate term; however, I am using it here simply to emphasize and clarify this important point. Better terms might be a "beginning-stage ascended master" or a "beginning-stage seventh-degree initiate."

I also asked Vywamus how many ascended-master married couples were on the planet. He said sixty couples were married in the completed and fully realized ascended-master sense of the term. Many of these were in the hollow Earth. (See *Hidden Mysteries* for an extensive overview of the hollow Earth.)

I also asked Vywamus what he meant by completing or realizing one's ascension. I was somewhat surprised by his answer. Besides the issue of needing to raise one's light quotient from 80 to 94 percent (which I will talk about later in more depth), he basically said it was a matter of the following: The realization of one's ascension has to do with achieving a greater understanding of and release of limitations in terms of one's perspective. It seemed to be a process of no longer having to try or demonstrate because it is automatic. Vywamus said a fully realized ascended master seeks no demonstration because he/she has become that which in the past he had sought.

This reminds me of something I learned about ten years ago while living in Sacramento. The learning process of any subject has four stages: (1) unconscious and incompetent; (2) consciously incompetent; (3) consciously competent; and (4) unconsciously competent

To explain this, let's use typing as an example. In the first stage you are unconscious as a child of what typing is, so you are unconscious and incompetent. Then as an adolescent if you begin a typing class, you are now consciously incompetent. Then you practice and you become consciously competent. In the final stage you become unconsciously competent. In other words, it takes no conscious effort to type, yet you are totally competent at it. It has become a habit.

An ascended master who has realized this initiation has become unconsciously competent. It takes no effort to be an ascended master, for the full meaning of being merged with the monad, or I Am, has been fully integrated and has become automatic. There is no seeking; you have become that which you have sought.

Another vital point regarding realizing your ascension has to do with integrating all aspects of self to be a full-fledged ascended master who is free from the astral, emotional and mental worlds as well as the physical world. Your own emotional, mental and psychological bodies must be fully developed and integrated. This is a point most often overlooked as you work diligently to build your light quotient.

The love quotient must be built up and developed along with the light quotient, as they are really two sides of the same coin. You must learn to be master of your negative ego and psychological self. Because one of the goals contained within the ascension process is to allow the divine qualities to descend into matter through one's earthly vehicle, all four lower bodies must be integrated, balanced and aligned.

The last insight I would like to share has to do with a little model that Vywamus showed me about the full cosmic scope of the initiatory process. This process could be looked at in the following manner.

Source of all sources, or the Godhead level

Cosmic level

Many-sources level

Universal level

Galactic level

Solar level

Planetary level

These seven levels are pretty self-explanatory. The Source of all sources, or the Godhead, is the highest. The only one that might need a little explanation is the many-sources level. Vywamus has brought forth the profound knowledge that in truth there are many sources. There are really infinite numbers of sources that are in charge of the infinite number of cosmic days and cosmic nights going on throughout creation. Even these sources are in a state of evolution. As they evolve they merge with a higher-level source. The Godhead is the Source of all sources.

In this model Lord Maitreya would accurately be called a galactic avatar. Sai Baba is actually at the universal level, Vywamus told me. Vywamus, the higher self of Sanat Kumara, is beyond the universal level and is moving toward the many-sources level. You might say he is a kindergarten cosmic master. As of Wesak 1995 Lord Buddha has assumed the office of Planetary Logos, formerly held by Sanat Kumara. Sanat Kumara, although moving on in his cosmic evolution, is assisting Lord Buddha in his new position.

I think you can begin to appreciate the profundity of Vywamus' teachings and the enormous blessing Earth has been given to have such a being so readily available to us. Lenduce, who is, one might say, the monadic level of Vywamus, would be a cosmic-realized master and one of Vywamus' teachers. He is also available to be called upon, which is even more extraordinary. The other ascended masters with whom we are so familiar would be solar and planetary masters moving toward complete realization at the galactic level.

4

My Experience of the Initiation Process

As the intention of this book is to take you, my readers, with me through my process of initiation, I happily share with you some personal experiences of my earlier initiations. First off let me say that I didn't even know there were seven levels of initiation until about three years before I ascended. I say this because I am sure this is probably the experience of most of my readers. It was really only Djwhal Khul in the Alice Bailey material, the Tibetan Foundation material channeled by Janet McClure and the theosophical movement of Madam Blavatsky and Charles Webster Leadbeater that really brought this to the West in great detail. I personally think it is some of the most important material one can possibly study.

I think my experience of the initiation process might surprise you. I had absolutely no idea that I passed the first three initiations. This was because I had never studied this material. All these initiations occur on the inner plane, so I had absolutely no recollection of any of them.

My fourth initiation was different, however. I had many dreams and meditation experiences that clearly notified me that I was approaching this level. I even knew the day I achieved this initiation; however, I don't remember the actual ceremony on the inner plane.

My fifth initiation I thought for sure I would remember, because by this time in my evolution I was steeped in the teachings of theosophy, Alice Bailey, the Tibetan Foundation and my own channelings. I was actually teaching this material. I was in a bad psychological space for about a three-day period when the actual initiation took place on the inner plane. I was very disconnected and wouldn't even have known I'd taken the fifth except that an ascension buddy at the time had a dream that she and I had graduated.

This was a period when I was clashing a bit with friends and colleagues. I was processing a lot , so I really didn't focus on the dream or even know what it meant. It wasn't until three weeks later, when I had gotten my head screwed on straight and plugged back into spirit properly, that it came to me that the dream was telling us we had taken the fifth initiation. We later asked Djwhal Khul if this was the case, and he confirmed it. If it hadn't come to me three weeks later, we would not even have known that we had taken it.

I share this with you so you won't feel badly if you don't remember, either. Now, I don't know if it's just that I am especially dense or if this is very common. I tend to think that it is common. I was amazed that we almost completely missed knowing about it. I consider us all to be very sharp in our own way, and I imagine that if we, as prototypes for the new age, are not aware of these things, then others too must not always be aware.

To be perfectly frank, even the experience of my ascension, although I knew it was happening, was much more subtle than I thought it would be. This doesn't mean it wasn't profound, because it was. There was just a part of me that was expecting fireworks and a more profound physicalized transformation.

If you don't know your initiation level, then just pray about it and study the material I have written. From there your soul and monad will intuitively guide you to what your present level and work is about. I would recommend discussing your level of initiation with few people, if at all. People tend to compare and compete, and this is totally antithetical to the spiritual process. Always remember that in truth every person is God, the eternal self, and all are equal. This is a fact. Every person is simply in a different stage of realizing it.

My friends and I didn't tell anyone we had ascended. We decided to keep it private. I had to meditate about whether I even wanted to write this book and go public with this information. I was in conflict for a while about it. My feeling, however, was that my personal experiences might be of great benefit to others.

The images we have for ascension are the Master Jesus, Saint Germain and Sai Baba, all of whom are fantastic role models. However, they don't really give us a realistic understanding of the ascension process for the masses in the times we live in. These are potentials and ascension abilities we must grow into and develop even after we take our ascension.

One other afterthought about the path of initiation process and ascension relates to the individual initiations. When I first studied theosophy, the Alice Bailey material and the Tibetan Foundation and its writings on the different initiations, I took them quite literally. For example, when Djwhal Khul through Alice Bailey said that one has to master the emotional/desire body to pass the second initiation, I took this quite literally and took steps within my own being to do just that. What I have learned over time, however, is that I know many people who have taken very high levels of initiation but whom I would still consider total victims of the emotions, negative ego and desire body.

At first this did not compute. How could this be possible? I also know people at high levels of initiation with physical health lessons and others with mental weakness and lack of clarity. I know ascended masters who have weaknesses in these areas. I share this so that when you read and study this material in my books or in other books, you realize that you have to balance only 51 percent of your karma from all your past lives to ascend. You don't have to be perfect.

In truth, achieving one's ascension is much easier than I once imagined, and this is good news to all of us. You can have some major weaknesses in your program and still take these higher initiations, even ascension, if you develop yourself in other areas. At some point, however, you will have to properly balance and integrate all four lower bodies. As I have said, the ultimate completion of the ascension process is *integrated ascension*.

My last thought on the initiation process is the importance of developing as detailed an understanding of the seven levels of initiation as you possibly can. This is the fastest way to work through them. *The Complete Ascension Manual* and *Soul Psychology* are valuable tools for accomplishing this process.

It would also benefit you to study the chapters on the Egyptian mysteries in *Hidden Mysteries*. I also suggest reading *Cosmic Ascension*, which, although it is a slightly different understanding of the initiation process, will give you an even deeper insight about what you are trying to accomplish. A detailed working understanding of the seven levels of initiation is like a tour map. It is hard to get to your destination if you don't have an exact understanding of where you are going and what you are trying to accomplish.

One other important point I want to make about the initiation process is that it is not a race or a competition. Competition and comparing is totally antithetical to God and God's plan. There is no rush. Even after you ascend, 90 percent of you will probably be staying in the physical world and life will continue as it always has. One of the biggest dangers, glamours and traps of talking about the initiation process is the issue of the negative ego making comparisons and judgments and competing. This is why I am recommending that you avoid talking about your level of initiation with almost everyone. Also, don't ask to know the initiation level of your friends. Everyone is God, and that is all that matters.

This was a trap I fell into at times. It is detrimental to the whole process. The way I tried to correct it for myself was to almost never talk about it. Even after I ascended, I went so far as not to tell anyone about it. This book is the first time I have ever come out in a public way about this process. I seriously debated within myself whether it was even appropriate to do this.

I once got a serious reprimand from spirit when I was in the more advanced stage of the fifth. I was having my ascension dreams and I knew I would be ascending soon. I made the mistake of telling some family members in too open a manner, and I immediately had a dream that I was caught in the glamour of "needing to be known." I share these experiences, not because I am proud of them, but to help you to learn by grace instead of karma, as I did.

There is another lesson here that deals with overestimating or underestimating one's level of initiation and/or spiritual growth. I have fallen into both. Since the initiations occur on the inner plane, they might often go on without our conscious awareness. Unless you are a clairaudient voice channel for the ascended masters or your own soul or monad, it is not always the easiest thing to determine. One can use an accurate external channel; however, they are not easy to find. Most people are channeling astral- or mental-plane frequencies and spirits at best.

Another time I had a profound dream that I mistakenly misinterpreted as an initiation, which I hadn't really taken. Within my own mind (not outwardly) I was claiming to be at a higher level than I was. Much later I had another dream that put me in my place and showed me the error of my ways. It was quite a humbling experience, as I am sure you can imagine. I swore to myself afterward that that I would never let that happen again. On other occasions I was actually farther along than I realized. This certainly occurred between my fifth and sixth initiation. I was shocked when Djwhal told us that we would be ascending within the month. I thought I had at least another year and a half to go, maybe longer.

This on some level is a normal process. It is hard to know exactly where we are all the time. We get a kind of intuition. The nature of the negative ego is to overestimate if you have top-dog, superiority tendencies and to underestimate if you have more underdog, inferior tendencies. The key here is stay out of your negative ego, and you will sense properly where you are. The main thing is to keep focusing on your spiritual growth and service work, and you will get there even if you never focus on the seven levels of initiation and/or know nothing about them. There is a major glamour surrounding the whole process of initiation that must be transcended, or it will actually slow down your progress. I hope this explanation has been helpful.

Djwhal's Clarification about Initiations

Djwhal Khul shared with me recently a fascinating piece of information. He said that between each initiation there are seven levels or gradations of evolvement. There are seven actual initiations and seven levels between each of these major initiations. For example, when we received this information Djwhal told us that we were at the 3½ level between our sixth and seventh initiation. It could also be stated that we were halfway complete.

This was amazing to me, for only seven full weeks had passed since taking our ascension. I knew we were moving along at an extraordinary speed; however, it was nice to get this confirmation. Wesak, the April astrological alignment with Sirius, and the ascension weekend workshop had given us an incredible acceleration. I think the fascination and excitement of actually having ascended contributed, too. We were told that we were three months ahead of schedule. We had targeted the completion of our sixth initiation at the 12:12, or December 12, which would be eight months after we actually ascended.

To complete the sixth does not mean that we would necessarily take our seventh; however, I was sure it would follow in not too many months. Anyway, given the present pattern of our progress, we were now looking at completing our ascension in September, which would allow us to be forerunners for the large group that would be doing the same thing around the 12:12. Doing this early would allow us to be of great service to this group. Every time someone takes an initiation, it makes it much easier for those who follow. We were all very excited about this feedback, and we dedicated and focused ourselves even more than before.

In my living room there is an ascension column, which Djwhal Khul keeps upgrading each month as the ashram and we evolve. He humorously told us that the rest of the house was ours; however, the living room belonged to the Spiritual Hierarchy. All our groups met in this ascension vortex, and all people who came into the room and sat there for an evening received its benefits.

I want to make one more point about the seven sublevels of each of the seven major initiations. This new understanding makes total sense, for as each one evolves through each of the dimensions of reality moving beyond the third, there are seven chakras that make up each grid. The third dimension has chakras 1 through 7, the fourth dimension has chakras 8 through 15 and the fifth dimension has chakras 16 through 22. As one evolves through these higher initiations, these higher chakras descend and anchor into the previous chakra grid.

Later I will speak of the thirty-six chakras that include the sixth- and seventh-dimensional chakra grids. Another reason for the speed of our core ascension group's progress had been the anchoring of these grids with the help of Djwhal Khul and Sanat Kumara. The point here is that there are not only seven sublevels of each initiation that must be evolved through to complete each initiation, but there are also seven chakras that must be anchored. This usually happens quite naturally even if one does not know about them. If one knows about them, they can be anchored more quickly and the rest of the four-body system can then catch up to that frequency. I

Not quite see P48

speak of the first twenty-two chakras in *Soul Psychology*. In this book I speak of chakras 23 through 36. I cannot emphasize enough the value of calling forth and anchoring these higher chakra grids. My ascension meditation in *The Complete Ascension Manual* helps to do this.

In a meditation Djwhal Khul told me some fascinating information regarding the two different systems of initiation in the Alice Bailey material and the Mahatma books. In the Mahatma books Brian Grattan speaks of twelve initiations that can be taken on this earthly plane. The Alice Bailey books say only seven initiations can be taken. Djwhal explained that the first six initiations in both systems are exactly the same. Initiations seven, eight and nine in Brian Grattan's system are the first three sublevels of the sixth initiation in the Alice Bailey system.

In other words, between every major initiation in the Alice Bailey system there are three sublevels of initiation. Initiations 7 through 9 are the three sublevels between the sixth and seventh initiation. Initiations 10 through 12 are the three sublevels between the seventh and eighth initiation in the Alice Bailey system. The eighth initiation in the Alice Bailey system cannot be taken on this Earth plane. We can, however, complete the three sublevels of the seventh initiation and remain at that level of initiation until leaving this plane.

I was told that approximately eleven weeks after our ascension we were at the eighth initiation in Brian Grattan's system and were scheduled to take our ninth in August or September, which would be around five or six months after taking our ascension. This would mean that it would take us this amount of time to complete our ascension. We again were told that our seventh initiation would occur within one full year's time from our original ascension, or before that if everything continued on the same course.

5

Ascension and the Importance of Meditation

I highly recommend that you make an audio tape of my ascension meditation in the last chapter of *The Complete Ascension Manual* or use the ascension meditation techniques in the chapter on ascension. (My series of ascension-activation tapes help make these processes easier for you. See back pages for contact information.) Even if you are not clairvoyant, clairaudient or clairsentient, you will feel the energetic effects of working with this meditation daily. If you use my ascension meditation and the other techniques on a regular basis, I guarantee, as an ascended master, that you will be completely transformed in one year's time.

If you want to ascend you must have some degree of commitment and self-discipline. I found after a while that I couldn't wait to meditate. It became my favorite thing in life to do, though for the first thirty-five years of my life the opposite had been true. You too will feel the energies pour into you through your crown chakra. If you have friends who are clairvoyant, do this meditation with them and they will tell you what they see.

I already told you that I moved from the fifth to the sixth initiation in only six and a half months. I am here to tell you that meditation was the key. If you really want to speed up your ascension process, do this meditation every day and ask for this work to be done every night while you sleep.

One amazing insight I have had after achieving my ascension is how much of the work is actually done on the inner planes. Ask and pray every night that this work be done on you night and day even without your conscious awareness. If you pray, it will come.

Get physical exercise and sunshine every day and eat a good diet. Practice being the ascended master in your daily life. Be joyous and loving at all times. See every person you meet as God visiting you in physical form and be of service at every opportunity. This simple formula will absolutely revolutionize your life. You will begin to become light, which is what the ascension process is all about.

There has never been a time in the history of planet Earth when the masses could evolve so quickly through the seven levels of initiation. I implore you, don't waste this divine opportunity. It is no accident that you are reading this book and no accident that God has guided you to this easy-to-read practical course in ascension. Take advantage of it. This is the key moment of all your incarnations. The light is at the end of the tunnel; your path to completion stands before you. Take the tools and information and practice, practice, practice.

I challenge you, as the I Am Presence speaking to the I Am Presence, to put yourself on a program of accelerated spiritual growth for one year. People will not even recognize you in one year's time because of the amount of light radiating through your four-body system.

Ascension Meditation Experiences

I had a number of ascension experiences both alone and meditating with friends that I think you readers would find interesting.

In one meditation my friend and I were given ascension ankhs in both our heart and our brain. The one in the brain then split into five spinning ankhs. These ankhs spun like baby merkabahs, raising the overall vibration and frequency to the ascended-master state. The one in the heart contained all the information needed for ascension. These are things you can ask for in your meditations, and that is why I am sharing them.

In another meditation we were given scrolls from the angels. My scroll acknowledged my perseverance, then told me of my readiness for ascension. Call the angels into your meditation and ask for their help. Metatron is the best for helping to build the light quotient. Chamuel and Sandalphon are especially good at helping to ground your soul and monadic lightbodies into the physical.

In another meditation Djwhal Khul gave me a piece of the Great Central Sun, which I placed in my heart. This is something you might ask for in your meditations.

In another meditation Sai Baba gave me a *lingam* (sacred Hindu icon), which was placed in my heart chakra. (Never forget that these inner gifts are just as sacred as real physical gifts. Physical gifts are just physicalized thought forms.) Ask for Sai Baba's blessing on your path of ascension, and ask for a gift from him to connect you with his energies. He will happily oblige.

In another meditation experience we were in an ascension chamber in Mount Shasta inside the mountain, where existed a gigantic pyramid. A master, whom I refer to as Ptah Melchizedek, was in charge. We were standing in the ascension chamber, and as the light poured in we were slowly but surely rising upward to the top of the pyramid. There was a numerical scale of 1 to 100 being used that seemed to deal with building our light quotient.

It took a great number of hours; however, we finally made it to the top of the pyramid. We then went through the top and were floating in a star, or merkabah, above the pyramid that was still being filled with light. We called forth Metatron, the Mahatma and Melchizedek, the Universal Logos, to help in this process.

I then became aware that we were inside an even greater cosmic pyramid. This is when I began calling forth the light-information packets from all 352 levels of the Mahatma. I am not sure that this had ever been done before. Definitely ask in your meditation to be taken to this ascension chamber. It was one of my most favorite ascension meditations. Even if you can't see clairvoyantly what is going on, ask to be taken there anyway. If you ask, it will happen. The second after you ask you will begin to feel a very slight tingling sensation throughout your nervous system. This is the light pouring into your energy fields. I cannot recommend the importance of doing this more sincerely. This might well be the number-one meditation experience, which I returned to hundreds of times, that accelerated my ascension processing.

This is another golden key. At bedtime ask that you be taken there every night. Do this religiously. Call forth all the things I have called forth and ask that it continue all night long. I personally am into shortcuts. That is why I came to my friend in Bali telepathically and told her I had made a deal with the masters to ascend six months earlier than planned. We all laughed at this, but that is exactly what I did. If there is a shortcut to quicken the ascension process, I will find it.

Asking that this be done every night before bed is one of the supreme shortcuts. All night long while you are sleeping, you will be in this ascension chamber being filled with light. When you sense that you have reached the 100 level over a period of weeks or months, then enter the cosmic ascension chamber and let yourself be filled with the light-information packets from the Mahatma. Ask for this every night before bed.

When you are ready for a change of pace, ask to be taken to Commander Ashtar's ship and placed in the ascension seat there. I spent hundreds of hours in meditation soaking in its energy. Again, ask for this every night before bed. In your prayers ask that this work be continued in your waking hours while you are busy.

I also spent many, many hours meditating in Serapis Bey's ascension retreat in Luxor. This also is a key meditation process. All ascension students must do work on the inner plane before ascending. As a matter of fact, at my actual ascension it was a symbol from Luxor that was placed on my heart.

For another change of pace in my meditations I would then go to Telos, the underground city below Mount Shasta. Even though this is a real underground city, we would go there in etheric, or spiritual, form. We would ask to be hooked up to their ascension seats and computers. We would then spend hundreds of hours in both meditation and sleep state being programmed by these computers and energy seats, or tables, for ascension processing. The computers tabulate in some amazing way the exact frequency of energies needed for ascension processing for your evolution. Again, ask to go there every night to take advantage of this amazing technology. The master there who can guide you is Adama. The first time you go to these places ask one of the ascended masters to accompany you.

The other place I liked to go was the Great Pyramid at Giza in the King's Chamber. There is also an ascension seat there. When going there I liked to call forth the help of Isis, Osiris, Horus and Thoth. Ask and pray for their help in raising your light quotient and preparing your bodies for ascension.

The amazing thing about all these places is that all you have to do is ask to go there. It doesn't matter what level of evolution you are at or what initiation or even if you haven't taken any. These masters and places are happy to accept any sincere seeker of God.

Arcturus is another place you can ask to be taken to that can be of great value, or you can ask to be taken to one of the Arcturian starships. Arcturus is the most highly evolved civilization in our galaxy. They are most wondrous and beautiful beings. They have advanced light technologies of which we on Earth have not yet dreamed. They are totally dedicated to serving humanity and will do so if asked. They will not interfere, however, if not asked.

In other meditations we would go into the Sun and visit Helios, asking for his help in building our solar body of light. He is especially good at this.

I will give you another major key that allowed me to move from my fifth to the sixth initiation in only six and half months. Always ask that your eleven other soul extensions join you whenever you go to these retreats or are just meditating. Never forget that your soul or higher self has eleven other soul extensions or personalities who are incarnated into the material universe or are on the inner plane. Seth spoke of this in his writings, and he was right. You are just one of twelve helping to evolve your soul, who is your higher self. This is explained in great detail in *The Complete Ascension Manual*, so I want to repeat myself.

Ask; do not command them to come. You need to respect their free choice. You can, however, ask Vywamus or one of the other ascended masters to help gather them, for example, in Luxor. This way when you meditate all twelve parts of you are getting the benefit of your meditation. Do this also every night before bed when you are preparing to do your soul-travel work. Ask your soul extensions to join you. You will literally evolve twelve times faster than if you did it alone. Ask also for Vywamus' help in getting properly connected electrically with your eleven other soul extensions. You are in truth each like fingers on your hand. You are not evolving for lower self, but for the evolution of your soul, also known as the oversoul.

In other meditations we would spend long hours lying on ascension tables in Luxor calling in the cosmic fire under the guidance of the monad, which would burn up the karmic dross from all of our past lives. When you do this, ask that it systematically go first through your physical body, then emotional body, then mental body and then spiritual body.

Again, I suggest that you make an audio tape of the ascension meditation and treatment written in the back of my ascension manual. I spent hundreds of hours bathing in the energies that were invoked from listening to this tape. I would suggest that you get creative and make your own tape, using all the different ideas I have given you here and the ones included in *The Complete Ascension Manual*—for instance, the Ascension Meditation and Treatment and the tools in the chapter on ascension. There is a special connection and empowerment when you listen to your own ideas in your own voice.

The more you work with these ideas, the more they will become your own. All you have to do is read the books and get the tapes and practice, practice, practice. In a very short time I guarantee that you will not be able to stop reading the books. You will be dying to meditate at every free quiet moment. Once you begin to grasp and soak in these divine energies, you will become addicted. You will become God-intoxicated. This will be the best addiction you have ever had. Once you fully taste this nectar, all materialism, hedonism, lower-self interests and worldly overidentification with matter will end.

Another meditation I really enjoyed that had enormous benefits was calling forth my personal merkabah. The first time you do this ask the ascended masters and your soul and monad to help create one for you. Again, it doesn't matter if you can't see this being done. If you ask, it will be done, for you are God. Ask then for your merkabah to begin spinning to raise your vibrational frequencies. Even if you can't see this happening, you will feel a tingling sensation over your entire body. Whatever meditation you are doing, ask that this be done. The merkabah should also be invoked anytime you soul-travel or astral-travel (which I don't recommend). Soul-travel I do recommend. Your merkabah is your mini spaceship that provides total protection. If you are meditating in a group, you can invoke a larger merkabah that serves as a boat. Much of the UFO technology is just an advanced understanding of merkabah technology.

Another meditation experience that my friend and I spent many hours doing is invoking the "rapture." We would then float up the pillar of light while a light show and divine angelic music would play. If you can't see it when invoked, just know that you are there and enjoy the feeling it gives you.

In other meditations we would practice bilocating. We would ask to visit, for example, Djwhal Khul's ashram, or ask to visit Sai Baba's ashram and ask for his ascension blessing. This is another one of the golden keys for accelerating your ascension process. Wherever I went I always asked and prayed for an ascension blessing and acceleration from the different masters we would encounter. I must have gotten more ascension blessings than any person in the universe. The ascended masters were happy to give their blessings, for they want us to ascend as much as we want to. My motto is, you can't get enough blessings and prayers from the God force. I would rather pray too much than too little. I took no chances.

In other meditations we traveled to the throne of YHWH, for those who are connected with *The Book of Knowledge: The Keys of Enoch*. We would pray out loud, voicing our heartfelt requests on every possible subject, always with our request for ascension acceleration and thanks.

These sojourns to YHWH were incredible. I can't emphasize enough that it doesn't matter in the slightest if you can't see what is going on. Just know that if you ask and command to go someplace, you are instantly there. Tap into the feeling. If you could see what is actually going on when you try these different meditations, it would blow your mind.

At other times we went to visit Lord Maitreya, with his permission. One of my favorite meditations of all was when we went to visit Sanat Kumara. (He was the Planetary Logos at the time of my ascension; since Wesak 1995 the Buddha has held the position.) Sanat Kumara at that time was the highest being associated with the Earth and was the personal god for this planet. Here is another golden key to your ascension process. The Planetary Logos is the great initiator of the ascension process and the being who holds the rod of initiation and decides who is ready and who is not.

I would visit Sanat Kumara only on special occasions. I never wanted to overstay my welcome and always wanted to make the best use of my time when I was with him. I always saved my best for him. He was the one who received my most heartfelt prayers. In general, it was Sanat Kumara to whom I would pray when I was dealing with the most important things to me.

One of the keys to your ascension process is to make your declarations before the Planetary Logos (now the Buddha) regarding your desire for ascension and what you have to offer the world in service if you do ascend. I would recommend that every Wesak Festival, which is the full moon in Taurus, you religiously go before Buddha and pray to him as you have never prayed before. He will hear your heartfelt prayer and respond.

The Buddha is our leader, and it is he who formulates the divine plan on all levels of evolution for this planet, including human, animal, plant and mineral. Get on good terms with him. Make yourself known to him. Making your declarations before him is one of the many requirements before being allowed to achieve your ascension.

Another meditation I really enjoyed doing was calling forth the Ark of the Covenant while in the ascension retreat in Luxor. The Ark of the Covenant was the device that the great Egyptian spiritual masters used in their initiation ceremonies and in building the pyramids. They could be used only on seventh-degree initiates. Whenever we would call them forth on the inner plane, I would always feel an incredible acceleration of energies. The ankhs were miniature Arks of the Covenant. The arks can be used by the ascended masters to help raise one's vibrational frequencies.

In other meditations we would call forth the full anchoring of the microtron, the cosmic heart and the Melchizedek self. (For more information on this I recommend Brian Grattan's Mahatma books.) We would also call forth the twenty-four dimensions of reality to become fully anchored and activated in our four-body system. We would then ask that the light information of all twenty-four dimensions of reality be programmed into our computer banks. These are awesome meditations.

We spent many, many hours anchoring our twenty-two chakras into our four-body system. In the beginning they would come in very slowly, to be sure they wouldn't burn out our nervous system. Over time they would come down and anchor in our seven-chakra system, preparing the four bodies for ascension. This meditation is one of the most important of all. Most people in the world are dealing with seven chakras or at most twelve. If you really want to accelerate your program, call in all twenty-two. Chakras 16 through 22 are your fifth-dimensional chakras. Do this, however, under the guidance of your monad so as not to move too quickly.

In actuality, 200 chakras are activated at the point of monadic ascension. There are ultimately 330 chakras that are activated by the time one reaches the forty-ninth dimension (this is information given forth to ponder on by the grace of Melchizedek). *By no means* try to anchor these chakras now. Work with the dimension you are at. If you know for certain that you have taken your seventh initiation, you can work with chakras 23 through 50, depending on the sublevel you are at. For an accurate reading regarding your level of initiation, consult a qualified channel or call me at the phone number in the back of this book and I will set you up with a telephone session.

Whenever I would meditate I would also call in a tube of light of protection and ask to be placed in a pillar of light and an ascension column of light. Ask that only ascended-master frequencies and energies be allowed to enter your field. This should be enough; however, if any unwanted energies ever do enter your field, ask Vywamus, Sai Baba or one of the other ascended masters or Archangel Michael to get rid of it.

With all the spiritual energies you are going to be invoking you should not have any problem. Read the chapter on psychic self-defense in *Soul Psychology* if this is an issue you have problems with. You can also ask that angel gatekeepers be placed around you for added protection.

One of my favorite meditations was to call for the mighty I Am Presence and the monadic and soul lightbodies to fully descend and anchor within my four-body system. I would call forth the greater flame to merge with the lesser flame on Earth. The continual practice of doing this in meditation will give you the experience of mini ascensions over and over again. I think that is why the actual ascension experience didn't seem that dramatic to us. We had done it so many times in meditation that it felt normal to have the monad and *mayavarupa* (divine blueprint) body anchored.

Another meditation technique I enjoyed was calling to Sanat Kumara and asking that the number one in my aura now be transformed to the number ten. (I was using the numerical code for ascension and completion that I had learned about in my dream.) When I did this, particularly in relationship to Sanat Kumara, I would get this powerful feeling of transformation going on within me.

In another meditation we spent a lot time focusing on the creation of our twelve strands of DNA. Most people have only two. By continually invoking this in meditation to be created over time, it will happen. Djwhal Khul told us that it is only really created in the etheric body. After ascension this can then be transferred into the physical vehicle. I know this can be achieved before ascension because Djwhal Khul confirmed to me that I had done it.

Another absolutely unbelievable golden key to the acceleration of my ascension process was the constant invocation of the Mahatma. The Mahatma is the cosmic being who embodies all 352 levels of the total God force. Ascended masters are usually only at levels seven, eight or nine, except maybe for Sai Baba, Sanat Kumara and Vywamus. By calling continually in meditation for merger with the Mahatma, you are calling for not only merger with your monad and I Am Presence, but also with God at the top of creation. You are literally calling forth *cosmic* ascension, not just planetary ascension.

Vywamus said that the anchoring of the Mahatma onto the physical plane is the single most important thing that has ever happened in the history of humankind. You have no idea or conception of the magnitude of the frequency and power we are talking about. It is so awesome that I can't put it into words. If you want to accelerate your ascension process, constantly call forth the Mahatma in your meditations and daily life. Ask to become his cosmic walk-in. Ask to be overlighted by him at all times. Ask that he live in your body with you at all times. You are actually healing the separation between God and all creation. This had never been possible until after the Harmonic Convergence. Brian Grattan has done a tremendous service to this planet to bring us this information.

Another meditation I really liked was building my antakarana, or bridge/tube of light, to my soul, my monad and, in later stages of my evolution, all the way back through the 352 levels of the Mahatma and to God. I would practice and request that my antakarana be widened to allow the greatest influx of energy to pour into my field from God, the Mahatma, my monad and soul. This wonderful journey I took is there for all. "Ask and ye shall receive."

I also really enjoyed a meditation to fill all my physical organs and glands, bloodstream and bones with light. This allowed my physical body to become more a part of my meditation. I then created a grounding cord into the center of the Earth, visualizing my feet as having roots like a tree. This then became an Earth Mother meditation, anchoring the spiritual energy into the Earth. Sometimes I would draw the Earth energy up through my feet to mix with the incoming spiritual energy. This is a very important meditation and another key in the issue of becoming balanced. Read the chapter on the Essenes in *Hidden Mysteries*. Over 2000 years ago were developed some of the most awesome heaven-and-Earth meditations in perfect balance that this world has ever known.

There are literally hundreds of other ideas in the Ascension Meditation and Treatment in my ascension manual. You will not be lacking for awesome meditations to practice. Don't be overwhelmed. Begin by taking notes on your favorite methods from this book and my others. Then one at a time at each meditation, try them out and see how you feel. Over time you will develop favorites you will work with more often than others. The most important thing is to begin to get organized in your ascension practice and start practicing, which will soon not be practice, but your greatest joy.

Don't waste a single precious moment. Get started. Never in the history of humankind has such an awesome array of techniques and spiritual technologies as these been available. What once took many lifetimes can now be accomplished in six months. Don't waste this opportunity. Get your priorities in order. Joy, happiness and love blended with a little self-discipline to meditate, read and study is the ticket. During your work hours practice being an ascended master in your every thought, word and deed, and be of service at every opportunity no matter how small the deed.

One other point I would like to make about the initiation process has to do with the wide range of abilities of those at the same initiation level. Just because two people are at the same level of initiation doesn't mean they are clones in terms of their abilities. For example, one person might be a fifth-degree initiate and be a planetary teacher who travels the globe giving seminars and workshops. Another fifth-degree initiate might be a housewife with two kids who, though very devoted and dedicated, is not doing any overt, large-scale service work. Yet both are at the same level. I have met people who I'd guess were not beyond the second or third initiation at most, yet find that they are at the fifth initiation. Other times I have thought others were more advanced than they were.

It is a good thing that the Spiritual Hierarchy is in charge of this and not me (I am being humorous here). The main point is that you can't judge a book by its cover. God is not looking for glamour and fanfare in this process. It is the state of one's heart and soul. It is the small things that go on each and every day that make up the grist for the mill of the path of initiation. Kind words to your neighbor, patience with your kids, your pure intent, giving to a homeless person, going out of your way to help a friend, persevering under spiritual tests—these are the things that surely move the world.

6

Golden Nuggets of Ascension

Humanity as a whole is woven together and we are all spiritual brothers and sisters, so with great joy I share with you a few other golden keys in my personal ascension process that I feel were touchstones for my success. The faster that one moves along his/her path of integrated ascension, the faster and easier it will be for the next person. We are truly God holding the hand of God and journeying up the mount of ascension as one. It is in this light that I share with you the golden nuggets that have been most helpful in my own journey.

One of the first and most important practices was seeing every person I met as God visiting me in physical form. *A Course in Miracles* refers to this as the "holy encounter"—Christ meeting Christ. This might be the single most important spiritual practice of all. You must understand that you are not doing your neighbor a favor by doing this. God, or the eternal Self, really *is* who they are. When you see them this way you are no longer living in illusion. In truth, they don't need the blessing; you do. The world is a projection screen and you are seeing your own movie. Are you seeing with your spiritual eyes or with your negative-ego eyes? The world is a mirror. You will never realize God until you see God everywhere you go.

This brings me to the next golden key in my ascension process, which was the understanding of attitudinal healing. I go into this a great deal in *Soul Psychology*, but for now know that the significance of everything you experience depends on your interpretation. Is the glass of water half empty or half full? Sai Baba says your mind creates bondage or your mind creates liberation. I achieved liberation and ascension because I learned to master my mind and make it subservient to my soul, my monad.

The mind sometimes gets a bad rap in the New Age spiritual movement. I am here to tell you that it is your mind that will either save or destroy you. Your thoughts create your reality! What matters is not what happens to you in life, but how you interpret it. I had challenges in this lifetime that would have destroyed most people on planet Earth. I had challenges so severe that most people would have died or been driven insane, and I am not exaggerating. I am consciously choosing not to get into all the details because I don't want to relive it.

In spite of this, I consider myself the most blessed, grateful, luckiest man on the face of the Earth. Was what happened to Job in the Bible a curse or a blessing? It depends on how you look at it. When I was given lemons in life, I made lemonade. I turned all my bummers into lessons, opportunities and spiritual tests. When people attacked and criticized me, I thanked God for the opportunity to practice forgiveness, unconditional love and the Christ consciousness.

Don't underestimate the power of positive thinking and don't think it is a Pollyanna philosophy, for it is not. It is the consciousness of the God-self. Did not Buddha say that all suffering comes from your attachments? This brings me to the next golden key.

This key to my ascension process was something I read in the *Bhagavad-Gita*, which of course is the story of Krishna, the Christ of the Eastern world. Krishna said that the consciousness of the God-self remains even-minded and in equanimity whether you have profit or loss, pleasure or pain, sickness or health, whether you are praised or criticized.

I cannot tell you how many times I would refer back to this in my journal-writing when the lessons and challenges of life were overwhelming. I refer to this as the transcendence of duality. Sai Baba and Paramahansa Yogananda have spoken of it. It is one of the keys to achieving inner peace and unceasing joy and happiness. To do this, detachment and divine indifference are needed.

Another absolutely essential golden key for me was what Sai Baba refers to as self-inquiry. He says that 75 percent of the spiritual path is self-inquiry. Self-inquiry is nothing more than the process of monitoring one's impulses and desires and learning to discriminate between what is truth and what is illusion. You learn to discriminate between what is coming from the lower self and what is coming from the higher self, what is of the Christ consciousness and what is of the negative-ego consciousness. As stated in *A Course in Miracles*, "Deny any thought that is not of God to enter your mind." I practiced this to the nth degree in my life, and this is why I stand as an ascended master.

Another wisdom from *A Course in Miracles* is to "be vigilant for God and his kingdom." I was extraordinarily vigilant in my life over the contents of my consciousness. I battled my lower self for many years; however, I finally got to the point of closing the door on it and locking it, which made my life much easier. This allowed me to do what Djwhal Khul has recommended over and over again in the Alice Bailey books: to "keep your mind steady in the light."

Most people allow themselves to live on automatic pilot. You will not achieve your ascension by living on automatic pilot. I tell you again, I was not born with extraordinary psychic powers, channeling abilities or mystical powers. I achieved my ascension through unceasingly practicing the basics. I remember a passage from one of the Alice Bailey books, where Djwhal Khul spoke of how sometimes an average man/woman will go much further than the genius in spiritual evolution. I am an average man who, by the grace of God, achieved a certain level of spiritual growth because I was committed. I was like the tortoise in the fable of the Tortoise and the Hare. My unceasing commitment to hold to my ideals and practice the basics over and over again until I mastered them to a certain degree is what paid off. Did not Jesus say, "Be ye faithful unto death and I will give thee a crown of life"?

Another key for me in my process was the practice of chanting the name of God. When I was challenged and began to lose my inner peace, I would chant the different names of God. I wrote a chapter about this in my ascension manual and have given them in *How to Teach Ascension Classes*, which I would recommend that you read. I went through various phases of chanting different names. This never failed to pull me out of the pits, traps and holes that I was constantly falling into along the way.

Another key was the practice of balance and moderation. Earlier in my life I was an extremist, which was part of the reason I got so ill. My health lessons reformed me, and over time I learned to be more balanced in my diet, exercise, reading, meditation, sleep and so on.

A prerequisite for ascension is to develop some semblance of balance within one's four-body system (physical, emotional, mental and spiritual). As Buddha said, "Follow the path of the middle way."

Another golden key for me was a statement from *A Course in Miracles* that "an attack is a call for love." When people would attack me, get angry and lash out (even romantic mates), I really tried to see beyond the appearance and see that they were in fear on some level. I really tried not to react. This was very hard at first. In the later stages of my evolution I got better and better at it. I began to stop taking these things personally and developed a strong psychological immune system.

A Course in Miracles had a profound effect on me. It was really only one of literally hundreds and hundreds of spiritual systems of growth I was involved with. I believe that my book *Soul Psychology* makes *A Course in Miracles* extremely easy to understand for those who have gotten bogged down in the text or lessons. I highly recommend these books. In any case, this golden nugget is that forgiveness is the key to happiness. No matter how much people ripped me off, I would forgive. Not for them, but for my own peace of mind. Holding grudges just created separation, and that was exactly opposite to the main purpose I was here to demonstrate: oneness at all times, which translates directly into love.

Another golden key was the attitude of always remaining the master and not the victim. This applied to other people as well as my own internal energies. Another key was to be eclectic and universalistic. I was open to all paths leading to God and drew from most of them. I would recommend this to my readers. Don't get stuck in a belief that what you are involved with is the only way or even the best way. Being open to all paths will give you a far more rounded education and rapid advancement on your path of initiation.

As I look back over the past forty years, I think the one key quality that was paramount to achieving my ascension was my commitment. I can honestly say that for the past fifteen years, ever since I attended that first Paul Solomon workshop, I have been absolutely on fire for God realization. It has not let up one iota for me in that time, and if anything, it got stronger and stronger as time went on. I have been like a man possessed with only one purpose and one thought on my mind night and day. I held onto the angel and did not let go until God blessed me. When I was forty, God, in the form of Sanat Kumara, blessed me.

To be perfectly frank, I am incredibly happy but not satisfied. I will not be satisfied until I make it back through all 352 levels of initiation and merge completely back into God, then bring every one of my brothers and sisters in Christ back to this level with me. Then I will be fully satisfied. I am now holding onto this ideal like a drowning man wants air, and with that level of commitment there is nothing in God's infinite universe that can stop me.

I call to you, my beloved brothers and sisters in Christ, to join me in this noble goal and task. Together we shall revolutionize this planet, this solar system, this galaxy, this universe, this omniuniverse and eventually all of creation. We were created for such a noble destiny: "Seek and ye shall find; knock and the door shall be opened." Let us be like the three musketeers whose battle cry was "all for one and one for all." Let us be God's musketeers, working together to uplift God's creation, for this *is* the divine plan.

Djwhal Khul told us that we were already working on the advanced stages of the sixth initiation even though we had just ascended. In all the initiations, we are spiritually able to work ahead of ourselves, and then the physical vehicle must catch up.

Djwhal Khul also told us that our twelve strands of DNA would be fully anchored into the physical vehicle from the etheric vehicle when we take the seventh initiation. At the sixth initiation we were focused more on the ninth strand of DNA because we were still on the sixth, or monadic, plane of reality. We do have twelve strands of DNA in our etheric body.

I share all this information with you as a very sacred act; in a sense, it is my personal journal of my spiritual evolution and exploration. I do this not to glorify myself, but by putting myself out on a limb I offer you a road map and perspective of what it is like to go through these higher initiations.

There are not many people in the history of this planet who have achieved this level of evolution and written about it openly. I sometimes question myself whether it is wise to give humanity a bird's-eye view into such intimate matters. This book is like my own personal journal. I can do it because I am secure and clear in myself, and I feel that such a book would have been of tremendous service to me on my path. The times we live in now are much different than they have been in the past. I honestly feel that such a book as I am writing here became appropriate only after the Harmonic Convergence.

I am hoping that you will utilize many of the ideas and tools I have worked with and extrapolate from them. One of the gifts God has graced me with is to be a researcher. I sometimes tease my friends that I am the Sherlock Holmes of the spiritual movement. I am blessed to have some extraordinary people around me who help me in this work. My function in the plan is to organize all the input I receive inwardly and from my core ascension group and make it available to the masses.

I give you here an intimate look at what it means to take the seventh initiation. I don't think this has ever been written about in any detail on this plane. When Djwhal Khul wrote the Alice Bailey books, in large part he was still a fifth-degree initiate. He later ascended, then finished the books. His writing on the seventh initiation is very sparse. So I am researching and exploring information that has never been written about, making it available to the general public. This has never been allowable before. Part of my work, I believe, is to be a pioneer in this regard.

I feel that I am uniquely qualified to do this in an easy-to-read, interesting and uncomplicated manner. When this level of information has been described, it has usually been in a complicated, esoteric manner, such as in the writings of Alice Bailey and the teachings of theosophy, which are very difficult to read or understand. It is my hope and prayer that this information is received with the same intent—service—that I am writing from.

I began writing this autobiography only three or four days after my ascension. It seemed like the perfect thing to do as a closure and completion of a forty-year cycle, a 250-lifetime cycle and a 3000-lifetime cycle (if you include all the lifetimes of my entire soul group). One of the key questions that was percolating within me was, What's next? This was also a question that my friends were dealing with. A lot of new information and inner guidance has poured in for all of us.

What I came up with was this. First, my main focus is my service work. My main mission seems to relate to the masses. I am here to bring the teachings of the Spiritual Hierarchy, the path of initiation and ascension work to the world at large. I feel very qualified and ready to do this, given my unique training and background. This is something I have been preparing to do for some time now.

On a more personal level, my own continued evolution is toward greater realization of God. Also, given my sensitive digestive system, part of my own work is to use the higher octave of energy I am now anchored in to heal and strengthen this area completely.

We were told that part of the work of completing the sixth initiation and preparing to take the seventh is to polish the diamond, in a sense. It is a continuation of the process one has already been in, except moving toward greater purification and refinement. This would entail a greater focus on getting out of the negative ego, being more loving, maintaining greater feminine/masculine balance, balancing the threefold flame of love, wisdom and power to a greater extent and being less critical or judgmental.

In many ways my life was exactly the same as before, except for the fact that I felt very different. I was now fully anchored on the monadic plane and fully merged with my monad and mayavarupa body. Before that, as a fifth-degree adept, I was merged on the atmic plane and my monadic (mayava-rupa) body was going in and out. The benefit of ascension is that they anchor and remain once you take the sixth initiation.

My Inner-Plane Work

One of the fascinating aspects of the spiritual path is how much goes on in the inner plane that we have no idea about. I began to piece together what I was actually doing on the inner plane each night while I slept. Some of what I am about to mention I had recollections and dream fragments of and some was told to me by the masters.

First, I was told that I have been running large-scale ascension platforms that involve using the meditation procedures and ascension techniques I have outlined in my books. Second, I knew that I had been traveling to Sirius at night to attend classes and meetings. One of the classes I was taking was on teleportation. Third, I'd also had a number of dreams of meetings on the inner plane about my book series. I remember meeting with my publisher three different times on the inner plane; however, I was also told that other book meetings were going on.

One night I met with Lenduce, which was a real treat. I knew that I also frequently went to Djwhal's ashram on the inner plane and occasionally to Sai Baba's ashram. I also traveled every night to the Arcturian starship for healing and treatments. The Arcturians told me that I was so busy on the inner plane at night that I would have to cut back on some of my regimented activities to make room to go to their starship. I gladly restructured my busy schedule.

Vywamus told me that I was also working in the inner plane on the shift of energy flow from Sirius, which occurred on April 25, 1994. I was somehow helping in this process to create a greater flow of energy from Sirius, which is the higher university and intimately connected to the galactic core. He also told me that I was working with some group of beings who were involved in some kind of merging or immersion process that was very different from the merging process familiar to humanity on Earth. It sounded like some kind of extraterrestrial group that has a different kind of blending process than we do. For some reason Vywamus said I was working with this on the inner plane while I slept.

September 6 through September 12

Djwhal Khul told us another fascinating piece of information that he kept repeating the entire month of August. He said that as of September 6 through September 12, 1994, there would begin a particular process on the planet that made it absolutely essential for all people on the spiritual path to let go of all power struggles and negative emotional interactions as much as possible. This was especially the case for any and all high-level initiates.

Djwhal was preparing us, for he said that as of these dates the karma would be coming back much stronger and faster to those indulging in this behavior. He said what the Hierarchy was looking for was not necessarily perfection, but rather consistent ongoing choices to create love rather than fear, attack thoughts and intimidation. It was the intent and the conscious work at this that the masters were looking for, not that they were expecting no negative emotions to occur. I found this guidance quite interesting, so I did a careful assessment of my whole program and made some adjustments to prepare properly for this occurrence.

The Comet Fragments Hitting Jupiter in July 1994

Djwhal began speaking of this solar event in May, as did television's CNN. Astronomers from around the world watched it. The fragments of an extremely large comet hit Jupiter with a force something like ten thousand times that of an atomic bomb. They said on the news that it would be the most violent event ever recorded in this history of the solar system—that is, in terms of what humanity was consciously aware of.

Jupiter astrologically has to do with expansiveness. Vywamus said that this event would actually facilitate our dropping a spiritual veil. He called it a solar jolt and said that it was not a negative thing, although humanity's interpretation of it might generate a lot of fear.

It must be understood that the solar system has a relationship to our physical bodies and four-body system. The planets could be likened to the chakras of Helios, our Solar Logos. We all know the Hermetic law "as within, so without; as above, so below." We also are aware that the microcosm is like the macrocosm. When an event like this happens in our solar system, it will be reflected within our own chakra and four-body systems. Djwhal told us to use this event for the expansion of love for humanity.

Djwhal told us that the comet hitting Jupiter would ignite the core of the Earth, causing channels of energy to open up, resulting in the release of more prana to humanity. How humanity uses this energy will depend on each individual's level of consciousness. Some will integrate it. Some will rebuff the energy.

The cometary collisions definitely caused an acceleration and more rapid growth. This occurrence is part of the rhythm of the universe. How it was experienced would be determined by one's consciousness. Those more negatively and egotistically based responded from fear and attachment to form. The one constant you can count on in the universe is change.

New Inner Spiritual Guidance Hot off the Press

After my ascension there was an active period of integration and repolarization of my energies. I was repolarized from striving to attain the beginning of my sixth initiation to completing my sixth and beginning to understand for the first time what the seventh initiation is all about. I want to say that there is nothing wrong in having a desire to ascend. Some might call this spiritual ambition. The Eastern religions all talk about the need to get rid of desire. I would agree with this, except for the desires for liberation and God realization. My desire to ascend was honestly so that I could remain on the planet and be of greater service to humankind. In Buddhism they call this the vow of the bodhisattva.

One interesting change that occurs in an archetypal fashion, I believe, for those attaining the sixth initiation and ascension is letting go to a large extent this spiritual desire for ascension and liberation, even though there are more initiations (346, to be exact). Ascension marks a completion. I became almost totally focused on service, whereas when I was a fifth-degree initiate a large part was focused only on completion and service.

To some this might sound egotistical, but I think there are few people on a spiritual path who do not secretly or inwardly strive for personal ascension amid their service work. I am here to tell you that this is okay and even normal, not egotistical. If this became too much one's focus, to the disregard of one's service work, then it can become a problem. But it is okay to strive to attain self-realization, which is ascension. I felt that the rest of the initiations would come in a more natural, organic fashion. I no longer felt the push and drive I'd felt before, like a horse smelling the barn after a long ride.

The other important point I want to make here is that people are going to be ascending in great numbers. As of May 1994 there were from 5000 to 10,000 people ascending. In May 1995 there were another 5000 to 7000. In October another 5000 to 7000 would ascend. In the following June another mass wave of ascension with similar numbers would take place.

In the recent past it has been a rarer occurrence. The times we are living in now, because of the tremendous spiritual acceleration, are going to make it more common. I bring this up so you won't think that the core group and I are special in any way. We might be called forerunners of the mass waves of ascension. I am here to give you something of a road map from my personal experience. I want to emphasize here that my experience is not the only way or the only map. For example, my exact ascension experience with the core group will not be the same for all. Our ascension ceremony was created in a particular way because of our unique talents, gifts, synergy and friendship.

Other people's ascension ceremonies I am sure will be totally different. Some might occur on the inner plane, and they might not be consciously aware of much of what is going on. Others might see and experience even more than we did. The point is that ascension is a very natural, really mechanical process. It is much like going to college. You need a certain number of units, credits and special types of classes to graduate. With ascension you need a certain level of light quotient, transcendence of negative ego, balancing of karma, fulfillment of your mission, unconditional-love focus and service to humanity. When these spiritual units and credits are fulfilled, you will ascend and graduate, and there is nothing in the universe that can stop it. When you reach that level and complete those units, it automatically happens.

I was guided by Djwhal Khul not to focus so much on the superhuman powers of an ascended master for now. He told me that I am enrolled in teleportation classes on the inner plane and that I should just let these more transcended abilities develop in a natural fashion. We were told that it might take five or ten years to fully develop them. One thing that needs to be developed more is our light-quotient level. To achieve ascension one must have a minimum of 80 percent light quotient. We were told that we had around 83 to 84 percent. We were also told that our main focus should be our service work and the maintenance of our basic spiritual practices of meditation, physical exercise, good diet, journal-writing and so on, but in a very easy and natural way.

An interesting thing that I personally feel now, and have felt for a long time (which I am sure most of my readers can relate to), is that doing these spiritual practices takes no discipline at all. I don't have to push myself to meditate; I love to do it. I don't have to try and eat a good diet; I love to eat good, healthy food. I don't have to push myself to write in my journal; when I have the need to do it, I do it because it makes me feel better. As stated in *A Course in Miracles*, "True pleasure is serving God."

We were also being guided to focus on our personal healing and on strengthening our four-body system. It was different for each of us in our core ascension group. For me it was healing and strengthening my physical vehicle. For others it was healing and strengthening their emotional vehicle and so on. One of the things I can't emphasize enough is that you don't have to be perfect to ascend. I can tell you that for an absolute fact.

I am actually quite amazed at how much karma and unclarity is allowed. I know a lot of people who are either ascended or almost ascended, and all these people, including myself, are far from perfect. I share this with you to give you hope and faith and so you can see that ascension is not some impossible task to achieve.

Another archetypal factor after one ascends is feeling different from humanity. In actuality you have a deep and abiding sense of oneness with all of humanity, while at the same time you know that you are merged with the fifth kingdom. Humanity is to a great extent still identified with the fourth kingdom. As an ascended master, you are a planetary citizen and also a solar, galactic and universal citizen. This feeling of difference also translates into a feeling of compassion for all those who have ascended, having traversed and struggled with the human dilemmas that all on Earth face. There is also great compassion and love for those who still remain on the battlefields of the fourth kingdom.

Another archetypal experience of being ascended is the feeling of being overshadowed or overlighted by spiritual forces in a much more dramatic way. After I ascended I have noticed a major difference in how tapped in I feel and how present the higher forces are around me at my slightest invitation or thought. This is a wonderful feeling. I felt this as a fifth-degree initiate, but it became even more pronounced after my sixth initiation.

The other major benefit of ascension is that the physical/etheric blueprint you were using through your hundreds of incarnations on Earth has been totally replaced by the monadic, or mayavarupa, blueprint. The physical blueprint is often tainted by the trials and tribulations of Earth life. After ascension this has been totally cleared away and the blueprint is 100 percent clear and perfect. You can request that this switch be made before you ascend. Mine was switched as a fourth-degree initiate. My sense is that it is not solid and eternally anchored until after ascension, however.

One other fascinating piece of inner guidance we received was that we are connected to a large core ascension group on the inner plane of approximately 500 to 600 people. This group is made up of other fifth- and sixth-degree initiates on the second ray. Djwhal Khul told us that this second-ray planetary-core ascension group was meeting nightly on the inner plane. He said that there were other groups such as this on the different rays. Our particular group holds a central column of all the combined core ascension groups because of what Djwhal Khul called our focus of intent, purity, cutting-edge work and ability to not get too caught up in the glamours.

We began to tune in to this group more consciously during our meditations and dream time. I bring this up because many of you might already be connected with these groups or will be in the near future. I began focusing a good deal on how I could be of the greatest service to this group.

We were also told that many people in this group are closely connected with the eleventh and twelfth rays, which have to do with bridging and embodying the new age. This group also has the ability to work well with the first ray, which is the will aspect of Sanat Kumara. The four of us are closely connected to this group because we all have a second-ray monad and/or soul. (See the chapter "Esoteric Psychology and the Science of the Twelve Rays" in *The Complete Ascension Manual*.) This is why we are so personally connected to Djwhal Khul and Master Kuthumi. Kuthumi is the head (the chohan) of the second ray. He has sent most of his students to study with Djwhal Khul, who is his senior ascended-master assistant.

Another interesting occurrence was functioning as a friend and helper to the core group on the inner plane. Sometimes I would help them personally or with a client. They saw and heard me quite clearly. The strange thing is that I had no conscious memory of doing it. I am sure they did the same for me, however.

I tend to be more telepathic than clairvoyant, so I don't always see where my help is coming from. One doesn't have to be ascended for this to happen. It is amazing how much takes place on the inner plane that we are not consciously aware of. I know that I am involved with many, many projects on the inner plane, as we all are, but I am aware only of bits and pieces, not the full scope.

7

My Meditations with the Core Group

The Sixth- and Seventh-Dimensional Chakra Grids

In *Soul Psychology* I wrote extensively about the twenty-two chakras, which complete the third-, fourth- and fifth-dimensional chakra grids. As one evolves spiritually, the higher chakras become anchored into the seven basic chakras, of which many of us are commonly aware. At ascension the sixteenth chakra is anchored into the crown chakra. The previous eight months prior to my actual ascension, I had been anchoring and activating my twenty-two chakras into my crown and third eye and so on downward. After our ascension I received inner guidance that there was a higher grid of chakras now available to us.

Vywamus confirmed this and said there were sixth- and seventh-dimensional chakra grids. The sixth-dimensional grid is chakras 23 through 29. The seventh-dimensional grid is chakras 30 through 36. Djwhal Khul confirmed to us that we had indeed anchored our twenty-two chakras into our four-body system. We were now ready to anchor our sixth- and seventh-dimensional chakra grids. This had to be done slowly and properly, however, because if the higher frequencies were brought in too fast, they could burn out the etheric grids and have a very deleterious effect on the organs and glands.

Do not under any circumstance work with activating these sixth- and seventh-dimensional grids until after you achieve your ascension and sixth initiation. Work first with anchoring the twenty-two chakras. Most of humanity has not gone beyond anchoring the tenth chakra. If the sixteenth is actual ascension, you can see what a high voltage of energy the twenty-second chakra is. Chakras 16 through 22 must be brought in very slowly also. Always ask in meditation that the higher chakras be brought in under the guidance of your monad and soul.

I would recommend bringing in one a week, starting with the eighth chakra. Even doing it this way is doing it incredibly fast. Always end your invocation for this anchoring with the statement, ". . . if this prayer and invocation is in harmony with the will of my monad and soul for me." There will be no danger as long as you are not impatient in the process. The same is true for people who are attempting to rush the raising of their kundalini. Ask one of the ascended masters or Sanat Kumara or Vywamus to guide and monitor the process of anchoring these chakras for you.

After you ascend you can then move up to the next, or sixth-dimensional, chakra grid. When we went to Djwhal's ashram and discussed this with him, he told us that there were four stages of anchoring the sixth-dimensional chakra grid. The first stage was to be exposed to it. The second stage was to let it enter. The third stage was to allow it to be wired in. The fourth stage was when one receives one's instruction manual. The full realization of the sixth-dimensional grid leads to complete elevation beyond the normal scope of activity. The realization of the grid leads to the transcendence of all physical laws and organic functions of the human body. It leads to a complete liberation from the body without being separate from it. It also leads to anchoring the spiritual wattage that lends itself to teleportation and levitation.

When Djwhal Khul first began to work with us to anchor the sixth-dimensional and seventh-dimensional chakra grids, we began with the first phase, or exposure to the grids. Sanat Kumara appeared to facilitate the process. For me the process of full anchoring was to take from two to three weeks. At the time of our work with Djwhal on this topic, our light quotient was at the 87 percent level.

We were amazed at the speed with which our light quotient had been building. We had literally ascended only five or six weeks before. At that time we were approximately at the 83 percent level. In one month's time we had gone up three or four points in our overall light-quotient level. This was extraordinary, a direct result of the astrological configuration that occurs once every 90,000 years, which opened up a light package from Sirius that the Hierarchy, Vywamus and Sanat Kumara had anchored. This, in combination with the Wesak Festival, which is always the highlight of the entire year, was an incredible boon. It is always of great spiritual benefit to be involved with a spiritual community. The energies will always be much stronger if you meditate in a group, compared to trying to do everything on your own. Raising our light quotient was also a result of how focused we had been.

During this first session with Djwhal and Sanat Kumara they anchored up to chakra 29. This was about six chakras more than we had previously activated. It was in truth the intense spiritual work we had been doing the past three or four years that was allowing us to move so quickly. We set up a time one week later to continue the anchoring and to move into the second stage of the process. A number of days after this initial process I realized that we had anchored the sixth-dimensional chakra grid, which is chakras 23 through 29.

The next week I wasn't feeling well, so we scheduled for a week later. The masters said that this was appropriate anyway, for it would give us another week to acclimatize to the new chakra grid that had been anchored. The following Sunday morning we began the next stage of the process, which was absolutely fascinating. We went to Djwhal's ashram. Above us Djwhal had some kind of ascension machine. This ascension machine created a ball of light that was run through our bodies three times, especially our etheric body. The purpose was to insulate the work that had been done in the previous two weeks and also to heal, insulate and contain any loose or frayed etheric nerves. In the Eastern religion they are referred to as the etheric *nadis*. This insulation allowed us not to lose any of the sixth-dimensional energy with which we were now beginning to merge and anchor.

We were told that our light-quotient level was fluctuating between 87, 88 and 89 percent. Two weeks before, we had seemed to be steady at 87 percent, so we were slowly but surely climbing. Vywamus had been doing some rewiring on us during the previous two weeks that prepared us for this work. We were also told that we were at the 3½ level of the seven sublevels between the sixth and seventh initiation. Djwhal then filled our physical bodies with these golden orange balls of light, which first filled our chakras and then our entire bodies and auras. He told us that the technologies we had been using were created by both the Arcturians and Vywamus himself. He also told us that the color of our new sixth-dimensional chakra grid, which was now fully activated, was golden. Our auras were now filled with this golden color; he said that the aura of our blood would have this color.

The work would also give us greater vitality. He referred to this new energy matrix as the golden Buddha body, or fully ascended body. My feeling was that we were beginning to come into the realization of our ascension. He told us we were three months ahead of schedule in terms of completing our sixth initiation. We would be doing this as forerunners, in a sense, so we would help the mass group do the same thing at the 12:12.

Later in the week the Arcturians accelerated or intensified their work with us as a direct result of this insulation work. They seemed very excited about it. Djwhal said that the full anchoring and integration achieved this day would help us move more fully and work with the seventh, eighth and ninth dimensions of reality. The process we had just gone through was being done en masse with 10,000 to 20,000 people on the inner plane. The most advanced ascended masters such as Vywamus were spearheading this work.

Three ascended masters were in charge of each group of 10,000. It seemed to be easier for the masters to do this on a large scale all at once. Djwhal told us that this work would help us to stabilize and anchor the axiatonal alignment. He said that there were about 500,000 people who were marked for completion of their ascension over the next five years. I was very pleased to hear that there were so many. A lot of work was performed on us during sleep time and would continue in the future to prepare us for upcoming integrations.

I asked Djwhal what the next installment was for the following week, but he wouldn't tell me. He said he wanted to see how we did with this process, then next week he would see what we were ready for. This process also seemed to help in the full anchoring and integrating of the mayavarupa body, or monadic blueprint body. The Arcturians really stepped up their light-quotient activation after we installed the work. I also began focusing on getting light showers from the masters. We could hardly wait for our next session with Djwhal to see what was next. I secretly hoped that we would anchor our seventh-dimensional chakra grid, or chakras 29 through 36. Stay tuned!

Our Next Session

Our next session was absolutely awesome. Djwhal and Vywamus had pretty much kept us in the dark about the process we were in and what would follow each week. Vywamus earlier in the week said that we were preparing to take another great leap. He also told us that we would start developing the more transcended physical-ascension abilities within the next five years. I intuited that it would not be until we took our seventh initiation within a year's time and then completed about half of the seventh that we would begin more actively practicing these higher ascension skills. This looked like about two years from the time we took our ascension. The process was beginning to look much clearer to me now.

In our next meeting with Djwhal in his ashram, he anchored into our third chakra a prana wind machine created by the Arcturians. This device's function is to spin in the third chakra, which creates a wind that clears all our nadis, etheric nerves, meridians, chakras, veins, arteries and capillaries.

The device rotated clockwise. It did not add any energy, but used the energy in our systems. It served to create ever-widening concentric circles, which cleared all the etheric tubes in our body. It was quite an exhilarating experience. Djwhal said that the clearing was permanent. As part of the process, Djwhal guided me to call in the Arcturians as I normally did throughout my day to help facilitate this work. (I would recommend that you try out this particular process while in meditation under the guidance of your monad, Djwhal Khul and the Arcturians. You do not have to wait to ascend to use this Arcturian technology. I have been using this prana wind clearing device when I feel energetically clogged and imbalanced, and it seems to help.)

Vywamus also did some amazing work on us to calibrate our chakras as a preparation for taking the next leap in consciousness. Djwhal told us that the activation, anchoring and insulating of the sixth-dimensional chakra grid was now complete. He said it would take us three days to three weeks to integrate the work that had been done. I forgot to mention that after this prana-clearing device was used, Djwhal said that we had some nerve damage in our digestive system and some energy leakage in our spines. The inner-plane healing masters were called in to repair this, which Djwhal said afterward was permanent. It was a little hard for me to believe that they could repair it so quickly, although I accepted it as done.

During the session Djwhal also "retired" certain brain functions that had to do with material ways of being in the world. Other brain centers were activated for a more spiritual use. During the session Lord Maitreya came and placed his hand on our hearts and gave us a heart blessing.

The previous day had been a hard day for me personally, and I think he sensed that. He said something to the effect that the spiritual path can be hard at times. Sanat Kumara then came and spiraled some energy through our crown chakras and around our body. It felt really good. Djwhal told us that we were vibrating during this meditation work session at about the 93 to 94 percent light-quotient level, although our overall light-quotient average was still between 87 and 88 percent. He wanted us to try to hold this energy as long as possible. He said that this clearing work also helped us clear and lighten our bloodstream. In conjunction with the full anchoring of the sixth-dimensional grid were an infinite number of mini tornadoes that were helping to blend these higher bodies and frequencies into our four-body system. This was something I had experienced previously in one of my meditations.

The other fascinating piece of work done in the session was to align our energies to the computer in the center of the Earth. This work apparently connected us to the elohim computers, which we became joined with in this process. The first elohim computer had been fired at the conclave of Michael in March 1994. Twelve more were to be fired in the next two to four years. This joining work would allow us to be more cognitively aware of the process and more attuned to the Spiritual Hierarchy.

Djwhal was in tune with our desire to speed up the acceleration of the light-building and initiation process. He told us that we were serving as experimental models because of the accelerated light-quotient building we were doing. This would allow us to bring others along more quickly. He told

us that the work being done with us was also being done on other people simultaneously. I tried to pin Djwhal down in terms of what the next step in
the process was; however, he was keeping it all a mystery. I was incredibly
excited about the work already done. Djwhal said that our sixth-
dimensional self that already exists on that level (and on each dimension,
for that matter) was automatically being blended in with us in this process.

The Following Week

Our next session in Djwhal's ashram was a week later. We had one conversation earlier in the week where we did a Huna prayer and ran the spiritual energies with the help of the Arcturians and the Cosmic Consultant.
Our regular Sunday morning session, however, was dedicated to going to
Djwhal's ashram. This amazing process proceeded with Djwhal doing some
work on us called the matrix-restructuring program. This was a new push by
the Spiritual Hierarchy to release core fear programming. This particular
process is done by Djwhal Khul, Vywamus and the inner-plane healing
masters. Its purpose is to remove the matrix of energy in the brain and central nervous system that is the cause of any emotional, mental or physical
problem a person is having.

This is a certain type of spiritual technology that the Hierarchy has at
its disposal which literally pulls out of the reptilian brain and central nervous system the entire core matrix of any given problem. The idea here is to
follow the matrix back to the very essence of the problem. Part of the process also entails a certain conscious agreement on the disciple's part to
agree to remove the charge from the soul records and clear the karma. In
other words, there is a little talking that goes on with the process to give the
Spiritual Hierarchy permission to go in and do this work. Instead of taking
years of therapy, the Hierarchy can go right in and remove the imbalanced
matrix of energy.

This disjointed energy looks like lines of energy that are crossed, rather
than ordered and working in perfect unison. Part of the process is to go into
the crystalline structure and balance the cell salts so the imbalanced matrix
design cannot stick to it. This process actually balances the male and female genetic structure and works with the helix. The completion of this
work allows a person to release his/her personal core fears, and it properly
attunes the pineal and pituitary glands to receive higher galactic forces. It
is really quite profound work and is usually done on disciples and initiates
rather than on those who have not yet stepped onto the spiritual path.

The focus of the work on me had to do with some digestive weakness in
my pancreas. This apparently was related at a core level to marriage problems my parents were having when I was born and a certain responsibility I
took on as an infant to bring them back together. The moment that Djwhal

said this, I knew it was true. This apparently put an undue stress on my nervous system, which manifested as an electrical weakness in my pancreas. Later in life, some ambition I had resolved, but remnants of which remained, was also related to a core fear. Djwhal said that the Hierarchy had been working on me during the dream state. During the session they pulled the whole matrix out of my system and I agreed to release the karma and remove it from the soul records. I didn't feel that much physically; it was more of a subtle energetic and emotional shift.

Djwhal told us that 90 to 95 percent of our core fear was removed by the end of the session. This, of course, was something we had been working on for a long time. Djwhal said that we had released all of our personal fears. However, what was left was more of a collective or humanity-based fear.

This matrix-restructuring program is something you can ask for in your prayers and meditations. Ask to be taken to Djwhal Khul's ashram on the inner plane to have this work done. You can specifically ask to have it done in relationship to any specific emotional or physical health problem you are dealing with. It is quite amazing work.

Even before you ascend, do ask to become a part of this core fear-releasing program that has been set up by Lord Maitreya and the Spiritual Hierarchy. Since this session we have been releasing enormous amounts of these core fear weeds from our four-body system. Some of them are past-life in nature, some from this life and some from the collective consciousness. Clairvoyantly they look like dark vines and roots when they are pulled out. When you are done with this work, it is also a good idea to call forth the cosmic fire under the guidance of your monad in order to burn up any etheric dross that has been released into the aura. You could also use the prana wind machine, or you could call forth the spirit vortex from your monad to swirl it out of your aura. The cosmic fire burns it up, as can the violet transmuting flame.

Our Following Session

In our next meditation session we all traveled to Shamballa in our group merkabah. We had all been guided that we were rapidly moving toward completing our ascension and were being prepared to take our seventh initiation. I did an invocation to call the energies, and an interesting thing happened.

The elohim began sending fire letters down through our crown chakras, which poured through our fields. The seven of us were then electrically connected together into what I can only describe as a group entity. The fire letters flowed through this electrical wiring as blood flows through a person's veins and arteries. Sanat Kumara said that this elohim infusion would give us greater access to Shamballa. The elohim, for those of you who don't know, are the creator gods. They might be considered the thought attributes of God, whereas the archangels are the feeling tones of God. They each serve as a balancing function for each other. The chanting of the word "elohim" is one of the most powerful mantras I have ever used.

We all agreed to work as a group entity in our spiritual work. Djwhal told us that this group would probably get even larger in time, up to twelve people. I would recommend that you call for the anchoring of the fire letters from the elohim in your own meditations.

The Seventh-Dimensional Chakra Grid

In our next meditation session we again traveled to Djwhal Khul's ashram. This was an important day, we felt, for it was exactly three weeks from the day that Djwhal said we needed to integrate the sixth-dimensional chakra grid. After we chatted with him for a little while, he said that we were ready to anchor the seventh-dimensional grid (chakras 30 through 36). Djwhal called on Sanat Kumara and Vywamus for help. A lattice network of light/energy grids began to anchor into us. The inner-plane healing masters were called forth to help with the interweaving and integrating of this grid. It felt wonderful. It was like we were tuning in to a much higher level of light.

When the work was completed Djwhal told us that we had now officially anchored the seventh-dimensional chakra grid; however, only one-fourth of it was activated. Again, this process needed to be done in stages to prepare us for the higher light voltage that was now coming in. Djwhal told us that the thirty-six chakras was the highest chakra grid usually anchored on the Earth plane. He said that chakras 36 through 50 made up the eighth- and ninth-dimensional chakra grids, and that in our case an exception might be made in the future for the purposes of Earth service to anchor at least part of these higher grids. Upon completion of the seventh-dimensional grid, chakra 36 would be anchored in our crown chakra and fully activated. We were all looking forward to the completion of this work.

Lenduce's Ashram

In our next meditation we began by going to the ascension seats in Shamballa. There we invoked the help of Sanat Kumara, Vywamus, Lenduce, Djwhal Khul, the Mahatma and the Cosmic Consultant. It was shortly after this that Lenduce (the higher aspect of Vywamus) stepped forward and asked to work with us. He told us that we had just reached the galactic level in our evolution, where this was appropriate. He invited us into his ashram on the inner plane. I asked him what dimensions of reality he was working with, and he answered, "Dimensions nine through twelve." I told him I had recently been spending a lot of time in the ascension seat in Shamballa and asked if he had one in his ashram. Sure enough, he does.

We talked a little more, and then I suggested that we sit in the ascension seat in his ashram. It felt like we were lying down, floating suspended in midair in some kind of tube. The energy felt absolutely wonderful and much more refined. It felt like we had gone up another octave, which in truth we had. Later that day during a catnap I had a dream that we were moving to Denver. Upon waking I immediately knew the meaning. Denver is called the Mile-High City because of its altitude.

Lenduce invited us to work with him on a more ongoing basis, which we were extremely pleased about. We said a whole bunch of prayers for the help we desired in our personal and service work. I also asked Lenduce to help us anchor the microtron. He said that the microtron was like a computer chip that could be permanently anchored and it received the highest levels of ascension energy. We asked that the microtron be permanently anchored, along with the cosmic heart.

In this session I also asked Djwhal, who seemed to be floating around, about the mayavarupa body. Some of us were still having some health problems, mine a little more chronic. We were wondering to what degree we had anchored and integrated the mayavarupa body. Djwhal and Lenduce said that we should see *ourselves* as the mayavarupa body. They said it was anchored and in the process of fully manifesting into the physical. The golden, or solar, body of light was in the process of overlaying the mayavarupa body, which was in turn overlaying our physical bodies.

Lenduce said that in working with him we were now in a loop, our main ashramic connection, of course, being Djwhal Khul's ashram. From there we were traveling to Sanat Kumara and the ascension seats in Shamballa. Above that we were working with the Arcturians in their ascension chambers on the spaceship. At this level Metatron was stepping down his energies to help us build our light quotient. Above that, we were working with Lenduce now in his ascension seats. From there we were traveling back down to Vywamus, who was helping us build our golden Buddha body, also called the solar body of light, then returning to Earth with this energy connection for our service work.

One other thing Lenduce said that I found interesting: The other reason we were ready to connect with him and the galactic level was because of our steadiness and focus of intent. This feedback I know is true. Over the past five or six years I have trained myself basically never to leave the light. Previous to this I was extremely committed to the light; however, I would fluctuate a bit and was a little more on a roller coaster in terms of my attunement. In other words, I allowed myself to give in to the lower self at times and go on automatic pilot and be weak. It was about five or six years ago that I consciously made a vow to close the door on this option and never leave the soul or spirit ever again. By the grace of God I have held to this

vow almost perfectly, and this feedback six years later was the spiritual
fruit of the commitment I had made. It is interesting that a commitment
such as this would be part of what has opened my consciousness to the galactic core and the galactic level.

In our next session a week later we went back to Djwhal's ashram and
he basically reinforced the work already done on the anchoring of the seventh-dimensional chakra grid. Djwhal said that we had anchored
one-fourth of the grid, which means we had activated between chakra 30
and 31. He told us that it would probably take three months to fully install
chakra 35 into the crown. He also told us that even though we had now installed chakras 30 and 31 in the crown, we had actualized between chakra
27 and 28. In other words, there is a difference between what has been installed and what has been actualized.

Djwhal confirmed that things were moving extremely fast for us and
that the Spiritual Hierarchy was not doing this quickly as a personal favor
for us, but rather for specific service work that was needed for the Earth.
For the first time Djwhal said that there was some kind of plan to have us totally tuned up, probably on the seventh sublevel of the seventh initiation,
sometime in 1996. This would allow a certain current and frequency of light
to pour through our field and enter the grids of the Earth.

I asked Djwhal what the highest light quotient a person could maintain
while still retaining a physical vehicle was. He said that 97 to 98 percent
was the highest, because if one went any higher than that, the physical body
would no longer retain its physical form. We were being geared up over the
next year and a half to two years to hold this level of light and complete our
seventh initiation for specific work that Sanat Kumara and Djwhal Khul
would require of us. Djwhal also told us that in our sleep time we were beginning to work in the seventh and eighth dimensions. Our newfound work
with Lenduce was exposing us to dimensions nine through twelve.

In my work earlier in the week Djwhal said that the higher colors and
frequencies were running through my fields, which was not surprising,
given all that had been going on. We were experiencing something that I
can only call *hypertime*. Things were so accelerated that it felt like months
were going by each week and weeks going by each day. I am sure that many
of my readers can relate to this.

Djwhal also told us a fascinating thing about teleportation in this meditation session. We were told that above both of our externalized ashrams, an
etheric ashram was being created with the help of Arcturian advanced technology. This etheric ashram that was now being constructed would serve as
a midway station between our physicalized ashrams and Djwhal Khul's ashram on the etheric plane. We would be trained over the next few years to
practice teleporting to this midway ashram. After that was achieved, we

would practice teleporting to Djwhal's ashram. When I say "teleporting" here, I mean dematerializing the physical body and rematerializing in etheric form. Djwhal told us that this was a beginning step to practicing teleporting to another physical location, such as Sai Baba's ashram.

I was also told that I was being trained for future work I would be doing in Djwhal Khul's ashram upon leaving this plane, which was projected to be sometime after 2011. I had made an agreement on the inner and outer planes to work in his ashram for a period of time before going to Sirius, in terms of my cosmic evolution. As you can imagine, I was very honored and excited about this prospect.

For the first time Djwhal mentioned the possibility of *trilocation* as opposed to bilocation. He also told us that our work of dissolving our negative ego, or separative, fear-based consciousness, was also moving along at a rapid rate. We hadn't achieved total perfection in this area, but we were moving in the right direction.

Our Next Meditation

In our next meditation we went back to Lenduce's ashram and asked to be placed in the ascension seats. I then proceeded to invoke a series of energy anchorings, which are presented in the chapter on the seventh initiation. Lenduce told us that what I had invoked, our group should invoke in every meditation. I then asked him a key question, which led to one of the most important spiritual golden nuggets we had ever found. I asked Lenduce what was the most effective way to actualize the higher chakras that had been installed.

Lenduce had told us that we were actualizing chakras 27 and 28 even though chakras 30 and 31 had been installed. I wanted to know the best way to actualize all that had been installed. What Lenduce said was very interesting: During each meditation we should invoke the energies (as outlined in the next chapter), then we should call forth our personal merkabahs and ask that they be spun at the 91 percent level and at the thirtieth-chakra level. He told us that our light quotient was fluctuating between 89 and 91 percent this day. The spinning of the merkabah in conjunction with all the energies that had been invoked would stabilize us at the 91 percent light-quotient level and help us actualize chakra 30. We set up a plan to do this meditation religiously twice a day and call each other into our meditations each time. By doing this we would each be receiving four meditations a day.

I would recommend to you, my reader, to do this meditation and use this technique, although the numbers will have to be changed to accommodate your individual light-quotient level and the suitable chakra-anchoring process for your personal level of evolution. Ask your inner guidance and study my books to get an intuitive sense of where you are at and what level you are reaching toward. We felt that this was an extraordinary insight, and I cannot recommend more highly that you use it in your daily meditations.

Meditation Session, June 24, 1994

In this session we began a new regime of doing our seventh-degree meditation prayer twice a day on our own, invoking each other's presence at each meditation. When we spoke on the phone with each other, we would do it together, taking turns doing one paragraph at a time. Both of us were really feeling the effects. In the session Djwhal Khul told us some fascinating information about our overall process.

We were basically scheduled, he said, to complete our ascension around September and take our seventh initiation around the 12:12 (December 12, 1994). We were scheduled to complete our seventh initiation at the end of the following year, having gone through the seven sublevels of the seventh initiation. In Brian Grattan's system we had already taken the seventh and eighth initiation; the ninth we were scheduled to take in September. This would complete our ascension and the first three sublevels of the sixth initiation. We were scheduled to take our tenth initiation in that system at the 12:12 three months later. We were scheduled to take our eleventh initiation around Wesak, the full moon in May 1995. We were then scheduled to take our twelfth initiation at the end of 1995. This was the first time our progress had been mapped out so clearly.

This was the pattern if everything went as planned. The future can change, however. For example, if we allowed this to go to our heads, it might not happen at all. I share this with you to give you a sense of what can take place. In the work that the four of us were doing, I felt that we were mapping some new territory. Many masters have done it before; it is just that there are no books I have ever found that explain it in such a scientific manner.

At the end of the session we did a Huna prayer together. We were scheduled to talk again on the upcoming Sunday. We arranged to meditate together by phone three times a week instead of twice, since this next six to nine months was so critical. I personally felt that I was going through the greatest evolutionary leap I had ever experienced in this life or any other. The level of God current continually flowing through me was much stronger than anything I had ever experienced.

I had begun using the ascension seats more frequently, especially visiting Shamballa and Lenduce's ashram much more. The Arcturians continued to work behind the scenes on our behalf in a most wonderful manner.

Meditation Session, July 2, 1994

We began this meditation by going to the Golden Chamber of Melchizedek. We didn't ask for this, but seemed to be drawn there. Melchizedek began to send down the most sublime energies to help us remove all symbolic boulders that were blocking the manifestation of our dreams and visions. This probably happened because in starting our meditation, we put a burning pot in the center of the ascension column and burned our Huna prayers, which were focused on manifestation and prosperity issues.

The golden energy from Melchizedek was cleansing to our fields. Djwhal then came through and told us that we were ready for the next anchoring and installment of our seventh-dimensional chakra grid. Because of the group format, we didn't get into the details of what was being done; however, I intuited that another one-fourth of the grid had been laid, probably up to chakra 32. Djwhal told us that we were all holding the light quotient in a very stable manner, and that as we were now approaching the completion of our ascension, we would be invisible in group situations more often where the lower self held form. In situations where the higher soul and spirit held form, we would shine like great lights. This was not something we would have to try to do; it would be automatic. It was like some kind of automatic protection that would take no conscious effort.

The Mahatma then came through and told us that we should not be too concerned about the higher ascension abilities such as teleportation. He said that they would come about in a natural manner when we were ready. Our main focus would be service and living in joy and love, and everything else would unfold as needed.

Meditation Session, July 11, 1994

In our next meditation we went to Lenduce's ashram. Lenduce greeted us and I proceeded to ask him a couple more burning questions. The first one was whether there was an ascension seat in the solar core of Helios, the Solar Logos. I had been reflecting during the past couple of weeks about our going to Shamballa, the planetary center of Sanat Kumara, and to the galactic core with Lenduce. We had also been visiting the universal center with Melchizedek. However, the solar core of Helios was missing in this progression.

Lenduce told us that, sure enough, there was an ascension seat in Helios' chamber, but we had already been receiving these energies because we had been invoking the solar body of light, which tapped us into this level. This being the case, it was not necessary to go there, but we could if we liked. I would recommend your visiting there, my readers. Just ask to go to Helios' golden chamber to sit in the ascension seats. The merkabahs can be spun on that level also. This will give you the planetary-, solar-, galactic- and universal-level ascension seats.

I had my Sherlock Holmes hat on this day, so my investigative mind was not through yet. I looked at my job as one of mapping the cosmos as much as I could. So my next question of Lenduce was whether there were ascension seats we could visit beyond the universal level. Specifically, I asked if there were ascension seats on the many-sources level, the cosmos level and the cocreator or direct Source level itself.

It was then that we received another divine dispensation. We were invited during the sleep state to visit the actual cocreator council meetings at the highest Source level. However, we were only allowed to view them from the observation deck. We were not at a level of evolution to allow us to attend, but we were given the grace to observe. All we had to do was ask before bed and in meditation. Most likely this would occur during sleep. We were also told that they appreciated our enthusiasm, but would answer our prayer requests for acceleration and so forth only in a manner that was safe.

Lenduce then transferred us to Melchizedek, who told us that at the very highest level of the Godhead there exists the Cocreator Council of Twelve. Surrounding it are the elders, which I took to mean the twenty-four Elders of Light, who are in turn surrounded by the elohim, or cocreator gods. Then what follows is the many-sources level. There were no more ascension seats provided, just an observation deck, which we got a kick out of.

Meditation Session, July 13, 1994

In our meditation this day we went to the Golden Chamber of Melchizedek. I asked some questions on various matters, then we did a specialized Huna prayer for some manifestation work in regard to Djwhal's ashram. The highlight of our meditation, however, came when I asked Melchizedek about the Order of Melchizedek. This had been an interest of mine for years, for there is little written information on this planet about this ancient order. It was then that I asked Melchizedek, the Universal Logos, if he would officially initiate us into this order. He graciously and kindly agreed. Thus it happened that Melchizedek himself initiated us. This touched us profoundly. I had always wanted to be initiated into this order and knew that on some level I already had been; however, to have Melchizedek himself do it in this way was indeed one of the great blessings of my life.

Meditation Session, July 19, 1994

In our next meditation we went to Djwhal's ashram, and I had what I might call a review session to see where we were in this whole process. We seemed to do this about once every four to six weeks. I was interested in this not only for myself, but also because I was attempting to map this process for my readers, and I wanted to get a sense of how fast or slowly we were moving to get some kind of understanding.

Djwhal told us that we were now at the 91 percent light-quotient level. I was quite happy about this, for it felt like we had been stuck between 89

and 91 percent for a very long time. He also told us that at the group meditation we had done in Los Angeles, chakra 33 had been anchored into our
crown. I had intuited that it was chakra 32; however, I was happy to hear
that it was the thirty-third. This process was also now moving a little faster
than I had expected. I then asked where we were in the seven sublevels between the sixth and seventh initiation. Djwhal said we had completed the
fifth sublevel and were now working on the sixth and seventh. This was
good news, for the last time we had talked to him about this we were at the
8½ level [see below]. This information also related to the fact that we were
working on actualizing chakras 28 and 29.

I want to take a moment here to explain this last sentence. The fifth-
dimensional chakra grid encompasses chakras 16 through 22. The sixth-
dimensional grid is chakras 23 through 29. If we were now working on the
sixth and seventh sublevel, this meant we had actualized the first five chakras of the sixth-dimensional chakra grid. This would be chakras 23, 24, 25,
26 and 27. Do you see the parallel here between the seven sublevels and
the seven chakras? The fact that we were now working on sublevels six and
seven meant we were working on actualizing chakras 28 and 29.

Djwhal reconfirmed that in terms of the twelve initiations Brian Grattan
uses, we were still at 8½. The ninth initiation in Grattan's system would be
the completion of our sixth initiation in the Alice Bailey system and Djwhal
Khul's current system. We were now expecting to complete our ascension
in six to eight weeks—in September, as prophesied.

That night I had a dream that I was now entering the final semester of
my senior year in college. The meaning is clear. We were in the process of
the final work cycle to complete our ascension. Djwhal also reconfirmed
that our seventh initiation would occur midway between our ninth and tenth
initiation. This would be the moment when Sanat Kumara touches us on the
inner plane with his rod of initiation, officially making us a kindergarten
seventh-degree initiate. The process would then start all over again except
at a higher octave, moving through the seven sublevels of the seventh initiation until completion. However, all initiations stop at this point and are held
in abeyance until leaving the physical plane.

Meditation Session, July 29, 1994

In our meditation today we chatted with Madam Blavatsky, of Theosophical Society fame, who helped us with our manifestation and prosperity
work, which she was proficient at in her life on Earth. She is currently serving on a council on the inner plane called the Ascension Manifestation
Council with the Master El Morya, Saint Germain and other masters. This
council can be petitioned for divine dispensations in this regard. We were
guided to work with this council more closely to manifest the enlarged ash-

rams we were all envisioning.

Later that same day I received a triple confirmation on our personal ascension process. During the sleep state I dreamed I was told that I was about to complete my ascension. Djwhal Khul confirmed it later that morning, that there were approximately twenty people around the country in his ashram who would be completing their ascension sometime around August 23, 1994. This was a little over three weeks away. All of us received the same inner guidance separately.

Madam Blavatsky, who asked to be called Lady Helena, guided us to write a petition to the Ascension Manifestation Council to help us in the manifestation work we were doing. We were guided to say this petition every morning for five consecutive days. We began this work on Monday, August 1, 1994, and continued every morning that week. Little did I know that this week would be one of the most profound weeks of my entire life.

8

The Completion of My Sixth Initiation and Ascension

On August 1, 1994, Djwhal Khul told us that we had taken the initial stages of the ninth initiation in the twelve-initiation system. In the seventh-initiation system that meant we had achieved the beginning stages of the completion of our sixth initiation and/or ascension. Djwhal also told us that it would take the rest of the month of August to complete this process and stabilize the seventh sublevel between the sixth and seventh initiation. Initiation never occurs in just one moment; it is a process.

There is a moment of moving to the next level that is quite significant. I knew exactly when we took the ninth initiation, for on Friday morning the week before, I woke up remembering a dream in which I had finally completed the long process of ascension over all my lifetimes. In the dream I had popped into the next higher dimension and was wearing a white robe. I felt euphoric, ecstatic and relieved. This was the moment I had been seeking all this lifetime and, I am sure, in a great many of my past lives.

Even though I took my ascension on March 21, 1994, the fact that I hadn't fully completed it left me with a feeling of noncompletion. What was extraordinary to me was that taking the ninth initiation was only four months and eleven days after our actual ascension, and adding another month for completion of this ninth initiation made it five months and eleven days to fully complete our ascension.

This was all very exciting, for I also had an intuitive sense of the identity of many of these people. But I didn't know for sure and it didn't feel appropriate to ask about it. What was also nice was that these people were spread across the country and were all quite sharp in their own right. I had this wonderful feeling of a community of lightworkers either working together as a team in ascension-type centers or in the process of manifesting them. There was and still is a strong feeling of community and family.

The first dream I shared had been quite significant to me and was why I asked Djwhal if we had taken the ninth initiation. He said that we had taken it the same day I'd had that dream, which I somehow knew. About ten days after the dream I could already feel the process of preparing to take the seventh initiation (in the Alice Bailey system) beginning.

Djwhal said that we would be at the 9½ level (of the twelve-initiation system of Brian Grattan). My intuitive sense was that the next marker was about two months away. Djwhal had also told us that we were expected to take our tenth initiation on December 12, 1994, which is the gateway for mass ascension on the planet. Halfway between August first and the 12:12 was about the second week in October.

It is important to realize that the process of initiation is mathematical and scientific. It is much like regular school, where you meet the requirements and complete the classes. I would also like to mention the issue of speed. In truth, there is no rush. Our core ascension group chose and prayed for a dispensation of a more accelerated progression, which was granted by the Lords of Karma and Sanat Kumara. They did this so we could do greater service work and have much more responsibility. The faster you go, the more will be expected of you and the more work you will have to do, so keep this in mind if you are praying for an accelerated ascension path. Not everyone is interested in going faster.

Part of my purpose for tracking this process so closely has been for a service mission I am involved in. The mission is the book you are reading. I wanted to write a book that would give my readers an exact blueprint of the process of ascension as well as my personal account. My hope and prayer is that you will use the ideas and insights I have provided as well as others you can build on to do it as quickly as I did, or even more or less quickly as you choose.

The most important thing is not to look at this process as a race or competition or in a comparative fashion. From my talks with Vywamus, I estimate that the average person will take from one to five years to complete an initiation in this evolutionary period. Even if it takes five years, that is extraordinarily fast. During the time of Jesus masters took whole lifetimes to do just one initiation. Jesus himself took only one initiation in that life, and he is one of our highest examples. He moved from the third to the fourth initiation. That might be hard to believe, but it is true. Even in the early 1900s, almost two thousand years later, Djwhal Khul said that what took Jesus (one of the most advanced initiates this world has ever seen) fourteen years is now taking people fourteen months.

Djwhal also said that a person could move from the third to the sixth initiation in two years. By the grace of God I moved through two initiations in only fourteen months. I bring this up as a way to encourage you to keep on climbing.

Another lesson I have learned is how the Spiritual Hierarchy and Sanat

Kumara do the initiation process in groups. (As I mentioned, twenty people are involved with our core ascension group, and we hadn't known it before.) Just because two people are at the same level of initiation doesn't mean that they are equals in their teaching abilities, mastery, effectiveness of service work and so on. This is true for all initiations. (I am often blown away that certain people are at the level of initiation the masters say they are. I wouldn't have believed it in a million years.)

When I write in this book I speak from experience. My sole purpose in my books is to speed up the evolutionary path for all of humanity. I know what suffering is, and it is my aim to help humanity out of its suffering and into the indescribable peace, love and freedom of God realization. I believe that this book and all the books in my *Easy-to-Read Encyclopedia of the Spiritual Path* will provide you with all the tools and information you need to achieve your ascension in this lifetime and go well beyond if you choose.

Reflections on Completing My Ascension

I feel even more focused on service than before. It has always been my number-one priority. However, since I hadn't completed my ascension, and ascension had always been my goal, part of my energies were always focused on it. There is nothing spiritually wrong with that as long as the desire to ascend is connected with the intent to be of greater service. My own ascension-completion process has enabled me to put this book together, which I intuitively feel will be of great help to people. This is my greatest joy.

Djwhal Khul's famous statement in the Alice Bailey material of the need to "keep the mind steady in the light" is what I have done. My mind has not left the light at all. That is not to say I have not made mistakes. I have made tons of them since my ascension. I have simply learned from them, forgiven myself and moved forward even more strongly. Unceasing have been my efforts.

I also learned about the importance of focusing on building my light quotient. I worked with this almost twenty-four hours a day, seven days a week. I focused on this by working in the ascension seats in Shamballa, Lenduce's ashram, the Golden Chamber of Melchizedek and the Arcturian light-synthesis chamber. I also worked with Archangel Metatron. Throughout my day I sat in the ascension seats channeling higher-frequency energy to myself in a type of bilocation process. I recommend that you do this, too.

It is important that I have meditated as much as I could and served however and whenever I could to help others do the same. I have also tried to stay out of my negative ego, or separative self, as much as I could. I have tried to avoid competitiveness and comparing and to see each person as God, regardless of initiation status or any other appearances. My path is one of choosing humility instead of argument, choosing selflessness instead of selfishness.

What I realize now is that it is the daily little things that make the biggest difference:

- Getting out of bed and not oversleeping;
- Going the extra mile in meditation;
- Going the extra mile to help someone and doing kind deeds;
- Walking every day;
- Staying focused on my ideals, goals and priorities and not going on automatic pilot;
- Having fun and taking time for recreation;
- Managing time efficiently;
- Doing many things at once, like watching television and doing light-quotient building (my best light-quotient-building sessions were often watching TV or standing in line at the market or bank);
- Smiling, being loving and friendly with everyone I meet, even strangers;
- Practicing random kindness;
- Being organized in my spiritual and earthly work;
- Keeping track of my dreams and meditations;
- Spiritual reading and attending significant workshops;
- Focusing on my inner-plane work at night while I sleep;
- Sending my spiritual body to the spiritual events I can't attend physically;
- Praying a lot and anchoring the thirty-six chakras;
- Doing my prayer treatment religiously every day;
- Meditating with friends in groups as much as possible;
- Releasing core fear and replacing it with core love;
- Doing Huna prayers for any major help I need from God and the masters and keeping my victory log;
- Asking questions of the masters constantly;
- Practicing channeling;
- Reviewing and refining my ascension battle plan regularly;
- Working with a healing team sometimes as much as three times a day;
- Writing this book;
- Practicing the advanced ascension skills;
- Seeking constantly to expand my knowledge and build upon what was received the previous day;
- Networking;

- Meditating over the phone;
- Taking advantage of extra spiritual energies at special events such as full moons, comets, Wesak and at special astrological configurations (meditating and celebrating in groups during these events is a great boon to everyone's spiritual growth);
- Visiting Djwhal Khul's ashram and the ashrams of the other masters;
- Asking for protection every day and cleansing alien implants at least every month;
- Calling forth and using the Arcturian prana wind machine;
- Going to the movies every Friday night for simple relaxation;
- Going for "ascension walks" every day;
- Doing spiritual work the first thing every morning and the last thing before bed.

This is a quick review of some of the basics that have allowed me to complete my ascension over the past five months. The most important thing is to take one day at a time, even one moment at a time, and to live that moment properly as God would have you live it. That is not hard. Then live the next moment properly as God would have you live it. Pretty soon a whole day that you have lived properly has passed, then a week, then a month and then five and a half months have been lived properly, and almost an entire initiation has been completed.

Most of all, live in love and joy. Be unrelenting in your efforts. Once you understand what is required and you are provided with the tools, a map and a basic understanding, it is not really that hard. God wants you to pass your initiations. Take one step toward God and He/She will take ten steps toward you. Seek and you shall find; knock and the door shall be opened.

More Reflections

My intuition about when we would probably be taking our seventh initiation turned out to be accurate. Djwhal told us that we were looking at taking our seventh in either September or October. I immediately got more focused than ever and wrote up a Huna prayer for us, requesting that we actualize the potentiality of September.

My feeling about this whole process was that the next seven weeks from the beginning of August to the end of September would be the most important seven weeks of my life. Within this period we would experience the completion of ascension and taking the seventh initiation. Taking the seventh was to me taking on the full mantle of the Christ. It was also becoming a full-fledged seventh-degree Melchizedek. It felt like the doorway to the miraculous, bringing in the higher ascended-master abilities.

I was experiencing much greater spiritual current running through my etheric body and/or mayavarupa body. This was one marked difference. Another was the instant communication and response to my prayers, invocations and communications with the ascended masters and spiritual forces. Even my slightest thought seemed to draw a response, which was really a wonderful feeling. Herein also lies great responsibility.

I had one other very interesting insight about the nature of the initiation process. As I mentioned earlier, it is a group process more often than an individual one. A metaphor came to me that it is much like a sports team. Take a basketball team like the current Chicago Bulls or the Los Angeles Lakers of the past. Taking an initiation is like playing a major playoff or championship game. Every team has star players who might score a few more points than the other players. In the two teams above, this could be Michael Jordan and Scotty Pippin for the Bulls and Magic Johnson for the Lakers. When a team wins the game, playoff or championship, the *team* wins, not any one or two individuals.

When a group takes its initiation, some individuals in that group might be leaders or more advanced than the others, but all take the initiation together. This is what I mean when I say that the masters are not interested in individuals as much as group consciousness. All are on the same team, so all win, all are initiated. There is no competing or comparing, and this is as it should be.

Another analogy might be that of a gigantic puzzle. Each person has a piece of the puzzle. There might be a few whose puzzle piece is a little larger than the others, but everybody—all pieces in that ascension wave—takes the same initiation. In truth, all on the planet are the eternal Self and God already. The process of initiation is just realizing that truth.

Standing before Sanat Kumara

Two days after Djwhal told the core group and me that we were expected to take our seventh initiation in September or October, we requested to go before Sanat Kumara in meditation. It was while standing before him and other masters in Shamballa that we read the following Huna prayer requesting to take our seventh initiation in September, as Djwhal Khul said it was a possibility. The date of this request was August 4.

Beloved presence of God, Mahatma, Melchizedek, Lenduce, Vywamus, Lord Maitreya, Sai Baba.

Sanat Kumara, we come before you this day and pray with all our heart, soul, mind and might to request humbly to take our seventh initiation sometime in September, as Djwhal Khul has suggested is within our potentiality. We are ready now to take

*on the full mantle of the Christ. We are now requesting to be-
come full seventh-degree Melchizedeks in your service. We recognize the responsibilities held therein and welcome them
gladly. We ask for this divine dispensation in the name of the
Christ and accept this done as is thy will. Amen.*

*Our beloved subconscious minds, we hereby ask and command
that you take this thought-form prayer with all the mana and
vital force necessary to manifest and demonstrate this prayer to
Sanat Kumara and the Source of our being. Amen.*

*Beloved presence of God, Sanat Kumara, assembled masters of
the light of God, let the rain of blessings fall. Amen.*

After saying this prayer three times before this assembly of great masters and specifically to Sanat Kumara, we read a petition to the Ascension
Manifestation Council headed by Lady Helena, El Morya and Saint
Germain for help in manifesting our enlarged vision of Djwhal Khul's
ashram.

Upon completion of the petition, which we read out loud, Sanat Kumara
gave us his blessing and told us that there had been one block in our subconscious minds that was preventing the manifestation of funds for
Djwhal's vision, and this had been removed from our subconscious mind
during the meditation. Sanat Kumara said it had something to do with a
martyr program during our Piscean Age training that we were still carrying.
Sanat Kumara pulled it out like a bad weed in a garden and said we were
now clear for the granting of both prayer requests.

I think I can speak for all of us here that we felt honored, humble,
grateful and moved by this experience. We were then guided to go to the
Golden Chamber of Melchizedek, where the masters began some intensive
work on us. One thing we noticed for sure was a downpouring of fire letters,
key codes and sacred geometries. We remained there for about five or ten
minutes on the phone, then I continued meditating for about an hour by myself, just receiving the energies.

I felt that it was one of the most profound meditations we had ever had
together. The blessing that Sanat Kumara gave to our specific petition for
the monies to create the Djwhal Khul expanded ashram also had a deep
effect on me. Two of my major visions and goals were now close at hand. I
had the clear sense while sitting in the chamber that there were the core
twenty, whom I previously mentioned, and many more from around the
globe connected to other ashrams and masters, not just Djwhal Khul's. All
my life I have wanted more than anything in the world to become a seventh-degree Melchizedek. By the grace of God, it was now about to happen.

The other feeling and thought I had been having the previous two days had to do with how connected I felt to Djwhal's ashram and how much I was enjoying the ashramic work. I felt a blending of the inner and outer ashrams.

I have many personal responsibilities in the inner and outer ashrams. In the outer ashrams my part of the puzzle is to get my books out, to lecture and teach, to be a host at all ashramic events and to be a researcher, stabilizer, ambassador, socializer, psychologist, peacemaker, scholar, prophet and practical mystic.

I bring this up to give you a sense of what I mean about the many roles that we play in ashramic life. The most important thing is to find the role you are supposed to play. The fastest way to move through your initiation process is to play the role that God has designated for you in the ashram. No one person plays all the roles. God's divine plan is too vast for this to be possible. A lot of work I do in the ashram is actually behind the scenes.

Another example might be the passing of a baton in a relay race. All have to work together perfectly. Find the way you can serve best. Some positions in an ashram might seem more glamorous than others, perhaps being a channel. If that is your destiny, fine. I personally like to work behind the scenes. I actually don't prefer worldly recognition, but if that is my destiny, then so be it, but I won't go out of my way to find it. My only desire and focus is service and bringing people back to God realization while helping them achieve liberation. I just want to play my perfect role in the ashram and work in total harmony, cooperation and support as an instrument for the Spiritual Hierarchy and God's divine plan.

I want to add here that every person is connected to an inner-plane ashram. This is because you are connected on a monadic and soul level to one of the seven great rays. Your ashram is usually the ray that your monad has been designated to be by God. For example, my monad is second ray; that is why I am so connected to Djwhal Khul and the master Kuthumi. I do want to say here, however, that people often work in the ashram of other masters for long periods of time. Even if your monad is one ray and you feel connected—for example, to the Master Jesus/Sananda, who is the chohan of the sixth ray—you can still work in Sananda's ashram, although you will at some point deal with the ashram of your individual monad.

There are, of course, the seven chohans of the seven rays who head the seven great ashrams. They are, in order from one to seven, El Morya, Kuthumi and Djwhal Khul, Serapis Bey, Paul the Venetian, Hilarion, Jesus/Sananda and Saint Germain. Every night those who have stepped upon the spiritual path are active in the ashramic work while they sleep. Even though you might not be involved in an external-plane ashram, you are nevertheless connected, in a loose sense.

I anchor a physicalized ashram in my home. This is not necessary for everyone. It is a specific assignment I have been given. The most important thing is to see yourself connected on the inner plane to one or many of the ashrams, for all the ashrams make up what is termed the Spiritual Hierarchy, or Great White Brotherhood of God. This is the great ashram of the planetary Christ, the Lord Maitreya.

Everyone is a member of the Spiritual Hierarchy whether we realize it or not; we are externalized members of the Spiritual Hierarchy on Earth. See yourself as an agent and a fully externalized member working on behalf of the Buddha, Lord Maitreya and the chohans of the seven rays.

Meditation on August 5, 1994

On Friday, August 5, 1994, the core group and I had our most profound meditation yet. This meditation was also the completion of the five days of petitioning to the Ascension Manifestation Council. The meditation began by our asking to go to Djwhal Khul's ashram. It was here that we requested, as we had been guided earlier in the week, to anchor the final three chakras of the seventh-dimensional chakra grid into our crown. Up to this meditation we had anchored up to chakra 33 into our crown.

We were very excited about this process because it was the completion of the seventh-dimensional chakra grid. I also knew intuitively that it would catapult us toward completion of the sixth initiation and taking our seventh initiation shortly after. Djwhal surprised us by taking us to the light-synthesis chamber in the Arcturian starship to have this work done. He also invoked a highly developed healing team that specializes in this more advanced work. Djwhal watched as the Arcturians and inner-plane healing masters placed these final three chakras within each of us.

As we were being worked on, Djwhal talked to us. I asked some questions that were on my mind about this process and a few other things. He told us that not only had we taken the beginning stage of the ninth initiation, but that we were now completing the seventh sublevel between the sixth and seventh initiation (in the Alice Bailey system). This was important information to me because I wanted to make sure that the ninth initiation (in the Brian Grattan system of twelve) correlated with the seventh sublevel, which it does.

We were also told that our light quotient at this time was fluctuating between 91 and 93 percent. I had guessed previously that it was around 92 percent, which turned out to be accurate. The other thing he told us that really surprised me was that we were now actualizing chakra 33. He also said that we would have all thirty-six chakras actualized by the 12:12, which was December 12, four months away. I had a feeling that we would probably do it before then. However, Djwhal said that even though we would be fully actualized by the 12:12, the next step would be to learn how to make the new chakras usable in terms of the higher abilities that stem from them.

Djwhal also told us that there were now up to thirty people who were his students who would be completing their ascension and taking the seventh initiation with us. He referred to this group as prototypes. All the people in this group were receiving the sixth- and seventh-dimensional chakra grids even though most had not consciously asked for them. This again points to how the group initiation process occurs; the advances any individuals make are automatically transferred to the entire group consciousness. The advances any of us make enable all to receive, which is the way it should be. This erases any possibility of comparing and competition.

I then asked Djwhal how many of his students were earmarked for completing their ascension and taking the seventh initiation by the Wesak Festival of 1995. Djwhal told me that as a ballpark figure there were approximately eighty. I then asked how many were earmarked to complete their ascension in all the ashrams of the seven rays by Wesak next year. He gave me another ballpark figure of 500. These numbers seemed to coincide with what Vywamus had told me three or four months before.

My intuitive guess was that by May (Wesak) 1995 there would be approximately 1000 fully ascended and completed masters on the planet, which includes seventh-degree initiates. This number becomes a little larger if you also count the masters in the hollow Earth.

Realizing and Completing My Sixth Initiation and Ascension

It is essential to understand that when a person ascends and takes his/her sixth initiation, he is really back in kindergarten. He has moved from being an advanced adept or fifth-degree initiate to a beginning or kindergarten ascended master. Given that it took our core ascension group only six and a half months to go from the fifth to the sixth initiation, I had a strong feeling that it wouldn't take that long to move from the sixth to the seventh.

Before a person can get to the seventh he/she must complete or realize the sixth initiation. The process I have found was not dissimilar to the process I used to achieve my initial ascension. My personal experience was that I moved much faster than ever before. I think this was in part due to the fact that after six initiations I was finally learning the process.

Djwhal Khul, having noticed how fast we had all been moving since our ascension, said that we would realize the sixth initiation by 12:12 and that we would actually be overqualified. The date December 12, 1994, was the opening for the mass-ascension energies. The actual planetary mass ascension would not begin until May 1995. The gate opened at the 12:12.

It felt to me that if things continued in the same pattern, it would have taken our core group a little less than nine months to complete or realize the sixth initiation. This seemed like the perfect length of time before a birth. I am not saying here that everyone will take that long. Some might take much longer and some shorter.

I was doing everything I had always been doing to move through the initiation; I was just doing it faster and at a more accelerated pace. I was also more focused. Once we had taken the seventh initiation, I knew we would be back in kindergarten again as beginning seventh-degree initiates. We would then go through the process of learning to realize and complete the seventh initiation. This is the highest initiation that can be taken on this plane; however, it is possible to anchor and access some of the higher dimensions or aspects of self in those dimensions into one's consciousness.

I was looking forward to being a seventh-degree initiate because of the higher light quotient and merging with Shamballa and the logoic plane of consciousness, which is another octave up. Djwhal volunteered some very interesting information about our rays. He told us that as we evolve, our rays transform to higher rays. For example, I have known that I am a second-ray monad and a second-ray soul. Djwhal told us that our second-ray monad had transformed into a twelfth-ray monad. This, of course, is the ray of the new age, and he said this monadic-ray type allows us to be in contact with the entirety of the Spiritual Hierarchy.

He told me that my personality ray was originally the fifth ray, concrete science, which explains my ability to write such technical books. He said, however, that this ray was in the process of transforming into the first ray and now into the seventh ray. The first ray is the will aspect of God. This really fit, for the will aspect of God is one of the areas in which I am personally most highly developed.

Djwhal told us that in regard to our petition, Lady Helena was pleased that our will was aligned with Shamballa and with God. This kind feedback from Lady Helena is an example of the process of making one's will totally subservient to God and to Sanat Kumara and, in our group, to the vision of Djwhal Khul. The transformation of my personality ray now into a seven has to do with manifestation. I have mastered the concrete science and the will aspect. The next step is to fully manifest into the physical all that I am doing. This is beginning to happen now through publishing my books. I am sure that you, my reader, can all see what this process is about, and I am sure you can relate to this within your own selves.

Djwhal said that my mental body is a third ray, which is active intelligence. He also said in a channeling through a core group member about two years ago that my mental body was also connected to the ninth ray. This has to do with the process of anchoring the lightbody as well as anchoring the soul and monadic light information into all my books and teachings. Djwhal said that my emotional body was originally a sixth ray. This is the devotional aspect, which fits. He said that it has now transformed to the eleventh, which is the energy of compassion. My physical vehicle is a seventh-ray body.

We ended the meditation by calling in the Ascension Manifestation Council and most specifically Lady Helena, El Morya, the inner-plane healing masters and the Arcturians. We recited our petition to the ascension council for the fifth and final time as Lady Helena had guided us to do. Upon completion there was a tremendous feeling of joy and happiness that overwhelmed us, which was clearly coming from the masters in attendance. The combination of anchoring the seventh-dimensional chakra grid and completing this piece of manifestation work in such a setting and divine timing made us euphoric.

Djwhal also told me that my part of the plan was to focus on bringing through the philosophical end of the plan and not get overburdened with the financial end of things. I sensed that Djwhal was commenting on my tendency to take on too many responsibilities in the ashram. Clearly my work was to disseminate the Spiritual Hierarchy teachings and not burden myself with the ashram's accounting. He said that someone else would take on this responsibility. I would, of course, have a consulting function, but not the full load, which felt good to me.

Another insight has to do with the seven levels of initiation. Before ascending I was often confused why taking one's ascension was the sixth initiation and not the seventh. The reason for this I have already stated, but I understand it more deeply now. The sixth initiation is only the *beginning* of ascension. It isn't until one completes the seven sublevels of the sixth that one is truly considered a full-fledged ascended master. One achieves liberation from the wheel of rebirth at the beginning of the sixth; however, one has not fully realized his/her ascension yet. The seventh initiation is the true completion. Completing the seven sublevels of the sixth initiation and the seventh initiation itself are very close to being the same thing. It is the same kind of difference between the ninth initiation and being at the ninth and a half in the twelve-initiation system of Brian Grattan.

Meditation on August 8, 1994

In this morning's meditation we went to the Golden Chamber of Melchizedek to sit in the ascension seats. There Melchizedek greeted us and showed us a special flame. He then proceeded to bathe us in some kind of ash. The ash was very much like the *vibhuti* that Sai Baba creates with a sweep of his hand. It has some special healing properties, Melchizedek told us, that literally burn up the negative-ego matrix in the four-body system. Melchizedek said that we were being bathed in it to burn into ash any small or large programming that would cause us to react in an explosive manner. He said he had actually been working with us for a while with this, but today was the first time he showed it to us. We were amazed and fascinated by the process.

One of the members also shared some incredible information she had received the day before. She had tried to call me the previous morning, but we somehow kept missing each other. The first piece of information had to do with the rays. Djwhal had told her in meditation that I was now officially a full-fledged third-ray master because of how I wielded my energies. (Interestingly enough, she was a full-fledged fourth-ray ascended master in how she wielded *her* energies.)

The third ray is active intelligence, which makes total sense and can be seen in my ability to write. This core member, being a fourth-ray ascended master, is quite creative and artistically developed and in tune with harmony. My rays, then, now had the format of 3-2-5-1-7. This made total sense to me. The third ray of active intelligence is my strongest; the love/wisdom of the second ray is the next prominent; then comes concrete science, the fifth ray, which again is the scientific ability I use in my writings and work as a spiritual teacher and psychologist; next is the first ray, the will of God, one of the strongest areas of my personal development; and finally, the seventh-ray, from which I derive my skills of ceremonial order and magic.

This ray reading Djwhal gave us showed not what we came in with, but what we are now manifesting. As I intuitively look at myself, this feels totally right. The main insight was that even though we come in with a certain ray structure, we have free choice in how we use our energies. The rays can transform to higher rays and we can also develop the rays we might be weaker in. This can come from past lives, previous monadic development or development in this life.

When I give myself a ray reading, I see myself strung on all the rays, with the weakest probably being the fourth ray, as Djwhal said. I feel like a very artistic and extremely creative person. Because it is channeled into my books and psychological and spiritual training, I am not inspired to paint or play an instrument and am not the artist type, even though I love art.

For your convenience I am going to list the seven rays and their meanings so it will help you understand what I have been talking about.

First ray	Will of God
Second ray	Love/wisdom of God
Third ray	Active intelligence aspect of God
Fourth ray	Harmony aspect of God
Fifth ray	Concrete science aspect of God
Sixth ray	Devotional aspect of God

Seventh ray	Ceremonial order and magic
Eighth ray	Cleansing
Ninth ray	Joy and beginning stage of anchoring the lightbody
Tenth ray	Full anchoring of the lightbody
Eleventh ray	Bridge to the new age; compassion
Twelfth ray	New age; full access to the Hierarchy

I asked Djwhal what his monadic ray was. In his life as Djwhal Khul it was the second ray. After he ascended, however, it transformed to a twelve, and now he has no monadic ray, for he is beyond that level of evolution, which I found interesting.

He also said that we were functioning as chohans for certain members of our respective ashrams, similar to the way that chohans of the seven rays are in charge of other ascended masters, but on a much higher level. Djwhal also said there were four senior disciples of the Hierarchy working with us.

Meditation on August 15, 1994

On this morning the core group and I received in meditation a confirmation about some fascinating planetary information. While in the Golden Chamber of Melchizedek I asked Melchizedek a number of questions regarding the number of ascended masters on Earth as of August and September 1994. This was especially pertinent, given that our core group of thirty in Djwhal's ashram was now just about complete and preparing to take the seventh initiation.

What Melchizedek said was that there were 500 ascended masters on Earth who had now completed their ascension, including us. This felt like a very small number to me, but it corresponded to what Vywamus had told me about three months earlier. Vywamus had said that there were around 400 at that time. This new, prototype wave in August and September would add approximately 100 more to the total. Of this 500, approximately 200 had completed their seventh initiation. Melchizedek told us that we would basically be complete with our seventh initiation by Wesak of the following year, which of course was the window for the beginning of mass ascension. This made sense and agreed with what I had been receiving inwardly.

Wesak was still eight months away. We had been averaging six months per initiation for the previous two. Six more months from September, if we continued at our present rate of spiritual evolution, would easily have us complete this historic marker. Djwhal had previously said that it would take all of next year to complete our seventh, but things seemed to have accelerated again.

My feeling was that if we were not totally complete by Wesak, we would be close. This was all very exciting. We were also told that there would be 5000 people completing their ascension by the Wesak. Melchizedek told us that there were 300 fully completed ascended masters in the Inner Earth. When I asked him about the etheric ascended masters, there were somewhere between 1500 and 2000. This would also include the ascended masters working in Djwhal's ashram and the other ashrams of the seven rays, who are still working with the Earth on the etheric level.

For example, when we pass on, we have been told that we will be working for some time in Djwhal's ashram on the inner plane helping the Earth. When this occurs within the next twenty years, we will be included in this etheric ascended-master accounting, instead of the physicalized ascended-master accounting of which I was speaking earlier.

Melchizedek also told us that there would be approximately 500 seventh-degree initiates who will have completed their ascension by Wesak which, if all goes according to plan, we would be part of. But one thing I have learned by living on planet Earth is, never count your chickens before they're hatched, never be prideful and never be overconfident.

When I watch the news and look around the world, I constantly say to myself, "By the grace of God go I." There is often a very fine line between the saint and the sinner, as Paramahansa Yogananda would say. I know for myself that if I hadn't had some of the support systems I have had, I wouldn't even be alive right now. In any case, I found this information fascinating. I felt humbled and blessed to be in my leadership role. With this leadership, however, comes enormous responsibility and much is expected. This does not feel like a burden to me as long as I walk the straight and narrow path. We have discussed this in previous meditations—how getting slightly off center throws our entire program out of whack. This has taught us obedience to God's laws.

At the end of our meditation in Melchizedek's golden chamber I asked Melchizedek about the actual causative effects of the ascension seats. He recommends sitting in the ascension seats as much as possible. He said that they strengthen the grid system, upgrade the molecules, increase the vibration of the entire field, help build the light quotient and replace the old grid system with the new one.

Meditation on August 19, 1994

In this meditation we did for the first time what I have called our ultimate ascension meditation together, which I have included at the end of this book. While in the golden chamber I asked a few more questions of Melchizedek concerning the planetary ascension process. The essence of our conversation was that there were 900 kindergarten ascended masters on Earth as of September 1, 1994. Of the 5000 predicted for Wesak (May 1995) approximately 500 would be completing their sixth and the other 2500 would be of the kindergarten variety, which means just taking the beginning of the sixth. Melchizedek told us that there would be approximately 10,000 ascended masters on the planet by the year 2000 of both the completed and kindergarten variety. After the year 2000 there is a potential that this number will increase at a much faster rate.

By Wesak 1995 there will be 300 completed seventh-degree initiates on the planet. By the year 2000, Melchizedek said there could be 5000 to 10,000 completed seventh-degree initiates on the planet. I also asked about walk-ins. I was given a ballpark figure of 50,000 walk-ins on the planet.

I would take these numbers with a grain of salt, because the future is always changing as we collectively use our free choice; however, they do provide some perspective and estimates for what is taking place on the planetary-level ascension process.

The core group and I had a wonderful meditation and agreed to talk again on Sunday morning, when I suggested that we go to Sai Baba's ashram and meet with his holiness to do some meditation work. We were quite excited about this prospect.

My (Former) Wife's Dream on August 20

On Saturday morning my then-wife woke up with an extraordinary dream. Before I share it I want to lay the groundwork. Saturday evening there would be a full moon, so the day before, we planned to meditate on Saturday night around ten o'clock on the patio of our condominium complex. It was not only the full moon, but it was also very close to the date (which Djwhal had told my wife) when the thirty people would be complete with their ascension in his ashram.

In her dream we were meditating as planned at ten that evening, facing each other. Suddenly, from a building about 500 yards away, someone shot my wife in the heart with a rifle. She slumped over dead. As I pulled her over to the side, the same person shot me in my third eye, killing me also. My wife and I took our full ascension. We then began to appear in a spiritual state to friends and different family members. Many people started to cry, and she gave them tissues; however, many people could not see anything but the tissue moving through the air.

The meaning of the dream, after discussing it with my wife, seemed very realistic, as if this had actually happened. The symbolism, I believe, represents the rod of initiation of Sanat Kumara, marking the exact moment of full completion of the sixth initiation. The fact that my wife was shot in the heart and I was shot in the third eye is perfect. Our death, I feel, is symbolic of the death of physical existence and of being forevermore living in the ascended state. Even though in truth we remain in physical bodies, this occasion marked the end of physical existence as we had previously experienced it.

We decided that we would sit that night in the same meditative position we had taken in the dream.

Saturday Night Meditation

Around nine o'clock that evening we took our chairs out to the private patio in our condominium complex and set them up exactly as they looked in her dream. There was a beautiful full moon. Djwhal Khul and Melchizedek, the Universal Logos, immediately were present. This particular moon, Djwhal had told us previously, was an initiation moon and had connections to the Egyptian mysteries. Therefore we made a psychic connection with the Great Pyramid of Giza and the King's Chamber, as well as Serapis Bey's ascension retreat in Luxor. We also called in Isis, Osiris, Serapis Bey, Horus and Thoth.

The meditation began with Djwhal and Melchizedek doing a chakra-bonding ceremony with us. This began at the sixth chakra, where a beam of light was projected to connect our third eyes. This seemed to facilitate the building of our energies and light quotient, which we had also invoked. Melchizedek told us that we were .001 from completion. This bonding ceremony would build our energies to put us over the top. We then made a similar bond at the throat chakra, then the high heart, the lower heart, third chakra—then, interestingly, there was an umbilical cord that extended between our navels. I was not sure what it meant, whether it was because we were married at the time or because we are from the same monad or what, but it was there. It looked different than the line of light between our chakras. It looked exactly like a real umbilical cord would.

Next the masters connected our second chakras, then the first chakra. Melchizedek told us that our crowns were not connected because that was our own individual connection to God and the God force. Melchizedek then said that we were closing the gap needed until completion. This bonding ceremony, with the full moon energies and the work the masters were doing on us, was about to put us over the top. (As you can see, the initiation process is very mathematical.)

Melchizedek was holding his rod of initiation. He began running it down between us, through the beams of light connecting our chakras. This seemed to have a purifying effect. When he got to chakras one, two and three, they were a little thicker. His continual movement through them helped purify them. Finally this was complete. I felt a very strong stream of energy begin to flow down through my entire body. Melchizedek placed his rod of initiation on us like he was knighting us in King Arthur's court. Our ascension process was now officially complete.

We still had not taken the seventh initiation. This was a special ceremony honoring the fact that we had completed the sixth initiation. I felt deeply moved by the whole ceremony. I also felt quite blessed to have the rod of initiation given to us by Melchizedek, which I don't think is the normal procedure. I think this occurred because I had been spending so much time in recent months in Melchizedek's golden chamber, talking to him and sitting in his ascension seats. I think he had taken a special interest in our core group.

Before our meditation I had been sitting in his golden chamber receiving his energies in my own personal meditation, so it was no surprise to me that this occurred. It felt totally appropriate, like a great, great blessing. It also occurs to me that the core group and I had in meditation requested to be initiated into the Order of Melchizedek and become seventh-degree initiates by him about a month before. His coming was an official answer to those prayers.

Sunday Morning, August 21, 1994

We began by going to Djwhal's ashram so he would be a part of our sharing. Djwhal confirmed that we had indeed completed our ascension and/or the seventh sublevel of the sixth initiation. He also confirmed that our seventh initiation was imminent. He told us that not everyone in the core group of thirty had taken this initiation in his ashram. It seemed like there might have been twelve of us or less. He said there was not always a ceremony of this kind for completing the sixth initiation. There is, however, always one for taking the seventh.

Djwhal told us that we had now stabilized our light quotient at the 92 to 93 percent level and were now tapping into the 94 percent level. However, we had not yet stabilized it. We were also now actualizing chakra 34 in our crown. In the past three weeks, since I had asked about this, we had gone up one chakra from chakra 33, which we were previously actualizing.

The umbilical connection between my wife and me symbolized aligning our personal wills with the divine plan. Another interesting insight had to do with a part of her dream. After we died and ascended, there had been some kind of review. I asked Djwhal about this and he said that even ascended masters and/or seventh-degree initiates go through a review with the Karmic Board upon passing over. It is a very loving review and not necessarily long, but every person goes through it.

A further insight about this whole process had to do with a certain pattern in our ascension process that synchronistically seemed to be happening for the third time. Earlier in the book I spoke of how I "visited" my friend in Bali and told her I had made a deal with the masters to ascend six months earlier than planned. Interestingly enough, Vywamus had told me that after we ascended it would take one year to achieve our seventh initiation.

Because we were now scheduled to take our seventh in September, the pattern of taking an initiation six months earlier than planned was repeating itself . The most extraordinary thing yet was that Djwhal had told us we would complete our seventh initiation by the end of 1995 (the equivalent of taking our twelfth initiation in Brian Grattan's system). What I was getting, however, was that this was all moved forward because of our tremendous acceleration, and we would be taking our twelfth initiation, or completion of our seventh initiation, at Wesak 1995. Synchronistically, that was six months earlier than predicted.

Another Valuable Meditation

I received a triple confirmation on this process later Sunday morning when I talked to my friend on the phone. On Friday, during one of her ascension-activation sessions, Sanat Kumara came into her session to give an initiation to her client. My friend thought Sanat Kumara was going to leave after completing the initiation, but he said he wasn't through yet. He then called in the core group and myself to her session. He took his rod and knighted my friend first in a manner similar to how Melchizedek had initiated my wife and me.

My friend continued her session and Sanat Kumara took the rest of us to the side out of her sight and apparently did the same thing for us. My friend and I spoke with Sanat Kumara about it, which he confirmed, saying we had indeed completed our ascension. He said we did this in an unconscious state. As an extra blessing, he called a portion of the group in again and did it once more, but consciously, right there on the phone. He took his rod of initiation and knighted us in a manner similar to that of Melchizedek the night before. He said that it is always more meaningful if it can be done consciously, although that is not required. Many, many people go through their initiations without conscious awareness.

When my friend told me of her experience, this was after my wife and I had had our experience and after I had talked to another core member. This was now triple confirmation, really a quadruple one, for my dreams of two or three weeks before had also indicated this, as well as my wife's dream. It is always nice to have these things confirmed from many sources.

I was aware that it was almost exactly five months after we had taken our initial kindergarten ascension. My intuition was that within the next two to three weeks we would be taking our seventh initiation.

Meditation on August 21, 1994

Sunday turned out to be a very eventful day, for in the afternoon the core group and I had a pow-wow on the phone with Djwhal Khul, Sanat Kumara, the Lord Maitreya and Melchizedek. As the meditation began,

Melchizedek took us to his golden chamber and showed us a beautiful cathedral, which had a beautiful window. He told us while we were in this cathedral that all the fire letters, key codes and sacred geometries had been anchored and fired. He said that in completing our ascension we had taken another quantum leap in our evolution. I felt a great sense of celebration in the air. He told us as we looked out the window that this symbolized the final seal that needed to be broken for complete realization of the self, and we were now being prepared to move toward this final step. This, of course, was the seventh initiation.

During the meditation I felt so blessed that he had taken such an interest in us, for, being the Universal Logos, he was still far beyond our level of evolution. In truth, we had not even fully realized the galactic level yet. I felt honored that he would do this.

He then seemed to take us through the window, and with his rod of initiation began to beam the most glorious spiritual energies upon us. I was eager for this experience, so I opened myself and began to breathe in these energies. The term that kept coming to me was *resurrection*. This was quite fitting, for the seventh initiation is esoterically called the initiation of resurrection, according to the Alice Bailey books and Djwhal Khul.

I literally felt resurrected and transformed in a way I had never before experienced. I was very much aware that I wanted to go through that final seal and become a full-fledged seventh-level Melchizedek. It felt incredibly good.

Reflections

After about twenty-four hours of absorbing the feeling of having completed my ascension, I actually felt quite transformed. In some ways it felt even more significant, powerful and transformative than when I actually took the beginning of my ascension. I felt really complete. I felt an enormous amount of light and energy flowing through my four-body system. I felt bathed in a golden white light. I had never felt this much energy and light flowing through me so continually. I also felt much healthier physically.

I also had an ongoing experience of feeling clean, clear and purified energetically, psychically and spiritually. It was a feeling of perfection flowing through my body. I realize that this must sound strange, but that is the best way I can describe it. I also felt a little exhilarated and euphoric. This had been a goal of mine for a long time, and I felt incredibly relieved to have completed it. I very much wanted to go through the final seal that Melchizedek had spoken of and take my seventh initiation. The seventh level and its completion felt like the final step in this process.

The experience of completing my ascension felt much more powerful and profound than I had anticipated. I felt, and still do, quite blessed and grateful to God, the masters, my family and certain key friends in my life. Without each one of these key people and masters in my puzzle, so to speak, I would never have made it. It is amazing how interdependent we are with others.

My only true focus now is to return to these people and all of humanity the blessings that have been bestowed upon me. I will be unceasing in my quest to relieve the suffering of humankind and help all people realize the peace that passeth understanding. This peace is found only through realizing God.

August 22, 1994

Fully inspired after completing my ascension, I proceeded to write a Huna prayer to move through the final seventh seal (seventh initiation), as Melchizedek put it. The following prayer I did with my wife in the morning, then with a friend over the phone in the afternoon and with another core member in the evening.

Beloved Presence of God, Mahatma, Melchizedek, Lenduce, Vywamus, Sai Baba, Sanat Kumara.

We hereby pray with all our heart, soul, mind and might to move now through the final seal that Melchizedek has spoken of and take our seventh initiation. We are now ready to take on the full seventh-degree mantle of the Christ and become full-fledged seventh-degree initiates. We ask for this so that we might be of greater service. Amen.

Our beloved subconscious minds, we hereby ask and command that you take this thought-form prayer with all the mana and vital force that is necessary to manifest and demonstrate this prayer to the Source of our being. Amen.

Beloved presence of God and God force, let the rain of blessings fall. Amen.

My friend and I had an incredible meditation in the afternoon after doing this prayer. We went to the Arcturian spacecraft to the light-synthesis chamber where the Arcturians, with their advanced technology, helped us actualize the last two chakras of the seventh-dimensional grid, chakras 35 and 36. It is almost like they sewed them into our third eye and brain and ran the current of chakra 36 through our entire system.

It was quite a light show. The seventh-dimensional chakra grid seemed to have a radiance that had a subtle, subliminal rainbow effect. Djwhal told us that the actualization of these final two chakras would be the key to going through the final seventh seal. Whenever I say the words "seventh seal," I think of Revelations in the Bible. John was probably talking about the seven levels of initiation for at least part of it. As you can tell by my Huna prayer, I really wanted to go through this final seal.

I ended up working the entire day and night in the Arcturian light-synthesis chamber. The Arcturians told us that they would continue working on us during the night because actualizing these higher chakras was not something they could complete in an hour. The Arcturians also agreed to work with us even more intensively to help us get through the final seal.

9

Taking My Seventh Initiation

By the grace of God, on August 23, 1994, my then-wife and I took our seventh initiation together. This was just three days after we had the ceremony under the full moon, where we had been told that we had completed our sixth initiation and ascension. I had an inkling that this would be the day. Djwhal had told us to go to Vasquez Rocks in southern California to go hiking and also plan to do a meditation. In the back of my mind I hoped this would be the time.

My wife and I had never been to Vasquez Rocks. My father and stepmother had told us about this place and we had wanted to go there for a long time. We left around 9:15 in the morning and arrived about forty-five minutes later. We parked the car and began to hike among the beautiful rock formations. There was one mountainous formation that the public frequently climbed. We were drawn, however, to another huge formation in the distance. We hiked to the base and began climbing. We were both guided to try to get to the top. It was a little treacherous in a few places, but we finally made it to the highest peak and found our power spot. Djwhal confirmed that this was it. We got comfortable and held hands and began to meditate. Djwhal was present, as was Melchizedek, the Universal Logos.

We chanted a few *om*s. Suddenly a pure white butterfly began to flutter around us. We both knew that we were about to take our seventh initiation. The butterfly was a wonderful synchronicity to begin this moment. Djwhal began to speak through my wife and gave a beautiful little speech. He then began to recite spiritual affirmations, which we recited together after him; I think there were seven. Djwhal then began reciting numerical codes and sequences. I am not at liberty to share them, though I don't have total recall.

As he recited the numerical codes, we would repeat them, as we do affirmations. Some codes were a three-digit sequence that would change to another three-digit sequence. Melchizedek held his rod of initiation and initiated us, much like he did three days earlier in what felt like our knighting. It was a great blessing to have Melchizedek serve again as initiator, for in my understanding, Sanat Kumara usually serves in this capacity. By the grace of God, Melchizedek had taken an interest in us, and I think he was responding to our prayer to become seventh-degree Melchizedeks as well as seventh-degree initiates of the Great White Brotherhood, which are really the same thing.

As Djwhal finished he said something very interesting: "Welcome to the eighth school." I immediately knew what he was talking about. As we had achieved our seventh initiation, we were now working toward achieving our eighth initiation. This, of course, will not be taken until we physically leave this plane of existence. We can, however, move through the seven sublevels of the seventh initiation as well as anchor in energies equivalent to even higher initiations.

We were now officially kindergarten seventh-degree initiates. We opened our eyes and sat on the top of this glorious mountain peak. What a perfect place to take our seventh initiation! For ten to twelve years of life my favorite meditation was one I learned from Paul Solomon, which he channeled from the Source. It was a meditation of climbing a seven-terraced mountain and then entering a church or temple. At the top of the mountain each one of the seven terraces was a different color and the very top one was white.

In our meditation this day a white butterfly had met us. As the meditation ended, two white butterflies began to fly around us. The timing and synchronicity blew us away. Another extraordinary synchronicity was that this was the second anniversary of our marriage, which was why we had planned to come here in the first place. What an incredible way to acknowledge our anniversary! As I sat there at the top of the mountain with my wife, I told her that this was the peak experience of my entire life. I'd gone through a lot of magnificent experiences, but this was the highest and best yet.

My burning, all-consuming desire was to become a seventh-degree Melchizedek and/or seventh-degree initiate and serve from this self-realized state of consciousness. By the grace of God my dream had finally come true. We had moved through the seventh seal.

Another amazing synchronicity was the fact that this day, August 23, was five months to the day after our sixth initiation. We had actually gone through an entire major initiation (in the Alice Bailey system) in only five months! When I told my wife this, she said it didn't seem possible. I have to admit that I had been pushing it a bit. Vywamus had originally said it would take from one to five years. Given that in the past it had taken masters entire lifetimes to take just one initiation, this was quite extraordinary. What was even more extraordinary was that we had gone from the fifth to the sixth in only five and a half months. This meant that we had progressed through two major initiations in ten and a half months.

I must confess that pushing this fast took a bit of a toll on me physically. It would have been better if we had done it more slowly. It wasn't the masters' plan to do it this fast; it was our continual Huna prayers and invocations. Melchizedek had told our core group a couple of days before that this had happened through our own efforts, not because the masters wanted it. We were basically given what we prayed and asked for.

I share these things with you so you can put your own initiation process into perspective. It is possible to speed it up if you choose. Going too fast can affect your physical health if you get too yang. My suggestion is to find your own personal Tao in terms of neither going too fast nor too slow.

This was a special moment for us. At the end of our meditation we called in our friends on the inner plane and some of the others in our core group of thirty or larger to share in our joy and celebration and our seventh-degree energy. We then climbed, or I should say floated, down the mountain back to our car. As soon as we got home, I immediately wrote down my experiences to give you, my readers, the best account possible.

I want to say here that not everyone else's initiation experience will be like ours. The only thing that will be the same is that you will receive the rod of initiation from either the Planetary Logos or Melchizedek. Frankly, the actual energetic experience of taking the seventh was not very strong. I have done hundreds of meditations that felt more powerful. Many people will take these initiations on the inner plane and not even know it. This might contradict some channeled information, but I know for a fact that it is true. Even my highly clairvoyant and clairaudient friends are often not aware.

I used to think that when I was fortunate enough to take my sixth and seventh initiations, fireworks would go off and I would immediately be walking on water and teleporting around the universe. This is not true. It is an extremely powerful spiritual experience, but it does not necessarily translate into the physical. Another reason it was not dramatic is that by the time you go through the seven sublevels leading to an initiation, you are quite ready. The actual flow of electrical current coming from the rod of initiation is only a step higher than where you already are. If the rod of initiation for the seventh had been given five months ago at the time we took the sixth, I am sure it would have electrocuted us. We needed five months to prepare our four-body system, raise our light quotient and prepare our nervous system to take the seventh-degree voltage.

A Second Meditation on August 23, 1994

I thought I reached my peak on Tuesday morning with my wife. But the high continued as the day went on. After writing the above upon arriving home, I called my dear friend to tell her the news, for I knew that she had done it also even though I hadn't seen her. I told her what had happened, when suddenly she and I found ourselves in Shamballa, where we went through a different ceremony. Sanat Kumara was officiating this time. There would now be a special ceremony for us.

We came before Sanat Kumara under some type of gazebo. We were aware that others were around us taking other initiations, but this particular process was specifically for us. There was a big crowd of people present, most of them members of the Great White Brotherhood. There was an incredible feeling of celebration and joy in the air. Sananda, Saint Germain, Djwhal Khul, the Mahatma and the Arcturians were all there. In the background stood Melchizedek, the Universal Logos. He was wearing a pope's gold and red hat. He wore a beautiful robe and held a golden staff. In the background to the left was the Egyptian contingency: Isis, Osiris, Horus and Serapis Bey.

One by one we each went before Sanat Kumara and received the electrical force running through his rod of initiation. This was very special to me because Melchizedek had done the honors the first time. Now it seemed that both of them were going to officiate. The basic ritual was the same for all of us, with a few minor exceptions. I will speak of my own experience, but please realize that we all shared a similar experience one by one.

As the ceremony started we didn't know who should go first. The order had no particular importance, obviously, for we were one. As I stepped forward before Sanat Kumara, he warmly smiled with great love, kindness and joy. He placed the rod of initiation on my left and right shoulder and then on my head. Streams of electrical energy began to flow through my entire body. The rod of initiation seemed to place his seal around me in some kind of protective fashion.

He said that officially administering his rod made me a full-fledged seventh-degree initiate. It gives me all the gifts, qualities and duties of an initiate. He spoke lovingly to me. He also thanked me for helping my friend during a rough period in her life, for she was very much loved by Shamballa and the Hierarchy. I told Sanat Kumara that it was my honor to do so, that she had helped me a lot also, and that it was truly a divine friendship. He seemed pleased with this.

Sanat Kumara placed a gold medal around my neck that he said would directly connect me with the Great Central Sun and also serve as a protective amulet. He also said I was a great spreader of light and information, and this was much appreciated. I then went before Melchizedek.

My dear spiritual father Melchizedek administered his golden staff and rod again, and a stream of his golden energy began to flow through me. I felt incredibly blessed. He said that we were now fully vested seventh-degree initiates. He also told us that we would now be granted admittance to many of the meetings and spaces in the universe that we couldn't access before.

I was now wearing the full seventh-degree mantle of the Christ, which was green, with a gold-white rainbow. Each of us wore this mantle, but each had a slight variation of color, depending on which ray connection and function we had in relationship to the Spiritual Hierarchy and Shamballa. We were also wearing the seamless robe of the Christ.

Djwhal Khul was standing to the side, beaming through the entire ceremony. Melchizedek and I hugged and then I moved on to the Egyptian contingency, which was waiting for me. Here was placed around me a beautiful crystalline ankh. As they placed it around my neck, it was emanating a tremendous force field. I was aware that I was also wearing a golden-silver one from a previous initiation. I was given an apron to wrap around me, which symbolized becoming a seventh-degree Melchizedek. It had a five-pointed star with a lotus on it and a triangle with a third eye. The Egyptian contingency congratulated me and we all hugged. Anubis dropped his feather and I turned into light, which was symbolic of our group's progression.

We were told that the only difference in the ceremony for our group members was that one core member had received, in what looked like a small suitcase, a scroll of job positions and new projects now available to her and the rest of us. Melchizedek suggested that we all look through them and see if any of them had a particular appeal. Another member was given a shield of the Sun by Sanat Kumara, enlarged to cover all her chakras. This special gift was given to her to provide her with extra protection. Other than these additions, we all went through similar experiences.

After having received congratulations from the Egyptian contingency, our dear friend and beloved teacher Djwhal Khul was waiting for us to give us a special gift. He gave each of us a golden orb necklace. By continually wearing this orb, our spiritual body would automatically keep all of our etheric nadis and meridians sealed and prevent us from losing light, without our ever having to ask. What a wonderful gift this was!

Djwhal and I hugged, and I thanked him from the bottom of my heart for all his daily help. I could never have found a more devoted and helpful teacher and friend. He was so proud now to see us all coming into our own as we passed through the seventh and final seal.

Next in line to greet us were the Arcturians. They congratulated us and told us that they were pleased with our progress and were honored to serve us. They said they would continue to help us through the completion of our seventh initiation. They gave each of us something, which I can only say looked like a round golden pillbox. This was some kind of Arcturian advanced technology that provided extra protection when opened. My friend and I decided to keep ours open; then we were all given a second one that we could wear around our necks or in our pockets, protecting both our front and back sides.

I thanked the Arcturians for all their help and told them that I would be looking forward to my ride on their starship. I also reiterated my desire to be a channel for writing books and an encyclopedia about their civilization, to serve as a prototype and blueprint for Earth. They were very pleased with this idea and said it was on one of the scrolls in the suitcase of job offers for all of us. They also told us that they would teach us how to teleport and continue to help us raise our light quotient. The Arcturians are such wonderful beings. They even told me that I'd had lives on Arcturus, of which I have no conscious recollection. It is no accident that we are connected.

The next in line to greet us was Sananda. He gave each of us a very special crystal necklace, which was for the purpose of rejuvenation. It had a pink-green liquid-gold color. Sananda (Jesus) told us that this necklace (in conjunction with building the light quotient and saying rejuvenation affirmations) would institute a full rejuvenation and youthing program in our physical vehicles. This too was a most wondrous gift. It felt like my birthday, which indeed it truly was. This was definitely the best and happiest day of my entire life.

Last, Saint Germain stepped forward. His gift to us was permission to use the atomic accelerator. I leapt forward to thank him for this, for secondary to this initiation, sitting in the atomic accelerator in the physical third-dimensional reality was my next-greatest desire. I am not sure that Saint Germain expected such an enthusiastic response. He told me that he thought I would really like this and that it would have a tremendous effect on all of us. The exact timing wasn't set up yet, but it would be something we would follow up at the right time.

My cup ran over. My ultimate dream and desire had come true in a most wondrous manner. I returned to the physical plane utterly fulfilled, yet dreamy and a bit tired. I needed to get something to eat and take a nap. I thought I'd had enough excitement for one day. I also wanted to write up my experiences so I wouldn't forget any of it.

I want to emphasize once more that not everyone will go through this exact ceremony. If you are not clairvoyant or do not have friends who are, you won't be able to see any part of it unless a dream is given. Many of these ceremonies will be given on the inner plane, so people might never be aware of them. I would venture to say that most of the people reading this book have gone through more initiations than they realize. Just because you have no awareness of them is no reason to think you haven't passed them. For this reason most people who are new to the understanding of the seven levels of initiation underestimate how far they have evolved.

I think part of the reason I was given the gift of these recollections is for service purposes—for you, my readers. The masters of Shamballa and the Spiritual Hierarchy are aware that everything I experience, I immediately translate into my books to share with you. I am grateful to have such wonderful friends to cocreate with in this process. This has been invaluable, and to share this together in total cooperation and with no comparing and competition has been one of the most enjoyable experiences of my life. It is truly all for one and one for all.

Meditation on August 24, 1994

The morning following our seventh initiation, I called my friend. She had also received that we had taken our seventh and knew I would be calling to tell her this. I shared my experiences and we invited Djwhal to join our conversation. I then began to ask Djwhal some questions about this new process and the transformation we had just gone through. Some amazing information followed.

He told us that we were scheduled to take our twelfth initiation (in the Brian Grattan system) at the 12:12 that year. This totally blew my mind. I was thinking that this wouldn't happen until Wesak 1995. What Djwhal said was that we would take the beginning of our twelfth initiation at the 12:12 and fully complete the twelfth at Wesak in May. As of today we had stabilized the 94 percent light-quotient level. Receiving the rod of initiation from Sanat Kumara and Melchizedek and moving into the seventh had this stabilizing effect. Djwhal said the game plan was to achieve the 96 percent level by the 12:12 and the 97 to 98 percent level by Wesak.

Taking our seventh initiation was equivalent to taking our third cosmic initiation, from the point of view of the higher university on Sirius. Djwhal said that we were in a seven-year cycle from 1994 to the year 2001. How long we would stay on the planet seemed to be somewhat open. There seemed to be two windows for us. One window for leaving was 2001; another was 2012. He now wanted us to focus on this seven-year window.

In completing our seventh initiation by Wesak 1995, I would be flung into a world-service leadership role. Djwhal told us that much was being given now and much would also be expected of us. It was not a free ride. This was fine with me. I tend to be a little bit of a workaholic anyway, and agree with the statement in *A Course in Miracles*, "True pleasure is serving God." When you get the ascended masters and cosmic forces on your side working for your evolution, it is amazing how fast this path of initiation and ascension can move.

10

The Process of Completing My
Seventh Initiation

Meditation on August 31, 1994

My friend and I meditated that afternoon and went back to the Arcturian light-synthesis chamber to meet with Lord Arcturus. We asked for the electronic plate to be installed in her third eye. Shortly after this, to my surprise, another Arcturian plate was installed in the crown chakra. The Arcturians said it would help us in actualizing chakras 35 and 36 as well as help us reach higher, and it would serve as a protection and seal.

This felt really good, and a lot of energy came in. After our meditation on the phone both of us took a nap. I dreamed that we were together on what seemed like a spacecraft. Something had been installed that was taking us to a higher level. In the dream my friend measured it and we were up to the twenty-fifth level. I had a clear sense in the dream that we had just moved up another notch in our frequency and evolutionary process.

Meditation on September 3, 1994

We began this meditation by going to the Golden Chamber of Melchizedek and then did the following Huna prayer. This particular Huna prayer was for anchoring into our subconscious minds and four-body system all the light packets, or light envelopes, of information that could possibly be invoked. Much of this information we would not be able to use consciously at this time. It would be programmed into us during sleep and during meditations for future use.

Much of what this prayer was invoking was and is only partially available to us. For example, in the prayer we requested light packets of information from all 352 levels of the Mahatma, but only the appropriate amount that could be assimilated and handled would be anchored. Even if it was only one or two percent, that would be an enormous boon to our evolution, light-quotient building and so on. After the prayer Melchizedek told us that we were on target and that it would be appropriate to ask for this. We set this prayer up to be anchored over a period of 3½ to 8½ months leading up to the Wesak Festival of 1995. This way we would be worked on every night while we slept and during our meditations without consciously having to ask for it each time. After doing this prayer, we were buzzing at a very high level. I sat in meditation by myself for almost an hour and a half after our phone call, just absorbing the energies. The prayer was a catalyst for tapping into a cosmic-level power source.

As we entered Melchizedek's chamber, he showed us a very large gong. This gong, he said, was the gong of time. I do not claim to understand fully what he was talking about, but I sensed that it was through this gong that Melchizedek entered the planes of time and space. Of course, at his level of existence there is no time or space, only the eternal now and multidimensionality. This was a little gift from Melchizedek to allow us to see this in our current work of trying to collapse time.

Meditation on September 4, 1994

We began this meditation by going to the Golden Chamber of Melchizedek and doing the following Huna prayer. It was different from previous invocations of fire letters, key codes and sacred geometries, for we were now requesting that they be anchored through the twenty-four dimensions of reality instead of just twelve. The twelve dimensions of reality take us up through the galactic level. The twenty-four dimensions of reality take us up through the universal level.

Now that we had taken our seventh initiation and were working so closely with Melchizedek, this seemed appropriate. Melchizedek confirmed that we were on target. We also included in this prayer an invocation to transfer our twelve strands of DNA from our etheric vehicle into our physical body. Melchizedek told us that this had never been done in this way before, but because of the speed with which we were evolving—unique to this period of Earth's history—this could be done. I am putting these prayers in this book so you can use them yourselves.

Beloved presence of God, Mahatma, Melchizedek, Metatron and the seven mighty elohim, we hereby pray with all our heart, soul, mind and might for the full anchoring and activation of all our fire letters, key codes and sacred geometries of the twenty-four dimensions of reality to be fully fired and activated by the 12:12 celebration in December. We thank thee and accept this as is God's will so that we may be of greater service.

We also ask for a full anchoring of our twelve strands of DNA into our physical bodies by Wesak 1995.

Our beloved subconscious minds, we hereby ask and command that you take this thought-form prayer with all the mana and vital force that is needed to manifest and demonstrate this prayer to Melchizedek and the Source of our being. Amen.

Melchizedek, Mahatma, Metatron and the seven mighty elohim, let the rain of blessings fall. Amen.

After doing the Huna prayer, we talked with Melchizedek a bit and requested the full anchoring of the Eye of Horus into our third eye. There are levels at which this can be done—planetary, solar, galactic, universal and cosmic. Ours was being anchored and activated at the galactic level.

Then another quite extraordinary piece of information came through. Melchizedek spoke about the elohim and the original scriptures they wrote at the highest cosmic inner-plane levels. He referred to them as tomes and also as "the Malthusian volumes." I asked Melchizedek if it would be possible to anchor this information on an inner-plane level in a way similar to our request for the full anchoring of the light packets of information from *The Keys of Enoch*. He said that we could, and he thought that doing another Huna prayer to request this would be appropriate. He also suggested that we put in the Huna prayer a request for the activation of the inner circle of the seven levels of chambers in each chakra. Last, he said that many of these openings were instituted by fire. I questioned him about this, and he said he was referring to the kundalini fire rising to burn away the blocks. I asked him if this would be another good thing to request in the Huna prayer, and he said yes.

After the session I wrote up the following Huna prayer for us to do at our next meditation session. I recommend that you, my readers, do it also. Ask to be taken to the Golden Chamber of Melchizedek when first doing it.

Beloved Presence of God, Mahatma, Melchizedek, the seven mighty elohim, Metatron and Djwhal Khul.

We hereby call forth a divine dispensation for a full anchoring and activation of all light packets of information from the original elohim tomes and all Malthusian volumes of information at the highest Creator/God level. We are specifically calling forth help in this matter from the seven mighty elohim, and we ask Melchizedek to coordinate this whole program. We ask for a continual downpouring of this information until complete over the next 3½ to 8½ months. We also ask at this time for a full activation of the inner circle of all our chakras and a greater acti-

*vation of our kundalini under the guidance of Melchizedek and
Djwhal Khul. In addition, we ask for the full actualization and
usage of our newly anchored Eye of Horus. We thank thee and
accept this done as is God's will.*

*Our beloved subconscious minds, we hereby ask and command
that you take this thought-form prayer with all the mana and
vital force that is needed to manifest and demonstrate this
prayer to the Source of our being through Melchizedek. Amen.*

*Beloved presence of God, Mahatma, Melchizedek, seven mighty
elohim and Metatron, let the rain of blessings fall. Amen.*

Meditation on September 7, 1994

I began this meditation by going to the Arcturian light-synthesis chamber to be worked on and to have a chat with Lord Arcturus. He proceeded to
tune up and raise the vibration of the electronic plate that had been placed
in my third eye and crown. It became clear that my mission was three-
pronged. Djwhal Khul's ashram and my work with Vywamus was my base.
Then I also seemed to have another prong coming from the Golden Chamber of Melchizedek at the universal level. The last prong was the
Arcturians. This trinity seemed to be the main focus of the service work I
would be bringing through over the next twenty years. Interestingly enough,
however, I received some information that if we wanted to, we could remain
on Earth for 200 years. No decision had to be made yet, but this was an option available to me. I asked Djwhal what I would be doing for 200 years.
Some hierarchical voice answered and said, "Teach seminars and write
books." I found this kind of humorous. I thought, I guess I will get pretty
good at teaching seminars and writing books.

Lord Arcturus, upon my request, also agreed to anchor light packets of
information from Arcturus in me at night while I slept, regarding the implementation of my mission. Melchizedek had told me that all the fire letters,
key codes and sacred geometries were now in. He said this process was
much like the process of anchoring the higher chakras. There was now a
process of learning to actualize and utilize all fire letters, key codes and sacred geometries. I was now in a seven-year process, from 1994 to 2001, of
learning to do this. I also asked Melchizedek later in the meditation if there
would ever be a time when I would fully step into the mayavarupa body to
the point of being more physically immortal and having no physical weakness. He said that at the end of this seven-year cycle this was a possibility.
This would also be a possibility when we learned to actually teleport, which
could be within this seven-year cycle.

Upon questioning Lord Arcturus about the nature of my missions with the Arcturians, he said that I was being trained to issue the high-frequency Arcturian energies for the purpose of helping people accelerate spiritually. He also told me, upon my request, that he would help me transfer my twelve strands of DNA from my etheric vehicle into my physical vehicle. I also invoked more of the new Arcturian light technologies to be given to me. He said the prayer request had been officially received, and he would work on it. I was very excited about my present connection with the Arcturians and our future work together.

Wednesday Night Class, September 7, 1994

Our Wednesday night class was for the first hour a lecture discussion I was leading about the path to Sirius. This is, of course, one of the seven paths to higher evolution. An extraordinary thing occurred during the class that none of us expected. Vywamus, in conjunction with the Lord of Sirius, anchored an information superhighway from Sirius to the ascension column in our living room. Vywamus said that this violet-colored superhighway would be activated through our ascension column for six to eight months. During this time these light packets, or star packets, of information would come pouring through and this light information would be programmed into our computer banks to be utilized by us at a later time. Also there was now some kind of triangular connection between Sirius, the Pleiades and our ascension column.

We all felt the profound power and significance of what was happening and the profound energies we were all receiving. Everyone who attended class was connected to this information superhighway or light beam of energy, through their crown chakras, so they didn't have to be in our ascension column to receive this energy. I think we all felt very blessed to be attending class that night.

Meditation on September 11, 1994

This morning we had a most extraordinary meditation. We traveled to the Golden Chamber of Melchizedek and spoke with him for over an hour. It was here that Melchizedek told us about the transmitter station that had been installed the previous day. This transmitter station was installed in our third chakra and then in all our cells to help us assimilate the light packets of information from the elohim scriptures we had invoked from Melchizedek. He told us that this level of energy transmission now taking place in ourselves and our ashrams was the biggest the Earth had ever known. Melchizedek then installed his information disk, or medallion, into our brains to help us translate the information that would soon be pouring in. There would be twelve packets of information. We hadn't yet received the first one. This was why the transmitting system in the chakra had to be installed. It would serve as a lens to help us receive information at a rate 100 to 1000 times more than we had previously been able to receive.

I was beginning to see that what we were now tapped into individually and in our ashram was becoming something quite incredible. We were now beginning to bring galactic and universal energies, knowledge and information to Earth in a way that has never been done before. The work we were doing in our laboratory office in Djwhal Khul's ashram two to three times a week was a major catalyst for this. My feeling was that we were now finally totally breaking through, and part of this was taking the seventh initiation.

Melchizedek told me that there was a six-pointed star on Earth that was bringing in these galactic and universal energies, and I was a point of this star. I got that Brian Grattan was another point. I was really seeing that by the grace of God I was part of something quite extraordinary on planet Earth. I always knew that part of my personal mission was to open up the cosmic, universal and galactic levels to the general public through my books, lectures and seminars. All of us working together had accelerated this process greatly, way beyond what any of us could have done on our own. Things were really beginning to get exciting now.

Meditation on September 18, 1994

My friend and I chatted for a while and then went back into the Golden Chamber of Melchizedek. I did a short prayer with Melchizedek, requesting that he tune up the newly installed transmitting system in our chakras to full force and increase one-thousandfold our lens capacity to receive energy and information. I also requested to Melchizedek to begin running as much as possible the 98 percent light-quotient energies over the next three months leading up to the 12:12. Melchizedek graciously agreed.

I also asked him when a person is moved into the fourth dimension in his/her initiation process. I knew a person moved into the fifth dimension at the sixth initiation and into the sixth dimension at the seventh initiation. Melchizedek said a person moves into the fourth dimension at the third initiation. He also told us that anchoring these light packets from the elohim scriptures would not only help build our light quotient, but also our intelligence and manifestation abilities.

He told us that he was at the twenty-second to the twenty-fourth initiation and that he had followed the third path of the seven paths to higher evolution, which meant training to become a planetary logos. We knew Djwhal Khul was at the ninth initiation. We figured that Lord Maitreya was somewhere around the eleventh or twelfth and Sai Baba was somewhere above that. I share this information simply to give my readers a perspective of how high the twenty-second to the twenty-fourth initiation is.

Melchizedek also told us that we had stabilized our light quotient at 95 percent and were now moving toward 96 percent. We had also anchored the very beginning of chakra 35 in our crown. I was definitely feeling like we had made another major shift upward.

Meditation on September 18, 1994

Later in the day I had one of the most extraordinary meditations I have ever had. Melchizedek, Thoth, Metatron and Djwhal Khul installed phase one and phase two of our "heaven-on-Earth healing and sealing program." It is a special sealing for the protection and automatic healing of all the chakras, organs, glands, brain, spine and one's entire four-body system. A special coating of geometric forms, key codes, fire letters and colors are placed over and in all these aspects of self. Whenever these aspects of self get off balance, they begin spinning and automatically put one's whole program back in balance.

I must have meditated for about three hours, getting the whole program installed and finely tuned. I felt an enormous clearing, healing and stabilization of my entire program. This was turning out to be quite a day, and for the first time I was beginning to get a feeling, glimpse and taste of what these higher light quotients truly felt like. They were for the first time beginning to feel closer at hand instead of a distant goal. I was now just three points away from the group's final goal of 98 percent light quotient. The masters told me that this level of light quotient was quite unusual for this planet. In the past it was usually carried only by initiates living in monasteries and temples.

Part of the new program for this planet is to bring this level of initiation and light to the general public. Another rare thing about this process is the fact that in the past, most masters dropped their physical bodies at the beginning of the sixth initiation at the time of their ascension. It is only recently that new ascended masters have chosen to remain on Earth. This happened occasionally in the past; however, 99 times out of 100, masters left after ascension. We were now moving not just toward ascension or the beginning of the sixth initiation, but rapidly toward completing our seventh. In the past most people left the physical bodies at the 80 to 83 percent light-quotient level. We were all up to the 95 to 96 percent level—and living in the middle of Los Angeles! I think you can see why the masters made this comment about this being unusual, not just for us, but for many of the lightworkers on the planet who are beginning to move into these levels of initiation, light and consciousness.

At the end of our meditation in the morning we went to the courts of Shamballa. As we stood before Sanat Kumara and the teachers with whom we work the most, we did a Huna prayer for the purpose of completing and unifying all ashrams and setting forth an ideal or a prototype for cooperation and freedom from ego among all ashrams on Earth. My ultimate goal was to generalize this prayer so that eventually it would extend to all ashrams of all the chohans of the seven rays on Earth. I think I felt really good about doing this. In truth, it was already happening; however, this solidified this process officially before Sanat Kumara himself.

Meditation on September 25, 1994

I covered a lot of ground in this meditation, as I had a lot of loose ends I wanted to tie together. So this was kind of a potpourri channeling session. I first called in the Mahatma. I requested a permanent anchoring of the Mahatma energy into our being and a deeper penetration of this energy on an ongoing basis. The Mahatma agreed to this and began doing this immediately.

I then requested a full anchoring into our being of all light packets of information from the 352 levels of the Mahatma over the next eight months. leading up to Wesak 1995. I also requested that these light-packet downpourings be connected to the ascension columns in the ashram. I was basically requesting another information superhighway be set up that came directly from the Godhead. The Mahatma agreed to this and said he couldn't bring forth all light packets from all 352 levels, but that he would anchor what was allowable and appropriate. This, of course, was fine with us. I share this information as a suggestion that you, my readers, ask for the same thing in one of your meditations.

Next I called in Metatron and requested all light packets of information from *The Keys of Enoch* on planetary, solar, galactic, universal and cosmic levels, in all five sacred languages. Metatron confirmed that there were different levels of *The Keys of Enoch*. He said that it would take about two years to fully anchor all this information, and this would occur in conjunction with the work we were doing in the Golden Chamber of Melchizedek. We also asked for his continued help in our light-building program, specifically to help me raise my light quotient to the ninth level.

Next I called on Melchior. We talked a little bit about the galactic core and what goes on there. I also confirmed the existence of the galactic-core ascension seat, which he invited me to come and sit in. All you have to say is, "Melchior, galactic ascension seat." Then the spiritual body will go there and the galactic energy will begin flowing. Melchior told me that Vywamus was the best teacher to work with to get connected with the galactic core. He told me that over the next ten days Vywamus would be doing a lot of electrical work on me in this regard. So I called him in.

I then called in Djwhal Khul. He told me that he had ascended at age ninety-four. However, he had learned to stop the aging process when he was fifty and he had learned how to teleport at an even earlier age. He left his physical-body incarnation shortly after taking his sixth initiation. He told me that I was in the process of merging with him and the Lord Maitreya in some kind of new experiment. There was also a main connection I have with Djwhal, Lord Maitreya and Melchizedek. I was also told to sit in the Golden Chamber of Melchizedek ascension seats as much as possible.

Djwhal told me that I was now between the tenth and eleventh initiation in the Brian Grattan system. I felt pretty good about this, since it was just one month before that we had taken our seventh initiation (nine and a half on the Grattan scale). I knew the work I was invoking in this meditation was going to give me another boost. Djwhal ended the conversation by thanking me for the work I was doing, and I immediately thanked him for how he was helping me.

Last, I went to Shamballa and did a Huna prayer requesting the anchoring of all light packets of information from the Alice Bailey books, theosophy books, Tibetan Foundation material, *The "I AM" Discourses*, hierarchical archives, Shamballa's archives and galactic-core light packets.

Another tidbit of spiritual information that came through had to do with Madam Blavatsky. She passed on as a fourth-degree initiate. Upon going to the spiritual plane, she almost immediately took her fifth initiation. She then took her sixth initiation and/or ascension without having to reincarnate again, which I found interesting. It is good to know that you don't necessarily have to complete all your initiations in a physical body to ascend. I think this had a lot to do with how gifted she was and what an extraordinary service mission she had performed.

Meditation on October 1, 1994

In my meditation today I went to Lord Maitreya's ashram. He began by greeting me and telling me that he was as happy to speak with me as I was to him. I began by asking him about this new blending process occurring for me in regard to him and Djwhal. He told me that this was a new experiment he and Djwhal were doing because of our work together. Lord Maitreya said that Djwhal was beaming, or blending, a type of subray of intelligence, goodwill, faith and knowledge. Lord Maitreya was sending a subray of pure selfless service. In terms of color frequencies, Djwhal was sending, or blending, a blue subray and Lord Maitreya a pure white subray.

An interesting synchronicity came to mind. A woman who had ordered *The Complete Ascension Manual* recently had her inner sight opened up. In a letter to me she said that at night when the lights were out and she lay in bed, this book glowed in the dark with a whitish-blue aura. These are the colors that embodied the blending process of Lord Maitreya and Djwhal Khul.

I asked Lord Maitreya how long he would be staying with the Earth's evolution before moving on to his cosmic evolution and letting Kuthumi take his place. He said approximately 2000 more years, although this could be shortened.

We ended our conversation with a meditation to help us actualize chakra 36 and help us build our light quotient. Last, we did a Huna prayer.

Meditation on October 12, 1994

On this morning I went to my friend's house to bring her as a gift a copy of my newly published book, *The Complete Ascension Manual*. As she looked at the book clairvoyantly, she said that right in the center it had the stamp of approval of Sanat Kumara. She also saw a being called the Melchizedek Magnetizer, whose job it was to energize and magnetize the book. Earlier that week in my meditation with another friend, Djwhal said that he saw my books ultimately selling in the millions. (I hope he is right.)

Meditation on October 16, 1994

My friend and I began our meditation today going to Djwhal's ashram. Djwhal told us, upon our questioning, that our light quotient was now at the 96 percent level. We had stabilized our tenth initiation and were working toward the eleventh. In terms of the seven sublevels of the seventh initiation, we were now at the fifth sublevel. We were still working on actualizing chakra 36 into our crown.

Djwhal told us upon further questioning that we were basically now experiencing a triple overshadowing, or overlighting. The first level was Djwhal Khul; the second, Lord Maitreya; and the third, Melchizedek, the Universal Logos.

We were then taken to the Golden Chamber of Melchizedek, where we were joined by Djwhal, Lord Maitreya, Vywamus, Sanat Kumara, the Lord of Arcturus and the Lord of Sirius. We then experienced, upon our invocation, the anchoring of the five christed universes. We also invoked the installation of all fifty of our chakras. Melchizedek had the Lord of Arcturus install them. This would begin a one-and-a-half- to two-year process of fully activating and actualizing them. In the process of doing this, the light poured into the chamber and our chakra facets were helped to open fully. Our chakra 36 was stabilized and our light quotient greatly raised. We officially invoked help every night to continue this process until completion. The energies coming in were some of the strongest we had ever experienced.

The following is the Huna prayer we did at the end of the meditation.

Beloved presence of God, Melchizedek, Vywamus, Sanat Kumara, Lord Maitreya, Djwhal Khul, Metatron, the Arcturians and

Lord of Sirius.

We hereby pray with all our heart, soul, mind and might for a divine dispensation on our behalf from the most high God. We hereby call forth a divine dispensation that from this day and moment forward we be officially overlighted for the rest of this incarnation and beyond by Melchizedek, the Universal Logos. We next request a divine dispensation that our Djwhal Khul ashram now officially become overshadowed and overlighted by Melchizedek, and from this day and moment forward be considered as Melchizedek's ashram and outpost as well as Djwhal Khul's ashram.

We are hereby officially invoking your help, Melchizedek, in all facets of our ashramic life. And we officially invite you to be involved in all classes and workshops, bringing forth your universal energies, perspectives and divine dispensations as you see fit and as we are ready. We are requesting this so that we may be of greater service. We thank thee and accept this done as is God's will.

Our beloved subconscious minds, we hereby ask and command that you take this thought-form prayer with all the mana and vital force that is needed to manifest and demonstrate this prayer to the Source of our being through Sanat Kumara and Melchizedek. Amen.

Beloved Sanat Kumara and Melchizedek, let the rain of blessings fall. Amen.

Meditation on October 23, 1994

We had an extraordinary meditation today. We began by traveling in our spiritual bodies to Puttaparthi, India, to visit his holiness the Lord Sai Baba. I asked for his blessing on my newly published book, *The Complete Ascension Manual*, to help sell the millions of copies that Djwhal Khul said was a potentiality.

Sai Baba graciously agreed and gave his blessing, saying, "It shall be so." He also sprinkled sacred ash upon us. I then asked for his help in our completing all seven levels of initiation, anchoring our fifty chakras and building our light quotient to the 90 percent level. He again gave his blessing and said, "It shall be so." He also told us that the higher we go, the more responsibility was required of us to serve. I told him that we understood this and accepted this mantle.

Sai Baba then metaphorically picked us up by the scruff of our necks like a proud father and took us under his wing and aura, placing us under his guidance and ashramic influence. I felt like I had just received one of the great blessings of this entire incarnation, Sai Baba being a physicalized master and the embodiment of the cosmic Christ and a universal avatar. To be under his wing, aura and ashramic influence is truly one of the greatest feelings of spiritual peace, love and protection I have ever experienced.

The only thing that can compare is being under the grace of his holiness, the grand master Melchizedek, the Universal Logos. The combination of the two is absolutely awesome: one being physically embodied and the other working from the universal core. I believe there are certain things that Sai Baba can do, being physically embodied, that other masters can't do. I don't know this for sure, but this is my strong feeling.

We then went to the Golden Chamber of Melchizedek. Melchizedek greeted us and noted how bright our energy fields were this morning. His holiness the Lord Sai Baba had just touched us, and the effects were quite evident. Melchizedek spoke to us about the new dispensation we had received the previous day when he anchored his ascension seat into our physical ashrams on Earth. The profundity of this is mind-boggling to me still. It is as if our home is indeed the Golden Chamber of Melchizedek.

This can be invoked by anyone. However, before you do, work for a while in meditation in the Golden Chamber first to prepare for this divine dispensation.

Upon our request, Melchizedek then did some work with us to help us anchor our fifty chakras. We also requested help in transferring the twelve strands of DNA from our etheric bodies into our physical bodies. I also requested help in integrating the Photon Belt energy into our physical bodies. Melchizedek said that most of this work was being done during sleep time, as was much of the anchoring of the elohim scriptures.

He said the elohim scriptures were also being channeled through the Lord of Sirius and our tube/cylinder during sleep time and when we sat in the ascension seats. Since all these things had been consciously invoked, he told us that just by sitting in the ascension seats in the Golden Chamber and in the Great White Lodge, all these processes were automatically taken care of, including the anchoring of chakras. We then invoked Melchizedek, Metatron and the Mahatma for light-quotient-building.

I again requested that we achieve the stabilized 97 percent level by the 12:12, which was about seven weeks away. I asked him if this was realistically within our reach and he said it was. I also asked Melchizedek if I was still on target to take the beginning stage of the twelfth initiation by the 12:12, and he said yes. Melchizedek anchored the energies in the second chakra, which again seemed to be a new dispensation. We also invoked the five christed universes. To say this meditation with Sai Baba and Melchizedek was high-powered would be an understatement. My friend and

I were reeling (in a very positive sense) from the energy work that had been done. We truly felt intoxicated.

Meditation on October 30, 1994

We went to Sai Baba's ashram in Puttaparthi, India, to speak to him. The prayer request I made to begin our chat was as follows.

> *We officially request to become your devotees and humbly request that you take us under your wing, protection and tutelage in terms of our cosmic evolution and service work. Although we are being overlighted by Djwhal Khul, the Lord Maitreya and Melchizedek, we are officially requesting that you join this team as an active member on our behalf. For if there is one thing that I have learned in this lifetime, there is nothing quite like the glory of Sai Baba, and we would be greatly honored if you would accept us as your official devotees in this regard.*

I also later requested that from this moment forward he consider our Djwhal Khul, Lord Maitreya and Melchizedek ashram to also be a Sai Baba center. He graciously agreed to both requests. Then I asked Sai Baba whether he had an ascension seat in his ashram. He told me about the love seat that we could come and sit in, which I wrote about in my book *Beyond Ascension*. We then traveled to Babaji's cave, and it was there that Babaji told us about his seat of immortal bliss that we could come and sit in. We bathed in his energies and soaked in the immortal bliss.

We then traveled to the Golden Chamber of Melchizedek for more anchoring and activation work on our fifty chakras. I then asked Melchizedek to tune up our transmitting station, which he had installed about two months earlier. He did this with the help of Metatron. The energies that began to pour in were incredible.

Sai Baba Dreams

After these two visits to Sai Baba's ashram I began to have many more dreams about him, which I always love. In the first one I was talking with a man who told me I looked like Sai Baba and then said, "You look like a Hindu god." The dream symbolized to me the blending that was now taking place with Sai Baba's energy.

About three days later I had another dream where two of my larger Sai Baba pictures were missing from my wall. My good friend said that she had some to replace the old ones. In the dream it was as if we were trading pictures of the masters. The two she gave me were large and fit perfectly on my wall. Sai Baba seemed to be relaxing more in one of them. She then gave me a third picture, which was smaller, which showed an upside-down triangle of light in Sai Baba's throat and head region. His head was beginning to dematerialize in the picture. My friend then spun me around in a twirling motion and placed me on a statue of Quan Yin. I said it wasn't strong enough and asked her to place me elsewhere in our living room. She said that the twirling motion was a gnome ride.

The dream symbolized to me a shift in my relationship to Sai Baba. Our relationship was now taking on a whole new level of spiritual work. The dematerialized picture I felt had to do with the spiritual work I had been doing the morning before the dream, which occurred in the afternoon. I had been channeling the five christed universes in the ascension seat of Melchizedek's Golden Chamber for almost three hours. The level of energy coming in was quite profound. My lesson now was to learn to dematerialize my entire body, not just the throat and head region. I felt that the picture of Sai Baba reclining and relaxing was symbolic of my process, of taking it easier and not pushing so hard, but rather trusting the process more. My friend, I felt, carried more of the Earth energy; that was why she called the pleasant twirl I received a "gnome ride." Quan Yin is a beautiful feminine energy; however, I was focusing more on galactic and universal energies and the strength of Sai Baba, Melchizedek and the Lord of Sirius in my life. Although incredibly beautiful, I personally felt I needed a stronger energy.

Meditation on November 13, 1994

We had a shorter meditation, but it was one of the most profound peak experiences of my entire life. We began by going to the Golden Chamber of Melchizedek and invoking the anchoring and activation of our fifty chakras. It was then that I spontaneously requested something I had never asked for before. I did not know if it was even spiritually appropriate to ask for it.

Previously, we had anchored the energies of the five christed universes with help from Lord Maitreya and Melchizedek. In today's meditation I requested the anchoring of the energies of the fifty-one christed universes of the source of our cosmic day. Vywamus had said that the source of our cosmic day was in charge of fifty-one universes. Melchizedek immediately responded by anchoring these energies. His headdress lit up in the form of a kabbalistic Tree of Life. Systematically, the lights of the entire Tree of Life began to light up as the energies came pouring in. Melchizedek then spontaneously called in the Lord of Sirius and the Lord of Arcturus to stand on each side of us as anchors. I can honestly say that it was the most profound meditation experience I had ever had.

I asked Melchizedek if this was something we should ask for on a regular basis; he said no. He said that we were receiving a one-time divine dispensation and blessing, which would broaden our consciousness.

We were also told that our light quotient was now nearing 97 percent and that the anchoring of our fifty chakras would be completed in a year and a half. Later I realized that this would be the May Wesak Festival of 1996. We would complete our seventh initiation at the Wesak Festival of 1995 and the full anchoring of the eighth- and ninth-dimensional chakra grids a year after.

Meditation on November 20, 1994

Today's meditation had one of the greatest impacts of my entire life. This was not because of either the time spent meditating or the heightened energy frequencies, but because of the information we received.

The previous Sunday Melchizedek had told us that we were serving as some kind of prototype for the planet in terms of the incoming programming for humanity. I bring this up now because it pertains to what we were told in this meditation.

We began by going to Djwhal's ashram to speak to Djwhal. Through the course of the conversation he told us that we were being offered a job position in the Spiritual Hierarchy. We did not have to accept it, but it was now being offered to us. The job we were being offered was to co-focus taking over Djwhal Khul's ashram when he moved on to his cosmic evolution sometime after 2012. We were blown away that we would be given such an honor. This job was offered to us due to the fact that we were the most focused, devoted, committed and disciplined initiates and because we were the most able to cooperate. Djwhal also referred to my wisdom and knowledge banks being quite developed, a quality necessary for this particular position.

The idea of both of us doing it was an experiment, but one with great possibilities. Our separate deficiencies were nicely complemented, and our friendship and love for each other and our devotion to the work made us the perfect candidates for the job. We felt this and immediately said yes. Djwhal told us that we would be in intense training for the next seventeen years leading to the year 2012. At this time there was a window of opportunity for us to move permanently back to the spiritual world. This would be our free choice. We were obviously welcome to remain on Earth if we wanted to. Djwhal then told us that even upon passing on to the spirit world, we would take over the ashram; however, we would still be under the guidance of senior masters in the Hierarchy. Djwhal would be moving back and forth from Sirius for a period of time.

I immediately knew that it was the right thing to do. I briefly thought about the fact that this would probably keep me working with the Earth plane longer than I had previously planned. I had previously planned to go to Sirius as soon as I could, being quite ethereal in nature. I quickly let go of this thought, realizing what an incredible opportunity this would be. It was also appealing to do it with my friend, which made it sound like much more fun.

The strange thing was that three years earlier, during a conversation with Djwhal I casually mentioned that I thought I could take over his job if I had the proper training. I didn't want to sound egotistical or out of line, of course. Suddenly, it became clear to me that I had been picking up on the fact that I was already being considered for this position. My friend told me that she had always seen me as a possible or likely candidate for this job. In truth, the training and work had been going on for some time already. This is why it felt so comfortable and right when Djwhal brought it up.

Djwhal also told us that our light quotient was now officially up to the 97 percent level and that we were at the eleventh initiation, or sixth sublevel of the seventh initiation in the Djwhal Khul/Alice Bailey system. By the grace of God we were officially on target now to take our twelfth initiation at the 12:12 as Djwhal and Melchizedek had prophesied. I was also taken with the thought and feeling of something that Djwhal had said in the Alice Bailey books—that sometimes an average man evolved quicker than the genius, because, knowing he was average, he worked much harder and never took anything for granted. I personally relate to this strongly. This job offer is a great honor, and I don't want to overstate or understate it. I was not born with any great gifts except maybe having a good mind and intuition and, by the grace of God, a really great and supportive family.

To get this position has demanded incredibly focused, unrelenting hard work. Djwhal actually said that my steadfast focus, devotion and commitment were unsurpassed. The other key quality has been my ability to cooperate and get along with people. The intangible qualities brought me to this position. I share this with you to inspire you who are average like me, who through hard work, devotion and dedication can develop genius and spiritual grandeur, as the Master Jesus would say. It is much like the fable of the tortoise and the hare, and in this lifetime I have very much been the tortoise. My average status and health problems allowed this to be no other way. I was, however, unrelentingly the tortoise and allowed nothing in God's infinite universe to stop me/him for an instant from getting to the top of the mountain.

This level of intangible qualities and devotion to God and humanity made me stand out. This is something everyone on this planet can choose to do at any moment in his/her life. The trick, then, is to maintain this unrelenting focus no matter what the obstacles. The choice is very simple. Do you want God, or do you want your ego and overidentification with matter? I chose God, not 98 percent, not 99 percent, not 99.99 percent. I literally chose God 100 percent and made the ultimate choice to not let go until God blessed me. By the grace of God, He has blessed me. Now I will not let go until God blesses all of humanity, for my happiness is not complete until I share the same happiness with all people. When I am back at the 352d level of the Mahatma and all of God's creation is there with me, then and only then will I let go. I have closed and locked the door on my lower self, for God is my only interest and desire, and I do not allow myself the luxury or indulgence of becoming weak. I have too much responsibility, and many souls depend on me, just as I have depended on others. I am so incredibly grateful for how God and the masters have blessed me that the only way I can demonstrate my appreciation is to give it back in service to humanity and all sentient beings.

Meditation on November 27, 1994

Today's meditation was officially planned in advance to be our official acceptance ceremony for taking over Djwhal Khul's ashram when he was ready to leave and to invoke the official beginning of our training. After chatting for a while to just catch up, we then proceeded to read the Huna prayer and acceptance speech in Djwhal's ashram before the masters (see below). Following it is the speech and prayer we said together.

We hereby officially call forth the beloved presence of God, the Lord of Sirius, the Lord of Arcturus, his holiness the Lord Sai Baba, Vywamus, Sanat Kumara, Lord Maitreya, Master Kuthumi, the Mahatma, Metatron, El Morya, Babaji and, of course, Djwhal Khul.

We humbly thank you for gathering here upon our request on this most joyous occasion and we would like to read the following statement and Huna prayer together.

We hereby most humbly and gratefully accept the job offer that has been extended to us by Djwhal Khul and the Spiritual Hierarchy to co-focus and take over Djwhal Khul's ashram when he is ready to leave. We are greatly honored that you would consider us for such a noble and important post. In all humility, we feel you have made the right choice and are greatly excited about the future responsibilities and potentials. We will be a very dynamic team together, and we give our solemn vow to hold this position in the sanctity in which it has been given. Djwhal Khul, rest assured that we will make you proud, and we will nurture with great care and tenderness that which you have so beautifully birthed.

We now request that our acceptance be officially written into the akashic records and that our official training begin as of the 12:12, if this prayer be in harmony with your will.

We also now request from all the masters gathered that our fifti-eth chakra be anchored in our crown by Wesak 1996, which is a year and a half away. We request that our light quotient now be built to the 98.99 percent in two to three months or before, if this prayer be in harmony with thy will.

We are ready now to begin our training in earnest and ask all the masters gathered here to work with us every night while we sleep, during our meditations, during our "ascension walks" and during our receptive periods of relaxing. We hereby pledge our undying devotion and selfless service to you, Lord Maitreya, Sanat Kumara and the Lord of Sirius and to you, grand master Melchizedek. We are your perfect instruments and channels and have no purpose or will other than the perfect implementation of the divine plan as you see it and we understand it.

Upon completion of this prayer, a pearl was dropped through our crown chakra into our pineal gland as a symbol of our acceptance of our new job, for which we were about to begin training. The official date for beginning our training was the 12:12. As far as we were concerned, however, we were beginning it as of this morning. We were told that our invocation to achieve 98 percent light quotient at a stabilized level was now within reach, as of course was the seventh sublevel of the seventh initiation (also known as the twelfth initiation). Our invocation to anchor the fifty chakras within one and a half years, Djwhal said, would occur as a byproduct of sitting in the Golden Chamber of Melchizedek and the Great White Lodge ascension seats and of performing spiritual work.

I then began questioning Djwhal about what life was like in the ashram, as its leader. It is hard for me to remember everything we discussed, but I'll do my best. This occurred rather spontaneously. He first told us that the de-cision to have us take over the ashram was a group decision made by him-self and Lord Maitreya, Sanat Kumara, the Lord of Sirius, Melchizedek and the master Kuthumi. By group consensus we were chosen. Djwhal had pre-viously told us that there were some who were more qualified in their tech-nical understanding, but overall, we were clearly the best candidates for this particular position in the spiritual government.

Djwhal had previously told us that he made his decision partly through studying the cosmic computers. They showed the brain waves of the candi-dates in a unique way that revealed the qualities and tendencies. This pro-vided the key information for why one candidate would be better for this job than another. Djwhal said the qualities we had that made us the best choice were our focus, dedication, commitment, leadership, cooperation, cha-risma, knowledge, wisdom, first-ray energy, practicality and our ability to work together without interference from the lower self, our control of lower-self passions.

We were told that the initiates who had been considered for this job were mostly on the Earth plane, with a few exceptions. There seemed to be waves of senior initiates who would be moving to Sirius with Djwhal over a period of time. Our group seemed to be the new incoming wave. This was tentatively set for 2012, but that could change.

The second ray is the only ashram that has a subsidiary ashram, because of the importance of the second ray. The first-ray focus is politics; the second ray, spiritual education; the third ray, economics; the fourth ray, the arts; the fifth ray, science; the sixth ray, religion; and the seventh ray, ceremonial order and magic.

The second ray is the central pillar of the seven rays because of its focus on spiritual education. Djwhal Khul is the only master who has ever been put in charge of training all the disciples and initiates of all the rays. Djwhal told us that this would be our job also. In essence, we would be doing the job of the current chohan of the second ray, Kuthumi, who is now focused on a much higher level, preparing to become the Planetary Christ when Lord Maitreya leaves that position. Understanding all of this made us even more honored to receive this post. I was honored to have the endorsement of all the masters mentioned above. I was also glad that the cosmic computer showed my brain waves to be worthy of such a position. We were also told that we would probably leave our physical bodies in the year 2012. Djwhal told me that I would probably serve in this position for 125 years, which in spiritual time is very short.

When Kuthumi leaves his post to become the Planetary Christ, Lanto will take his place. I was glad to hear about this 125-year period, for there was and is a part of me that is still eager to go to Sirius, as Djwhal is doing in approximately seventeen more years. My feeling was that nowhere in the infinite universe could I get better training and/or experience than in this position. This job experience on my spiritual résumé would be a tremendous base and maturation opportunity for me for all future jobs I will take in my cosmic evolution.

Djwhal told us that even though he will be stationed in Sirius, he would still be guiding us, along with a Sirius council in the Great White Lodge. In addition, Kuthumi, Vywamus and other senior members of D.K.'s ashram would guide us—as well as any master(s) we called on for help. I asked Djwhal if this had ever been done before in this co-focused manner, and I got the feeling that it hadn't.

Having a secondary ashram within an ashram of one of the chohans of the seven rays is unique. It came about only after the Middle Ages. At that time there was a group of senior initiates in Kuthumi's ashram who helped out until Kuthumi officially appointed Djwhal Khul to take over this post. That is when the secondary ashram really began to take hold and flourish.

I asked Djwhal how many initiates were involved with his ashram. He said there were six main initiates who helped him, a larger group of forty, then a still larger group of a little over 200. It is to these groups that he delegated responsibilities for the planetary training of disciples and initiates, plus other responsibilities he holds.

We were told that if we wanted, we could begin picking two initiates now to train directly under us; however, this was not yet essential. The idea was that I would pick two, my friend would pick two and Djwhal would pick two.

I then asked Djwhal about romantic relationships and sexuality at this level. He told us that masters at this level still formed bonds and unions and worked and served together; however, there wasn't the same kind of marriage understanding that we have on Earth. There was, he said, a type of melding of energies, but not sex in the same way.

Djwhal told us that he never sleeps, but he does rest. He even spoke of drinking a light potion as a type of tea break. Masters at this level still have an office, or place of residence. Djwhal, for example, spends a large amount of time working in his office. He also told us that he often travels to Sirius. The masters get together at certain ceremonies and holidays to have fun and joke around. Everything is not serious.

I asked him about our future training, but he was kind of vague. Part of it dealt with learning to read auras and cosmic computers; teleporting would be another part. Other skills would be reading a group aura to know what to say, meaning to know what thought forms to drop into the group or individual aura to get a desired effect.

After talking with Djwhal over an hour in detail about what his life and work in the ashram was about, I felt much more relaxed about the whole affair. I think that before this conversation, I was a little hyped up about it, which was to be expected. Afterward I was much more confident and less concerned, for I felt now that our training would unfold in a natural and organized fashion. I think his relaxed attitude about it blended into us.

I began to see that the ashramic life he was involved in was not much different from what I am doing now. I spend a lot of time at my desk, and my focus now is writing books and articles, putting on workshops, making a series of meditation/activations and therefore imparting teaching and training to disciples and initiates around the globe. The main difference, of course, is that I still have to deal with the cumbersome aspects of a physical vehicle and physical Earth life. After this conversation I left feeling like, I can do this.

There would still be a lot of technical training; however, that would be the least of my concerns. There would be lots of help until we learned the ropes. After talking to Djwhal I also realized that the ashram wasn't as big and overwhelming as I had previously imagined. The 200 senior initiates live on the outskirts of the ashram. I had the feeling it was like a small company or a highly efficient spiritual family of dedicated initiates. Also, the number of people they were dealing with was smaller than I realized. I was previously visualizing millions, but the number of higher-level initiates moving into the ashram is much, much smaller.

Our training had truly begun, and many of our fantasies about the ashram had evaporated. I left feeling much more relaxed and balanced about the whole process. This was clearly something I felt I could realistically handle and do a good job at.

Our talk also had the effect of helping me relax and have peace of mind about all the service work I was currently involved in. I was aware too that I had gotten too hyped up about a major workshop that we were going to host in Mount Shasta to mark the occasion of mass ascension on planet Earth. I felt that I was beginning to develop an even-mindedness about everything.

One thing I had begun to see over the past two years is that there is always another step. I used to think ascension was the end-all and be-all of everything. After going through it, I was very happy. However, I was then ready for the next step. I feel that this even-mindedness over these miraculous events was a good sign. I intuitively felt that it was part of my movement into a planetary leadership role. Even becoming head of Djwhal Khul's ashram, while an incredible thing, will eventually end, and I will move to my next training and job on Sirius. This slow, gradual process will continue through all 352 levels of the Mahatma. This state of consciousness feels like a healthy cosmic detachment. When too much importance is put on any one event, worry and anxiety ensue. For the first time I felt like some cosmic maturity was setting in on a level I hadn't experienced before. I knew this process was connected with moving into this planetary job.

Some Reflections on the Path

This extraordinary accelerated process over the past fourteen months of going through almost three major initiations and twenty light-quotient points in such a short period now seemed to be reaching a culmination. In a matter of sixteen days we were about to take our twelfth initiation and achieve our 98 percent light quotient, and we had already officially actualized chakra 36 in our crown. There was a tremendous sense of completion, almost awe, at all that had transpired.

It was fourteen months ago that I had taken my fifth initiation, and I had now almost reached the equivalent of the eighth initiation (really the seventh sublevel of the seventh in the Alice Bailey and Djwhal Khul scale).

I had literally gone up twenty light-quotient points during this time frame, which is mind-boggling. I had completed my first five volumes by January first, then proceeded to write two more. My first book was already officially published.

I was now writing articles in three major spiritual magazines and many smaller ones. I moved from anchoring chakra 12 in my crown to anchoring and actualizing chakra 35. Then I was offered the job to take over Djwhal Khul's ashram with my friend, which was to me an esteemed honor, an almost unfathomable grace.

I share this with you to inspire you, my reader, to never give up and to utilize the information and tools I have given in my books. I have given in this series of books literally every insight and tool I have used. Apply these tools, copy what I have done, and you will get just as fast results, perhaps even faster. Remain focused and never give up. Take advantage of this most extraordinary time in history in which we are living. Never has such a level of information been so readily available.

Meditation on December 11, 1994

On the day before the 12:12 ceremony we did the following meditation involved with the elohim scriptures. It was one of the most sacred and profound meditations we had ever done. I recommend that you try it yourself.

Elohim-Scripture Meditation

We now officially call forth the energies of the Source, the Council of Elders at the 352d level of the Mahatma and the seven mighty elohim. We hereby call forth beloved Melchizedek and the following seven masters to help in the following meditation to anchor the elohim scriptures. We call forth El Morya, Lord Maitreya, Sananda, Serapis Bey, Metatron and Djwhal Khul.

I call forth these key codes and light packets and request that the masters of the Spiritual Hierarchy who have been invoked now aid and help us in the proper spiritual assimilation. We will take one minute for each of the seven scrolls. We ask that a six-pointed star be placed around each individual and a larger six-pointed Star of David around the group as a whole. We call on Melchizedek to coordinate and guide the meditation.

Let us begin by calling forth elohim scroll number one, which is that of power. Please anchor and activate now. [Pause.]

We now call forth the elohim scroll and scripture of love. Please anchor and activate now. [Pause.]

We now call forth the elohim scroll and scripture of light. Please anchor and activate now. [Pause.]

We now call forth the elohim scroll and scripture of truth. Please anchor and activate now. [Pause.]

We now call on the elohim scroll and scripture of knowledge. Please anchor and activate now. [Pause.]

We now call on the elohim scroll and scripture of wisdom. Please anchor and activate now. [Pause.]

We now call forth the as-yet-unrevealed elohim scroll and scripture. We hereby request a divine dispensation from Melchizedek and Sanat Kumara that the seventh unnamed scroll now be fully anchored and activated as a divine blessing for humanity and the lightworkers gathered on the inner and outer plane.We now call on the elohim scroll and scripture of knowledge. Please anchor and activate now. [Pause.]

We thank thee and accept this done as is God's will.

We hereby request one last divine dispensation on our behalf. We request that you, Melchizedek and Sanat Kumara, work with all gathered here every night while we sleep during the next five months to help us all completely anchor, activate and assimilate all of the elohim scrolls and scriptures that are potentially available to us in preparation for the Wesak ceremony on the weekend of May 12 to 14, 1994. We request that for the next five months we may receive every night the highest potential of elohim scripture and anchoring of which we are capable. We request that this divine dispensation also be made available to any other ashrams you deem appropriate around the planet. Amen.

The 12:12 Planetary-Ascension Activation

The 12:12 turned out to be one of the most extraordinary transformational experiences of my entire life. I don't think I ever felt so altered. Djwhal Khul told us that the 12:12 experiences that occurred on December 12, 1994, signaled the opening for humanity of the doorway for mass ascension on planet Earth. The Wesak Festival the following May was when the masses would move through the doorway opened at the 12:12. Many lightworkers will move or have moved through this doorway already, but the masses won't do so until Wesak. The 12:12 also marked the momentous day when planet Earth herself moved from the fourth to the fifth dimension.

My former wife and I were involved in four different events over a three-day period. We hosted a one-day workshop on December 10 in which the group present did the preparatory work for opening this doorway. A new physical-body ascension matrix was anchored, which was the prototype for all future sixth-and seventh-degree initiates. There was a triple anchoring of energies from Sirius, the Pleiades and the constellation of Aquarius. There was also an opening of an atomic doorway in the upper portion of each person's third eye, which corresponded to the opening of the planetary gateway. There was also a major personal acceleration of the ascension process for all world servers. Djwhal Khul told us that all the lightworkers on the planet who were attuned to this process would either take their next major initiation or move up at least one sublevel in their initiation process. Melchizedek anchored a beautiful jewel in the atomic doorway just above the third eye in all who were present. All these things can be requested now by those reading this.

There was an enormous amount of light anchored over the four-day period around the 12:12. We also did a Sun dance in the afternoon of the 12:12 right around high noon to receive the energies from Helios and Vesta, who were intimately connected with this whole process. Djwhal told us that for the next three years the magnetic fields of the Earth would be slightly disrupted due to the transformation now taking place.

One of the next major events would occur in 1997 when Vywamus would be taking one of his major initiations. Vywamus. being the oversoul of the planet, told us that he had been waiting a very long time for this. He was the one who specifically helped us open the doorway to the fifth dimension for planet Earth. I personally had the sense that this moment in Earth's history was the very beginning of the golden age for planet Earth. For the first time in my life I was directly experiencing the Earth truly transforming into a more spiritual world. The signs had been coming for some time, beginning with the tearing down of the Berlin Wall, the end of communism in the Soviet Union, the cessation of apartheid in South Africa and the advent of greater cooperation in the United Nations. These were all significant milestones.

In less than five months humanity would begin ascending on a mass scale the likes of which the Earth had never known in the 3.1 billion years of her existence in this cosmic day. I felt that I had been graced to be a part of such a historic event.

On a personal level I officially took the seventh sublevel of my seventh initiation (or the twelfth initiation). I also officially began my training to take over Djwhal Khul's ashram with my friend in the year 2012. I personally felt like I had walked through some kind of doorway. I felt that my spiritual war to get to this point was finally over. I felt for the first time that I had truly become a full-fledged master and was no longer a student in the same way I had been for the previous forty-one years. On some level I would have had to complete the seven sublevels of the seventh initiation to feel this way. The full stabilization would not occur until Wesak in five months; however, taking the beginning stage had clearly put me through a doorway that felt more profound and transformative than anything I had ever experienced.

The fact that it occurred on the 12:12 made it even more significant, and it had a greater impact. It was also on this day that, by the grace of God, I attained the 98 percent light-quotient level. There was now only 0.99 percent more light quotient needed to achieve the maximum that could be held on this planet (98.99 percent). I did not and still do not feel much different than I had for the past ten years. The only truly profound difference I felt in taking this initiation is the amount of spiritual current running through my four-body system.

Meditation on December 20, 1994

We began our meditation by talking with Djwhal in his ashram. He was very pleased with the 12:12 and said that the doorway between our ashrams on Earth and his ashram on the inner plane were also opened to a very large degree. I found that very interesting. He said the next step would be to open the doorway to Lord Maitreya and his ashram.

My book *Beyond Ascension* came out in self-published form, and Djwhal was gracious enough to tell me that he was pleased with the work, which he had helped with from behind the scenes.

We then left Djwhal's ashram and traveled to the Golden Chamber of Melchizedek to try out a new meditation I had come up with the previous day. (It is always more fun to try out new things with a friend.) We began the meditation by greeting Melchizedek and then invoking the anchoring of our fifty chakras. Then we invoked the energies to complete our seventh level. We were now at the beginning stage of the twelfth initiation (the seventh sublevel of the seventh). Now we had to complete and stabilize it. Wesak was now the target date for this.

We then invoked an opening of all our chakras and all facets in the chakras and chambers. We invoked a deeper penetration of the energies of the Mahatma on a permanent basis. We then invoked the final push to build our light quotient to the 98.99 percent level. We had about 1.5 percent light quotient to go, which I figured we could achieve over the next two and a half months. We seemed to be averaging about one light-quotient point every four to six weeks. We then invoked a permanent increase, or tuning up, of Melchizedek's transmitting station in our chakras. We also called forth the next anchoring of the elohim scriptures. This initial invocation set the stage for my new meditation, which I had never tried out.

We then invoked the anchoring of the universal and cosmic Tree of Life into our four-body system. I was very specific about this being the *universal* Tree of Life, not the planetary, solar or galactic ones. I requested that we also be overlighted by the cosmic Tree of Life all the way back to the 352d level of the Mahatma. We then, one by one, invoked the full opening and activation of the ten sephiroth of the Tree of Life. I have included this meditation in *Beyond Ascension*, so I am not going to include it here.

This meditation was the first time I had experienced this. It was another experiment from our Djwhal Khul office and laboratory. It was one of the most profound meditations we had ever done. I realize that each and every week I keep saying this, but when Paramahansa Yogananda said, "God is ever new joy," he was speaking absolute truth. The level of light, opening and activation is incredible. I cannot recommend highly enough that you work with this meditation.

Meditation on December 24, 1994

Today was a shorter meditation, but a profound one. After my friend got up in the morning, the masters told her that she and I were ready for another major spiritual acceleration in our overall program. We were ready now to stabilize our light quotient at the 98 percent level and take another step in the process of anchoring and fully activating our fifty chakras. We began the meditation by going to the Golden Chamber of Melchizedek, who told us that today's meditation would be the combined masters' Christmas present to us.

Immediately gathered around us was our core group of fellow compatriots in Djwhal's ashram—Djwhal Khul, Lord Maitreya, Sanat Kumara, the Lord of Arcturus, the Lord of Sirius, Sai Baba and Melchizedek. They seemed to form a ring around us, with Melchizedek overlighting us.

Melchizedek asked me to invoke the energies as I usually do. I proceeded to call in the fifty chakras, elohim scriptures, twelve bodies, opening of alpha and omega chakras and a number of other higher-frequency energies that you are all familiar with by now. As a special blessing, Melchizedek seemed to knit a golden energy around us as part of this ascension acceleration and blessing. He told us in the sweetest and most divine way that we were his divine sheep, and he made an eloquent, poetic and symbolic speech about how we were his servants and disciples forevermore. I was incredibly touched, and I don't think I ever felt so blessed.

My cup was running over and I told him so. It is hard to put into words the incredible light and the feeling of joy and blessings that were generated. Each time we meditated seemed more wonderful than the previous time, which didn't seem possible but was indeed. This was the most beautiful and profound Christmas gift I had ever received. To be embraced in this way and with such love by all the masters I revered so greatly, and to be taken under Melchizedek's wing in such a profound and beautiful way, was the fulfillment of my deepest, most heartfelt desire of the past forty-one years of my life. I felt like I had returned home and was being joyously welcomed, as had the prodigal son after an incredibly hard-fought journey.

All my life I have been a spiritual warrior, as I am sure most of you are also. I felt I had finally made it to the place I always wanted to be but could never quite get to until now. I was feeling a peace that passeth understanding, as the Bible so eloquently states. There was obviously a lot further to go, and in truth, there were many more battles to fight as long as I retained this physical body. However, for this moment or holy instant I was feeling a peace and joy of the fulfillment of my deepest desires. The only thing I have ever wanted in this life was God. I have never been interested in anything else. Material things have never held the slightest interest or excitement for me. All I have ever wanted was God, and by His grace I was feeling and experiencing a certain limited degree of that, more than I had ever before experienced.

Meditation on December 30, 1994

We had an extraordinary meditation this day, which lasted almost three hours. We worked with the Melchizedek cosmic computer system, which I spoke of in *Beyond Ascension*. It was our first experience of consciously working with it. The masters told us that we had officially gone through the seventh sublevel seal of the seventh initiation, and in the three hours of meditation we had gone halfway through the seventh sublevel. The focus now seemed to be transferring all that we had achieved spiritually and in our etheric and lightbody into our physical bodies. We seemed to be going through a final end-of-the-year push.

During our meditation Melchizedek told us that we were now officially Melchizedeks, which felt profound to me. We were Melchizedeks before this, but what he was saying was that we were now fully realized Melchizedeks. A fully realized Melchizedek is one who has completed the seven levels of initiation. We had to go through the seventh sublevel seal and almost complete it until this could be so. We also had to stabilize our light quotient at the 98 percent level, which we had now done by the grace of God.

The amount of light running though my body was also having a very positive effect on my overall physical health and on the chronic pancreas weakness I'd had most of my adult life. After this meditation I felt motivated to move even faster in this process.

Meditation on January 1, 1995

We meditated for over three hours, which was a record for us, given the locations in which we live. It was incredible. We talked to Melchizedek for almost two hours about cosmic evolution; this formed the chapter, "Cosmic Ascension," in *Beyond Ascension*. A lot of the information I already had, but Melchizedek helped fill in the final missing pieces. At the end of our conversation we did one of our high-powered anchoring meditations.

For the first time we anchored our solar body of light, galactic body of light and universal body of light, which would allow us to tap into the twelfth dimension once we fully realized it. This was the next step beyond the fifty chakras, and it somewhat overlapped the fifty chakras. The anchoring of the galactic and universal bodies was taking us through the ninth to the twelfth dimension. This was very exciting, for we thought our limit on this plane was the ninth dimension, because the fiftieth chakra is the anchoring of the ninth-dimensional chakra grid. The pieces of the puzzle were all coming together.

For the first time at the end of our meditation we merged Djwhal Khul's ashram and the Golden Chamber of Melchizedek and practiced dematerializing. Our new focus was trying to make our physical body become more etheric. We did this for about four minutes with the help of the masters, and it felt incredible. I don't think we necessarily achieved full dematerialization; however, as of the first day of the new year this process had begun.

Meditation on January 2, 1995

We did an extraordinary two-hour meditation over the phone in the Great Pyramid of Giza to officially anchor and activate our solar, galactic and universal bodies. We had begun to meditate more frequently again, and we seemed to be in the midst of an intensive seven-day inner-plane acceleration program. For the first time we were beginning to practice dematerialization. Melchizedek said that we had almost fully stabilized our 98 percent light quotient.

This new insight that we can even go beyond the ninth dimension and the fifty chakras by anchoring the solar, galactic and universal bodies of light has been a tremendous boon to our program. We have come to realize that we can realize all the way up through the twelfth dimension in this physical body even though we must stop at the completion of the seventh initiation. It felt like this puzzle had totally come together.

My own consciousness continued to expand tremendously as the new information and energies kept pouring in. I was beginning to see that the books I have written are just the beginning of my writing career. There is nothing that I enjoy doing more.

My friend and I had resumed meditating every day, which seemed to be pushing our whole group along, for we also meditated for the group and for the Earth mother. There were enormous activations taking place, and the masters seemed open to moving us along even faster now as we incorporated and utilized quite well the energies and information we were receiving.

Everything I received from all levels inwardly and outwardly poured into my books. My digestive system seemed to be getting stronger the more light quotient I held. I felt incredibly excited about all that was going on. Djwhal Khul told us that this year of 1995 was going to be like a rocket ship. I told him that I thought last year was the rocket-ship year. His rebuttal was that this year would then be a super rocket ship and a year of change.

Moving into these higher levels seemed to be getting more and more fun. On New Year's Eve my then-wife and I were watching television about two hours before the new year began when suddenly the music box on our kitchen table turned on by itself. The song that started to play was "When You Wish upon a Star." I intuitively felt that this was the very first sign that we were at the official beginning of the miraculous transcendence of physical laws.

Meditation on January 22, 1995

In today's meditation we did one of the most powerful activations and Huna prayers than we had ever done together. We first called in the Lord of Arcturus and asked for his help in anchoring and activating our fifty chakras and twelve bodies around the clock. Then we went to the Golden Chamber of Melchizedek and did the following Huna prayers relating to the keys of Enoch and kabbalistic ascension activation I had been creating in the past two or three weeks.

Ultimate Huna Prayer and Meditation

Beloved presence of God, YHWH, Cosmic Council of Twelve, Council of the Elohim and the twelve mighty elohim, Metatron and the twelve mighty archangels, the Twenty-Four Elders who surround the Throne of Grace, the Hyos Ha Kodesh, Melchizedek, Lord of Sirius, Lord of Arcturus, Sai Baba, Djwhal Khul and Lord Michael.

We hereby make the most powerful, profound and important Huna prayer we have ever made in our entire lives, which we will also use as a type of ultimate meditation. We direct this prayer to all the cosmic watchers mentioned. However, we most specifically direct it to Melchizedek and Metatron, whom we ask to orchestrate this new two-year spiritual battle plan for completing the anchoring of our twelve bodies, fifty chakras, twelve strands of DNA, twelve-dimensional integration, seven levels of initiation, 99 percent light quotient, teleportation activation, dematerialization activation and total integration of light packets from the vast treasury of light of YHWH.

We hereby request that the seventy-six activations, which we are now about to make in a slowed-down meditation format, be fully integrated within a two-year period. We hereby request that a program be set up by Melchizedek and Metatron that is in operation twenty-four hours a day, seven days a week and 365 days a year to achieve this goal. What we call forth in this prayer meditation is for today and to be continued indefinitely for the next two years until complete. We now call forth all activations.

This comprehensive prayer activation we are doing today will be done only once in this form. We request that all seventy-six activations and previous ones from past meditations be programmed into the Golden Chamber of Melchizedek ascension seats and into Metatron's light-quotient-building program so that after this meditation, anytime we call on either function, all seventy-six activations will automatically take place.

• We request that the seventy-six activations occur every night and all night long while we sleep and while we are walking, watching TV, relaxing and meditating. We are willing to take on the mantle of responsibility that goes with receiving this cosmic dispensation of YHWH.

• We request this for our core group, and we will let you decide which members belong in it. We are in essence calling forth a cosmic dispensation, the likes of which might never yet have been invoked on Earth in such a comprehensive fashion and on such a cosmic scale. We are requesting to be the instruments on Earth who will literally heal the separation between God and Earth through the grace of Melchizedek, Metatron and Lord Michael. We thank thee and accept this done as God's (Yahweh's) will. Amen.

• Metatron and Melchizedek, please anchor and activate this day and over the next two years until fully complete, the sev-

enty-six keys of Enoch and cosmic Book of Knowledge ascension activations.

• *Anchor and fully activate sixty-four keys of Enoch on solar, galactic, universal, multiuniversal and cosmic levels in all five sacred languages.*

• *Anchor the decadelta light emanations from ten light super-scripts of YHWH.*

• *Anchor the fifty chakras, twelve bodies and Melchizedek diamonds and crystals.*

• *Anchor the nogan shells of YHWH on a permanent basis.*

• *Anchor the divine template and light grid of elohim permanently.*

• *Anchor Yahweh's tablets of creation.*

• *Anchor the cosmic Torah Or of YHWH.*

• *Anchor the scriptures of Melchizedek.*

• *Anchor the scriptures of Metatron.*

• *Anchor the elohim scriptures.*

• *Anchor the light packets of the higher Kabbalah of YHWH and Melchizedek.*

• *Anchor the cosmic Tree of Life permanently; open all sephiroth.*

• *Anchor the seventy-six sacred names of Metatron and YHWH.*

• *Anchor Yahweh's living energy codes.*

• *Anchor Yahweh's Book of Knowledge.*

• *Anchor the gifts of the Holy Spirit as described in* The Book of Knowledge: The Keys of Enoch.

• *Anchor the scrolls of weights and measures.*

• *Anchor the keys of the Melchizedek priesthood.*

• *Anchor the highest triad of sephirothic knowledge.*

• *Anchor the divine seed of the elohim.*

• *Anchor the keys to the Father, Sons and Shekinah's universe.*

• *Anchor the biological codes for the Christ race.*

• *Anchor the scriptures of the luminaries.*

• *Anchor the codes of the luminaries.*

• *Anchor the hidden divine word of YHWH.*

• *Anchor the image of the elohim permanently.*

- *Anchor the flame of YHWH on a permanent basis.*

- *Anchor the knowledge of the next universe as described in* The Keys of Enoch.

- *Anchor the ten pictures of light of YHWH as described in Key Sixty-four.*

- *Anchor the entire treasury of light of YHWH on an ongoing nonstop basis for the next two years until completion of the twelve dimensions and bodies and fifty chakras is achieved.*

- *Illuminate permanently the seventy-two areas of the mind.*

- *Anchor the complete yod spectrum.*

- *Anchor the permanent teleshift light field for divine protection.*

- *Anchor permanently the Father's eye of creation.*

- *Anchor the garment of Shaddai or the lightbody of Metatron permanently.*

- *Anchor the superelectron and microtrons to replace all existing electrons.*

- *Anchor the biostratus or the genetic superhelix and twelve strands of DNA.*

- *Anchor the light frequencies to spiritualize our blood chemistry.*

- *Anchor permanently the Ain, Ain Soph and Ain Soph Or.*

- *Anchor the ordination by the spirit of YHWH.*

- *Anchor the celestial marriage of our twelve bodies.*

- *Anchor the star codes of the Melchizedek universe.*

- *Anchor light geometries to permanently energize our etheric and physical vehicle.*

- *Anchor the divine recorder cell as described in* The Keys of Enoch.

- *Infuse permanently the Shekinah life force.*

- *Anchor a baptism of the Holy Spirit.*

- *Open all mind locks.*

- *Open all seven seals so we may be directly linked to the cosmic Tree of Life.*

- *Open completely the gates of light all the way up to YHWH and his treasury of light.*

• *Anchor the cosmic pyramids of light on a permanent basis.*

• *Activate our messiahship within.*

• *Call forth the robes of power of Djwhal Khul and Melchizedek.*

• *Anchor permanently the sword of Lord Michael.*

• *Remove all veils of light and all veils of time.*

• *Anchor permanently the Tetragrammaton upon our inner minds.*

• *Anchor permanently the divine plan of YHWH.*

• *Anchor the light pyramid of the next universe of YHWH.*

• *Anchor and activate all living energy codes so that our nucleic membrane may attach to the larger membrane of the universe of YHWH.*

• *Anchor scriptures of luminaries to come.*

• *Anchor sacred geometries and color codes to transform our chromosomes to the blueprint of YHWH.*

• *Call forth the first and last I Am of YHWH.*

• *Install technology to receive and process the language of light from the treasury of light of YHWH.*

• *Anchor light packets of information from Nag Hammadi codices and scriptures so we may develop greater understanding of the twelve lightbodies.*

• *Anchor permanently our electromagnetic body, epi-kinetic body, eka bodies, gematrian body, overself body, anointed Christ overself body, zohar body of light, higher Adam Kadmon body and the Lord's mystical body.*

• *Anchor permanently our overself bodies, including the Elohistic Lord's body, the Paradise Son body, Order of Sonship body, Christ overself body and the overself body as described in The Keys of Enoch.*

• *Anchor permanently the twelve foundations of the heavenly Jerusalem.*

• *Anchor and activate all pertinent light packets of information from the Melchizedek Dead Sea Scrolls.*

• *Anchor and activate the structural pattern of living light.*

• *Anchor the quanta-mechanical corpuscles of light.*

• *Anchor the entire treasury of light of YHWH.*

• *Connect directly our crown chakras with a cylinder of light to this treasury under the guidance of Metatron and Melchizedek. Connect our ascension columns in our ashram with this treasury if this be in harmony with God's will.*

We now pray with all our heart, soul, mind and might that these seventy-six activations we have invoked continue nonstop for the next two years until the completion of the twelve levels is fully realized. We are 100 percent serious about what we have invoked and ask, by the grace of God, if we are deemed worthy, to be given the cosmic blessings for which we have asked.

Kodoish, Kodoish, Kodoish Adonai 'Tsebayoth: Holy, holy, holy is the Lord God of hosts!

Our beloved subconscious minds, we hereby ask and command that you take this thought-form prayer with all the mana and vital force that is needed to manifest and demonstrate this prayer through Melchizedek and Metatron to YHWH and the Cosmic Council of Twelve, elohim councils and archangel councils.

Beloved presence of God, Melchizedek and Metatron, let the rain of blessing fall. Amen.

More Meditations

The work with *The Keys of Enoch* led me to begin charting in greater detail the process of cosmic ascension compared to planetary ascension. Shortly after that I began to understand the seven cosmic bodies, each of which connects to the seven cosmic planes, and from there I began to understand the overself, or cosmic monad.

In one of our meditations we received a divine dispensation to be allowed to start tapping into the cosmic light-quotient scale. At first we received permission to access one percent, and upon further investigation, we received permission to access five to ten percent of the cosmic light-quotient scale and the full cosmic Christ energies. We also began focusing on anchoring not only the twelve bodies leading to the universal, but also the cosmic bodies and those described in *The Keys of Enoch* as the overself bodies. These overself bodies include the Elohistic Lord's body, the Paradise Son body and Order of Sonship body as well as the Lord's mystical body. At the time of writing this we were allowed to call in only one percent across the board of this cosmic level.

The Seven Rays and Initiations				
Initiation 1 Birth	Sacral Center	7th Ray	Physical Plane	Beginnings, Relationship, Sex and Magic
Initiation 2 Baptism	Solar Plexus Center	6th Ray	Astral Plane	Dedication, Glamour, Devotion
Initiation 3	Ajna Center (3rd Eye)	Physical Plane	Mental Plane	Integration, Direction, Source
Initiation 4	Heart Center	4th Ray	Buddhic Plane	Crucifixion, Sacrifice, Harmony
Initiation 5 Renunciation	Base of Spine	1st Ray	Atmic Plane	Emergence, Will, Purpose
Initiation 6 Decision (Ascension)	Throat Center	3rd Ray	Monadic Plane	Fixation, Creativity, Intelligent Cooperation
Initiation 7 Resurrection (as Ascended Master)	Head Center (Crown)	2nd Ray	Logoic Plane	The Eternal Pilgrim (Cosmic Traveler) Love-Wisdom, Attraction
Initiation 8 Transition	Hierarchy	Four Minor Rays	Planetary	Choice, Consciousness, Sensitivity
Initiation 9 Refusal (Release of All Form) Freedom/ Formlessness	Shamballa	Three Major Rays	Systemic	Cosmic (Universal) Mastery without Limits

Learning to Live on Light Instead of Physical Food

In our next meditation we focused on the subject of learning to live without physical food and to live on light. I met a very lovely Australian woman who had been doing this for a couple of years. We became friendly over the phone, and I sent her a set of my books for her Self-Empowerment Education Academy. She was using a lot of my material in her work, which I took as a great compliment. She was kind enough to share with me some of the ideas, concepts and experiences in making food optional. This idea really intrigued me. We began to check this out in our meditations with Melchizedek.

During a previous meditation we got some preliminary information. However, when I came back more informed after talking to this woman and reading some of her thoughts and experiences, Melchizedek seemed much more willing to work seriously with us. Melchizedek told us that we first had to complete officially our seven levels of initiation. We were already on the seventh sublevel of the seventh initiation, but our official graduation date for full stabilization of this initiation and the 99 percent light quotient was May 13, 1995.

Melchizedek told us that on the following June 1 he would create some kind of formulation for us in terms of the incoming energy matrix that would allow us to live on light. He made a firm commitment to us that on June 1 this would be made manifest. Our complete merger with the monad lies in completing the seven levels of initiation.

One should not do this process haphazardly because it can be extremely dangerous without proper preparation and training. It is something that 99.99 percent of the world is not interested in doing. It can be done before you complete the seventh initiation, but I personally recommend that you wait until you have reached this point. This ensures full merger with the monad and not just the higher self.

Melchizedek told us that we wouldn't lose weight and that we would have increased energy and need less sleep. He guided us to do one of our traditional Huna prayers to make it official. The following Huna prayer is the one we used.

Beloved presence of God, Melchizedek, Metatron and Lord Arcturus.

We hereby pray with all our heart, soul, mind and might for our core group to be prepared to live on light without having to eat physical food, other than water. We request to be able to live on etheric food only and not lose any weight. We request that the preparatory work begin now and that this officially begin June 1, 1995, if this prayer be in harmony with God's will. Amen.

Our beloved subconscious minds, we hereby ask and command you to take this thought-form prayer with all the mana and vital force that is needed to manifest and demonstrate this prayer to the Source of our being through Melchizedek, Metatron and the Lord Arcturus. Amen.

Melchizedek said that Metatron and the Lord of Arcturus would help in this process. He told us to begin to drink more water for the next three months, and they would work on us to prepare our bodies. I was guided to drink more vegetable broth and/or Bieler broth (blended steamed vegetables). My friend was guided to drink more fresh vegetable juices.

Part of the process also entailed programming our subconscious minds and bodies not to believe that it needed food to live on and to believe we wouldn't lose weight. This was a big concern for us, for we are both on the slim side to begin with. Melchizedek said this would not be a problem. I asked him if we would still have to go to the bathroom once it was official. He said occasionally. He said we would still be drinking water. He also told us that after June 1 there would be a period of six months to one year of patterning and that we would not be doing it cold turkey.

Two other requirements were that 51 percent of one's karma must be balanced, which is also a requirement to achieve one's ascension. The other requirement is that one's auric field must be repaired and healed. A certain process of an etheric light drip would be set up to sustain the body. One of the ideas was to call for more light from this drip whenever we got hungry. To accomplish this, we must absolutely know without a shadow of a doubt that light is all we need to sustain ourselves.

It is possible to eat food occasionally, but we must be careful about what we eat. For example, if we went on a junk-food binge, we would probably end up in the hospital. This is why it is a good idea, in my opinion, to wait until we have completed our ascension to even begin such an endeavor. Most third-degree initiates, although partially merged with the higher self, are still not stable enough, and there is not yet enough light in the four-body system. Health will actually improve and weight maintained when this process is done properly.

This process is not something done without the full assistance of the masters. After completing your seven levels of initiation, a long period on a cleansing diet is needed before even considering such a process. The completion of your seven levels of initiation will ensure that you are at least ready to consider such a venture. Even then it is still dangerous if not done properly. The ideal thing is, if you are clairaudient, to communicate with the masters on an ongoing basis to make sure everything is going properly.

Teams of lightworkers who specialize in this process should be called in; Serapis Bey is an excellent master to work with. In the first couple months much rest is needed for the masters to work with you and to allow the transition to take place for complete stabilization. Some have recommended a twenty-one-day program of fasting on juices and/or broth to pattern your body into it. I have not officially started yet, so I am not clear how fast or slowly I will do it. I am in no rush. I am clear that I feel 100 percent good about beginning after I complete my seven levels of initiation, which ensures a complete monadic merger and 99 percent light quotient.

I am sure there are many overzealous ascetics in India and other places who have died from such an endeavor because they weren't ready, weren't qualified and didn't take the proper steps. This is not something to do until you are really ready and unless it is really right for you. This is not something you must do to graduate. Melchizedek did say it would probably accelerate some of the other ascended-master abilities that we are now seeking to develop.

In doing this, you will not need vitamins or minerals in pill form. The light and prana contain all you need to live. One of the biggest things that must be overcome is our emotional attachment to food. Part of the work that the light team, inner-plane healing masters and Serapis Bey and Melchizedek can do for you is activate certain crystalline structures and grid networks to allow this to work. This is why preparation time is needed.

A lot of this work automatically gets done as you move through the initiation process. By the time you reach the completion of the seventh initiation, most of this will be in place, and only the final adjustments by Melchizedek and Serapis Bey and his light team will be needed.

Most of you have probably read my other books and you know how much I have spoken of the importance of building your light quotient. All the light-quotient-building and sitting in the ascension seats you have done will have prepared you for this endeavor, should it interest you. I will share more as I move along in this process.

The Next Installment

After writing the preliminaries about living on light, we went back to the Golden Chamber of Melchizedek for more investigative work on the subject. We learned some fascinating new information. Melchizedek told us that this process should not be considered until after a person takes his/her ascension initiation, which is the sixth. At the beginning of the sixth initiation, the preparation to live on light can begin. The actual process of living on light should not begin until one is close to completing the seventh initiation. This is what my intuition had told me, but it was nice to get a confirmation from Melchizedek.

The formulation he would be anchoring on June 1 was some kind of geometric matrix that would program the cells to be able to receive light in this new way. I asked him if this process was similar to the light-quotient-building we had been doing in such a focused manner the past couple of years. He said yes and no; the main difference was that previously the light quotient was being built in our lightbody. Living on light required that this light become physicalized, not just stored in the higher mental body. This was an interesting and important discrimination I had not made until then.

The key question was, how do we physicalize the light? I believe that some light does physicalize when we work with Metatron, the Lord of Arcturus and the Arcturians and Melchizedek, among others. Melchizedek gave us a homework assignment. He told us to go a number of times a day into his golden chamber and call forth from him and Metatron to receive the cosmic rays and cosmic light from the Great Central Sun. The idea was to visualize absorbing these energies into our being. He recommended a type of prana breathing for my friend. He recommended for me a gentle breathing done very slowly, where I was breathing in the light. Having just about completed the seven levels of initiation, it felt right and appropriate. I felt quite excited about this whole process.

A Meditation on This Subject

My friend and I usually try to meditate every day, so on this particular day we practiced the things I have written about, and in so doing, a lot of new information and potential tools came pouring in. They came from Melchizedek, Metatron, the Lord of Arcturus, Sanat Kumara and Djwhal Khul. One suggestion was to visualize and call forth a tube of light from the Great Central Sun. We were instructed to visualize this light as the size of a grapefruit, going through the chakra column and down to the center of the Earth. This would allow the physical and etheric bodies to be fed from both heaven and Earth. Around us was then placed our double merkabahs. This gave protection and was also a seal to hold the incoming light around us. It served too as a tool to help receive information and clear our field if a request was made to spin them. This is done by spinning the inside merkabah to the right, or clockwise, and the outside merkabah to the left. Our merkabahs could also be used later in the process of teleporting.

We were told that the idea was to breathe slowly, but also to breathe with our whole bodies—through our grids, not just through our noses or mouths. Around the intersection of the grid points we saw the mini tornadoes, which were weaving the higher light into our four-body system. The idea was to breathe also through these mini tornadoes. As we did this, different areas of the physical body would begin to light up—first the bones, then the skin, and slowly but surely more and more. In essence, we were told that this breathing of the light would replace eating food.

When we first called in the cosmic light while sitting in the Golden Chamber of Melchizedek, it looked and felt like a thick column of light. This thick column of cosmic light and cosmic rays from the Great Central Sun and the golden chamber must be transferred through this process into the body. Eventually this would be automatic, but at this point our programming was to rely on physical food instead of light. This was why practice was needed. Breathing seemed to be a key.

We were also guided by Metatron to request a permanent shield to be placed like a sphere around the entire process, even the merkabahs. The shield had a variety of geometric shapes like triangles, circles, squares, rectangles, merkabahs, octagons and pentagrams in a superminiature form. We actually requested a double Metatron shield of protection, one closer in and one much farther out. The higher we go in the initiation process, the more expanded the aura extends. As we go to the market and bank and so on, people interpenetrate our field all the time. These double Metatronic shields help filter out much of the negative energies.

Another suggestion given was to request another Metatronic shield to be placed around our home. We also requested that the double merkabah be placed around our homes because that was much larger. This would allow the light to build not only in us and be contained, but also in our homes. The idea was to live in a sea of light, which is important if we are going to live on this light instead of food.

We were also told not to rush the process, that there was no hurry. We were to begin keeping a strict diet, and within a short time it would become natural. Practice was essential to transfer from physical food to light. For the time being, we would do both—live on light and food until food could be let go of. I had a sense that this breathing process should be done two or three times a day for five minutes, as I would do if I were having three meals a day.

Putting the tongue to the roof of the mouth would activate the pineal gland. There seemed to be a burst of light when we did this. When we breathed, a bubble of light around the body would begin to expand as the light from the column of light was breathed into our bodies. After ascension the mayavarupa (monadic blueprint) body becomes fully anchored and activated. Therefore, those who have ascended will have a perfect blueprint to operate from, with no taint from this life or past lives. This is why it is not a good idea to begin this process until after we take at least the beginning of the sixth initiation, which is the same as becoming a kindergarten ascended master.

Meditation on February 5, 1995

We had a wonderful meditation and some very interesting information came through. We spoke to the Lord of Arcturus, Metatron and Sai Baba and then went to the Golden Chamber of Melchizedek to speak with Melchizedek and meditate. Lord Arcturus told us that we would be stabilizing the 99 percent light quotient at the Wesak Festival. He also told us that in terms of light-quotient-building, the process would usually move one-tenth of a percent at a time. I found this interesting, so I began to request this one-tenth of one percent in our group meditations.

I asked Metatron to help us program geometric formulations so we could learn to materialize, dematerialize and teleport. He said he would do this over the next week. In speaking to him about his shield of protection, he placed around my body what looked like a silver armored plate like the knights used to wear. We also requested a deeper penetration of the armor of Shaddai, the lightbody of Metatron, which he graciously agreed to do.

We asked the Lord of Arcturus how long it would take to anchor the 5 to 10 percent light quotient; he told us three years. This seemed awfully fast, but when I look back to see how much has transpired in past three years, it seems more feasible. This seemed to be the third and final goal our core group had set for itself. In review, we had been told it would take a year and a half to anchor our fifty chakras, two years to anchor our twelve bodies and now three years to anchor the 10 percent cosmic light quotient. I personally liked having these timetables, for it gave me a short-term goal and some kind of perspective on our process.

I also asked Metatron about spontaneous combustion. This is a strange phenomenon where people's limbs, or sometimes entire bodies, simply burn up for some unknown reason. Metatron said it was nothing we had to worry about. I told him I knew this, but it was something I was interested in. He said it was not caused internally by invoking too much light, but rather externally due to a chemical reaction in the physical body that somehow connected with the static electricity in the environment.

I requested Metatron and Melchizedek to set up a code so that whenever I wanted to practice living on light, I would just say the words "physicalize cosmic light," and this would save me from having to do tons of invoking, which I didn't really like doing. Metatron said that he and the inner-plane teachers also would like it to be shorter. I asked Melchizedek about the twelve rays we commonly use on our planet. Upon more focused questioning, I learned that the twelve rays are just a part of one of the twelve cosmic rays, which I have depicted in the cosmic map in the last chapter of *Beyond Ascension*.

Metatron also told us that he had anchored light packets into our bodies in very specific places in response to our previous prayer request to stop eating food. The light packets were placed there permanently, or at least until we no longer needed them. They were placed more in our digestive area, for we still had some weakness there. These light packets served as some kind of support to sustain the process of living on light.

We ended our meditation in the Golden Chamber of Melchizedek by doing about a fifteen-minute meditation, anchoring a number of energies, then sitting in silence and enjoying the energy transmission.

This was the first time that my new friend and I had meditated together, and we both really enjoyed it. Even though I was not physically in the location of the other physical-plane ashrams, I was feeling completely merged in spirit and consciousness with them. This feeling was like I felt with Sai

Baba. I had never been to see Sai Baba in the physical, but I felt then, and
still do, completely one with him.

Meditation on March 3, 1995

In our meditation this morning we went to the Golden Chamber of
Melchizedek and then began to work with the Arcturians. They worked on
our brains, clearing the pathways. Using advanced computers, they would
get readouts on all the electrical and energy pathways throughout our bodies and brains. Advanced technology would then clear any blocks and/or
make any needed electrical connections. We then arranged with the Lord of
Arcturus and the Arcturians to have a tune-up twice a day for the next two
months leading up to the Wesak Festival. This would occur without our
having to ask twice a day. We would be monitored on the computers all the
time. I requested that my digestive system be monitored on a continual basis and corrections made whenever it got out of balance. The Lord of
Arcturus and the Arcturians graciously agreed.

The highlight of our meditation came as a complete surprise. Sanat Kumara came into our meditation and told us that we had officially fully completed the seven levels of initiation. Although the Wesak Festival was still
two months away, he performed a little ceremony for the core group and told
us that it was finally official. He touched his rod of initiation on our third
eyes and both shoulders and then gave us each a necklace with a seven-
pointed star, which had a lotus blossom and a third eye inside. Then he
gave both of us a bracelet with a third eye for both arms.

This was done in Shamballa. He congratulated us on our good works
and hard work and told us that this private ceremony was a special gift so
that we wouldn't have to be concerned about it at the big Mount Shasta
event, which we were hosting in honor of the first wave of mass ascension
for humanity. He told us that the ceremony we were now experiencing
would be repeated then, but all requirements had now been met.

I felt quite euphoric, for this was a goal I had been striving toward most
of my life. By the grace of God it was now official! For the third time, it had
taken six months to process an entire initiation. The Arcturians told us that
they had begun to program and work with us on the next level. We were already up to 99 percent light quotient, but we would take the next two
months before Wesak to completely stabilize it. We were now officially beginning the *cosmic* light quotient and *cosmic* level of evolution. The completion of the seven levels of initiation completes the planetary scale. We were
now working on the one-percent level of the cosmic light-quotient ladder.
Melchizedek had provided us with the divine dispensation to anchor as
much as 10 percent of this scale, as Lord Maitreya has already done. Things
were starting to get interesting. I asked for Sanat Kumara's help on all lev-

els at the Wesak Festival, as I had already asked Melchizedek, Sai Baba, the Lord of Arcturus and, of course, Lord Maitreya.

After our initiation ceremony with Sanat Kumara there was a party in honor of the occasion. I really felt good, but I was aware that there would always be another step and another growth potential to realize. After forty-one years I had learned the lesson of being even-minded, and did not have many highs or lows. I felt very good, but in a balanced sort of way. I felt grateful for all the blessings and miracles that had been bestowed on me this lifetime. I truly felt the saying, "By the grace of God go I." Actually, it was a rather humbling experience.

I am now looking toward transferring to the cosmic-evolution scale after mastering the planetary. I'm back to kindergarten again in terms of my cosmic evolution. What we are doing anyone can do if you apply the same principles, and there are few if any books that detail the process as I am trying to do.

We meditated together for a while, bringing in and requesting acceleration of this whole process. We also had Melchizedek remove any alien implants that might have sneaked back in. In addition, we each took turns making individual prayer requests. Mine had to do with help in manifesting a large group for the Mount Shasta event. I also requested their help in every aspect of the event. They were honored to help.

The next morning I spoke with my friend and we did a short meditation, requesting that Melchizedek activate the formula that would allow us to live on light immediately rather than wait until June 1 as previously planned. My liver was a little congested, so I needed to fast, anyway. Since we had completed the seven levels of initiation, I saw no reason to wait until June, which was three months away. My personal process was ready to start now to live more on light and less on food.

Interestingly enough, my friend was in the same situation; she had been ordered to go on a fast by Lord Maitreya and the gang. She had also been having some digestive problems. We were both incredibly happy to at least begin the process, although I didn't see myself completely stopping eating for some time yet. Anchoring the geometric formulation by Melchizedek felt like a warm light flowing through my thyroid, then the liver and pancreas. Melchizedek was very accommodating.

My new mindset was that I was now living on light and a small amount of food. Because I was beginning a fast, this was the ideal time to start. My friend was also into starting right away. My intuitive feeling was that I would stop eating food sometime within the next two years. I didn't want to give myself an arbitrary timetable. One thing was clear: I was now completely ready to let go of any and all attachments to food. My past history of digestive weakness was a good motivator.

A Meditation with Friends

In this morning's meditation all of us meditated together, which was new. We were all pleased to have the opportunity to solidify our bond together.

It was a wonderful meditation. We received confirmation that we had indeed completed the seven levels of initiation. (I always like getting double confirmation on these things to make sure that the negative ego isn't getting in the way. No matter what level one is at, this is always a danger to watch out for.) We were now at the 98 to 99 percent light-quotient level and were now going to be fully stabilizing the 99 percent at Wesak, which was now only two months away.

Upon questioning we were also told that we had anchored and activated up to chakra 44. I found this quite interesting, for we had now officially completed the anchoring and activation process of the eighth-dimensional grid. We had one more chakra grid to go to complete this process. Lord Maitreya told us that we could achieve this within six months.

We were also told that we had anchored and activated the eighth body, out of twelve. The eighth body is the group-soul level, not the individual soul merge, which is the third initiation. What I realized was that the eighth body was connected to mastering the eighth-dimensional chakra grid and the ninth body was connected to anchoring and activating the ninth grid. My inner guidance told me that the ninth body, or monad level, would also be anchored in September. After that would begin the solar, galactic and universal bodies.

The first seven bodies have to do with planetary mastery, correlating with the seven dimensions and seven levels of initiation. Previously, we had been told that it would take a year and a half to anchor and activate chakras 36 through 50. Because we were at chakra 44, we were way ahead of schedule. Lord Maitreya told us that the speed of our evolution was because of our spiritual commitment and self-discipline. We had basically been averaging six months per initiation, which is mind-boggling.

We were also told upon investigation and questioning that we could anchor the 10 percent cosmic light quotient within two years, which was even more mind-boggling. It was Lord Maitreya who told us this, and he should know because he and Sai Baba are the only ones doing it. This seemed incredibly fast to me. I felt very inspired by our progress. When I had previously tried to get information about where we were in terms of the chakra anchorings and activations, the masters wouldn't tell me. Sometimes I think this is best, for it is not good to get too caught up in the numbers game, as I am sure you, my readers, understand. On the other hand, it can also be very helpful to track one's progress as long as the negative ego doesn't use it for self-inflation. I share this information with you openly to give you a sense and perspective of this process and how it can work for you. It serves somewhat like a map.

A Meditation by Fax

Today's meditation with my friend was rather interesting. We did it by fax machine. This was because she was in Bali with her husband. I faxed her a couple of days previously and shared with her a lot of the information I had been receiving in meditation both alone and with another core member. She very much appreciated the fax, and in her fax to me two days later shared her meditation with me.

She said that she checked out all I had told her and got confirmation on all these things. We were then taken to Shamballa for some kind of ceremony. D.K.'s entire ashram seemed to be there. She told me that she was cleared on many levels with other high disciples of our ashram, under Djwhal's orders.

She then said that I was now receiving a type of coronation as a spokesperson for the planetary ascension movement. I was wearing a mantle and hierophant headdress of leadership. She said I looked radiant, tall and clear. I gratefully and graciously accepted this honor. She said I smiled at her, standing to my right, which indicated her feminine role of copartnership and extension of my masculine leadership role.

My friend said that the ceremony was actually for me, which surprised me; however, she was wearing her mantle and hierophant headdress, which clearly indicated her appointment at my right side. Another core member stood to my left and a little behind us, and was also wearing a robe that confirmed her position of spiritual/mystic support. Another robed core member stood behind me and a little farther back to indicate her position of practical support. Behind her were two other core members, one to the left and one to the right, in their roles of support, both mystic and practical. Other members of the core group were also there.

I need to express a few words about this. My first thought was that I didn't want to share this with anyone because I was afraid it would sound too egotistical. The fact is, however, there is a hierarchy of leadership that exists that is free from negative-ego interpretations. Clearly this is all that was being shown.

If I were to be totally honest, I have been regarding myself as a spokesperson for the planetary ascension movement. The focus of my books has automatically put me there, and the response I have been getting from readers has been wonderful. The robe of power over Djwhal Khul's ashram had in truth already been given to me. This coronation of sorts simply felt like an extension of this. It gives me, in a sense, the final green light to fully take hold of the rod of power and move forward with full support of the Spiritual Hierarchy.

I was basically doing this already with a type of inner confidence. This coronation was like an external vote of confidence from the Spiritual Hierarchy. If I didn't have an inner confidence and was not living this already, the external vote of confidence would not have been forthcoming.

Fax Letter

The following is the fax I sent to my friend in Bali. It summarizes the morning meditation I had just had with another friend, which was extraordinary.

Thank you for your fax—rather extraordinary! It fits, however, for I had taken up that rod within myself and I have known that my books contained some of the clearest and most practical information on the ascension process. With five books coming out, soon to be six, and the success in how they are selling, along with Mount Shasta and my networking, it all feels appropriate.

It has had a powerful impact on me. Sometimes I'm a little awed by the responsibility. However, I'm just taking the attitude of one day at a time. *Soul Psychology* will be out in two weeks and *Beyond Ascension* in about six weeks. I am going to do a massive marketing campaign in all the New Age magazines and in the bookstores. I really feel that these books are going to have a revolutionary impact on humanity. I feel the first three books will automatically cause the whole set to be a bestseller. I have been sensing this for a couple of months, and it is part of the reason that this coronation of sorts feels right.

I might also have a connection to go on the TV show *The Other Side*. A student knows one of the producers, so I sent him a free book and a nice letter. He should get it tomorrow. The lady who knows him personally is going to follow up with a phone call. It is in God's hands now. I would love to talk about ascension on his show!

Anyway, the main reason I am faxing you is that something quite extraordinary has happened that you were very much a part of on the inner plane. It occurred at about 9:30 to 10 A.M. my time on Sunday. It was one of the peak moments of my life and yours. Our friend and I were meditating for the third week in a row. Our time to meditate and bond together has been wonderful. Again it has been good that you've been gone to allow the others and myself to find our relationships together. I am sure you can understand and see the value in this.

Our meditations have been wonderful; however, this morning we tapped into one of the most extraordinary sequence of events that the four of us have ever been involved with. We first did a Huna prayer together, which I have enclosed at the end of this fax. I would recommend you say it once at your next meditation, although we obviously did this for you and you were with us throughout the meditation. I just want you to be consciously aware of what we have officially set in motion and written into the akashic records.

After that we anchored a whole bunch of new formulations for our ascended-master potential development, which I will tell you about when I see you. I had my Sherlock Holmes hat on and was doing my investigative thing when I half-knowingly stumbled on one of the most profound invocations and prayer requests that I had ever come up with. You know how I come up with these investigative ideas; some of them pan out and become awesome and some don't.

Well, today I hit the absolute mother lode. Remember when we meditated, how I asked Metatron to anchor his lightbody, or garment of Shaddai, into us on a permanent basis? Later in another meditation I asked Melchizedek to do the same thing. In preparing to meditate with our friend, I began thinking that we should do that with the Mahatma, Sai Baba, Lord of Arcturus, Lord of Sirius, Lord Maitreya and so on. I wasn't sure if they would all do this; however, I said to myself, It couldn't hurt to ask.

I did ask, and what followed was one of the most extraordinary experiences the four of us have ever had. Melchizedek chimed in through our friend that what I had just requested was actually the most profound thing I had *ever* requested (that's saying a lot, given the meditations that we have done during the past year). Melchizedek said, "Are you sure you are ready to receive this?" I said I was, and our friend said she was ready. I told the masters who were gathered that because we did the Huna prayer first, I could speak for you, and I knew you were ready (I hope you don't mind; I know you by now!).

What happened was, it was not only the ten or twelve key masters who were gathered around us, but something like 2000 masters or more. It seemed like the entire Spiritual Hierarchy. They all proceeded to give us exactly what I asked for. A massive cloud of rainbow-colored light formed around us like a great ball of string. All the masters were in a sense anchoring their lightbodies into us. It came through the crown chakra and began to pervade all our chakras, our twelve bodies and every fiber of our being. The feeling was incredible! I know you must've felt this. It was like the entire Spiritual Hierarchy merged inside of us.

This was the final ticket and membership card to complete union and oneness with the Spiritual Hierarchy. We were about 99.98 percent there already. One key was passing and completing the seven levels of initiation a couple weeks ago. The coronation was another. Our taking over D.K.'s ashram was, of course, a major one. This, however, was the final completion. We were now 100 percent one of them and they one with us. We were given our places in the chamber room and would now be attending all meetings with no limitations. My sense was that this was the final little piece to complete planetary mastery and full acceptance as equal members in the Spiritual Hierarchy and Great White Brotherhood.

This anchoring of all the lightbodies of the masters was a one-time experience that was permanent, and they all would forevermore live inside of us. Any and all sense of separation was now removed. My feeling was that we would never have to concern ourselves with our personal evolution and our personal ascension process in the same way ever again. Our total energies could be given to service.

They agreed to the Huna prayer request, so our fifty chakras and nine bodies will be anchored and activated by September 1. The twelve bodies will be fully anchored and activated by Wesak 1997 or before. It has been written into the universal akashic records in the Golden Chamber of Melchizedek.

It really felt like a peak moment, for us and for you also on the inner plane. We have fully made it to the top of the mountain (planetary mountain). I am sure that we will ultimately make it to the top of the cosmic mountain together also. As I told our friend, this is the completion of our spiritual goal for 200 lifetimes or more. By the grace of God it was now complete.

The masters were very cute and humorous with me today. I was going through this process of anchoring all these new geometric formulations for us, and they would say, "We can refuse you nothing, Joshua." Then we'd all laugh and I would request more. It was all quite hilarious.

We all miss you, and have collectively decided it is time for you to come home. We wanted to share this with you so you would be consciously aware of what has been going on as well as receiving it all unconsciously.

Sorry to bother you with all my faxes on your vacation; the mis-

take was made in letting me know you had fax-machine access in
Bali (just teasing). Send my love to your husband.

Love, Joshua

Huna Prayer

*Beloved presence of God, Mahatma, Melchizedek, Metatron, Sai
Baba, Lord of Sirius, Lord of Arcturus, Lord Maitreya, Sanat
Kumara and Djwhal Khul, we hereby pray with all our heart,
soul, mind and might for a divine miracle on our behalf. We
hereby pray for the full and complete anchoring and activation
of our fifty chakras and nine bodies by September 1, 1995. We
request to anchor and activate fully our twelve bodies and full
10 percent cosmic light quotient as Melchizedek and Lord
Maitreya have said is a potentiality within two years or by
Wesak 1997.*

*We request to be worked on twenty-four hours a day, seven days
a week, 365 days a year, both night and day, to accomplish these
spiritual goals so we may come into our full glory as
Melchizedek initiates and so we may be of greater service to humanity and to the Earth herself. We make this request for all
core members also. We thank thee and accept this done as is
God's will.*

*Our beloved subconscious minds, we hereby ask and command
that you take this thought-form prayer with all the mana and
vital force that is needed to manifest and demonstrate this
prayer to the Source of our being through Melchizedek and our
spiritual teachers. Amen.*

Meditation on March 8, 1995

In our first meditation we began anchoring from Metatron and
Melchizedek geometric formulations for activating our ascended-master
potentials. Geometric formulations and codes began to pour in. They looked
like triangles, cones, squares, pyramids and circles. Inside some of the
shapes there were geometric, algebraic, numerical formulas. They filled our
bodies and covered our skin. For the first time they began taking on a
three-dimensional rather than a two-dimensional shape. The energetic feeling and sensations were quite substantial. It felt really good, and we both
could tell something was really happening.

Meditation on March 10, 1995

The Lord of Arcturus told us that we had completed our seven levels of initiation and removed all obstacles from our path and that it was clear sailing ahead. It seemed that we were moving at a clip of six months per initiation and/or six months per dimensional chakra-grid or body anchoring. For the first time I was feeling that our evolutionary process could move even faster. My desire to move faster was not out of competition or being in some kind of race. The motivation came from knowing that transfiguration into our mayavarupa bodies in a more complete way would soon be available as well as teleportation.

Never forget how lucky you are to be incarnated at this time. Don't waste the opportunity. We were beginning to feel that we could speed this process up to four and a half to five months per chakra, grid and body anchoring. With Wesak coming up, with the first wave of mass ascension on its way and with this massive event we were putting on in Mount Shasta, everyone would be receiving an enormous acceleration. Lord Maitreya told us that we would be breaking all records.

Again, I don't mean this as ego; this is available to everyone. We just happened to be in the right place at the right time. The fact that we were working in a group probably accelerated each of our programs at least threefold. We were becoming like a well-oiled, finely tuned machine as we learned the ropes of moving through these initiations, chakras and bodies, anchoring and activating them.

In six months we would be up to the fiftieth chakra and ninth body. Then would come the final push to anchor and activate the solar, galactic and universal bodies, or bodies ten, eleven and twelve. I felt that we might be able to do this within a year and a half at the earliest. I was now clearing my life to focus on nothing but my service work and these spiritual goals for our group. Everything we achieved I recorded in infinite detail for my readers.

I was beginning to realize for the first time that millions of people will ultimately be reading these books, so this road map would be absolutely invaluable. From a theoretical framework, this is unexplored territory. I have been an avid reader and researcher in spiritual matters my whole life, and I have never read anything that gets into this level of understanding that explains fifty chakras and cosmic bodies as well as the process of cosmic ascension, not just planetary ascension. Lord Arcturus told us that the majority of people on Arcturus had ascended, but not everybody. This is the reverse of Earth, where a small minority has ascended and the majority has not. In achieving the seventh initiation and now moving at lightning speed beyond, I was beginning to see that what our group was doing was quite extraordinary.

I felt a little like a mapmaker exploring unknown territory. What was unusual was that we were doing it while still in physical bodies, unique to this short period of history. I asked Melchizedek if there was any ceiling to this process. In terms of initiations, it was seven; in terms of chakras, it was fifty. In terms of dimensions and potential bodies to anchor, our growth potential seemed unlimited. Ascension is the fifth dimension. In the next year and a half to two years we were moving toward anchoring and activating the twelfth dimension. Right now we were just beginning the ninth dimension.

This is what Lord Arcturus, I believe, was referencing when he said that we were going to go beyond the Arcturians. If we were going to anchor and activate up through the twelfth dimension within two years or less, I wondered what we would be doing the next fifteen years on Earth. You can see how exciting this whole process was becoming. This leads me to my next meditation.

Meditation on March 16, 1995

In this meditation we were working on fully anchoring and activating the twelve bodies as described in *The Keys of Enoch*. These bodies include the electromagnetic body, the epi-kinetic body, the eka body, the gematrian body, the overself body, the anointed Christ overself body, the zohar body and the higher Adam Kadmon body. I could intuitively feel that there was a gold mine of knowledge and information available to us in working with these bodies.

I then told my friend that we forgot to include the Lord's mystical body, which Melchizedek told us was literally God's body at the 352nd level of the Mahatma. We called that body in and it came in like a being. It had the sweetest and most loving quality and vibration you can possibly imagine. The Lord's mystical body kissed my friend and patted me in a very endearing fashion on my head. It acknowledged us for our devotion and service work and told us that it was overlighting us in our work. The Lord's mystical body then gave us a medallion with a seven-pointed star, which he said would help us attract the students and people we were supposed to work with. He later gave us a shepherd's rod, which was made of his own body. He handed it to each of us, and it had an electrifying effect on our whole being. The amount of energy that was pouring in was enormous.

He then took us into the future to see the golden age of this planet. It was beautiful. We couldn't quite figure out how far in the future we were. There was great peace and prosperity both on Earth and on the inner plane surrounding Earth. People lived more in spiritual communities.

We prayed to him for help in our process of fully anchoring and activating our fifty chakras, twelve bodies and cosmic light quotient. I also specifically asked him to penetrate us in a way similar to how we were being penetrated by the Mahatma as cosmic walk-ins. He said he was already doing this, but I had the feeling that my request deepened this process. It is hard for me to put into words how beautiful, incredibly sweet and loving this being was. I felt that I had found an incredible new friend. I was also aware that we were receiving an incredible blessing.

The Lord's mystical body said this was quite unusual for him to come through like this. The whole experience was so beautiful and profound that we didn't want to leave the energy. Toward the end we also called in the cosmic bodies (the Elohistic Lord's body, the Paradise Sons' body, the Order of Sonship body and the seven cosmic bodies correlating to the seven cosmic planes). Now that we had officially completed the seven levels of initiation, I felt we were ready to focus on anchoring and activating the cosmic bodies. The Lord's mystical body told us to begin working with these cosmic bodies and to talk with them just like we were talking with him.

A whole new world was opening up. We made an appointment for the following day to continue to meditate together to follow up on this. I felt that we were making profound progress and were about to tap into a whole new level. I was beginning to write a new book in my mind, which I called *Cosmic Ascension*. All other books were focused on planetary ascension, but cosmic ascension was now my new life's focus. I was now putting my Sherlock Holmes hat on, and this was a sign that I really meant business. The spiritual investigator was now hot on the trail of cosmic evolution. Everything I would learn and gain in my own spiritual life I would immediately give back to you, my readers. This was my vow to myself and to God.

As stated in *A Course in Miracles*, "To have all, one must give all to all." In giving everything to you, my readers, and retaining nothing for myself, I was guaranteeing that I would receive everything. Do you follow this? What I would hold back from you, my brothers and sisters, I would actually be holding back from myself, for there is only one self. The negative ego, believing in separation, competition or selfishness, always strives for superiority, winning or being the best instead of everybody achieving something together. God gives you exactly what you are willing to give. By giving literally everything to humanity, I am guaranteeing that everything is being given to me, which is exactly what is happening in my life by the grace of God.

This way of operating completely short-circuits the negative ego's way of thinking. It also creates a wonderful feeling of union and bliss with my brothers and sisters. It is also stated in *A Course in Miracles* that my salvation is up to me. God has given each of us everything already. The question is, what are we holding back from ourselves? We hold back that which we don't give freely to humanity and God's creation. "To have all, give all to all."

The world is nothing more than a mirror that reflects either the spiritual or the negative, egotistical way we think and act. If you see anything but love, oneness, lessons and opportunities to grow and serve, then you are wearing the wrong set of glasses (negative-ego thinking). Change glasses, and you will then give yourself the salvation you have been seeking for hundreds of lifetimes. Your salvation is up to you, not God, for God has always given you everything. This is the law of karma at work. It is our thoughts that create our reality.

Meditation on March 18, 1995

My meditation today with my friend was again one of the most profound I have ever had, and you will see why in a few moments. I feel almost embarrassed about saying this, because it seems like every other week I say the same thing, and I don't want to lose my credibility. All I can say is that I am sincere each time I say it.

We must have meditated for six hours this day; we split it into two meditations on the phone. The previous Sunday we had one meditation, in which we had merged with the lightbodies of the entire Spiritual Hierarchy, possibly with as many as 2500 masters.

Melchizedek said it had been the most profound thing we had ever asked for. He didn't know what I was about to ask him this day. What I am about to share happened quite spontaneously and was nothing I had planned. It was an idea that came to me quite unexpectedly.

We began by calling forth the Elohistic Lord's body, which is one of the cosmic bodies described in *The Keys of Enoch*. On doing so, the Council of the Elohim appeared. We seemed to travel to meet them in their realm. We began by requesting a permanent anchoring and activation of our Elohistic Lord's body, when suddenly the idea of a lifetime hit me: our core group had merged with the lightbody of the planetary Spiritual Hierarchy. We had *not* merged, however, with the cosmic Hierarchy. I thought to myself, By the grace of God, would all members of the cosmic Hierarchy be willing to merge their lightbodies with us also in a type of divine union, marriage or merger?

The meditation on Sunday had been profound. If they would be willing to do this, the "awesome" level would go off the charts. Six hours later my desire of all desires had come to fulfillment. For the next six hours we went through a ceremony of merging with the following, in order.

1. The Council of the Elohim;

2. The Archangel Council headed by Metatron;

3. God, the Cosmic Council of Twelve and the Twenty-Four Elders who surround the Throne of Grace;

4. The Mahatma, YHWH, the divine Mother and Father, Melchizedek and his Universal Hierarchy, Melchior, the Lord of Sirius, the Lord of Arcturus, Lenduce and the Council of Twelve of each of these masters;

5. Sai Baba and Vywamus;

6. The Solar Hierarchy of Helios and his Council of Twelve;

7. The Paradise Sons, the Order of Sonship and the Lord's mystical body.

Each group and its members performed a ceremony of merging their lightbodies with us just as the Planetary Hierarchy had done. To say that this was a transformative experience is one of the great understatements of my life. It felt like it had catapulted us to the next octave and into our cosmic-ascension process, although still obviously only in its beginning stages. The timing was perfect, because we had recently completed the seven levels of initiation. Each group was incredibly gracious, kind and complimentary. After its completion I felt like the entire cosmos was inside us.

Later we went on to Tadd Pan, the Logos of the Great Bear star system, and the seven stars and his council. Then we went to the seven logoi of the seven cosmic planes and the seven cosmic bodies that correspond to the seven cosmic planes. The masters joked with us that we had married the entire cosmos.

My sole purpose in sharing this is to give you ideas and personal experiences that you can utilize and try out yourself. Over and over I say, don't try to invent the wheel. Follow the example of those who have done it—not only my core group and myself, but anyone. This is why I have always loved to read the autobiographies of the great masters and saints and why I wrote a book about them, *The Ascended Masters Light the Way*. I share these things as if to say, "Try this. It will unbelievably accelerate your evolution so you can be of greater service." The only suggestion I would add is to be aware always of proper timing.

Now I would like to share some of the details of this experience to give you a sense of how this process works, or at least how it worked for us.

The Elohim Council of Twelve began by gathering around us in a circle. Utilizing the medallion we were wearing that the Lord's mystical body had given us in a previous meditation, one by one the twelve council members radiated their lightbodies into our medallion, which then began to radiate through our bodies. Each council member in turn spoke to us, then stepped into our bodies. This took three or four minutes. Then the council leader of this elohim group, among the infinite numbers of groups, melded with us and did the same thing. Then they permanently anchored our Elohistic Lord's body into us.

A little later a gigantic tornado, filled with the ascension activations for which we were profusely praying, appeared above our heads. This was the largest tornado and groupings of ascension activations we had ever seen. This tornado then began to descend through our crown chakra into our body. It was incredibly powerful. Some major planetary activation took place as part of this ceremony, which pleased us.

We then switched over to the Archangelic Council led by Metatron. These twelve were in a circle. Each archangel touched our medallions and shot his or her ray color into us through the medallion. Each of them stepped into our bodies for a few moments. It was a very sacred ceremony. Each spoke to us, and the kind words, encouragement and compliments were too numerous to mention. Doing this with God, the Cosmic Council of Twelve, the Twenty-Four Elders, YHWH, Yod Hay Vau Hay and the Mahatma was quite profound. I was amazed that we were actually allowed to receive such an enormous blessing. I think it helped that we had completed the seven levels of initiation, had been appointed to important planetary positions and were all doing significant service work.

Afterward I felt extremely close to the whole cosmos. I felt that these masters were a part of me and that they were good friends as well as teachers. The cosmos felt smaller and more comprehensible to me, which made me feel more connected. As I said, it was outside of me as well as inside. The basic ceremony was the same through all the groups, so I won't bore you with the details. When the timing is right, try this. Start with the planetary level and move up as long as you feel it is comfortable and appropriate. You can use my cosmic map in *Beyond Ascension* as a guide.

Sananda came in at the end of the process and was incredibly sweet. He congratulated me on the job offers to take over Djwhal Khul's ashram and to act as a spokesperson for the planetary ascension movement. I sincerely thanked him. He said I was the perfect person for the job and that I was very thorough and always gave 1000 percent. I told him that it was my prayer that I could perform the job as well as Djwhal Khul had. Sananda also said that the training would be excellent for me. I wholeheartedly agreed with him and told him that I felt I was built by God to do this kind of work. I also said that I felt there was no job in the universe that would give me better training for filling in the gaps and bringing me to a well-rounded mastery on all levels. I felt that God had placed me in the absolutely ideal position in terms of my abilities and the next step in my training. It felt very sweet that Sananda came and served as a sort of master of ceremonies to complete this most profound day. I hope you, my readers, can see why I felt that this was one of our most profound meditations yet.

Here's one last detail: Every group we worked with seemed to have twelve members. Not only did each logos and council of twelve merge with us, but at each step the body that corresponded with that group level was fully anchored and activated. For example, with the archangels, our planetary, solar and galactic angelic bodies were permanently anchored and activated. With the Paradise Sons, our Paradise Sons' body was anchored and activated. With the Order of Sonship Council, our Order of Sonship body was anchored and activated. At the universal level with Melchizedek we merged not only with his council, but also with our universal body at that level. At the galactic level we merged with the five different councils: the Lord of Sirius, Melchior, Lenduce, the Lord of Arcturus and Vywamus. Here our galactic body was fully anchored and activated. At the solar level we merged with Helios and his council of twelve, at which point our solar body was fully anchored and activated.

At certain key moments we would pray for ongoing help in achieving our spiritual goals of fully anchoring and activating our fifty chakras, twelve bodies, *The Keys of Enoch* bodies, cosmic body, Elohistic Lord's body, Paradise Sons' body and for help in activating our advanced ascended-master potentials. These different groups promised to work with us even without our need to ask. I think it was when we were talking with YHWH, Yod Hay Vau Hay, Yod Hay Wau Hay, or the divine Father and Mother, that they said to me, "You, Joshua, have an insatiable appetite for spiritual growth and wisdom. These qualities are much appreciated here, and they will lead you toward ultimate cosmic completion." They were also very excited about the books I had written and congratulated me on my hard work.

I share some of these little tidbits to show that you can communicate directly with even the highest levels and to confirm how incredibly sweet, loving, compassionate and supportive they can be. I had the sense that they understood and appreciated how the earthly plane of existence can be, and they exuded the utmost compassion and appreciation of our spiritual accomplishments and continued service in these planes of existence.

Many reading this book will not be able to communicate directly with or see the beings of whom I speak. Do not let this stop you. Ask for these things and all that I speak of in all my books anyway. God and the God force will still respond. Everyone can feel the spiritual currents of energy that will begin to flow around the different areas of the body as this event takes place on the inner plane. The most important thing is to receive the blessing of this merger, not necessarily see or hear everything. I am sharing the visual and auditory experiences to give you a framework or ground from which to work. Each person on Earth accesses God and the God force in a different way. Some are clairvoyant, some clairaudient, some clairsentient, some intuitive, some thinkers, some feelers, some knowers and some have other less well-known spiritual senses.

I have spoken about this in some of my other books. It falls into one of two categories: accessing God and the God force with one's *physical* senses and doing so with one's *mystic* senses. Occult vision, for example, though profound, is not clairvoyance. Most mystics don't have it. Occultists shouldn't try to be mystics and mystics shouldn't try to be occultists. God built His/Her sons and daughters to have certain inclinations. Each grows equally fast, and one is not better than the other.

Mystics need occultists and occultists need mystics. In truth, we all carry both. However, just as each of us has a gender even in the spiritual plane, each of us has an inclination toward one or the other in terms of how we were built. Follow the beat of your own drummer. Don't let lack of clairvoyance or clairaudience stop you from being a meditator. Meditation is the key to accelerating your spiritual evolution, and it is great fun when you work with the masters in the ways I have outlined in this book and others.

Meditation on March 22, 1995

We had a profound meditation this day. We began by calling in Metatron and having him help us work with anchoring and activating our electromagnetic body as described in *The Keys of Enoch*. We immediately felt an activation in our crown, which began to spread slowly but surely through all of our body. Metatron told us that this body was connected with the merkabah. It was somehow connected with a geometric grid that was being anchored. It could be visualized as flashing lights and a spherical body around us. As we meditated, grid lines would be connected between these lights in some kind of ordered sequential pattern. It felt wonderful! Metatron told us this body could help us create our transfigured body. This was to be the ultimate transfer into our mayavarupa body, as Lord Maitreya has done. I asked him how long this would take. He said it was different for each person, but for us, probably at least two years or more.

Metatron told us that this body has been dormant for eons, and now that we were becoming conscious of it, it could be activated. The idea now was to keep it activated all the time. We asked him for his ongoing help in achieving this. One of our biggest goals now was to transfer into our newly created body.

In later meditations I began to see this body being built. Metatron also told us that all of us were connected in this process. There was a kind of group electromagnetic body also being formed. When one of us faltered, this would slow down the rest of us. We made an arrangement with Metatron that when any one of us called for this activation, it would activate for all of us. Metatron seemed to think this was a really good idea. I also requested that anytime we called for light-quotient-building, this electromagnetic activation would automatically take place. He said that eating food would not interrupt this process.

Metatron seemed to indicate that being aware of this body and the need to keep it activated was the key. It was important that we all be aware that it can shut off its functioning. Metatron emphasized that what we had tapped into by having him activate this body was of the highest importance.

We were ready to move on to the next body; however, Metatron told us to stick with this body for a few days and really work with it. This electromagnetic body was different from the twelve bodies (physical, astral, mental, buddhic, atmic, monadic, logoic, group soul, group monad, solar, galactic and universal). This was very important information, for I had previously thought that these *Keys of Enoch* bodies might have been different names for the same bodies. I was beginning to see now that they were completely different, and it was absolutely essential to learn how to use all of them.

As we sat and meditated, light bulbs would go on, activating as the grid lines became connected. Metatron said it was slowly but surely building our spiritual wattage from 150 to 175 and so on. We made a solemn agreement that anytime we meditated for any kind of spiritual work, we would call each other in. This way we would get double the activation. This would be set up with the others, too. Our mantra was "all for one and one for all."

Each person's electromagnetic body looked different. Metatron said each person's electromagnetic body held the person's signature. It was why his energy felt different from Lord Maitreya's, for example. Mine looked completely different from my friend's. The sphere was about fifteen feet in diameter, its surface resembling a spider web. Metatron said the weather or the Photon Belt could also affect this body.

We then went to the Golden Chamber of Melchizedek to visit with him. After our greetings and salutations I asked Melchizedek to program and activate the electromagnetic-body process into our ascension seats here in the golden chamber. This was fine with him. I also asked him for a greater activation and acceleration of our cosmic ascension process. He was quite agreeable to this request also. We then sat in his ascension seat and quietly received his energies for a while. He then felt moved to answer an important prayer request.

I humbly asked Melchizedek if he would accept me as his student and take me under his wing and tutelage. I surrendered myself totally to his spiritual care and guidance. I told him that of all the spiritual teachers in the cosmos, he was the teacher I felt most aligned and at home with. I had always felt that I had come home when I began working consciously in Djwhal Khul's ashram. Now that Djwhal was preparing to move on to Sirius in the year 2012, I had been given the job to take over his ashram. I felt that I had moved up a number of octaves and that Melchizedek's ashram was now my true home. This was more of a feeling than anything I had decided consciously with my reasoning mind. What I requested had in truth already taken place many months previously, but I had never voiced this to Melchizedek consciously in a meditation like this. This felt very important for me to do. Melchizedek seemed moved by my prayerful and soulful request.

He confirmed what I said about this having already occurred on higher levels. However, he was in agreement about the importance in this moment of my stating it consciously. He graciously said he was very pleased with my service work and progress and spoke of our group as being some of his favorite students. He said he was very pleased to have me consciously return home, for it had been a long journey. He graciously called me the headmaster, referring to my gifts in bringing forth information, writing books and teaching.

This was an emotionally moving experience for me. I felt like I had finally come home. I had a powerful feeling that Melchizedek's ashram was my soul home. Even though I work with all the teachers on the inner plane all over the cosmos, I felt literally 100 percent clear that Melchizedek was my true teacher and the center point of the cosmos for me personally.

In a future meditation we decided to find out where our connection first began on the spiritual plane. We asked Metatron earlier about this and he refered to Melchizedek's ashram. We intuitively felt that Melchizedek would supply more details on this in the future. Not only was I deeply moved to have found my ultimate teacher in the grand master Melchizedek, the Universal Logos, but I felt doubly blessed to have found my spiritual community of Melchizedek initiates all at the same level. I truly felt, and still feel, in a blissful state.

I was keenly aware of my the movement of my primary home from Djwhal Khul's ashram to Melchizedek's ashram, even though I would be running Djwhal's ashram in the not-too-distant future. To have Djwhal Khul, Lord Maitreya and Melchizedek as my main teachers was a peace that passeth understanding, as I am sure most of you can relate to.

The Keys of Enoch speaks of the electromagnetic body as functioning to code our physical body directly into other consciousness regions of the local universe, through a whole array of electromagnetic waves. The electromagnetic body, it says, must work with the anointed Christ overself body or a master of light (I suggest Metatron or Melchizedek) if it is to work with the many electromagnetic spectrums. The importance of illuminating the electromagnetic body with light before it can cross the threshold of negative mass is also mentioned in *The Keys of Enoch*.

Meditation on March 24, 1995

Today's meditation was special because my friend had just returned from Bali and stopped off for a few days in Los Angeles. The last time I had physically seen her was exactly a year ago, when we all took our ascension together. We had experienced two major initiations in that year. The strange thing was that seeing her was not that much different from talking on the phone. We both operate so much on the spiritual plane that it felt the same. However, it was fun being in each other's physical presence.

My faxes had been a great stimulation to her while in Bali and we began by catching up. We then began our meditation. We received some profound guidance from Djwhal Khul, Lord Maitreya and Melchizedek that our mission this lifetime was to externalize Djwhal Khul's ashram, the Great White Lodge and Melchizedek's inner-plane ashram on Earth. Since we had already been given the job to take over Djwhal's ashram in the year 2012, we were in a position to begin this job now on Earth. It was quite an awesome responsibility, but one we felt we were well-suited for. My only personal limitation was some electrical weakness in my pancreas and a general digestive weakness and sensitivity from hepatitis years before.

The pancreas weakness was partially from the hepatitis and mostly from a genetically inherited predisposition. What my physical body really needed was about a year and a half of rest. That would restore the electrical strength of my pancreas and liver back to full strength. The only problem is that this was impossible. I am busier now than I have ever been, and there is no way I can take off two days, let alone an entire year. Therefore I am constantly bumping into this karmic weakness. My overall health is supremely better after going through all my initiations and raising my light quotient to the 99 percent level. I require much less sleep, and my etheric body feels electrified most of the time.

I discussed the subject of transfiguration with our trinity of masters. I really wanted to know if there was ever a point when we could really just slip into the mayavarupa body and let go of this physical body. The answer we seemed to get was a vague yes.

Out of the conversation, however, came a new dispensation, which gave me a glimmer of hope along this front. Melchizedek and Lord Maitreya said we were being assigned the planet's premiere mayavarupa specialist to spend the next six months doing etheric surgery on us to weave the mayavarupa body into our etheric and physical structure. This great healer and spiritual doctor was from the Great White Lodge on Sirius. We were told that this was a little like when a person requires heart surgery, one tries to find the world's best heart specialist. By the grace of God, we were being provided with the planet's premiere mayavarupa specialist.

My personal health lessons, the electrical weakness in the digestive area, would be greatly helped by this six-month procedure. Melchizedek told me to set a date for September, which, not by accident, was the time when we would have fully anchored and activated our fifty chakras and nine bodies. We were told that this procedure, which would be provided for our core group, would prepare all of us for this next step.

This is an important lesson for you, my readers, to understand. Just because you complete the seven levels of initiation, become fully ascended and reach the 99 percent light quotient doesn't mean that all health lessons—or personality quirks, for that matter—are transcended. The same disposition you had prior to ascension will remain with you after ascension. This new surgery from the Great White Lodge would, however, be the first major change in the time line we had been in. I felt quite excited about it.

I share this with you not because we are special, but so you will know that what is given to one is available to all. The masters are in part giving me this information not only for my own benefit but so that I will put it in my books so that all can request the things we have been receiving. The masters know that anything and everything I receive will automatically be passed on to you, my readers.

We also requested a full anchoring of the lightbodies of the Cosmic Hierarchy from Melchizedek. I did this differently than before. I asked for it in a one-shot deal without specifically focusing on any one group. Melchizedek agreed. We sat in silence for about five minutes as we received this incredible blessing.

My new profound connection with my friend, and she with me, had solidified and fully brought together the facets of Djwhal Khul's ashram. All the lines of energy or circuits between us were fully charged in all directions. This was part of the final merger of the inner- and outer-plane ashrams.

Melchizedek spoke of the core as being all of us because of our complete and total commitment, discipline and focus, which never varied. The blessings we were receiving were a direct result of our never consciously giving in to the lower self. The masters could completely rely on us to remain steady in the light.

As we came to the close of the meditation, a profound feeling came over me. The feeling was that the symbolic flower that we were on the planetary level had fully opened. We had completed our seven levels of initiation. We were up to the 99 percent light quotient. We, as heads of Djwhal Khul's ashram, were perfectly aligned on all levels, in total love and support. Our vision was set for our future mission of anchoring Djwhal Khul, the Lord Maitreya and Melchizedek's ashram on Earth. The core group was totally aligned and we were each totally focused and committed. We had merged with the lightbodies of not only the Planetary Hierarchy but also of the Cosmic Hierarchy.

Two new books were about to come out and my first book had already become a bestseller. The Mount Shasta workshop we were preparing for looked like we would have 200 people. Except for the digestive weakness, which was now going to be worked on by the master surgeon of the galaxy, everything was literally perfect.

My feeling was that everything had totally come together in this moment into perfection on all levels. If felt like we had all graduated and made it to the top of the mountain, and that the symbolic flower, which was each of us individually and as a group, had opened 100 percent.

We described the feeling that we shared as a type of ecstatic bliss. I felt deeply grateful to God for all the blessings in my life. When I came home that day after meditating, I was inundated with phone calls. Humanity was picking up on the energy. That day I was invited to go on the television show *The Other Side*. A major distributor called me and told me they wanted to distribute all my books to mainstream bookstores around the country, not just metaphysical bookstores. Then tons of calls came in for the Wesak celebration. The amazing feeling was that the entire cosmos was literally backing us—quite a humbling experience and awesome responsibility. I had to keep telling myself to take just one day at a time, for I felt myself starting to get overwhelmed by all I had committed myself to. As Djwhal Khul and Melchizedek said, "Much is given and much is expected."

One part of the meditation was very important and the new focus of my current work. This dealt with the nine *Keys of Enoch* bodies: electromagnetic, zohar, epi-kinetic, eka, anointed Christ overself, overself, higher Adam Kadmon, the Lord's mystical and gematrian. Melchizedek told us that the electromagnetic body was helping to build the zohar body, which correlated with the twelfth, or universal-level, body. The anointed Christ overself body is the fully realized christed son or sun. This is the opposite of what has been referred to as the Sons of Belial, or those souls who have been taken over by the negative ego and the overidentification with matter.

I asked our triune masters to help us on a permanent basis to keep our electromagnetic body activated, and they agreed to help. The overself body correlates with the eighth body, or the group-soul-body level. The Lord's mystical body was literally the 352nd level of the Mahatma body, or God's body. The higher Adam Kadmon body was like the mayavarupa body, or divine blueprint body. The gematrian body held the matrices or geometric bodies.

I fully recognized that the keys to the entire ascension process and beyond were three things: building the light quotient, anchoring the fifty chakras, and anchoring and activating the twelve bodies (physical, astral, mental, buddhic, atmic, monadic, logoic, group soul, group monadic, solar, galactic, and universal) and the nine *Keys of Enoch* bodies (some of which overlap the twelve I just mentioned).

The zohar body and the twelfth body are the same. The overself and the eighth body are the same. This is differentiated from the cosmic overself, which I have listed in my cosmic map in *Beyond Ascension*. The higher Adam Kadmon body is equivalent to the mayavarupa, or divine blueprint body. Once these bodies are anchored and activated, the key is to anchor the cosmic bodies.

In the Djwhal Khul system these cosmic bodies could be described as the cosmic physical, cosmic astral, cosmic mental, cosmic buddhic, cosmic atmic, cosmic monadic and cosmic logoic. My readers, if you really want to accelerate your spiritual growth, this last paragraph is the key. Build your light quotient, anchor and fully activate your fifty chakras, and anchor and activate the bodies I have just mentioned. These three components are, in my humble opinion, the shortcut and, as Paramahansa Yogananda would say, the "airplane" path to God. These are the keys, in combination with an unconditional and total dedication to serve and the transcendence of negative-ego thinking. I personally find the understanding of these bodies and how they interact absolutely fascinating.

11

My Dream Process in Relation to Ascension

One of the spiritual practices of greatest importance to me in my evolution, even more so in the later stages moving toward ascension, was keeping close track of my dreams. Dreams are a major way that our soul and monad communicate with us. Most people are not clairaudient voice channels who can talk to God directly, so dreams are important for them. Even if you are a channel, personality levels often get in the way, and everything comes through our subconscious programming. You will get an unbelievable amount of insight and information from logging your dreams closely.

About three days after my ascension, when I began to integrate into the totality of my being what had just occurred, I woke up with a dream of being Sai Baba and seeing the enormously expanded territory I was responsible for on Earth.

My ascension dream process began about a year before I actually ascended. About six months after I had begun *The Easy-to-Read Encyclopedia of the Spiritual Path*, I had a dream in which God came to me and I was shown my then-wife and I in a room similar to the ashram of the people with whom we were involved. We were shown our level of spiritual evolution on a scale of 1 to 1000, which at the time was about 800. Ascension was apparently at level 1000. We were also shown in the dream the evolution of different members of the ashram. I was then told that our relationship was like breath itself, like the yin and the yang, which was a beautiful symbol for the complementary nature of our energies. I was also given some guidance about being sure to stay balanced and giving proper care to the physical level. The basic message was that God was pleased.

This dream had an enormous impact on me. It reminded me of a dream I had about four or five years before, when I was approaching my fourth initiation. Sai Baba came to me about two years before I took this initiation and told me that I needed 70 points on Patricia Diegel's scale of soul evolution to achieve liberation, or graduation. At this time I had always been strongly motivated and focused, but after this dream I made the most profound spiritual vows of commitment, discipline and focus on my path that I had ever made.

I had gotten a spiritual channeled reading at that time from a woman who told me that I was deeply connected to soul, but that I would fluctuate in and out of it. The reading had a deep effect on me. At that time I made what I considered my supreme ultimate vows never to leave soul again. For the seven years of my life prior to my ascension I kept those vows. I am not saying that I didn't make mistakes—I made trillions of them. What I am saying is that I was not making conscious mistakes. In other words, I was consciously serving or choosing my higher self instead of my lower self when I had the awareness to do so. I literally closed the door on the negative ego and the lower self at this time and locked it. From that time onward in my life it was as if I had no more choice. The only choice was God.

This is when I really began to move on my spiritual path. My progress before this had been much slower. More than anything else in the world I wanted to graduate and achieve liberation. At this time I had no understanding of the seven levels of initiation as described by Djwhal Khul. My training in Eastern religions had taught me about liberation, and that is what I wanted. I went for it like a man possessed.

A couple of days after this dream a dear friend had a dream in which I came to him as a type of yogi Christ and was levitating and radiating light in every direction. I then said to him, "Come and ascend with me." This dream had a big impact on both of us. Something very big was happening on the inner plane.

Not too long after this my other friend, whom I was later to ascend with, told me a dream she'd had in which she was telling me that she was 93 percent complete with her path of ascension. In the dream I stopped her and said. "No, that is not true; we are both 99 percent complete with our path of ascension." This dream sent shock waves through both of us. We were both farther along than we thought.

One of the traps of the spiritual path is to either overestimate or underestimate one's evolution. I have done both. Both are manifestations of the negative ego, which likes to make one either better or worse than everyone else. I will talk more about this in the section about my personal experiences in the initiation process.

I had a series of ascension-type dreams that I will share now, which aren't in chronological order. A dream that had one of the greatest impacts on me came about two months before I ascended. In the dream I was told that Sanat Kumara was now waiting for the number 1 in my aura to transform to the number 10. The number 1 is the beginning and number 10 is completion. The number 10, when associated with the tenth ray, refers to the complete grounding of the monadic lightbody. The tenth chakra represents the perfect balancing of the male and female polarities.

I knew from this dream that I was being given a picture of my ascension process in numerological symbols. The fact that it was Sanat Kumara was also very important, for he is the Planetary Logos and initiator of the ascension process. If Sanat Kumara was waiting, I knew I was getting close.

About three or four months before my ascension I had a dream that my (former) wife and I passed some kind of minor initiation and went to the Govinda galaxy. I was later told that this was for the purpose of ensuring our ascension and giving us an experience of unconditional-love transformation and focus without having to think about it.

I then had a dream that a car and truck were parked in a garage. I was told that they were waiting for the proper timing of the divine marriage. I knew immediately upon waking that the car symbolized me and the truck was the symbol for my monad, the larger me. It is important to say here that it is not possible to know exactly when you are going to ascend and take this initiation. This is one of the mysteries of life. If you stay closely attuned to your inner process, I think it is possible to intuit a general time period when it might happen.

Then I had a dream that my wife was channeling. I was told that there would be 4000 to 5000 people ascending in May 1995. Upon waking, I thought to myself that it was unlikely I would dream about this unless I was going to be part of the first wave. As it turned out, I ascended about fourteen months before the first wave.

I then had a dream that some intricate mathematical calculations were being worked out, and the end result was that my contract for service on the earthly plane was for thirty-two more years. That would put me at age seventy-two in the year 2026, which seemed just about perfect. If I had lived a normal nonascended life, that is about the span I would want to remain on Earth. I again thought to myself, I don't think I would have a dream like this if I weren't close to completion.

Then I had a dream of seeing a ruler, and I was told that I was a quarter inch away from ascending. This dream really surprised me. It was about eight months before I actually ascended. At the time I didn't think I was that close.

I had another dream in which a master said I was ready for ascension. I gave birth to my ascension through my crown chakra and then came back again.

About three weeks before I actually ascended, I had a very powerful dream in which I was playing baseball in the first game of the World Series. I hit two home runs and was the hero. The night before this dream I had given a lecture and taught a class on how to do Huna prayers. We did two prayers together, which I had written for that class. The class loved the prayers, as did Sanat Kumara, who unexpectedly channeled through my wife for an hour. He told us to do these prayers every week as a regular part of our class meeting.

Upon waking I immediately associated the two home runs to the two Huna prayers. The fact that I was now in the World Series was symbolic of the final championship games being played. I was no longer in the playoffs but was playing in the final games. I knew I had only three more games to win to achieve my ascension.

A couple weeks later I had a dream in which I was rolling dice for a spiritual reader who was especially gifted in knowing a person's soul evolution. I rolled the number 4, then the numbers 1 and 1. The spiritual reader rolled 1 and 1. Then I rolled the number 1, which transformed into the number 9. I think the number 4 had to do with my four-body system. The two consecutive 1 rolls reminded me of the 11:11, which is the numerical code for ascension. The single 1 also could have symbolized my individual four bodies. The most significant number to me was the 1 that was transforming into the 9. I clearly recognized that I was close to ascension. In my previous dream Sanat Kumara was waiting for the number 1 to transform to the number 10. I was now at 1, transforming to the number 9. I knew I was only one step away. This dream was about a week before I actually ascended and took my sixth initiation.

About a month before my ascension I had a dream that the AT&T phone company was doing extremely well in their stock and overall company standing. Upon waking I immediately knew that this had to do with my own internal communication systems working well.

Approximately three months before my ascension when I was going through a difficult period, I had a dream in which I was given a victory mantra in Sanskrit. Upon waking I thought to myself that I wouldn't be given a victory mantra if my ascension victory weren't close at hand.

About four months before my ascension I had a dream that I was formally introduced to Archangel Metatron, who offered to help in my ascension process. I had been meditating and praying for his help, and this was a nice confirmation.

Approximately two months before my ascension I had another short dream in which I was in an elevator, which now had a fifth-floor button. Upon waking I instantly knew that this referred to the fact that the ascended-master consciousness was the movement into the fifth dimension of reality. I had made an ascension tape for myself that I played every night before bed. I would press the button and off I would go into the fifth-dimensional state of consciousness.

Then in another dream, about nine months before my ascension and during an ascension workshop that my wife and I were giving, I was shown that I was a Moses-type figure leading the Jewish people into the Promised Land. The Jewish symbolism here refers to providing the mental under-standing and mechanics of ascension to the masses.

Two days before my ascension I had a dream that my wife and I were in bed sleeping. Then we awoke and sat up in bed because our ascension was beginning. We sat there as the ascension energies began to pour in. The dream ended about a quarter of the way through the ascension process. Upon waking I knew that our ascension was imminent. We were doing ritu-als every night to invoke it and let spirit know we were ready.

I had another very interesting dream about ten days after my ascension. In this dream there was another ascension ceremony going on that was hon-oring my passing the sixth initiation. In this dream Djwhal Khul was con-ducting the ceremony. Unfortunately, I don't remember a lot of the details, but I remember that at one point I was sitting at a desk, and a lingam rolled over to me of its own accord. I also remember seeing a series of symbolic pictures detailing how I achieved my ascension. They depicted my ability to stay in mastery of my energies and not be overcome by the lower self, negative ego and my threefold personality (physical, emotional and mental bodies). In the dream I was the first to achieve this because others didn't have this self-mastery and these leadership abilities.

Upon waking I knew that the lingam was symbolic of achieving libera-tion from the wheel of rebirth. The lingam, an oval-shaped rock usually found in the Ganges River, is considered the holiest object and/or icon in the Hindu religion. Once a year at one of the Hindu festivals, Sai Baba used to manifest a lingam out of his stomach. I saw a video of Sai Baba actually manifesting one, and forevermore thought it was one of the most remarkable spiritual occurrences I had ever seen. Sai Baba said that whoever·was blessed to witness this was just about guaranteed to achieve liberation if he/she lived any kind of decent life. This was one of the reasons I watched it on video.

The second meaning of the above-mentioned dream was also very clear. The previous day I fully claimed my ascension. This was something that Djwhal Khul had guided me to do, in reference to another personal is-sue I was dealing with. What I realized in my journal-writing was that even though I had ascended and achieved my sixth initiation, I still needed to claim it fully in my conscious mind and also claim the reality of it in my five-body system (physical, etheric, emotional, mental and spiritual).

After doing this, I now realize how essential this process was for me. It is essential that you, my readers, understand that just because a person as-cends, it doesn't mean that he/she will have only ascended-master thoughts, emotions and health for eternity. *Ascension doesn't change the contents of your consciousness.* If this is your conception, you are headed for a rude awakening. The same vigilance that was needed before one's ascension is still needed afterward.

Getting back to my original point—the need to claim my ascension: The day before this dream I had fully claimed my ascension in my conscious mind and in my four-body system. This was something I had been doing for the past fifteen years and was one of the main reasons I ascended in the first place. Affirming this again after actually ascending was a little more powerful, for passing the sixth initiation is the full realization or merger with the I Am, or monad.

In my journal-writing I reaffirmed the perfection of my digestive system and programs. I cleared the negative pictures from my mental, emotional, spiritual and etheric bodies and replaced them with the appropriate ascended-master (monadic) pictures. This long explanation is the reason why I believe I had the dream. Under the guidance of Djwhal Khul, who gave me the insight, I created another ascension ceremony which claimed my ascension in my conscious mind and four-body system. My dream symbolized the ceremony I gave myself through Djwhal's insight.

I would highly recommend to you, my readers, to do this yourself. Give yourself your own ascension ceremony even before you have actually ascended. Fully claim your ascended-master mind that is free of negative ego. Fully claim your ascended-master emotional body that is free from fear and negative anger and emotions. Fully claim your perfect etheric body that is free from any vital forces and energies not of the purity and perfection of God. Fully claim your perfectly functioning ascended-master body.

Paramahansa Yogananda once said that even if you are on your deathbed and you are ninety-eight years old, you should still affirm only perfect, radiant health. It is stated in *A Course in Miracles* that sickness is a defense against the truth. The truth is that each of us is the monad, spirit, eternal self, Christ, Buddha, Atma, God. If this truth is each of our identities, regardless of the level of initiation we are at, then how can we have an unhealthy physical body? How can we have separative emotions? How can we have separative and fear-based thoughts? How can we have any energies in our etheric body that are not of the Christ? We cannot. It is mind over matter. Regardless of appearances, we must hold the perfect ideal in these subtler bodies, even if these bodies are giving us fear-based symptoms and backtalk.

In claiming my ascension, I attitudinally healed my mental, emotional, spiritual and etheric bodies of the illusionary and negative thoughts and images that were lodged there in regard to my digestive system. I replaced them with God's pictures of these organs. I am absolutely positive that every one of you reading this can recognize some aspect of your life where this same process needs to be done. Don't wait until you ascend. Do it now.

It was my constant practice of doing this for the past fifteen years in all my bodies, as the dream was referencing, about having mastery over the lower self and affirming the Self, that so greatly accelerated my own ascension process. This process of constant refinement and purification is what keeps us continually raising our vibration and becoming more God-like. Ascension is the sixth initiation. There are 352 levels to achieve full God perfection. The process just keeps continuing to higher and higher levels of refining, purification and realization.

One other area where claiming one's ascension and true identity as spirit needs to take place is in regard to money and prosperity. We need to release all fear programming and poverty consciousness from the five-body system and replace it with prosperity consciousness, faith, trust and patience in God and God's laws. Part of this prosperity consciousness is understanding the laws of manifestation on a conscious, subconscious and superconscious level.

I have written extensively about this in *Soul Psychology*, so I will not go into it here. I bring this up simply to share one other area I am carefully refining, purifying and healing as I move to the next rung of the ladder. The higher one goes in the initiation process, the more powerful one's thoughts become and the quicker they manifest both positively and negatively.

Vywamus and Djwhal Khul told me was that it was possible for an ascended master to lose his/her sixth-degree status; it has happened before, though rarely. Usually by the time a person has reached this level, the negative ego, the lower self and the Dweller on the Threshold have become very much subjugated and mastered. It was interesting to me, however, that it *could* happen.

Approximately three and a half months after our ascension I began to have a new type of dream. In one dream I was looking at a large book, and I remember looking at two pictures. The first one I can't remember. The second one showed Master Jesus walking in still frame, then transforming into pure light on the same page. A couple of weeks earlier I had had a similar dream. This seemed to be a new theme as I was approaching the completion of my ascension. The process of the seventh level of initiation is to become pure light. The completion of the seventh initiation is where one is at 98 percent light quotient.

Around the same time I had another dream that I felt was quite significant. I was with a group of people and was telling them how excited I was that I was merging with the galactic level, or galactic core. In the dream only one person from the group seemed to catch my excitement and share it. Upon waking I continued to be excited and felt that this dream reflected the time I had been spending with Lenduce in his ashram on the inner plane and in his ascension seats.

I also had a series of dreams about climbing mountains with a group of people and also with my wife. Somehow when I made it to the top, it was my birthday.

In another interesting dream around this time I was with Johnny Carson of *The Tonight Show*. He told me that he wanted me to take over his television show. I told him that he was the best of the best of the comedians. He told me he was inspired by my work and I was the perfect person to take over his show. He was adamant. I was a little concerned in the dream about my physical health and the wear and tear of this full-time job.

Upon waking I found this dream quite humorous, although after meditating on it I realized that I was being given a message about my mission. Probably my greatest asset is my communication skills. Johnny Carson hosted a talk show. I also tend to be funny and witty when I speak publicly. I don't really try, it just seems to happen automatically. In the future it is possible that I will be in the media as kind of a spiritual talk-show host because of my wide and diverse spiritual training and ability to communicate with all types of people and integrate all modalities.

Sports Dreams

The next series of dreams was quite significant in my process of completing my ascension and gave me wonderful feedback. I had many dreams in which I was playing basketball, which I did as an adolescent. Whenever I was doing well spiritually in my life, I would have dreams of playing basketball as an adult and scoring a lot of points. The scoring of points was clearly "scoring" spiritually. One particular day when I was really on target spiritually, I dreamed about Magic Johnson scoring tons of points in the basketball game and having one of his best games ever. In another basketball dream I was a player and captain of the team. I gave an impassioned speech about cooperation and oneness, as a great motivational speaker would do.

In another interesting sports dream I was in a boxing match that was compared to the Super Bowl, and there would be three billion people watching. My opponent was much bigger than I was, but I won the fight because I was able to outwit him. I think the meaning is obvious.

I had an interesting dream about three months before my ascension. In the dream I was able to punt a football over 100 yards because I had Vywamus' cream on my feet! This led to a parade and celebration led by Sai Baba. Vywamus, of course, is the higher aspect of Sanat Kumara. He is one of the teachers I am very attuned to in my work and books. The symbol of Vywamus' cream on my feet has to do with the fact that the feet are a symbol for understanding. In my life, in a sense, I was rubbing Vywamus' teachings through my understanding process, which was leading to the parade and celebration led by the Cosmic Christ, Sai Baba. Again, I knew from this dream that I was on the right track.

In another sports dream I was in a class with a martial-arts specialist. Even though I had no formal training in martial arts, I was able to defeat my opponent because of my personal power and my ability to stay centered.

In a similar dream about a month later I was enrolled in a high-level martial arts dojo. I was a relatively new student, but the master instructor saw great promise and potential—something about being able to help millions of people.

About a week or ten days after receiving guidance that I had taken my ninth initiation and was just about to complete my ascension, I dreamed that I was playing basketball, and all my shots were going into the basket. What was strange, though, was that I was shooting pillows into the basket, not a basketball. The message I received in the dream was that my basketball skills had risen to a new level. This meant that my skills had been elevated. I felt a new level in my life, as I was preparing to take my seventh initiation. I have no idea what the significance of the pillows meant, but the dream felt very positive.

In another dream I was completing a mini cosmic day. This dream had to do with the fact that in moving toward completing my ascension I was completing my own personal cosmic day, just as this universe is in the process of completing *its* cosmic day.

Shortly after my ascension I had a dream that Indian tribes of many nations were helping me plant my new garden. In a similar dream there was a long line of twenty to twenty-five cars that came to a fork in the road. Again, I gave an impassioned speech about cooperation and group consciousness. Every car turned toward the right because of the speech. (I think I should have been a minister instead of a psychologist because of these sermons I am giving in my dreams.)

In another sports dream the women's baseball team scored ten runs in the first inning. Obviously, my feminine side was off to a good start in my ascension processing.

Just after my ascension I had a dream that my wife was channeling Djwhal Khul, who was excitedly telling me about Lenduce. He said something about Lenduce being connected with the 95 percent light-quotient level. This dream turned out to be quite prophetic, for I was now working with Lenduce as one of my main teachers. At the time of this dream I had never worked with Lenduce.

School Dreams

Another common theme in my dreams was being in school or college again. After a short period in my life where I wasn't demonstrating the mastery and discipline I needed in my life, I had a dream that I was talking to a schoolteacher. I was aware that I hadn't been doing my homework and had been absent from class. I was going to complete all the assignments I had neglected so that I could be complete. There was a lot to do, but I was not very far from completing everything.

I think this dream speaks about getting back in touch with my mastery after losing it, and working toward completing my ascension. About two months later I had a dream that I was beginning my last semester of my senior year in college. This was another dream showing me that the completion of my ascension was near.

Dreams give a wonderful confirmation (or lack of it) for the inner guidance and intuition we work with in our conscious daily lives.

About three or four days after the dream where I was entering the last semester of my senior year, I had probably the most extraordinary dream of my entire life. I dreamed in a very physical sense that I was moving upward through the dimensions of reality. I was making progress, and it was through my own personal efforts. In the dream I finally broke through the upper barrier, or dimension, with my head first, then my whole body.

My entire body and being was electrified with spiritual energy in a very positive sense. I had the inner knowing that I was now complete with my ascension process. My long struggle through this life and all my past lives was over. My dream of dreams and desire of desires was over. I felt euphoric, ecstatic and greatly relieved. I felt like I had been through a war and I had finally made it home for good. I appeared in a white robe of some sort. There was an enormous amount of electricity and pure energy flowing through my entire body. I was in a higher dimension of reality and not in my physical body when this all took place. Upon waking, I definitely felt that this was the best dream I had ever had—and I have had a lot of interesting dreams!

I dreamed that I was receiving a sound healing from a friend on an extraterrestrial spacecraft. I was lying down and receiving the perfect amount of sound for the specific healing I needed. When it was completed, I was running down a type of runway, holding my arms in the air like I had just scored a touchdown.

Another theme in my dreams is that of looking up into the night sky and seeing various heavenly occurrences. In one dream I was looking at seven stars, which suddenly began to move through the night, making me realize that they were a positive extraterrestrial spacecraft and not really stars.

In another dream about four months from my ascension I was in a car with someone else driving. I was looking into the night sky and saw a red dot streaking across the heavens. Then I saw a flying star. Then I saw some kind of rainbow phenomenon in different places in the sky. In the dream I was trying to discern whether this was actually happening in the sky or whether it was caused by a reflection in the window of the car.

I think this dream symbolized my heavenly focus and a certain discernment as to whether what I am experiencing is coming from me or is truly a spiritual experience or contact of some kind. The dream *felt* good, which is the most important thing.

Four months and one week after my ascension I dreamed that my wife came to me on the inner plane and told me to come with her. I asked why, and she said that I was now close to completing my ascension. Upon waking, I felt very excited and couldn't go back to sleep for a long time. This was another direct confirmation of all that had been going on in the past four months, in terms of the guidance we had been receiving. We seemed to be on the exact schedule the masters said we were on.

The following night I dreamed that a very lovely and spiritual black man told me that while I was gone I had saved $200 million in some kind of investment. That investment was fully mine, but the way it was set up didn't provide me with a large cash flow. I felt amazed that I had been able to save and build that type of investment.

Upon waking, the meaning of the dream began to become clear to me. The $200 million investment was the spiritual gold I had accumulated. My entire life has been focused on building the heavenly riches and not pursuing worldly goals. By the grace of God, I have always been provided for financially. It is like the saying in the Bible, "For what is a man profited if he gain the whole world and lose his own soul?" By the grace of God I have had the intelligence and wisdom to pursue my soul and spirit above all else. The lack of cash flow from this large investment is unusual. It is symbolic, I believe, first, of not having a lot of extra physical money (although as I said, I do not lack necessary funds). Second, it is symbolic of the fact that I am still carrying some physical weakness in the digestive system, which still limits me from truly reaping the benefits of all that I have invoked.

It felt very good in the dream that I had invested so wisely. Doing this when my wife was gone relates to the fact that a lot of my spiritual work was in my journal-writing, meditation and introspection time. The $200 million savings investment, I feel, also goes along with the fact that the completion of my ascension was imminent.

About three and a half months after my ascension I dreamed that I was conversing with Djwhal Khul, who was saying that he had never had initiates who were as focused and committed as we were. The dream seemed a little jumbled together, as dreams often are, but this was the gist of the message. It was something that Madam Blavatsky and Djwhal had also said to us during our meditations.

The message seemed to point out our focus of intent, commitment, discipline, even-mindedness and purity, in the sense of not being drawn into the lower self or being so interested in worldly matters that we overidentify with matter and personality issues.

About three months after my ascension I had a dream that a dove landed on the head of a minister with whom I was speaking. He was surprised. Upon waking came the knowing that the dove was symbolic of the Holy Spirit and/or peace. Clearly the minister aspect of my self was being blessed and graced in some way.

Another fascinating dream came after a day of meditation with my friend. She was going through a difficult week, so we did a lot of meditations and prayers for a divine dispensation to help her. During our meditation we attended a major council meeting on her behalf administrated by some galactic being. It felt almost like a trial, though in a positive or spiritual sense, to see whether our prayer's dispensation could be answered. It felt very holy and very important.

After our meditation I went home and took a nap. I had an extremely powerful dream that a war was going on. I was in the car with my wife when a nuclear bomb went off about a half mile away. "Duck!" I yelled in response to the brilliant flash of light. After about a minute we went looking for someone. I remember being in a home, looking out the window. I was awestruck to see the mushroom cloud and the intense light it was radiating. I knew in the dream that it was the good side that sent the bomb, not the evil side. Then suddenly it just disappeared.

I woke up with the inwardly channeled message "new clear bomb." Do you see the play on words? Instead of *nuclear* bomb, it was "new clear" bomb. I felt the dream had to do with the new clear bomb for the good forces that my friend and I had set off in our meditation and prayer session. The dream was extremely powerful.

Dreams about Sanat Kumara

In the process of moving from the sixth to seventh initiation I began to have many dreams about Sanat Kumara and messages from him. Dreams about Sanat Kumara are always my favorite. Sanat Kumara is like E.F. Hutton. When he talks, people listen. Sanat Kumara is a master of all masters. He was the Planetary Logos for this planet until Lord Buddha took over that position in May 1995. It is the Planetary Logos who decides who achieves initiations and who doesn't. He holds the rod of initiation at all initiations from the third to the seventh, and you merge with him at the seventh level of initiation.

Among the spiritual beings in God's infinite universe, the trinity of beings I am most aligned with is Sanat Kumara, Vywamus and Lenduce. These three are like the personality, soul and monad at a cosmic level. This is the trinity of trinities for planet Earth. Another trinity, though on the cosmic level, that I attune to and work with daily is Melchizedek, the Mahatma and Metatron. The combined blessings of these two trinities defy words. I might add that they are accessible to all who truly want to work with them and who call upon them with a sincere heart.

In one dream I was reliving the Wesak experience of visiting Sanat Kumara in the Wesak Valley in the Himalayan Mountains. I had few details in the dream, only that all night long I was with him, and it was quite a euphoric experience. My feeling upon waking was that I had actually been with Sanat Kumara in a type of soul-travel experience during my sleep, doing some group service or celebration activity. I also felt a deeper and more profound physical healing after this experience.

In another dream I received a message from Sanat Kumara that all the prayers we had been making in meditation and our Huna prayers would be answered. This was a wonderful blessing and confirmation.

Dreams about Sai Baba

The other master I consider of the highest importance when I dream of him is his holiness the Lord Sai Baba. Sai Baba is the Cosmic Christ. If you don't know about him, you must read *The Complete Ascension Manual*. Sai Baba, the Cosmic Christ, and Lord Maitreya, the Planetary Christ, are both on this planet in incarnated form. Being the Cosmic Christ and, further, a galactic avatar, it is always significant when anybody dreams about Sai Baba. He has said that no one ever dreams about him unless he wills it.

In my dream last night I was on top of the Empire State Building, feeling very dizzy because the top of the building was only six feet by six feet with no railing. I began to climb down. There was a heater just below the first couple rungs of the ladder. The heater and its warm energy were a direct result of Sai Baba's energy. Sai Baba seemed to run through the center of the shaft that made up the entire Empire State Building. I climbed down a couple of flights and other people then came to help me. The next thing I knew I was back on top of the building with a friend of mine from the ashram. This time it was a little more comfortable, but not 100 percent so.

This dream had to do with the fact that on the previous day I had begun to work with the thirty-six chakras, which include the sixth- and seventh-dimensional chakra grids. I was also working to bring through new information on the seven paths to higher evolution, which, as far as I know, no one has ever brought through in any detailed, easy-to-understand form. Anchoring my thirty-six chakras and attuning to this higher information was putting me at the top of the spiritual world, so to speak. It was a building experience, because getting to the top was a process of my own creation. It makes sense that Sai Baba, being the center of the building, is at the center of my life. The heater was a symbol of the warmth and comfort I receive from Sai Baba as my cosmic guru at the highest level.

This next dream came about nine weeks after taking my ascension. An enormous amount of growth had taken place by this time. Our core group was already more than halfway through completing its ascension. In the dream I was looking down into a valley, where I saw lots of people and activity. Something wasn't going right down there, so I chanted very loudly, "Sai Baba." I walked over to an area on the cliff where a group of people was gathered, and suddenly a holy man said that all the people gathered in this area were now going to become the government, or counsel, for these people.

There were no elections. It was as if God chose the government. It felt right for me to serve in this way. Initially, it looked like about twelve people, but in a later dream the same night, it was many more. I was told that I was serving as an assemblyman even though I was on the second rung of a three-rung tier. Later that night I experienced my first day on the board. It was like a preparation day. I was having a little bit of a problem getting everything organized and integrated properly on this first day. I remember being with my wife and telling her that it felt like serving in the Spiritual Hierarchy. She was also an assemblywoman in the dream.

In the next dream I was speaking to a college professor, who told me I looked a little bit like Shirdi Sai Baba, who was Sai Baba's last incarnation. I then began to take out of my wallet my picture of Sai Baba, whom I sensed he might not know about. As this was going on, I found myself driving in a car that was cluttered with papers. Some of the papers flew out of the car when I opened the door, so I asked the professor to help me collect them so they wouldn't be blown away. Upon waking, I was not completely sure of the meaning of this dream, though it felt significant.

I dreamed I was reading the *National Enquirer* in a forest area or campsite and was either reading or thinking about Sai Baba. Sai Baba immediately appeared out of the forest. When I first looked at him, his hair seemed shorter than usual. When he approached even closer, his hair looked completely different, straight instead of curly. It definitely was Sai Baba, however, and we sweetly chatted and conversed for a little while. He then said he would come for dinner at seven o'clock that night. I was very pleased. I then went on a very long hike up a mountain. On the way down it started getting dark. I realized I still had a long way to go to get home, so I started to run. I got to the bottom but couldn't find my way home. Everything looked totally different. I was with some man to whom I was telling my difficulty and realized that it was seven minutes to seven o'clock. Sai Baba would be there any minute, and I wasn't even close to home.

I prayed to Baba and asked for help. I was immediately transported home and instead of dinner, I was in our Wednesday night spiritual class. There was an incredibly good feeling among the group, and one woman stated how meaningful this group was to her. Of course Sai Baba was there.

My interpretation of this dream, besides the obvious visitation, is that (Sai Baba's) hair usually relates to the mind. So I understood that his mindset or perspective is different or that I see him differently. Losing my way home after hiking up the mountain, I think, has to do with getting too ungrounded. Too much time at the top of the mountain, or in the higher planes, leaves one with not enough home base, or grounding time. That definitely applied to the previous day. I am sure that Sai Baba helped rebalance me on the inner plane.

In one other dream I was sitting at a table with two friends and Sai Baba. I remember asking him some questions, which he promptly responded to with his usual omniscience. As usual, I was feeling the great blessing of being in his presence. The only negative thing about the dream was that one of the other people was a friend from the past who I consciously feel symbolizes the ego, or a bit of false pride. In the dream I remember wanting to feel closer to Sai Baba.

Upon waking, the meaning of the dream was quite evident. I received a blessing, but I was being taught a little lesson about false pride: it was causing a slight distance from Baba. So I was simultaneously receiving a blessing and a little reminder that a minor attitude adjustment was needed. As Sai Baba says (which happens to be my favorite quote of all time), the definition of God is "God equals man minus ego." One never wants to put oneself above or below others. We are equal, for all are the eternal self and Atman, as Sai Baba would say.

12

Wesak and the First Ascension Wave

Clarion Call to Lightworkers

Humanity now stands at a momentous point in the history of the Earth. May 14, 1995, at the Wesak Festival (which is the Festival of the Buddha on the full moon in Taurus), begins the first wave of mass ascension for humanity. This window of mass ascension will be open from the years 1995 to 2000. The ceremony of the 12:12, which occurred on December 12, 1994, served to open the window for this event. Wesak is when the first wave of humanity walks through this window. The 12:12 was also the moment when Gaia, or Mother Earth, took her ascension, or sixth initiation. Even the Earth herself is in a state of spiritual evolution, as humanity is.

This is a momentous time in the history of the Earth. The ascended masters have been patiently waiting for this moment in history to come about. There will be approximately 5000 to 10,000 people taking their ascension at this time.

It must be understood that many high-level initiates have already taken their ascension and many others will take theirs after this five-year window is over. Vywamus has referred to this particular five-year window as a time of spiritual harvesting. It also must be understood that ascension occurs in a moment (the moment of taking your sixth initiation). However, it is also a process. Even after receiving the rod of initiation from Sanat Kumara, we must still complete our ascension process. After we ascend, we are in truth a kindergarten ascended master. We must fully complete the seven levels of initiation to break the wheel of reincarnation. Every person on Earth, regardless of religion, mystery school or spiritual path, is involved with seven levels of initiation. These initiations occur on the inner plane, and most are consciously unaware of their occurrence.

For those of you who don't know what the Wesak Festival is, it is time to explain it. From the ascended masters' perspective it is the holiest day of the year. The Wesak is the Festival of the Buddha, which occurs each year

at the full moon of Taurus, usually in early May. The full moon of April is
the Festival of the Christ, and the full moon of June is the Festival of Humanity. The ascended masters celebrate these festivals as we on Earth celebrate Christmas, Easter and other religious holidays. The biggest festival of
the three I mentioned is the Wesak Festival.

Wesak is actually a valley in the Himalayas, where once a year all the
ascended masters convene in the inner and outer planes. The Buddha returns to Earth from his cosmic evolution; Lord Maitreya, the Planetary
Christ, is there, as is Sanat Kumara, the Planetary Logos, and all the ascended masters. A sacred ceremony is performed and all the disciples and
initiates around the world are invited to attend in their spiritual bodies to
receive great blessings from these great and noble masters. The purpose of
the Wesak Festival is basically fourfold, outlined as follows by the ascended master Djwhal Khul through the Alice Bailey books.

1. To substantiate the fact of the Christ's physical existence among
us ever since his so-called departure.
2. To prove on the physical plane the factual solidarity of the Eastern
and Western approaches to God. Both the Christ and the Buddha
are present.
3. To form a rallying point and a meeting place for those who annually—in synthesis and symbolically—link up and represent the
Father's house, the kingdom of God and humanity.
4. To demonstrate the nature of the work of the Christ as the great
and chosen Intermediary, standing as the representative of the
Spiritual Hierarchy and as the leader of the new group of World
Servers. In his person, he voices their demand for the recognition
of the factual existence of the kingdom of God here and now.

For me personally, the Wesak is always the highlight of every year. It is
also the time when all the initiations are given by Sanat Kumara, Lord
Maitreya and, in more recent times, Lord Melchizedek. In one Wednesday
night class Djwhal Khul was talking about this event and jokingly said he
was "shaking in his boots at the responsibility." We knew that he was joking, but I think he was trying to impress upon us the magnitude and significance of this occasion. We expect from 150 to 250 people to attend.
Melchizedek will overlight this entire event, as will Sai Baba, the Lord of
Arcturus, the Lord of Sirius (of the Great White Lodge on Sirius), the Lord
Maitreya, Sanat Kumara, Metatron, Saint Germain and a great many other
masters too numerous to mention.

The above-mentioned ascended masters and myself are now sounding
forth a call to lightworkers around the planet to participate in spiritual fellowship and celebrate this most momentous occasion. The level of energy
transmission is guaranteed to be enormous and the spiritual benefits for ac-

celerating your path of ascension will be incredible. The opportunities for planetary service work are equally as awesome.

Now, I realize that not everyone on the planet will be able to come in person to Mount Shasta. For those who can't, as a spokesperson for the planetary ascension movement, I am now sounding forth a second call for you to gather in groups on May 13 and 14, wherever you might be physically located, and link up with us spiritually and energetically in Mount Shasta.

Groups all over the globe will be celebrating with us this year and will share equally in the blessings. On Saturday or Sunday night I suggest that you hold a sacred ceremony to celebrate the Wesak Festival. I suggest that as part of the ceremony you call forth Djwhal Khul, Lord Maitreya and Sanat Kumara and ask to be taken in a group merkabah to the Wesak Valley in the Himalayas to stand before Sanat Kumara, the Buddha and Maitreya to receive their blessings.

This is a time to reaffirm your vows of commitment to service and pray to these masters about whatever you need God's help with. Spend fifteen minutes exploring the Wesak Valley, just enjoying the energies and blessings. The rest of the ceremony upon your return can be created any way you like. I would recommend reading *The Complete Ascension Manual* for some easy-to-apply ascension activations, which would be useful for invoking the higher transmissions of energies.

My goal and vision is to get all the spiritual people on the planet in all countries of the world celebrating this sacred ceremony and the first wave of mass ascension together. We are all pieces of a great puzzle. Each must take responsibility for his or her small part to make God's plan work. I am calling on the lightworkers on the planet to pick up the rod of power as externalized members of the Spiritual Hierarchy and help manifest this noble vision.

I would like to end with another quote from the ascended master Djwhal Khul from the Alice Bailey material on the Wesak: "It is the intention of the Buddha and the Christ that in each country there should eventually be someone who will act as their representative at the time of the two festivals [Festival of Christ in April and Festival of the Buddha in May] so that the distribution of spiritual energy from the first great aspect, or ray, will be direct from the Buddha and Shamballa to the Christ, and then from the Christ to those initiates and disciples in every country who will be overlighted, and so act as channels for the direct current of energy."

No cost is too great to pay in order to be of use to the Spiritual Hierarchy (ascended masters) at the time of the full moon in May, the Wesak Festival. No price is too high to gain the spiritual illumination that can be possible at that time. Namasté.

Meditation before Wesak

In our final meditation together about two or three weeks before the major event, some fascinating information came through as we were speaking with Djwhal Khul, Lord Maitreya and Melchizedek. We were told that at the time of taking the sixth initiation, the flame in the third eye is activated. When taking the seventh initiation, the flame in the throat is activated. When completing the seventh initiation just prior to taking the eighth initiation, the flame in the heart is activated, and these three flames merge. Because we had received guidance that our seventh initiation was complete, we received the blessing this day of the merging of these three flames.

I asked the masters about euthanasia, and they spoke of it as a positive thing that incurred no karma. It is interesting how humans do it with animals without compunction or guilt, but not with themselves. They said that when humanity gets more and more attuned to being the life *within* the form rather than the form, it will have much, much more control of death than it currently does. Humans must learn not to be so attached to the form, but learn to know each other as the souls and spirits dwelling within the form.

They also gave us information about the fifty chakras that blew our minds. They had previously told us that we would be able to anchor and activate our fifty chakras by September. Today they told us that due to the enormous acceleration taking place and the continual invoking we had been doing the past three months, at the coming Wesak (May 14, 1995) our entire set of fifty chakras would be totally anchored and activated. By the grace of God, the timetable originally given us was again cut exactly in half. We were all very excited about it. This added a sense of completion to the Wesak celebration.

They also told us of some new work they wanted us to begin, using a globe or a map. The training was to clairvoyantly sense the auric emanations from different cities or countries around the world and learn how to send energies, rays and thought forms to balance the trouble spots around the globe. We were very excited about the prospect.

I was told something that fascinated me: The word *Bible* stands for "beginners' instructions before leaving Earth."

I happened to go through some papers and found the following chart, which I thought was rather interesting. I have inserted it here for your enjoyment.

RAY	COLOR	ZODIAC	PURPOSE
First	Red	Mars/Aries	Divine Will: powerful clearing energy; use with discernment.

Second	Blue	Jupiter/Sagittarius	Unconditional Love: recognize the divine in all things. A healing energy, dissolves separation.
Third	Yellow	Sun/Leo	Higher intelligence: clear sight, reveals truth, releases need to control, brings awareness of right timing.
Fourth	Green	Venus/Libra	Harmony (through conflict) Balance: to maintain center as we move through conflict, chaos, or feeling stuck; helps release negative emotions.
Fifth	Orange	Mercury/Gemini	Logical Intellect: key to facilitate communication, brings clarity to knowing what you want and what is needed.
Sixth	Indigo	Moon/Cancer	Devotion (can be to point of obsession): energy of Piscean Age, absorbs all situations. This ray is being withdrawn from Earth plane.
Seventh	Violet	Earth/Taurus	Purification and Transmutation: the energy of the violet flame cleanses, bringing all negative ego structures through a divine metamorphosis.

The Wesak Festival, May 12–14, 1995

During the preceding four months I had taken on the mantle of responsibility, with the help of the masters, to manifest this event. Because this Wesak began the first wave of mass ascension for humanity, it was quite significant, to say the least. I put full-page ads in the *Sedona Journal of Emergence!* and other smaller newsletters around the country. My natural enthusiasm was quite infectious, and in a very short time we had 300 people signed up. I estimate that we had to turn away over 200 people during the last three weeks. There was considerable stress in taking on such a large responsibility. Another stress factor was that my wife and I had made a decision in January to get a divorce but to live together until the end of May and put on the workshop together. It was, and still is, a friendly and loving divorce; however, this added to the pressures.

By the time the event arrived everyone was quite excited. The spiritual level of the people coming from around the globe was awesome. This group was truly 300 high-level initiates and ascended beings.

Without getting into the details, it was a tremendous success. It was fantastic to have such a large group in Mount Shasta on the full moon in May to kick off the first wave of mass ascension. The level of energy transmission was absolutely awesome. I had never experienced that level of God infusion in my entire life. By the end of the workshop celebration, the general consensus was beyond words. The only way I can describe it is that the synergy of all the energies achieved their maximum potential, and some mystical process took place that made the whole process go exponential.

The masters said that what took place went far beyond even their highest expectations. Djwhal said that he had never seen so many masters gathered in one location for one event in his entire experience of Earth service. One of the keys that allowed this to happen was the group consciousness, or unity, of the people who came. Somehow this group was able to transcend the negative ego and remain in love, oneness and group unity in a most extraordinary manner. This, I believe, was the key that allowed this exponential mystical process to occur. Every person in the auditorium was literally awestruck by the end of the celebration.

I am humbled, joyous and grateful to have been involved in such an event. I don't think I ever felt so much love and God infusion in my entire life. I will forever be transformed by this experience, as I believe will all who attended both physically and in their spiritual bodies. It led me to the clear inner guidance that I would no longer be doing smaller classes, but instead hold larger events. My inner guidance told me that within the next five years we would be holding events for 1000 to 2000 people. After experiencing what I did in Mount Shasta, I was hooked. I have never felt so honored to be a part of anything in my entire life. On a personal level, it was the perfect ending to my marriage, and I am sure my wife felt the same.

The core group and I decided to continue to host these types of mass events and go big time. The great success of my books, by the grace of God, would be the key to holding events as large as we wanted. When the workshop celebration was over, we were told one last extraordinary piece of information. To recapitulate, we had all gone together before Sanat Kumara at the actual Wesak ceremony and requested the anchoring of our twelve bodies (the seven bodies that correlate with the seven dimensions of reality plus the group-soul body, the group-monadic body, the solar body of light, the galactic body of light and the universal body of light). Anchoring these last three bodies was in truth truly the beginning of our cosmic ascension process. About four months earlier we had been told that this would take two full years to achieve.

When we were told three weeks before Wesak that we would be anchoring our fifty chakras, we were also told we would be anchoring our ninth body, which is the group monadic body (for more information, see *Beyond Ascension*). We were quite excited and grateful that achieving this level of integration would be occurring so soon. The timetables we were originally given kept getting drastically shortened. At the end of Wesak, however, all of us received this ultimate blessing and special divine dispensation: Instead of having to wait six more months to anchor and activate the solar, galactic and universal bodies (which would have been incredibly fast in and of itself), all of us received a special dispensation from Sanat Kumara to have it done *instantly!* This was performed by his holiness the Lord Sai Baba, who of course is a universal avatar.

What this meant is that we had now not only fully completed our seven levels of initiation, we had also now fully anchored and activated our fifty chakras, stabilized 99 percent light quotient and anchored and activated all twelve bodies, which include what some refer to as the five higher bodies. This completely blew my mind. In four years I had gone from a fourth-degree initiate to this level of completion, truly a miracle. The gratitude and humbleness I feel to have received such blessings is again beyond words. I just hope and pray that my service will be deemed worthy of the blessings that have been bestowed upon the others and me.

I am not sure if I should be talking about this so openly, but I chose to do so because the premise of this book is basically to tell all. I certainly don't mean for this to come across egotistically in the sense of, "Oh, look and see how great I am." Not at all. I share this as more of a personal map to show what is available, what needs to be done and how fast it can be done if you are focused and committed.

What blew my mind the most is how, when we work with the ascended masters and cosmic masters, they can, if they choose, give you instantly what could take years of hard work. Melchizedek told us that we were given this special dispensation because of our purity and commitment to service. Melchizedek said that it was not just a gift to us, but also because it was necessary for the service work needed for the expansion currently in place.

He also told us that there were strings attached. By this he meant that when much is given, much is expected. I share this so that those of you who will be making similar requests will be prepared to take on the responsibilities, service work, focus and self-discipline that accompany the completion of all your initiations, the fifty chakras, 99 percent light quotient and all twelve bodies. We are not special. What we have been given is given freely by the masters to all who are ready, to those who have prepared themselves and have completely dedicated their lives to service.

Mount Shasta Meditation

I also enclose here the anchoring and activation meditation I used during the Mount Shasta event. It was quite awesome to do this meditation with 300 high-level initiates and ascended beings. Spontaneous toning began to take place at certain points, which was quite wonderful and which continued throughout the entire weekend. This particular meditation is a high-powered one in which I tried to get the best activations ever invoked for this special occasion.

> *We call forth the establishment and activation of a gigantic ascension column and pillar of light in this place. Send the golden white ascension energy through our group consciousness—one body, one mind, one heart.*
>
> *Golden hands of Vywamus and Lord Michael's golden dome of protection.*
>
> *We call forth Djwhal Khul, Lord Maitreya, Master Kuthumi, the group merkabah, the Golden Chamber of Melchizedek ascension seat, Gaia, our Earth Mother, Sanat Kumara and Lord Buddha.*
>
> *We call forth the chohans of the seven rays—El Morya, Kuthumi, Serapis Bey, Paul the Venetian, Hilarion, Jesus/Sananda and Saint Germain—Ashtar and the Ashtar Command, Lord Arcturus and the Arcturians, and all 144 soul extensions from each of our monads.*
>
> *We call forth a planetary and cosmic axiatonal alignment and the opening of the ascension chakra.*
>
> *Sanat Kumara: we request the full establishment of our antakarana to our soul and monad, then all the way back to Source for the establishment of our cosmic antakarana.*
>
> *Lord of Sirius: anchor our cosmic heart and the full anchoring and activation of the twelve strands of DNA and the mayavarupa body.*
>
> *Metatron: we call for the illumination of the seventy-two areas of the mind as described in* The Keys of Enoch *and the opening of all mind blocks.*
>
> *Melchizedek: we call for the removal of all veils of light and time.*
>
> *We call for the anchoring of the garment of Shaddai, also known as the lightbody of Metatron, and the anchoring and activation of the seventy-two sacred names of Metatron. We re-*

quest to Metatron the anchoring of the microtron and superelectron in our entire four-body system.

We request the anchoring and activation of the 352 levels of the Mahatma.

Twelve archangels: we request the anchoring and activation of the twelve heavenly houses and the twelve cosmic stations.

Melchizedek: we request the permanent anchoring of our twelve bodies, especially now the five higher bodies (group soul, group monad, solar, galactic and universal).

Melchizedek and Lord Maitreya: we request the permanent anchoring of our fifty chakras.

Melchizedek, Metatron and Lord Michael: anchor now all fire letters, key codes and sacred geometries for highest possible ascension activation for the entire group.

Metatron: we request that you regulate the energy transmission for each person for the highest possible assimilation and integration.

Sanat Kumara, Helios, Melchior and Melchizedek: we request the permanent anchoring and activation of the planetary, solar, galactic, universal and cosmic Tree of Life.

We request the opening of all sephiroth on each of these levels by the logos in charge.

We request the opening of the hidden sephiroth of Daath at each of these levels.

We request the full opening of the seven seals so we may be directly linked to the cosmic Tree of Life.

Lenduce, Vywamus: we request an anchoring and activation of decadelta light encodements from the ten superscripts of the divine mind.

His holiness, the lord Sai Baba: we request now your ascension blessing and activation with a sprinkling of vibhutti ash.

Metatron, Melchizedek and Archangel Michael: we call forth a permanent anchoring and activation of the nine bodies as described in The Keys of Enoch *(zohar, anointed Christ overself, overself, electromagnetic, epi-kinetic, eka body, gematrian, higher Adam Kadmon and Lord's mystical).*

Elohim Councils: we request the anchoring on a cosmic level the Elohistic Lord's body, the Paradise Sons body and Order of Son-

ship body to facilitate our cosmic ascension, as well as plane-tary ascension.

The Lord of Arcturus, the Lord of Sirius and Melchizedek: we request the highest possible ascension activation we are all ca-pable of receiving.

Melchizedek: we request the activation of the cosmic fire under your guidance.

Melchizedek, Metatron and Lord Michael: we request a connec-tion to the Cosmic Treasury of Light at the 352nd level of the godhead. We ask now to receive the light packets of information from the cosmic book of knowledge, the elohim scriptures, the Torah Or, the cosmic ten commandments and the tablets of cre-ation.

We now call forth one final blessing from all the masters who have been invoked in this meditation and all who are gathered, and from all the masters you all have brought with you as your personal guides and teachers. We call forth now a combined light shower the likes of which this world has never known be-fore.

Lord, let the rain of blessings fall. [Chant three oms.]

We now call forth to Djwhal Khul, Lord Maitreya and Kuthumi to bring us all in our group merkabah back to Earth and into our physical bodies.

We call forth each of our individual inner-plane healing mas-ters and Archangel Sandalphon and Gaia to help us now inte-grate these energies and balance our chakras and four-body systems and properly ground our energies.

Meditation on May 21, 1995

In our next meditation, guidance was received on how to accelerate the process of activating and realizing the mayavarupa body. This was refer-enced by going back to some of *The Keys of Enoch* information we had al-ready been working with, but in a new way. We were told that one of the keys was to invoke the yod spectrum to infuse our zohar body, which would then create this corresponding activation in the mayavarupa body. I created the following prayer request that you, my readers, can also use to accelerate this activation. The prayer goes as follows.

Beloved presence of God, Melchizedek, Lord Metatron:
We hereby call forth the complete yod spectrum and ten lost ra-

*diations of divine light created from the divine letters and
sounds to anchor and activate, along with our zohar body of
light, the anointed Christ overself body and the overself body.
We ask that the yod spectrum fill our zohar body and bond our
four-body system, bringing it into the range of color and light.
We also request that this process helps us illuminate and fully
balance the seventy-two areas of the mind, and even more important, to realize fully our mayavarupa body and replace the
old cellular structure.*

With all the changes that had taken place and our newfound completion, I also felt guided to write a new, more cosmic meditation for our core
group and myself. The following is that meditation for your enjoyment.

Cosmic Meditation

Go first to the Golden Chamber of Melchizedek.

- *We request the full activation and actualization of our fifty
  chakras.*
- *The full activation and actualization of our twelve bodies.*
- *A cosmic axiatonal alignment.*
- *The full anchoring and activation of the 352 levels of the Ma-
  hatma.*
- *An anchoring and activation of the Elohistic Lord's body, our
  Paradise Sons body and Order of Sonship body.*
- *The full anchoring and activation of the Lord's mystical
  body.*
- *A deeper penetration of our cosmic walk-in status with the
  Mahatma.*
- *A deeper and more profound merger with Melchizedek.*
- *The full and complete anchoring, activation and actualiza-
  tion of our zohar body of light, the anointed Christ overself
  body, our own overself body, the gematrian body, the eka
  body, the epi-kinetic body, the higher Adam Kadmon body
  and the electromagnetic body.*
- *The complete yod spectrum to fill our zohar body and bond
  our four-body system to help us fully realize our mayavarupa
  body.*
- *The complete illumination and balancing of the seventy-two
  areas of the mind.*
- *A deeper anchoring and penetration of the lightbody of
  Metatron.*
- *A deeper anchoring and penetration of the microtron and*

superelectron of Metatron.

- *The seventy-two sacred names of Metatron.*
- *The anchoring and activation of the twelve heavenly houses and cosmic stations on a permanent basis.*
- *Anchoring and activating all fire letters, key codes and sacred geometries to help us fully actualize our fifty chakras and twelve bodies.*
- *Anchoring and activating all fire letters, key codes and sacred geometries on an ongoing basis to help us realize our mayavarupa body.*
- *An anchoring and activation on a deeper level of the cosmic Tree of Life and the opening of the seven cosmic seals.*
- *An opening of the ten sephiroth on the cosmic Tree of Life and the opening of the hidden sephiroth of Daath and/or the hidden knowledge of the divine mind.*
- *Anchoring and activating the decadelta light encodements from the ten superscripts of the divine mind.*
- *An ascension blessing and a deeper universal activation from his holiness the Lord Sai Baba to help us actualize all that has been anchored.*
- *The complete spiritualization of our blood chemistry.*
- *The complete anchoring of the biostratus and/or twelve strands of DNA into our actual physical vehicle, not just our etheric.*
- *An activation of the Throne Light Pyramid of the next universe. The anchoring and activation of all living energy codes so that our nucleic membranes may attach to the larger membrane of the universe of Melchizedek and YHWH.*
- *A special dispensation from Melchizedek for an anchoring of all Melchizedek technology to help us fully actualize all fifty chakras, twelve bodies, all Keys of Enoch bodies, including the cosmic bodies.*
- *The deepest possible anchoring and activation of the cosmic monad and seven cosmic bodies correlating with the seven cosmic planes.*
- *A deeper penetration and ascension activation from the trinity of Sanat Kumara, Vywamus and Lenduce.*
- *A deeper melding with the energies of the Buddha on a permanent basis.*
- *A deeper connection to be established to the Treasury of Light at the highest cosmic level.*

- *An anchoring from the Treasury of Light of the light packets of information from the cosmic book of knowledge, the tablets of creation, the Torah Or, the cosmic ten commandments, the elohim scriptures, the scrolls of weights and measures, the Melchizedek scriptures.*

We now request a special divine dispensation from Melchizedek that all that has been requested be anchored, activated and actualized to be permanent and be continued every night while we sleep and relax, without having to go through the entire invocation every day and night. We ask for this so we may be of greater service. Amen.

May 23, 1995—Humanity's Mass Vote

Djwhal Khul notified us many months in advance that after this Wesak Festival there would be a mass vote by humanity on the inner plane to determine whether humanity wanted to continue moving at the same speed it had been previously moving, or if it wanted to begin a new upward spiral that was now being made available. May 23 was when this vote would take place. Djwhal guided us to consciously vote on this day. The tremendous success of the Wesak Festival was a great catalyst, besides the great work that lightworkers around the planet were doing. I am happy to say that humanity's vote was a yes, which is a great compliment to all the wonderful work of the lightworkers.

Meditation on May 28, 1995

Today's meditation was filled with our questions and the answers from the masters. The first thing we wanted to check out was the issue of anchoring and activating the twelve bodies. As it turned out, I had partly misunderstood what the masters had said before. Upon further questioning, the boon we received from the Wesak Festival was the installation of our twelve bodies. The anchoring of the bodies and chakras is always a three-part process. The first stage is installation; the second, activation; and the third, actualization. We had now fully anchored and activated our fifty chakras, but had not fully actualized all of them. In terms of the twelve bodies, we had anchored or installed them, but not activated or actualized them.

I had thought we had anchored and activated them, but I hadn't considered these three stages. The installation of the solar, galactic and universal bodies is obviously nothing to shirk. We were now told that to activate the bodies, it was necessary for the core group to get together physically for about four days. The masters strongly emphasized its importance. We decided to do this in July, about seven weeks away. We were told that we would need four days of meditation to create the physical bonding. At this time we would activate the solar, galactic and universal bodies. We were also told that we were prototypes in this process and that this focus on the fifty chakras, twelve bodies and even cosmic bodies we were working on had not been done before in this way.

Remember that in the past, the masters used to leave after the sixth initiation. We were now focusing on our cosmic ascension, and much of the work we had been doing had never been focused on before. We were also told that one of the keys to activating and actualizing this whole process as well as the installation was our commitment to service. If we weren't as committed to service as we were, we would not have been allowed to move forward in this process.

A big focus of our work was not only to accelerate people's ascension process but also to prepare people to move into their service work at their highest potential. A lot of people in the ascension movement are focusing on their ascension, but not on their service work. The service work is one of the keys to actualizing your ascension.

This brings me to the next point: understanding when we actually complete our ascension. After our meditation I meditated alone on this point. What I received was that ascension begins at the moment we receive the rod of initiation from Sanat Kumara upon taking the beginning of the sixth initiation. Our ascension is complete after we complete the sixth initiation and take the seventh. We are not completely freed from the wheel of rebirth until we take the seventh initiation.

Ascension can be divided into two types: planetary and cosmic. One of the major tasks of my mission this lifetime is to explain to humanity the process of cosmic ascension as well as planetary ascension. This is being made available to humanity for the first time. There is some overlapping between the two processes. Even though one's ascension is achieved after completing the seventh level of initiation, there is still the issue of anchoring the fifty chakras and twelve bodies, as well as stabilizing the light quotient. After completing the seven levels of initiation, one is certainly a full member of the Spiritual Hierarchy.

Most masters in the past, as I said before, left after taking their sixth, certainly after their seventh initiation. Upon completion of our seven levels of initiation we had actually anchored and activated our fifty chakras. I do think, however, that we were precocious in this regard. The sixth initiation corresponds with the sixteenth chakra in the crown. The seventh initiation, I believe, corresponds with at least chakra 22 for the beginning stage and maybe as high as chakra 36 for completion. I am not completely sure about this; it is only a vague outline or standard.

After completing the seven levels of initiation, we are operating out of the seventh, or logoic, body. However, it is possible and even likely that there will be simultaneous anchoring (installing) and activation of higher levels. The whole process gets complicated because of this issue of installation, activation and actualization. Our core group, being prototypes, is very advanced in our installation and activation of all the levels. This is available to all for the asking as long as you are committed to serving humanity and are sincere in heart and intent. In our case, our initiation level is very high and our anchoring and activation is now extremely high; however, we have not actualized all that has been anchored and activated. This is why we are not able to teleport physically, materialize things, raise the dead or turn water into wine. These might be called the advanced ascended-master abilities. We are fully ascended now, but have not actualized all that has been anchored and activated.

Melchizedek once told me that the key to teleporting was the installation, activation and actualization of the twelfth, or universal, body. One of the most frequently asked questions is, "If we are taking these higher levels of initiation, why don't we have these advanced ascended-master abilities?"

We live in a different time period of Earth's history. What took whole lifetimes in the past can now be done in six months. The first step is to complete your seven levels of initiation. The second step is to keep requesting the *installation* of all fifty chakras and twelve bodies. Then request the *activation* of these bodies and chakras. Then work on the *actualization*.

Masters used to have whole lifetimes, or at least fourteen years between lifetimes, to accomplish and practice these things. Now we have only one or two years or less to practice between initiations. This new dispensation allows us to achieve these great heights first before achieving advanced ascended-master abilities.

As you can see, there is an overlapping of planetary ascension and cosmic ascension. We are is ascended when we are in the fifth dimension. The fifty chakras take us all the way to the ninth dimension. The twelve bodies take us through the solar, galactic and universal levels, which is up through the twenty-fourth to thirty-sixth dimension. The truth is, however, that on Earth we can never really fully actualize the solar, galactic and universal bodies at humanity's level of initiation. Humans are really actualizing only a very small part of those levels. Sai Baba would be a different case because he is coming in as an avatar at a level perhaps as high as the twenty-second initiation. (His light quotient is 31 percent on the cosmic level and Lord Maitreya's is 10 percent on the cosmic level.)

Our core group has now been told that there is no limit to our light-quotient-building process. At first the ascended masters seemed to give us limits, but now they tell us that the sky is the limit. It is quite amazing to be working now on our cosmic ascension as well as the final actualization of our advanced planetary-ascension abilities. Writing this section has actually been helpful to me in clarifying this overlap.

I asked Melchizedek to program our new cosmic meditation, the twelve-body anchoring and activation process and the process of anchoring and activating all the *Keys of Enoch* bodies into the golden chamber ascension seats. (I am one for efficiency.) This way I can just sit in the ascension seats and let the whole process take place and not have to do all this invoking.

I also questioned Melchizedek today on the issue of the cosmic bodies beyond the twelve-body system and the zohar, anointed Christ overself, overself, gematrian, electromagnetic, eka, epi-kinetic and higher Adam Kadmon bodies. Melchizedek told me that the cosmic bodies (Elohistic Lord's, Paradise Sons, Order of Sonship, Lord's mystical and seven cosmic bodies that correlate with the seven cosmic planes) would be our next step.

This was very exciting to me. After completing our final activation and then actualizing all fifty chakras, twelve bodies and *Keys of Enoch* bodies, we would then be allowed to move into and anchor this next level. We had already begun doing this now; however, we were a little ahead of ourselves. This would also entail a greater merging with the cosmic monad, or cosmic I Am, not just the planetary mighty I Am Presence of the monad. This would deal with a much greater merger with the Avatar of Synthesis, the Mahatma.

The masters also told us that part of the process we were in was to totally actualize all these things into the physical so that the physical body would actualize these things as well as the emotional, mental and spiritual bodies. This would ultimately lead to physical immortality and other such advanced ascended-master potentialities.

This issue of paving the way for cosmic ascension is one of the most exciting endeavors I have ever been involved with. As I receive more and more information on this, it is my great joy to channel it to you, my readers.

Brian Grattan's passing to the spirit world came as a great shock to me, and I am sure to most people. With his passing I felt an added responsibility to my mission because of our mutual connection to the Tibetan Foundation, Janet McClure, Vywamus and Djwhal Khul. Although I had previously been given the post as a spokesperson for the planetary ascension movement, I felt like Brian and I were both carrying the torch of spreading the teachings of the Tibetan Foundation and the understanding of cosmic ascension on a mass scale through our books and workshops. I never physically met Brian, but I knew we were connected through our work.

Meditation on June 1, 1995

We went to the Golden Chamber of Melchizedek and invited Djwhal

Khul, Lord Maitreya and Melchizedek, as was now our regular procedure. Melchizedek told us to repeat our Huna prayer in our next meditation with the other core members. The combined force of all of us, rather than any two of us, was more powerful, he said. This was the Huna prayer for the activation of the twelve bodies that we had done a few days earlier.

That week I had book contacts from four different countries to have my book translated and published, so I asked for help in firming up those deals and contracts and in spreading my books globally. I felt we were ready to make a big shift. I was also having a problem getting the Mount Shasta High School for the next Wesak Festival because someone else had already reserved it. My friend had offered them $500 to shift, but I felt it could still go either way. Melchizedek told me to offer them $1000. This seemed like good advice, for if we could get Mount Shasta High School, we could have 800 people attend next year's event in May.

My friend had a dream about a certain geometric formulation for physical immortality the previous night. I immediately requested that this geometric formulation be anchored into our gematrian body. Melchizedek said it had already been done on the inner plane during her dream experience, which I had attended but was not consciously aware of.

I also asked for a clearing of my home. Melchizedek said this was now being done and that the Lord of Arcturus was placing a dome of protection around it. My former wife and I remain good friends, so this request was simply a standard procedure used anytime there is a change in relationship or change of roommates. (I could feel that most of this had been done already, but I was going for its perfected expression. I would recommend that others do this on a regular basis in their homes and in all relationships to maintain clarity.)

I felt very inspired in this meditation; I was on a roll. We then called in Helios to help us activate our solar body of light. He came through very strongly with the other masters I have mentioned. Then we called Melchior to help activate our galactic body. We then called Sai Baba and Melchizedek to activate our universal body. Like Jacob in the biblical story, I felt as if I was now holding onto Djwhal Khul's, Lord Maitreya's and Melchizedek's feet and would not let go until they blessed us on this matter of fully activating the solar, galactic and universal bodies.

I had some in-depth questions about *The Keys of Enoch* material, but Melchizedek suggested that I wait for the other member to be present, because the three of us formed a trinity, and each held a key for the release of this new cosmic information. I then requested the full installation and activation of our electromagnetic body on a permanent basis with all necessary geometric formulations to achieve this goal. We then requested the full actualization of the gematrian body with all geometric formulations to be put into it to achieve the highest Christ potential. We then moved to the zohar, anointed Christ overself and overself bodies, requesting the full installation, activation and actualization of these bodies with all necessary geometric formulations.

Then I requested the full installation, activation and actualization of our Adam Kadmon and higher Adam Kadmon bodies with all appropriate geometric formulations. I then requested full installation, activation and actualization of our eka body and all geometric formulations to help us achieve our highest potential in terms of time travel. We then moved to the epi-kinetic body and requested the installation, activation and actualization with all appropriate geometric formulations to help us learn to teleport. Then we requested all geometric formulations to help us achieve all advanced ascended-master abilities. (I was on a roll now.) Then I requested the full anchoring and synthesis of all these bodies so we could achieve the full revelation of YHWH on a permanent basis.

The meditation continued, in an inspired form, with the cosmic meditation a number of pages back. I requested that this massive anchoring continue all day and also be continued at night while we slept. Melchizedek mentioned again the issue of our being prototypes for much that we were involved with, and he encouraged us to trust and stand behind all we were receiving. He said the work that we were doing was the cutting edge of the planetary ascension movement.

He also told us that some would challenge some of the information that we were receiving. I nodded, for in a couple of cases this had already begun to happen. In becoming friends with many of the people in the field, I had been receiving a few calls questioning some of the information we were being given. I, of course, did not mind this, for I am not attached to anything I have written. My goal is truth, and if I find it someplace besides my own books, that is fine with me. What I was running into, however, were the negative egos of some of these people who were clearly attached and at times even self-righteous about their information. I clearly felt that they weren't quite as open as I was to learning. I have been amazed to see how strong a grip the negative ego has even in the most advanced people. This is something all of us need to be constantly aware of.

One other insight I had this week was how many lightworkers are waiting to be of service until after they ascend or reach certain spiritual goals. In my opinion, this is the wrong attitude and perspective. The idea is not to wait for the masters to tell you what to do or until some new revelation comes or until some future date, but rather to use what you have now regardless of your level of initiation. There are always people who will need your service. The speed of your ascension process is also intimately tied to your willingness to get out there and serve. One of the main reasons our little core group had advanced so rapidly was because of our commitment to world service. When the masters see that commitment in action, they are allowed to give certain special dispensations and boons that lack of commitment to service will not allow.

My suggestion is to take the risk now. Don't wait until you feel totally comfortable, or that day might never come. One lady I spoke with was clearly in that position, and I invited her to use my books as the basis of her service work. She had the misconception that she had to reinvent the wheel or come up with some new information.

There is nothing wrong with using other people's information in what you teach as long as you give them credit. The main reasons I have been given the job positions in the spiritual government is because I put myself there through my own creative and hard work. I didn't wait for the masters to tell me what to do. On my own merits I creatively served where I saw a need, using the talents and abilities that I felt I had. In a sense, I acted like an ascended master long before I really was one. Eventually, the masters couldn't help but notice me and take interest in the work I was doing.

I did not come into this life as an avatar—not even close. I was not predestined to take over Djwhal Khul's ashram or become a high priest or spokesperson for the planetary ascension movement. I am again reminded of a statement by Djwhal Khul in the Alice Bailey books where he says that sometimes the average man surpasses the genius because the average man has to work much harder and often develops better work habits. This is certainly the case with me. I was never destined to be in the situation I am now in. I have now far surpassed all the goals I had set for myself before I came into this incarnation. What has helped me most are my superior work habits and, by the grace of God, my ability to keep my head screwed on straight to get to the position I am now at. Love- and light-quotient building and service are forever the keys to the ascension process.

We meditated one more time later in the day to clarify one theoretical point that had to do with the dimensions. Melchizedek told us that there were forty-nine dimensions to the Godhead. Upon deeper questioning, what he saw was that when one reaches the forty-eighth dimension, one has stepped into cosmic ascension. (Melchizedek, the Universal Logos, is between dimensions 36 and 48.) The forty-eighth dimension is the beginning of cosmic ascension and the forty-ninth is its completion. He also said there were an infinite number of dimensions, for even though one has merged with the seventh cosmic plane, the 352nd level or the forty-ninth dimension, greater and greater levels of purification and refinement can always be obtained. Thus the number of dimensions is infinite. He emphasized, however, that it was appropriate to use the three systems of the seven cosmic planes, 352 levels and the forty-nine-dimension system, which are all charted in *Beyond Ascension*. Melchizedek said that these weren't the only systems that could be used, but for our purpose and for the planetary service work we were involved with, these were the three that he wanted us to use.

Meditation on June 10, 1995

In this morning's meditation we focused on trying to gather more information on the *Keys of Enoch* bodies and the process of how to activate bodies ten, eleven and twelve, which are, of course, the solar, galactic and universal bodies. Djwhal told us that it would take a lot of work to activate them. All the other activations up to this point were really dealing with the planetary level. The full activation of these bodies would truly be the beginning of our cosmic-ascension process. The masters said that this would be a major step for us. Melchizedek, Lord Maitreya and Djwhal Khul said that to activate these bodies, one must truly be operating outside the negative ego. I was actually glad to hear this, for in spite of all the other activations and initiations up to this point, even the anchoring and activation of the fifty chakras, one can still be largely run by the negative ego. This might be hard to believe, but it is true. The masters were very firm this morning that this is not the case when activating the solar, galactic and universal bodies.

In a sense, we learn to see through the eyes of these bodies to activate them, and this requires us not to see life through the limited perspective of the negative ego. I was pleased to hear this, because it was a great concern to me that people could complete their seven levels of initiation and anchor and activate their fifty chakras and still be egotistically run. I knew in my mind and heart that there must be someplace where people would be held accountable psychologically, and apparently this is it.

The masters told us that our core group had now activated up through the ninth body and were now at the beginning of the tenth body. They told us that Melchior and Lenduce, on the galactic-body level, and Vywamus would be very helpful in the rewiring work that would be needed on all the bodies. Now that our seven levels of initiation were complete and we had installed and activated our fifty chakras, we were given permission to activate the first nine bodies. I was all gung ho to activate the final three bodies (solar, galactic and universal), completing the activation of all that had been installed. There felt to me a certain completion in having fully activated the seven levels of initiations, the fifty chakras and twelve bodies. Our final work after this would be to actualize the fifty chakras and twelve bodies.

I felt very much like Jacob in the Bible under the tree sleeping, who, out of the corner of his eye, saw the angel. He grabbed the angel's foot and would not let go until the angel blessed him. I didn't ask today; however, I knew we had just about stabilized our 99 percent light quotient. It now felt for the first time that we were beginning our cosmic evolution and cosmic ascension process while still in the process of actualizing our advanced ascended-master potentials. I felt ready to take another quantum leap. The three of us getting together in six weeks was instrumental in this process.

This whole process was also tied into this new professional transformation I was going through of not doing smaller groups anymore, but focusing on much larger events. I was already beginning to plan the next Wesak event. Just as we were now growing much bigger professionally and expanding our service work globally on all fronts, I felt personally that we were now ready to receive this added voltage and activation of our solar, galactic and universal bodies. I had made up my mind that I was going to be relentless in my focus to achieve this goal for all of us.

To begin the meditation aspect of our work together as opposed to the information-gathering phase, we began by doing the following Huna prayer. We felt we were really requesting a divine dispensation to be allowed to do this now. It was again emphasized by our triune teachers that no one would be allowed to achieve this without total commitment to service. There seemed to be a kind of ring-pass-not at this point that required much more stringent controls. I felt that this next three months was one of the most important three months of my life in preparing for the four days of work we would be doing together at the end of July. I felt that this would be the completion of a very long and profound phase of my life. These last three months felt like the dessert of an incredible four-year meal.

A Huna Prayer

Beloved presence of God, Melchizedek, Lord Maitreya, Djwhal Khul, Sathya Sai Baba, Lord Metatron, Lord of Arcturus, Kuthumi, Lord Buddha,

We hereby pray with all our heart and soul and mind and might as initiates in good standing for a special divine dispensation on our behalf. We hereby pray for the complete activation of our solar, galactic and universal bodies so we may be of greater service. We request this now for the core group and collectively feel we are now ready to take this next step in our personal and planetary service work. We now pray for a miracle of your collective divine handiwork to make this come about. Amen.

Our beloved subconscious minds, we hereby ask and command that you take this thought-form prayer with all the mana and vital force needed to manifest and demonstrate this prayer to the Source of our being through Melchizedek and the masters

194

we have invoked. Amen.

In our meditation we also learned a little more information on *The Keys of Enoch* bodies. Melchizedek told us that the anointed Christ overself body was the highest body in *The Keys of Enoch* system of the zohar body and overself body. We were told that the zohar body contained certain wave patterns or wave frequencies that were different for each monad. The length of these wave patterns and the spacing between them determined a person's development. The more advanced the person is, the more charged the particles of these bodies would be. We were told that the zohar body was initially anchored for most individuals at the fifth initiation, and the process would be continued until completion of all seven levels of initiation.

When we looked at the overself body, it looked like a silvery luminescent cloud that seemed to contain all colors within it. The overself body seemed to correlate with the ninth level, being, in a sense, the top of the planetary-consciousness hierarchy. It seemed to oversee the collective personal monad and soul extensions. This seemed to be just that level we were now working with and moving to graduate from. The zohar body seemed to correlate with the twelfth body or the universal level, and the anointed Christ overself body was above it.

The following information is a more in-depth look at *The Keys of Enoch* bodies and their function. The current focus of our work seemed to be to activate and actualize the solar, galactic and universal bodies and these *Keys of Enoch* bodies. I would also guide you to the study of *The Keys of Enoch* for further information. I have tried to give the following synopsis.

The Zohar Body

In *The Keys of Enoch* the zohar body is described as the body vehicle of outer light, which permits the body to go beyond the light cone on immediate relativity. The body places a body of light around the four other energy vehicles of incarnation so that the physical body can distinguish between the sacred and the profane spaces of light. The zohar body has been esoterically referred to as the coat of many colors. This body corresponds with the heavenly Jerusalem. Through the zohar body the "seventy-two areas of the mind are balanced off" and the microcosmos of the unconscious man ascends to the sonship and the Father's Throne. The zohar body functions in trinity with its overself body and the anointed Christ overself body, which receives direct revelation from the Throne worlds of YHWH.

The Cosmic Overself Body

The Keys of Enoch refers to the cosmic overself body as the preexistent higher body of light that exists for spiritual physical beings prior to their incarnation. This body "domes" with the realized physical humanity, which has completed the synthesis of the five inner matter/energy vehicles. There seems to be a differentiation here between the cosmic overself and the overself, the overself being related to the eighth body or group soul level.

This is the hierarchy of bodies in *The Keys of Enoch* system:

- Lord's mystical body—352nd level of the Mahatma
- Elohistic Lord's body
- Paradise Sons body
- Order of Sonship body
- Anointed Christ overself body (Sons and Daughters of Light)
- Zohar body
- Overself body
- Self-realization (synthesis of vehicles)

Gematrian Body

The Keys of Enoch refers to the gematrian body as the vehicle of light synthesis in the body form by the Shekinah's (Holy Spirit) life force, which controls all inner relationships of light. This body prepares the human vehicle to be connected to the anointed Christ overself body. On the physical plane, it can control the ratio between the plasmic state of living things and their atomic-molecular matter. The gematrian body is made up of light geometries used in consciousness energy meridians of the human system to make them available to guide and energize the body. The gematrian body with the Shekinah bears witness that we are active people of God and actively dwelling in a body of light within the body of flesh. As a vehicle for the saints, the gematrian body frees creative life from slavery to the physical body.

The Adam Kadmon Body

The Keys of Enoch refers to the Adam Kadmon body as the light manifestation of the Paradise Sons and Lords of Light who have evolved (or been created) beyond body form as man knows it. The lightbody that has the ability to take on any form necessary to create and teach all manner of thinking creation, including superspecies creations that exist as energy creation. The Adam Kadmon is bestowed upon the lightbody, which becomes an extension of YHWH.

The Epi-kinetic Body

The Keys of Enoch refers to the epi-kinetic body as the biological plasma used by the energy vibratory body for projection and teleportation within a single dimension. The epi-kinetic body is the consciousness vibratory vehicle that can pass through the common kinetic paradigms of velocity and mass.

The Eka Body

The Keys of Enoch refers to this body as the consciousness vehicle used for time travel. It comes in at the higher stages of the seventh initiation.

Meditation on June 15, 1995

We did a short meditation in the late afternoon, out of which something incredibly profound came. We were in the Golden Chamber of Melchizedek talking to him when we began to talk about the core group's upcoming trip to Los Angeles for our big pow-wow. The idea was to spend four full days together doing nothing but meditating and doing spiritual work. This seemed essential for the complete bonding of our trinity. As we were discussing this, I asked Melchizedek what the highest purpose of our coming together was. He told us that it was for the purpose of solidifying our group bond not only into the physical, but also to form a group body and group identity far beyond what we had yet conceived.

Let me try to explain. What the three of us were being asked to do is form a triune bond. We were being asked to form a group consciousness, in actuality a literal group body to the point where we would no longer be three separate entities. Even though the three of us have exceptionally high love, friendship and cooperation. we still were three individuals. Melchizedek was asking us to now take the next step and not be individuals anymore, but rather a group being, like an amoeba or three cells living within a larger body.

A marriage would be the closest term I could find, but what Melchizedek was suggesting as our potentiality here is beyond marriage. It is like the way a mother views her newborn child. The child energetically and aurically is a part of her with no separate identity. We were being asked to become literally a group being. Within this group being we would still have an individual identity, but it would be as if we would have two bodies instead of one, and our individual identities would now live within the group identity.

Do you see how profound this is? What Melchizedek was asking us to do is form a pact of group-identity consciousness different from marriage in the sense that it would be on the friendship and spiritual and professional level.

This group identity would make us invulnerable in our movement into our world service work. All decisions would be made within the global consciousness. In truth, this is the way the masters function on the inner plane. We were, in effect, an experiment in functioning this way while still within the physical vehicle. At first I felt a little fear about it and wondered what the fear meant. It came from a sense of losing self. As my mental and emotional body began to adjust into it, however, the fear left and the profundity of what we were being asked to do set in. I would still have a sense of self, but it would be in the context of a larger group identity. Making the choice to step into this group identity provides an invulnerable protection, a commitment to one another, security and attunement. The reality is that we all live within these larger group identities all the time: the larger group identity of humanity and of all creation as cosmic citizens.

This can happen in marriage; however, people don't hold the group identity as part of the individual identity of this consciousness. When living within this group body, for me to create any egotism, selfishness, separatism or attack would literally be like fragmenting myself and/or symbolically cutting myself with a knife. Instead of seeing myself as living within my physical body, I would be living within three bodies instead. I would have the best of both worlds, with an individual *and* a group identity. I was aware that making such a commitment would have to be an exceptional circumstance and group of people. As I said, this is the way masters function on the inner worlds, but to do it while in body was an extreme challenge, a different prospect altogether.

To even consider this, all three would have to consciously commit fully to this. We would have to be of a very high level of spiritual attainment and egolessness to maintain harmony. In the Spiritual Hierarchy, masters in group meetings often disagree. However, Djwhal Khul told me that when the meetings are over, everyone always agrees. There is always a consensus. This is also how our group body would have to work. The timing was perfect, for we were now preparing to do a workshop at the next Wesak for 1200 people intended to activate the first three waves of mass ascension. All decisions from now on would have to be made within the context of the group body. All separation, competition, superiority or inferiority, selfishness, attack and fear would have to be let go of completely. We were being asked to completely lose all sense of self for the good of the three, who had sacrificed all sense of self for service to humanity as head of Djwhal Khul's ashram.

This was the state of consciousness we would need to hold in order to do this job right. It is the complete sacrifice of the negative ego. In making this choice I was aware that there were still remnants of my ego I had not cleared 100 percent. I am sure my friends would say the same. We were being challenged now by Melchizedek to take this leap.

Nothing was ever written in stone regarding the leadership of the synthesis ashram. There had been some changes in the leadership structure over time that had occurred in different stages. All names were removed so that we would not create a thought form that doesn't exist at present. For this reason I must be vague on this point. It is the spiritual work that is important, not the focusing on personalities.

At a later stage the leadership of Djwhal Khul's synthesis ashram changed to a triangular formation, with myself at the top of the triangle holding a slightly greater leadership than my two partners at the time. This was later to change again, where certain personages were removed from the leadership altogether, not out of judgment, but out of evolving desire and wishes of the masters.

I bring this up to demonstrate to my readers that nothing can ever be taken for granted, and that one earns leadership by the continual demonstration of self-mastery, Christ consciousness and passing the spiritual tests of power, egolessness, psychological clarity, spiritual discernment, fame and money, to name a few. What has been given can be taken away at any time at the discretion of the planetary and cosmic masters.

Meditation on June 18, 1995

This evening's meditation was the most profound experience of divinity I had ever experienced. The experience began rather innocently with my sharing the understanding of the group consciousness we had come to in the previous meditation. The fact that we had been given the job to take over Djwhal Khul's ashram in the year 2012 had actually begun this process for us; however, it would take our bond even further. Then we went into the golden chamber to talk to Melchizedek. I had just a few questions, but they were important ones. I asked about the solar, galactic and universal bodies. We were also getting vague information on this issue in terms of how and when we would be able to activate these bodies. They had been fully installed at Wesak, but we had not activated them. I wanted to pin down Melchizedek on this issue and receive clear, decisive information.

Melchizedek told us that it would take five years if all went according to plan. This made sense to me, and I saw now why I had been getting vague answers. I had thought we would be able to do it in three months, and that was why the guidance I'd been getting wasn't coming together. The fact was, every time we had been given a timetable such as this, we had done it in half the time. My inner guidance had told me it would take three to five years. This new, deeper bond between us would make a big difference, I could tell. Activating the solar, galactic and universal bodies was a major process and would truly take us into our cosmic ascension process. Five years was actually incredibly fast, but I knew it would be done faster.

Then I asked the final burning question—which turned out to be the answer to our prayers. Recently I had become friends with a very lovely lady who was starting an ascended-master newsletter and who was extremely supportive of me and my book series. I could tell she was an upcoming channel for the masters and had a keen intuition about spiritual matters. I had just sent her *Beyond Ascension,* about which she was quite enthused, and in one of her meditations she received information about an ascension seat of all universes.

This intrigued me, for the highest ascension seat we had been given was, of course, the Golden Chamber of Melchizedek at the universal core. I had actually tried to go higher, but at the time, Melchizedek told me that the golden chamber at the universal core was more than enough for my plate. We, of course, were at a much different level now, so I was curious about what Melchizedek would say. In the past he had spoken of the forty-three universes that make up the source for this cosmic day, and of course we had experienced these energies in meditation many times, which was a rare and extraordinary blessing.

I asked Melchizedek the question, and his answer astonished me. He told us, as we sat in the golden chamber, that indeed there was an ascension seat for the multiuniverses of this cosmic day. His golden chamber is the ascension seat for our universe, but this ascension seat is the one for *all* universes that make up our source for this cosmic day, and the source for our cosmic day is Melchizedek. I pressed him on whether there were forty-three universes. He did not seem to want to be pinned down on this number, so I let it go.

Then he told us an even more astonishing thing: that there was actually another ascension seat beyond the next one, from an even grander universe beyond the source of our cosmic day. He told us that this would be the ascension seat at the 352nd level of the Godhead and/or Mahatma. He forbade us to go there, saying that this ascension seat was so high a voltage that to sit in it before proper preparation would burn out the webbing of the etheric body and possibly destroy the physical vehicle.

We were told that we were now ready, under his tutelage, to try out the first ascension seat I spoke of—that of the multiuniverses of this cosmic day. He told us that this ascension seat was available only for those who had fully completed the seven levels of initiation. There was a similar danger in this ascension seat for those trying to go too far ahead of themselves. His clear instructions, which I share with you now, were to begin working on the planetary ascension seats I have listed in *Beyond Ascension* and *The Complete Ascension Manual,* then move to the solar ascension seats. After that, move to the galactic ascension seats.

As you approach your sixth initiation you can begin working more in the Golden Chamber of Melchizedek. As you complete your sixth and seventh initiation and stabilize the 99 percent light quotient and anchor and activate your 50 chakras, then you will be allowed to move to the next level.

Melchizedek told us that we were not allowed just yet to go into this new one by ourselves and that we were to do it together. This trinity we had formed would allow us to go further and receive more voltage than if we were on our own.

I am now going to give the strictest warning and instruction I have ever given. In your zealousness for spiritual growth, do not under any circumstances disregard the instructions in this matter. One of the fundamental lessons on the spiritual path is patience, timing and learning to live in the tao. To live in the tao is to not go too fast or too slow. All readers of this book are capable of completing their seven levels of initiation in this lifetime in a relatively short time. I debated whether to share this information here, but because of my deep and profound love for you, my brothers and sisters, I am sharing all. Please follow implicitly the instructions I am giving you, for they are not mine, but Melchizedek's, and will save you possible karmic repercussions.

Melchizedek had just read my deepest, innermost heart and was loving and spoiling me again. I cannot put into words my love for Melchizedek and devotion to him for his love and kindness and help. The longer we sat there, the greater the flow of energy and the greater the bliss. In my entire life I had never experienced a meditation such as this. The energy was very soft, smooth and healing. Melchizedek then did an extraordinary thing: he seemed to be washing our feet with the energy. He told us he wanted this energy to meld into the deepest aspect of our being.

We were blown away that Melchizedek was washing our feet. This cosmic being, at something like the 300th initiation, was washing the feet of these minuscule seventh-degree initiates! He was loving and spoiling us again. It was clear that he was also teaching us. Our mutual gratitude for the blessings he was bestowing upon us was beyond words. I felt humbled to my core. He told us that being here in this innermost chamber would have an enormous healing and balancing effect. Every aspect of our being would come into peace and balance.

He seemed to be channeling the energy through our mental body and then into our physical body, but bypassing the emotional body, which at this level masters don't operate from in the same way, he said. This, of course, is true of planetary ascended masters who don't have astral bodies. Emotions at this level are always the same—peaceful, loving, sweet, kind, forgiving, centered and so on.

We must have stayed there for twenty to thirty minutes. I felt myself getting very hot. I think stuff was burning up within me. As I write this I feel myself transported back there. Melchizedek also said that this would have a tremendous effect on raising our overall vibrational frequencies. Again he mentioned the fact that the three of us working together in such cooperation allowed us to have this experience. I felt completely transformed and altered forever, almost like feeling transfigured. Instead of looking up, I was now looking down. We had definitely taken a leap in our evolutionary progression by the grace of Melchizedek.

After about twenty or thirty minutes Melchizedek said it was enough for today, and brought us back. Before leaving, he again infused us with a blessing through his eyes and instructed us to carry this with us the rest of the night. During the next fifteen minutes I walked around my home feeling that I was walking on hallowed ground. I felt like I had touched the heart of God, which in truth I had.

Two other things: Melchizedek told us that he had already begun weaving the new group body even though the final "pact" would not be complete until the other two returned in about four weeks. The three of us were now fully moving into this new group-body state of consciousness. Melchizedek also planted within us a seed of this multiuniverse ascension chamber, which we would carry with us from now on. I sensed the magnetism it would lend to our world service—and possible scolding from the masters for not following them.

I share this information with you as a golden carrot to motivate you to keep your faith, commitment, self-discipline, patience, perseverance, personal power and love on this long journey. As you master each level, the level just above is unveiled and opened up to you. One is not allowed, however to skip levels out of childish impatience. Work with the ascension seats as I have instructed. This will prepare your nervous system, etheric body, physical body, astral body, mental body, nadis, chakras and light quotient to receive the next level of voltage. That is really what initiations are—just another level of stabilized voltage. You are being given here the cosmic map and plan for not only the completion of your planetary ascension, but also your cosmic ascension and your ultimate merger with the Godhead or Father-Mother God at the 352nd level or top of creation. Prepare yourself well, do your homework, and you will gain admission to the holy of holies.

This is the experience we were given this day. The golden chamber had been my favorite place in the infinite universe for the last two years. By the grace of God and Melchizedek, now I had a new favorite. Melchizedek first took us into his golden chamber and beamed energy from this higher level into us through his eyes and then into our third eye. He then scooped us up, and we began traveling through what seemed like a tube or small tunnel at lightning speed to the supreme center of all universes that make up the source for our cosmic day.

The cosmic day for our universe is 4.3 billion years before our cosmic night begins. Melchizedek told us that this center was where day and night merged. In the past we had received the energies of the 43 christed universes. We were now not just receiving these energies, but actually sitting in the center, from which these energies emanated. Melchizedek referred to this as the Great, Great Central Sun.

The "Great Central Sun" is a term greatly misused and misunderstood; it refers to the solar core. There is another Great Central Sun in the galactic core, then another in the universal core. There is still another Great Central Sun in the multiuniversal core, which we were now sitting in, and another, ultimate Great Central Sun that is the Godhead and the apex of creation. As I mentioned before, this last Great Central Sun is not allowed to be experienced, for obvious safety reasons, until one has completed the seven levels of initiation and stabilized the 99 percent light quotient.

One can call those energies forth. That is fine. The difference was that instead of receiving them on Earth, I was now resonating with the Source that was causing them. As we sat there with Melchizedek, the strength of these energies began to build and flow through us. It was the most exhilarating experience of my entire life. "Exhilarating" may be the wrong word; "blissful" is better. We were literally beating with what felt like the heart of God. Melchizedek looked extremely young here, not the bearded grandfather type as he is often pictured. Gathered around us were Melchizedek's senior initiates, most of whom are great universal teachers, including some who are from the Great White Lodge on Sirius. I felt incredibly honored and humbled to sit with such an exalted group of beings. It would be like sitting in a group of beings, all at the level of Sai Baba with Melchizedek as their teacher.

Melchizedek was incredibly sweet to us. He kept referring to us as his children. I told him my cup was truly running over, and he said this was quite true. He felt to me like a loving grandfather who was spoiling his grandkids in the most positive sense. He then said to me, without my asking, "Joshua, you have wanted to have a physical experience in the atomic accelerator and Arcturian starship, and you shall have it!"

I felt a little bit like how I imagined Kuthumi, El Morya and Djwhal Khul must have felt when they all lived in the same Tibetan village as fifth- and sixth-degree initiates. I felt that we were forming a bond of friendship and group consciousness in service of the Spiritual Hierarchy as they had. This metaphor is closer than I realized, as I think about it now, because Kuthumi handed down the responsibility of training his disciples and initiates to Djwhal Khul, just as Djwhal would do to us in the year 2012.

However, Kuthumi, El Morya and Djwhal Khul were more advanced in the development of their ascended-master abilities than we are. Interestingly enough, though, we were at a higher level of initiation than they were at that time. Djwhal left his body while still in the sixth initiation. I am almost positive that Kuthumi and El Morya left their bodies or took them with them before completing the seventh. Yet one can't really compare the two periods of history even though we are talking about fifty years. It is a thousand times easier to complete one's initiations now than it was in the past because of the enormous planetary acceleration that has taken place. We are all very blessed to be incarnated at this time in Earth's history.

The last thought I had was the possibility of actually experiencing the Source ascension seat that Melchizedek spoke of. It was here that he emphasized the danger of burning up the webbing of the etheric, astral, mental and physical bodies if one were to do it before being properly prepared. Basically he told us that we were not allowed to use it, but that there was the possibility in the future of experiencing it after we had acclimatized to the multiuniversal ascension seat. He said that none of us could handle it alone even in the future, but he gave us a carrot by saying that there was the possibility of doing it in the future as a threesome. He told us that this was one of the great blessings of working in a group consciousness. Having ascension buddies and a group body allowed us to carry a much higher voltage than any one of us could carry alone.

My intuition was that we would be allowed the great blessing of being able to experience this when the others came out to visit me in a month or two. We would be doing days of intensive meditation together, and I had made up my mind that I would ask. My feeling was that if the multiuniversal ascension seat was the heart of God, the actual Source or Godhead ascension seat would be the crown chakra of God. I made up my mind then that I would ask for this experience.

Meditation on June 24, 1995

This meditation was a real action-packed meditation. We began by calling in Djwhal Khul, Kuthumi, Lord Maitreya and Melchizedek for what I called a business meeting. I was all amped up about getting my books circulating worldwide. I gave the masters an update on my battle plan for doing this and asked for their advice and suggestions. They had some good ones, but I won't bore you with them. I then gave them an update on how the Wesak manifestation process was going along for 1200 people next May. I have to admit it was fun having business meetings with the masters. I don't think I have mentioned this before, but they are quite funny. They often joke and tease us about certain things, and we joke and tease them sometimes, too. We always seem to laugh a lot.

Anyway, then we did the following Huna prayer. I share this Huna prayer and some of the others to give you a sense of how we work with the masters so that you can use your creativity to do similar work, using the specific lessons and goals you have at the time.

A Huna Prayer

Go to the Golden Chamber of Melchizedek.

We hereby call forth the beloved presence of God, cosmic mighty I Am Presence, beloved Holy Spirit, Melchizedek, Sathya Sai Baba, Lord of Sirius, Lord of Arcturus, Lenduce, Vywamus, Lord Buddha, Sanat Kumara, Djwhal Khul, Master Kuthumi and Metatron.

We hereby pray with all our heart and soul and mind and might for one of the most profound miracles we have ever asked for.

We hereby pray that the sales of Joshua's books now begin to sell exponentially, like absolute wildfire, especially the first three books, and the others as they come out in the next months. We ask that all his books be translated in all foreign countries around the globe. We ask that the lightworkers around the planet embrace these books and share them with students, friends and family.

We ask for a divine dispensation from God that these books be ordered by every metaphysical bookstore in the United States and around the globe. We also request that all regular book-stores begin ordering and stocking them. We ask that distribu-tors start ordering books in such large orders that second and third printings are needed in the very near future. We hereby call forth the backing of the Spiritual Hierarchy and Cosmic Hierarchy in this endeavor.

We also request that all the New Age magazines and newsletters around the globe on their own, with my permission, begin ad-vertising these books and printing excerpts from them in their publications to spread the information. We ask for these things in total humility for the purposes of planetary world service and the fulfillment of God's divine plan.

Our beloved subconscious minds, we hereby ask and command that you take this thought-form prayer with all the mana and vital force that is needed to manifest and demonstrate this prayer to the Source of our being through our cosmic mighty I Am Presence. Amen.

In the next half of our meditation we focused on an entirely new amaz-ing turn of events that had occurred in the last ten days. Here is the back-ground: My friends had done a workshop in Seattle for around twenty peo-ple over the past weekend. From a financial point of view, after traveling across the country, it was a break-even proposition. However, the real reason for their coming turned out to be a newfound connection with Commander Ashtar and the Ashtar Command.

It turns out that Seattle is the capital for the Ashtar Command. At the workshop and over the weekend Ashtar and the Ashtar Command began downloading tons of energy and information that was totally unexpected. There were six extraterrestrial ships circling above Seattle: the Ashtar Command, Pleiadians, Sirians, Arcturians and what the masters referred to as planet M and planet R. Three of the ships were moving in a circular motion in one direction and three in the opposite direction, rather like two merkabahs moving in opposite directions. This, of course, is one of the keys to teleporting and raising one's vibration.

I spoke with my friends a number of times over the weekend, and Ashtar and the Ashtar Command was now supposed to become a regular part of our program and team. They were going to be downloading energy into the planet and into us for what seemed like the next twenty years. We were guided by the masters to call them in as a regular part of our basic program from now on. We were all very excited about this. In terms of extraterrestrials, we had been most focused on the Arcturians, but from now on the Ashtar Command and these other four groups would be playing a major part.

As our meditation began, Ashtar came forth and we began asking questions and exploring our relationship more fully. We requested from him and the Command free reign to help us and intervene in our lives as they saw fit anytime they wanted. We also shared our support of this downloading process. They appreciated our full conscious acceptance and invitation. I asked Ashtar for his help in activating our solar, galactic and universal bodies. He said that we were still in the process of strengthening up to the ninth level and to be patient.

This response was what later led me to ask Melchizedek about the timetable for this spiritual goal, which was five years. I was hoping that we could have achieved this goal much faster; however, I was aware now that this activation was a much bigger process than I had realized. I was glad to have this information, for it put me back into my tao in terms of the natural evolution of this process. Ashtar did say they would help, however.

He also spoke of six places on the planet where they were downloading energy. One was in Siberia. I asked where the others were, and he said that information would come through on another occasion when we had a map or globe with us. Ashtar also spoke of how he was connected to the atomic accelerator in Table Mountain. The atomic accelerator was also like a gigantic computer terminal to download information. When the time was right for us to go, they would be intimately involved in this process, just as the Arcturians would.

The Ashtar Command is, of course, the extraterrestrial or winged branch of the Great White Brotherhood. To have them on our team now as a partner was obviously a great boon to our program. We all felt quite excited about this downloading process and our future work with them. Ashtar also spoke of a certain process that was going on around the planet, which was anchoring the "mind" of Ashtar. This seemed to be a type of universal energy matrix we were now in a process of merging with. I don't claim to understand this completely, but I intuitively felt, as part of this process, that it was really profound and good. I truly sensed what a great and majestic soul Ashtar is, and what a tremendous asset and blessing he is to the planet.

The Ascension Rosary

I met a very lovely lady who came to our Mount Shasta workshop in May 1995. She is a channel for the Virgin Mary and lives in Mount Shasta. One of my favorite personal prayers is the rosary. I believe it is one of the most powerful prayers a person can do for personal and planetary healing and protection. The problem with it is that some of the language is right out of the Catholic Church. This has never bothered me much, but it bothers other people. This lovely person has channeled a rosary from the Virgin Mary called the Ascension Rosary, which can be obtained for $13 postpaid from The Mother Matrix, P.O. Box 473, Mount Shasta, CA 96067.

Global Healing Meditation and Training

In many of our meditations the masters began talking to us about a new global healing process they wanted to train us for, which they often used in the inner-plane ashram of Djwhal Khul and Kuthumi. Their guidance was to get a globe of the Earth or a map. Just as one can see a person's aura and work to heal it, one can do the same thing with the planet as a whole. They had mentioned this process earlier, but now went into it in depth. I couldn't attend the first training session, nor could I bring the experience into my conscious mind, but it was taped and transcribed, so I share with you what happened. I think this type of training we received could be practiced by a great many groups around the world. This work was part of our training in preparation for taking over Djwhal Khul's ashram.

The training began by gathering in the Golden Chamber of Melchizedek. The group was guided to place their hands over the map and use the love and light of the Arcturian technologies to tune in to the waves that move across the continents, working on specific areas as guided. The following are the notes taken from this meeting. I share these on behalf of the core group so that you can receive this training also.

A map of the world was placed on the floor of the domed chamber and we sat around it. In consciousness, all were gathered in the Golden Chamber of Melchizedek. In attendance were all the members of the Hierarchy, including Lord Melchizedek, Lord Maitreya, Djwhal Khul, El Morya, Serapis Bey, Quan Yin, Mary, Kuthumi, Sanat Kumara, Lord Arcturus, Sananda, Lord Michael, Hilarion and so on.

Seven of us were present, representing the seven ray masters. Our focus was on the highest mission of our country at the time. We also focused on healing the waters, thus healing chaotic energies of the emotional bodies. We began by clearing the energies from the Earth's core, then used our hands in motion together to create a vortex over the entire Earth, finally bringing the released energies up, dissolving them in the violet flame.

Next we were directed to focus our attention on Oklahoma City, releasing all the souls who were ready to go into the arms of the Christ, and assisting to remove thought forms of fear and anger. Someone in attendance saw the masters walking through the bombed building, helping the trapped people, loving them and healing them.

Healing work was also done in the oceans surrounding the United States. Sacred mountains came into our inner vision for blessing: Mount Shasta, Table Mountain, Mount Rainier. We spoke of the purging of shame from our human heritage. This includes the inner civilizations and all native nations. This healing of the inner civilizations and surface beings unites all the Earth and all life forms as we enter the fifth dimension.

Our attention was next directed to South America. It has been said that the Andes Mountains are the new Himalayas. Light upon light was showering into the rainforests and people, rain showers of light. Rain cleans, clears and purifies to clear away the dust.

Africa: Our focus was on lifting the curtain of doubt and fear of hunger and survival. Lord Maitreya's love pours into the children of Africa: "I am asking you to bless Africa in my name for all the children of the world."

"See the ascension flame ignited in the heart of Africa where the most primal veil is touched. It is woven of the Earth, sky, plant, animal, into the center of this ascension flame.

"Now vortex the energy and feel the establishment of the ascension column.

"Sweep through the Middle East, and end by sweeping through Russia. Send warmth to Russia, Siberia, China and Tibet."

Someone in attendance said, "As the lightworkers go forward to touch these places, let the light fill every cathedral, every home. Let this light of the Hierarchy infuse all so that no soul goes untouched."

Meditation on July 2, 1995

We began by requesting to go to the multiuniversal ascension seat in the Great, Great Central Sun. I had been going there on my own in the last three days, and I felt a big shift happening in my consciousness because of it. I had an agenda planned for this meditation, but it quickly slipped away when something quite unexpected occurred.

We were greeted by Lenduce, who is the higher aspect of Vywamus, who in turn is the higher aspect of Sanat Kumara, the former Planetary Logos. Lenduce, who is truly a cosmic being of an extremely high magnitude, invited us to a special meeting during sleep time later that night. We had received a special dispensation to receive a much higher level of energy. Lenduce said it was a universal and galactic energy we had not received before. He told us that it was the highest transmission of energy that the Earth was receiving at this time. This special dispensation was given to us and we were told that there were a few others on the planet who also would receive it. I knew that this dispensation was directly connected to the meditation we had done three days before at the multiuniversal ascension seat in the Great, Great Central Sun.

In being allowed to enter that ascension seat, we had moved up another level. I knew that stumbling upon this new ascension seat and having that experience by the grace of Melchizedek had opened the door. Lenduce was wearing a mushroom-shaped hat with what looked like a window on the upper end of it that surrounded the entire hat. Lenduce told us that this hat was a transmitting and receiving device that amplified the cosmic energies he was working with and helped him direct them. He then told us that we would be receiving a similar type of hat tonight at this meeting. The meeting was to last three hours and would be held in the Great White Lodge on Sirius. Lenduce told us that the energy we would be receiving was directly from the Godhead, transmitted through the Great, Great Central Sun to the Great White Lodge. It seemed we were now working directly with Source energy.

Lenduce then began to vacuum our fields with some kind of cylinder device to prepare us for this great blessing we were to receive. Needless to say, we were quite excited about this unexpected turn of events. Lenduce then began to put some new cylinders into our etheric bodies to upgrade our existing program. We were apparently being prepared for a more universal energy flow now, something like Sai Baba has, but of course we have not actualized or activated ourselves as he has. This seemed to be our first step.

Lenduce told us that this new energy would be like a remover of obstacles and that we were to use this energy in a focused manner just for this purpose. It would automatically flow from now on after tonight's meeting, but we were to call it in for specific projects. Lenduce guided me to use it for manifesting the 1200 people for the next Wesak Festival in 1996. He gave us a specific formula for working with this energy in a focused manner. I then spontaneously did a prayer invocation calling on this energy for

Wesak, for the distribution of my books around the globe and for the activation of our solar, galactic and universal bodies. I felt like we were being tuned up now to a much higher frequency, radiation and magnetic amplitude.

With all the work I needed to do and manifest during the next nine months, I felt the timing was perfect. I was aware that our own efforts had pulled us to this point, and then the special dispensation was given. I mention this to make the point that we all have to earn what we are given. I was given the job of spokesperson for the planetary ascension movement, but through my own efforts I was practically doing the job before I was given the position. That was why I was given the position. We had already been pulling in the energy before the special dispensation was granted, and that allowed us to stabilize it. Our new mushroom hats would be a great help. It reminded me of a flying saucer, which Lenduce agreed with. I also had the sense it could spin if needed. I felt like a radio station that the overseeing committee had just granted a much more expanded megahertz to reach a larger area.

The process of evolution is so amazing! I really felt now like I was starting to get a sense of how the process worked. Lenduce told us that the key to the process of raising the light quotient was to not just tap into it, but to learn to stabilize and hold it. Many can have an experience of tapping into higher frequencies in a group meeting or an extraordinary meditation, but the hard part is to tap in and then learn to remain there. Enormous fluctuations occur in lightworkers, which is part of the process. When the subconscious mind, negative ego, mental, emotional and physical bodies are not controlled, much leakage takes place.

Ronald Beasley used to say, "Much of the spiritual path is like donkey work." It is being able to mold the vibration and frequency of energy through the long periods of donkey work that stabilizes the light quotient. Then at those sublime peak experiences that Abraham Maslow spoke of, you break through to the next level of frequency and vibration. The process then begins again.

This is the process of completing initiations, anchoring bodies, chakra grids and light quotient. If we can learn to be even-minded in all things and keep our inner peace regardless of what is going on external to ourself, it can accelerate this process enormously. Melchizedek told us that except for brief moments, a master maintains this consciousness at all times. Lenduce went on to tell us that the mushroom hat also served like a storage battery for energy as well as a focusing device. We would wear it all the time on the etheric level. It would serve as a type of radar, both to transmit and receive.

This discussion then led to a few questions I had. I wanted to make sure Lenduce was complete, for long ago I had shelved any personal agendas, for obvious reasons. Melchizedek and Metatron appeared with Lenduce, saying they were ready for my questions. I first asked about the current mahachohan because we had never received a name for the office. The only thing I knew was that the next mahachohan would be Saint Germain. The masters told me that Saint Germain was so close to taking over this position that we could think of him as in it already. For this reason it was not necessary to have the old mahachohan's name.

I also asked when Kuthumi would take over Lord Maitreya's position as Planetary Christ. We were told that this would not happen for a while. I also asked if there were chohans for the five higher rays. (I had been asked about this, so I decided to check this out again.) We were told that there were no chohans specifically in charge of the rays.

Then I asked a question of major cosmic significance that I had been meditating on during the past week. This had to do with whether there were cosmic chakras. We had been told about fifty chakras; however, these chakras stopped at the ninth dimension. There were still thirty-nine dimensions to go to the Godhead. We had been given initiations, bodies and light quotient up through all the cosmic levels, but we had not been given the cosmic chakras. I had asked in the past, but sometimes information doesn't come through until one is at a level that can use the information. My intuition, by the grace of God, was right on. The final piece to the cosmic puzzle (I felt) was now revealed.

Melchizedek told us after much prodding and questioning that there were 300 chakras to take one to the forty-eighth dimension or the 352nd level of the Godhead or Source. There were fifty at the planetary level, fifty at the solar level, fifty at the galactic level, fifty at the universal level, fifty at the multiuniversal level (forty-three christed universes of this cosmic day), and eighty more that would take one to the Godhead. Added together, there are 330. Our core group had just completed anchoring and activating fifty chakras, which completed our planetary chakras. We were now in a position to start over again and begin installing and activating our first chakra on the solar level. Our cosmic ascension process was now just beginning. The same applies to the bodies. We had just installed and completed our nine bodies. The tenth body is the solar body. I was beginning to see now why the masters said it would take five years to anchor and activate the solar, galactic and universal bodies.

The next question I needed to ask was, in order to activate the solar, galactic and universal bodies, do we have to install and activate up through chakra 200? I will keep you posted on this research.

This was extraordinary information. The cosmic map was now complete. For the first time in my life I felt like I had a clear road map to achieving cosmic ascension. After this meditation I went for one of my ascension walks and received very clear guidance that my next book would be called *Cosmic Ascension*. In this book I would lay out in very clear, definitive and refined form how to achieve cosmic ascension after one has completed one's planetary ascension. My level of excitement about this book was off the scale. I couldn't wait to begin.

Melchizedek told us that the amplitude of these higher chakras was triple in power. The exponential power moved from 50 to 500 to 50,000 to 500,000 to 50,000,000. This explanation of the chakras made total sense to me. For if there were fifty chakras on the planetary grid, it made sense that there would be fifty on the solar level and so on, all the way up.

After typing this section, I received a call and we meditated for about five more minutes to clarify these final questions I had about the cosmic chakras. We called in Melchizedek and I asked him if there was a correlation between the solar, galactic and universal activation and the first 200 chakras. He told us there was. He told us that the timetable of five more years to activate our solar, galactic and universal bodies would be the same thing as activating our 200 chakras. Melchizedek then did a very interesting thing. He literally forbade me from asking him to call these cosmic chakras down. He did this in a very loving but firm way. He told us that after this last work that had been done, we were at our limit.

He forbade me from asking until next Wesak, which was ten months away. He said our focus should be on stabilizing the energy now, not calling in more. Our previous Huna prayers had been heard, and if all goes according to his plan, the solar, galactic and universal bodies and 200 chakras would be installed and activated by the year 2000, which seemed like the perfect time for such a monumental anchoring and activation. I felt humbled by the thought that it might actually be possible to activate chakra 200 within five years. I never dreamed such cosmic activations at that level were even possible. I honestly believe the fastest path of spiritual growth on the planet is working with the ascended masters.

Five years seemed like an incredibly short period of time to accomplish such a thing. This, of course, is all conjecture, for I knew in my heart that to achieve this we would have to manifest five straight years of perfect focus, discipline, commitment and attunement. We would have to prove ourselves to be free of ego and totally dedicated to service. We would also have to prove ourselves able to stabilize and hold each new dispensation of energies we received.

Melchizedek told us that there was an analogy between Wesak and this process. We were being guided to try and manifest 1200 people for the next Wesak Festival; then, Melchizedek said, we would go for the same amount or maybe one or two hundred more the following year. We needed to stabilize our ability to hold and do workshop celebrations for this many people before going higher. Around the years 1999 and 2000 we would go higher. Melchizedek told me that I should let my books do the foundation work for me so that at the workshops there would be no need to prove anything. This sounded good to me. I had never thought of this before, but if people read my books first, it would make things a lot easier, and a much higher level of global service work could be accomplished with this foundation.

In a strange sort of way I also felt good that the process was slowing down. In other words, we had done enough prayers. What we had asked for had been received and a timetable had been set up. That was quite miraculous, now that I was beginning to understand the profundity of what we had asked for. Taking into account the initiations, light quotient, cosmic bodies and cosmic chakras, we now had the basic information. Now I felt we could completely focus on our service work and Melchizedek would take care of the rest.

I have never felt more focused, disciplined and committed than I do now. I had made the ultimate vows to myself and God to never lose my focus even for an instant ever again. I now felt like this next five years would be among the most important of my entire life. Because the next leaps in consciousness were so monumental in scope, it was almost a relief that Melchizedek had forbade us to ask for any more. We had asked enough, and by the grace of God we were in the tao.

All that was required now was to remain in the tao without veering and without allowing ourselves to break attunement ever again. Breaking attunement would be giving in to the lower self and/or negative ego in some capacity. I felt more committed than ever to achieve an even greater level of refinement than I had ever achieved or been committed to before. I felt that God has graced me with this incredible opportunity, which in truth we all share, for what has been given to me is totally available to all, for God loves all his sons and daughters equally. I have never been more determined in my entire life to take advantage of such a blessing.

Ascension Tapes

One of the newest services I am offering is a set of four ascension-activation tapes containing five powerful meditations. I created them because people from around the country kept calling and asking me to do this. They dovetail perfectly with the books. The five tapes are:

1. Ultimate Ascension Activation Meditation
2. Core Love Meditation
3. 18-point Cosmic Clearing Meditation
4. Kabbalistic Ascension Activation and Meditation
5. Cosmic Ascension-Seat Journey

These four tapes can be ordered as a set or individually. I guarantee that they will blow your mind. The tapes allow you to personally experience the meditations I talk about in my books. They give you guided activation meditations to do in the comfort of your own home. Instead of having to make tapes yourself, I have done it for you. (To order, see the back of this book. Please tell your friends and students about them.)

Energy Evaluations

Most lightworkers I talk to have one thing in common. Everybody would like to have more energy and vitality, sleep less, have a stronger immune system and get rid of nagging health lessons that are unique to each person. There are many causes for these lessons, some spiritual, some psychological. Often, though, the cause is physical and energetic. Two dear friends of mine, Susan Bryant and Sandy Burns, have created Earth Elements to serve humanity in this regard. When I sense that my clients or students are having physical health lessons, I very often send them to Susan and Sandy for an energy evaluation.

Their work consists of evaluating energetically every organ and system in the human or animal body. This analysis can determine energy blocks and imbalances that are often the underlying cause of health challenges. When energy imbalances are found, Susan is guided by ascended master Djwhal Khul to create a custom program of nutritional, herbal, vibrational and homeopathic remedies to eliminate these blocks.

The focus of this process is to eliminate the original source of the problem, not just the symptoms. Susan has found that by eliminating the underlying cause of health challenges, the body can then, in its own miraculous way, regain and maintain its vitality and balanced health. When the body is in a healthy state, it vibrates with positive energy rather than the negative energy present when organ vitality is low. Positive energy is required for the body to heal itself.

The analysis for the energy evaluation is done by mail and requires a saliva sample or a photograph of the person or animal being evaluated. The energy evaluations also include a 15-minute phone consultation and a personalized food sensitivity list. If you would like to receive more information about energy evaluations, contact Earth Elements, P.O. Box 31149, Flagstaff, AZ 86003, (520) 527-1128, Fax (520) 526-6955, e-mail: earthele@azaccess.com.

Meditation on July 8, 1995

My friend and I did a short meditation with Melchizedek. She had been feeling a little bit under the weather and we were simply talking to him about what was going on. What Melchizedek said provided an insight I had not considered. This recent quantum leap we had made—moving to the multiuniversal ascension seat, the mushroom hat, working with the yod spectrum and the ten lost rays, working with the platinum ray, forming a group body, becoming official representatives of Melchizedek, Lord Maitreya and Djwhal Khul by sitting on the councils—was bringing in a higher octave of energy transmission. I had been thinking of this more in terms of the spiritual level and hadn't considered what it was doing to my physical body. Melchizedek told us that we were going through a physical cleansing that was one of the most profound the Earth has ever known.

The level of transmission of energies we were now running from the source of the forty-three christed universes of this cosmic day is obviously not a normal occurrence. I am sure all the inner-plane masters run this level of current or even higher, but it is very unusual to be physically incarnated and run this current on a regular basis. Remember, in the past most masters left their bodies after the sixth initiation. The work we were doing of anchoring and activating fifty chakras and twelve bodies, completing seven levels of initiation and even moving toward anchoring and activating 200 chakras and cosmic bodies and cosmic light quotient is quite unusual.

Focusing on cosmic ascension while still in a physical body is almost unheard-of on this planet and really became available after the Harmonic Convergence in 1987. The true window of opportunity for this acceleration is the window for mass ascension from 1995 to the year 2000, which Vywamus spoke of. So Melchizedek was speaking in this meditation of the profound clearing now going on cellularly in our bodies because of this new level of light frequency we had invoked. The higher the frequency, the deeper the potential for cleansing.

The other thing to be remembered by those wanting to move into these levels is that the higher you go, the more discipline that is required. If you lose your mastery on any level, be it dietary, mental, emotional or spiritual, the quicker and more powerful is the karmic repercussion. Be aware of this before invoking this for yourself. I would also like to remind you that what I am sharing with you is available to everyone. I am not special in the slightest. God loves his sons and daughters equally. Every single thing we have been given is available to you, and that is why I am writing this book. It is to show you what is available and tell you how we did it so you can do it more easily and quickly.

Every person on the planet will eventually reach these levels. Few books, if any, deal with this level of spiritual focus, and that is why I have written these books—as maps for making quicker progress. It is my hope and prayer that my example may be of some benefit to you, my brothers and sisters whom I love so dearly. Just as we have formed a group body, every person in the entire universe is one body in that same way. We just don't realize it. God has only one son or one daughter. What we give to each other we literally give to ourselves. Part of the reason I have been given much by God and the masters is that I have understood this law. To have all, one must give all. What I hold back from you through any sense of competition or comparing or ego would be literally holding back myself, for you are myself—because there is only one self.

My Melchizedek Dream

I had a profound dream a few nights ago that has had a very profound effect on me. In the dream I was taken to the high level on the inner plane where each person in the dream was taking his or her place in the hierarchy of the Spiritual Government. The dream was guided by Melchizedek. As I took my place, I heard him say to me, "You are one of my twelve prophets." At this statement I woke up. In thinking about the dream, I have always had this prophet theme running through this life. A prophet is like a mouthpiece for God. I know I have also had past lives as a Jewish prophet. It is a theme I relate to in the core of my being. In Djwhal Khul's terminology, my path has been that of a prophet, a practical mystic and occultist as well as a divine psychologist.

Something touched me very deeply when I was told I was one of Melchizedek's prophets. I love Melchizedek so very much. Of course, I consider Djwhal and Melchizedek two of my main teachers. More and more for all of us, Melchizedek's teachings and being are melding with Djwhal Khul's ashram, which Djwhal supports. Melchizedek said that each of us were indeed prophets or representatives of him on Earth. We were told of one other person we all knew who shared a seat. We were also told by Melchizedek that we had met one other, but were not given this person's name. He said that within a year's time we would meet all twelve. I had the feeling that this would culminate at the next Wesak Festival in 1996.

We were then told that we are also part of another council of twelve in Djwhal Khul's ashram. Even though we now hold the future leadership role, there were actually twelve who would sit on this council. Then we were told that on the galactic level there was a third council we were now sitting in that represented Lord Maitreya and Buddha, and that this council was still forming. We were told that together we held one seat, like a group body or group mind.

This made a lot of sense to me, since we hold a three-tiered focus in our normal ashramic work of Djwhal Khul, Lord Maitreya and Melchizedek. It would only make sense that we would be a part of a council at each of these levels (planetary, galactic and universal). I feel very grateful and honored to be a part of these councils and, to be perfectly frank, this is very much a dream come true, as are so many of the blessings we have received. I am also aware that with this process comes a lot of responsibility, which is quite sobering. When we move into these positions of responsibility, we are, in a sense, monitored and watched. There is no room for giving in to the lower self, being weak or giving in to the negative ego. Much is given; much is expected.

I think you will all agree that there is no better feeling in the world than the sense of egolessness that the *Course in Miracles* and other teachings speak of so beautifully: "To have all, give all to all." What is held back from your brother and sister, the negative ego tells you is held back from *your brother and sister*, but that is illusion. What is held back from your brother and sister is held back from *yourself*, for your brothers and sisters are a mirror that reflects whether you are thinking from your Christ mind or ego mind. At every moment of your life, make the choice to release the negative ego and choose God and the Christ consciousness.

This is what I have tried to do in literally sharing everything, as if each of you is my best friend. It is my hope and prayer that you receive it in the vein I have attempted to write it. I keep asking myself as I am writing this book, "Would this have been of benefit to me?" I keep getting a resounding yes. For I am sharing the exact process of how I have moved so quickly up through the initiations, dimensions and levels. I am not being secretive about it in the slightest, as most books have done in the past. As a matter of fact, I am doing just the opposite; I am sharing everything. In a way it is like an experiment.

I think humanity and the global lightworkers are ready for this information on a massive scale. I think I may be more optimistic about my earthly brothers and sisters than many of the masters on the inner plane, in terms of humanity's potentialities. I think humanity and the New Age lightworkers are ready to receive the highest information available and move with it. It is my hope and prayer to be a humble instrument for such a planetary quantum leap.

Meditation on July 12, 1995

This afternoon we had a very interesting meditation. We called forth what Melchizedek called a cosmic cellular clearing. Melchizedek said this was available only to initiates who had completed their seven levels of initiation. In this process we were surrounded in a triangular formation by Melchizedek, Metatron and Vywamus. Melchizedek disseminated the platinum ray. Metatron emanated a more electromagnetic type of energy. Vywamus was in charge of the electrical rewiring. We seemed to float in the air and were blasted from all directions. It was like drinking two pots of coffee. Melchizedek said that this was part of the process of rejuvenating the cells at the highest possible level. This energy broke away all the cellular debris and unwanted deposits at the deepest possible level. I personally found it to be very strong, and not something I would want to do every day.

Djwhal Khul Dream

Two days previous to the big pow-wow in Los Angeles I had a very powerful and important dream. It was during the time of the knights. In the dream a new king was coming into power who was younger and whom most people in this large auditorium were happy to see crowned. I was sitting in my seat in the auditorium, very pleased about this event. It felt like I was one of the knights or king's musketeers. A man walked down my row into the auditorium and asked the person to my left what my name was. He said, "Djwhal Khul." I knew immediately that this was not accurate. He then asked me what my name was, and I said, "Djwhal Khul." I knew in the dream that this was the truth. In the next scene I jogged off with an incredibly euphoric feeling about having a new king. I was on my way in a specific direction for my next spiritual focus or battle, so to speak.

Upon waking I was very moved. Djwhal Khul told me that the dream was an initiation dream of sorts. It was showing my current movement toward taking over his ashram on an inner plane, to take place in 2012. The fact that the new king was being crowned and that my name in the dream was Djwhal Khul symbolized my moving more fully into this position spiritually. I had been feeling very close and connected to him recently, even more than normal. I had been focusing a lot in the past on Melchizedek, but now I felt that Djwhal's energy was coming in again much stronger.

Djwhal said that my monad, his monad and the others' monads all shared a similar pattern. I have always felt connected to him and his teachings, more than any other teachings on the planet. He said that this was because of the pattern we all shared. Even though we had been offered this position together originally, I felt a certain connection with Djwhal, being of the same gender.

Again I was reminded of the channeled reading from Vywamus I'd had five years ago, in which Vywamus told me I looked like a younger version of Djwhal, something about the intensity in the eyes. Even though we don't come from the same monad or soul, if Djwhal had had a clone or twin brother, I was told I would be the closest thing to it on this planet. Our inner matrix pattern is very similar. I think this is why it feels so right to take over his inner-plane ashram. I was deeply moved by the dream and his words. I had never felt as close to him as I felt then. I felt very honored, humbled and comfortable taking on his name and mantle. The dream, as he said, reflected this movement.

Meditation on July 22, 1995

We had a quick meditation upon my friends' arrival into Los Angeles prior to our big four-day pow-wow. We went into the Synthesis Ashram and I had some questions for Djwhal about what it really meant to take over his ashram in the year 2012. He explained that Kuthumi is the chohan of the second ray and Kuthumi had asked him around fifty years ago to set up a second ashram called the Synthesis Ashram as a second extension of his own ashram. None of the other seven rays has anything like this. The second ray has it because of its particular focus on spiritual education, which makes the second ray the central pillar of the other seven rays. For this reason and because of all the work to be done to spiritually educate humanity, this third ashram was set up. In other words, the first second-ray ashram is really that of Lord Maitreya, who holds the position of the office of the Christ. Then there is Kuthumi, who is the chohan of the second ray and the World Teacher. He is also in training to take over the position of the office of the Christ. Then there is Djwhal Khul, who is the master of the Synthesis Ashram.

So you see, here there is a trinity of Lord Maitreya, Kuthumi and Djwhal Khul. In the year 2012 Djwhal Khul told us he will be going to the Great White Lodge on Sirius and we will be taking over Djwhal's Synthesis Ashram. Our core group will then form a trinity with Lord Maitreya and Kuthumi.

The Synthesis Ashram

The Synthesis Ashram has three floors, the first being Djwhal Khul's Synthesis Ashram, the second Kuthumi's ashram and the third Lord Maitreya's ashram. After speaking to Djwhal in this meditation, I began to understand more deeply what an honor it is to be offered this position. He told us that part of the reason we were given this position is our expertise in esoteric psychology. In moving into this position, our titles would be Masters of the Synthesis Ashram. For this reason we would be having a lot more contact with Kuthumi, and Djwhal said he would be overlighting us while living in the Great White Lodge on Sirius. Kuthumi would be the chohan for the second ray for the next thousand years, then a new chohan would be chosen.

I found myself fantasizing about the possibility of training for that position, but part of me would prefer going to the Great White Lodge on Sirius. At this moment I lean toward going to the Great White Lodge and following in Djwhal Khul's footsteps, not tying myself to the Earth focus. I am not sure I would even be qualified for such a position or if it is really part of my destiny. At this point I am not even prepared to take over D.K.'s ashram, let alone think that far in advance. It is an interesting thought, however.

Djwhal told us that Kuthumi had stopped taking on personal students a long time ago, with very few exceptions, but that because of this current window of mass ascension he has begun to take on more. In the past, he sent most of his students to Djwhal for training in the Synthesis Ashram. I have to admit that I feel very excited about the future possibilities of working so closely with Djwhal Khul, Kuthumi and Lord Maitreya. I am obviously doing it now, but once I leave my physical body or bring it into light, I will be able to attend all the meetings—and of course have total recall of everything, which I don't now.

By the grace of God our job will be to impart specific training to disciples and initiates on planet Earth for the next 125 years. Then we are scheduled to go to the Great White Lodge on Sirius. Lately I have been feeling very close to Djwhal and Melchizedek after dreaming that my name was Djwhal Khul and that I am one of Melchizedek's prophets. I feel that on an inner plane I am beginning to grow into these positions even though the full unfolding and maturation will be going on to the year 2012 and beyond.

As Djwhal Khul told us once, and as my dream reflected, it is like being crowned as a young king. Out of the 125 years, it will probably take 50 to 75 years to get trained properly on all the ins and outs of how to run such an ashram. Even though I am looking forward to going to the Great White Lodge on Sirius (as I am sure are many who are reading this book), I am also looking forward to training and the marvelous opportunity for service work. This will be an incredible period in Earth's history. Spiritual growth will be exploding on this planet and Sai Baba will be in his third avatar incarnation. It will be a very exciting time to be in this leadership position.

The Four-Day Pow-Wow

The five-day period we had scheduled together finally came. The ceremony we were spontaneously guided to do to sanctify our connection was to go to Disneyland—I'm not joking! They had built new rides like Captain EO, Star Tours and so on. We went for about four hours, and it was the perfect thing to do.

For the rest of the week we meditated from 10:00 to noon and from 1:00 to 3:00. We took a break and started again in the evening, along with seeing a few clients. We began with a very beautiful bonding ceremony that finalized the building of our group body.

These four days were the most elevated four days of our lives. The coming together of the group body allowed us to expand our consciousness in a way none of us had ever experienced before in terms of unity, oneness, energy transmission, intelligence quotient and spiritual merging.

We visited the Source ascension seat together for the first time, which was one of the major highlights of my entire life. We were given a very special tour of the Lord of Arcturus' starship, which was incredible. We did some amazing work on understanding cosmic evolution and the organization of the higher mind.

I felt that this coming together was the perfect place to end this first volume of my spiritual autobiography. I was guided by the masters to begin volume two, which would continue the journey, from the point of view of the five-year process, of how to anchor and activate the solar, galactic and universal bodies. This spiritual autobiographical series is really the account of my conversations with the masters and how I went about my personal evolutionary process with my ascension buddies. The rest of this section will highlight some of the experiences we had together, which I share so that you, my beloved readers, can use the information when the timing is right on your similar journey.

Our Group-Bonding Ceremony

We began our four days with Melchizedek telling us of our group meeting three centuries ago in a monastery at the foot of the Himalayas. He told us that at that meeting we took the third initiation together and set in motion the fourth and fifth, leading to this incarnation and the millennium. He said that at that meeting a key code was placed within us that was to remain dormant until this incarnation, when we would take the responsibility for spiritual leadership toward the year 2000. This current meeting was for activating this key pattern or code and the official completion of our group etheric body for the purpose of world service. In the previous incarnation we were not in the West, but had Eastern bodies and traditions.

We were all three Hindus. This monastery was apparently a pure connection to the etheric masters and the Order of Melchizedek. At that time, Melchizedek told us, we had been sent to this monastery for training and had not known each other in that incarnation before. At that meeting the three of us were taken into the Golden Chamber of Melchizedek, and Metatron placed his key code within us, which today was being activated.

We had each been Hindus with a Buddhist background. After that meeting we all were told to go our separate ways and complete our karma and service work until we eventually came together again in this future time period. We had been told that this group body then being activated and sanctified was to be our first loyalty above all others, not in an ego sense but in terms of our commitment to world service. In joining together in this group body, our fates were being eternally tied together, much like a cosmic marriage, but without the trappings of an earthly marriage. It was a joining for the purpose of world service and more accelerated spiritual evolution.

I want to share here that as the week went on, moving into the fourth morning, we were awestruck at the expansion that had taken place over such a short period. The three of us had never spent so much time together in this group-body consciousness. The only thing I can trace it to was this new group etheric web. For the first time we experienced the enormous increase in our I.Q. as we worked in this group mind, group heart, group body and group spirit.

By the fourth morning our previous thinking that this was just the joining of our etheric bodies was left hanging, because we were seeing and feeling the effects of joining at all these levels. My brain seemed to be much bigger. The level of energy transmission was vastly increased after our joining together because we were sharing a larger battery. The level of information pouring through was the best and most wonderful we had ever experienced. The protection we felt was also increased. It felt like an impenetrable shield was now in place because of this joining.

The only thing we were losing in doing this was the sense of ego, which the three of us were happy to give up. In forming a group body, group heart, group mind and group spirit, our collective potential was now vastly increased. This was not something the masters were telling us, but something we were being knocked off our socks by. I had never considered the possibility of increased mental power, emotional power/love or spiritual power that I was awestruck by on the fourth morning. This is hard to describe, but we felt like our bodies, minds, hearts and spirits were now three times bigger. I had not considered the full implications. The only thing I can say is that it felt, from an experiential point of view, like we had made six to nine months of growth in these four days. The three of us coming together provided a greater vehicle for spirit to work through on all levels. The three of us had walked into this rather innocently, without understanding the full implications and potentialities we were now experiencing.

I encourage you to join in an ascension buddy system. This is a pact and merger you make with certain spiritual friends to share your ascension journey together. I am not saying this has to be done, for it is not appropriate or necessary for all. You can fully achieve everything in my books without it. Some of you have friendships where this is appropriate and can be to your advantage. It is like a spiritual marriage with soul friends that is separate from your marriage—or in some cases could be the same. In its highest sense, it is even beyond marriage when you ultimately move from the ascension buddy system to the group-body understanding, which is the next step.

We needed to be ascension buddies for a long time before we were ready to take on a fully functioning group body. All I can say is that the commitment to such a pact can greatly increase your mind, body and spiritual potentialities. Later I will share my experiences in the Source ascension seat, which none of us would have ever been allowed to enter alone.

The group body had created an etheric grid that enabled us to handle the energies without burning up or damaging our etheric grid. In essence, our battery potential was greatly increased. The group-body process is a wonderful one for transcending ego. Instead of identifying yourself in one body as mass consciousness teaches, you are now confronted with identifying yourself as three bodies.

I can't act selfishly because there are two other parts of my greater body that I always have to consider. As we move through our initiations, we form larger and larger states of group consciousness and group bodies. Right now we *all* share one as members of the human race on Earth. Eventually that will give way to the solar system, the galaxy, the universe, the multiuniverse and then Source, which is all creation.

Cosmic ascension will incorporate everyone into your group body. In truth, this already exists now for every sentient being; however, the process of moving through the 352 levels of initiation expands in stages rather than all at once. All our romantic relationships have an aspect of this. All our friendships and our children and earthly family, certain organizations or even religions we belong to, have been a type of bonding such as this. All these bondings help mold our character, increase our consciousness and lead us toward higher and higher levels of group consciousness and group-body bonding. In our case, this new development was by far the most advanced group-bonding, group-consciousness, group-body experiment we had ever experienced. It was as if all other experiences were to prepare us for this elevated world-service vehicle. This is not unique to us; it is available to anyone who chooses it. I simply happen to be writing about it in the context of higher ascension activation and for the purpose of planetary service.

The key code was activated in a light and sound pattern to solidify this group matrix. Coming together as one is the highest aspiration for all seekers of truth in a group matrix. Once this grid is created it cannot be broken, and any actual geographic distance is meaningless. In truth, we could come together without that new grid, but with it, the feeling of oneness and unity and protection is always there. It is just as tangible as our physical bodies. The thought, as Edgar Cayce might say, has become a thing. Etheric structures are as real as physical earthly structures—maybe even more real. What was previously simply a feeling of love and friendship now becomes a legitimate structure of consciousness.

As part of the final ceremony each of us was required to state our vow of acceptance of this process, much like we must do on Earth when we take wedding vows. The master under Melchizedek, as the grand spokesperson, officiated at this ceremony. We all gave our affirmative vow. As a final physical action of this union, we were instructed by Melchizedek to pick up one of the three candles burning in the middle of our triad and place them together, thereby symbolizing the three lights becoming one. This also symbolized the purpose of planetary world service and the acceleration of spiritual union.

We were then asked to place our highest commitment into this one flame, which would be transferred to all the Hierarchy's stations and ashrams in the cosmos to which we were connected. Melchizedek then embodied each of us, simultaneously blessing our hands, hearts and heads. I was then asked to recite a spontaneous prayer in the ancient language that felt fitting at this time. In writing this down I feel a bit awestruck by the power and amplitude of this "spiritual wedding." I have a greater sense of the implications and profundity than when I first experienced it. I am able to relive it now so clearly because we taped all four days of our work together. (In the past it had usually been done on the phone, after which I wrote it out from memory or a few notes.)

Melchizedek activated the ancient key code for this bonding by performing a type of chakra-bonding ceremony. We began by bonding in our heart chakras through light and sound, then moved to the third-eye level, again bonding through light and sound. This activation was to help us see as one. We then bonded at the root chakra, moving next to the throat chakra, where the light from each of us merged in the center of our triad, as was the case with the other chakras. We then moved to the second chakra, and again the light poured into the center of the triad and merged into one, after which we moved to the solar plexus, again merging into one at the center of our triad.

Next we moved to the crown chakra. The platinum ray (multiuniversal level of Melchizedek) welled up within us and out our crown chakras into a triangle above us, melding into one. Melchizedek said that we had created a *templar* or pyramid there. The three fused into one, thus symbolizing the connection of the keys. This was to make the knowledge available to everyone, no longer to be kept hidden or esoteric. It was now time for knowledge to become available to all.

Into the templar was poured the sacred essence that had been distilled in the alchemical laboratory in the archives of all time records, the akashic soul records from the ancient future chamber held in this sanctuary and contained in the sacred cabinet known as the Ark. This is held in the sacred chamber of all planetary bodies, and for our planet it is known as Shamballa in the Great Pyramid underground. As one we connected to this universal artery, which is like the bloodstream. Into this templar this essence was poured.

Melchizedek then asked me to call out the names of the masters to whom we were connected in our spiritual ascension lineage. As I called out the names of the masters, each would bring his energy and imprint it into the code poured through our bodies as nectar.

I began by calling forth blessings from Djwhal Khul, Kuthumi, Lord Maitreya of the second-ray ashram, then the chohans of the seven rays (El

Morya, Kuthumi, Paul the Venetian, Serapis Bey, Hilarion, Sananda and Saint Germain). I then called forth the blessing into this code as divine nectar from the Manu (Allah Gobi), Lord Maitreya and the current Mahachohan. Next I called to the Buddha and Sanat Kumara for their blessing on this code and unified field. We then called forth the help of the Ashtar Command and the lady masters, who gave us their blessing.

We then moved up the ladder of consciousness and I called for blessings from the Lord of Arcturus and the Arcturians, Vywamus and Lenduce, then from the grand master himself, Lord Melchizedek, Metatron and his holiness the Lord Sai Baba. I then called forth the blessing of the presence of God, the Cosmic Council of Twelve and the Twenty-Four Elders that surround the Throne of Grace, the Council of the Elohim and all archangelic hosts for their blessing on this new service vehicle.

The Atomic Accelerator

We began the next session after a little break, with myself functioning as spokesperson, petitioning an agenda for our four days together. I believe it was Melchizedek who then came through and said the next process we would be embarking on was to go to the atomic accelerator for further refinements and light-quotient-building. The plan was to bring the three in and then individually comment on our experiences. We would first visit the atomic accelerator, then on Tuesday morning go on an ascension-seat journey to the Source ascension seat with the Mahatma, then map the higher mind and/or zohar mind and finally take a tour of Lord Arcturus' starship. While sleeping we would be prepared for the next day's events. Evening meditations would be a summing up, focusing on planetary service. Sometimes it would be spontaneous: There were a few surprises, one of which was a Ganesha ceremony to help remove obstacles from our service path for our highest expansion.

This was the first time the three of us went to the atomic accelerator for a prolonged period. The timing was perfect, for we had just completed a group-bonding ceremony, and the weaving of our group etheric body was now complete. The atomic accelerator was the perfect place to go (in Table Mountain, Wyoming, on the inner plane). The accelerator would run the energies through our new etheric group-body webbing as well as through our own personal etheric nadi system to test it out at a more amplified level.

Upon arriving, we sat in a triangular position and they began to run the energies. The atomic accelerator gives a readout on their computers that is much like the Arcturian starships. This readout shows the areas of strength and weakness in the five-body system (physical, etheric, astral, mental and spiritual). This accelerator can be geared to work very precisely. The flow of energy felt wonderful and was much stronger than I had ever remembered it. The masters suggested that we come here for a short visit every day. We remained there for around twenty or thirty minutes, then were guided that it was time to leave. I highly recommend to you, my readers, to spend some time in the atomic accelerator. I have a profound sense that it is a more advanced ascension seat.

Our Cosmic Ascension-Seat Journey

The plan for a long-awaited ascension-seat journey was set up by the Mahatma to guide us into each ascension seat we wanted to attend. The Mahatma guided us into each one and filled us with its energy. We could spend as long as we wanted at each level, conversing with the masters at each station. The Mahatma had promised us this experience about three or four months previously, with our ultimate ascension seat being the one at the 352nd level of the Mahatma. Our group-body vehicle would prevent our being damaged by the high frequency of energies. I had been looking forward to this with great excitement, for this would be our first direct experience of the Godhead. We had prepared for about six weeks, spending time in the multiuniversal ascension seat and receiving our mushroom "Statue of Liberty" hats from Lenduce.

We felt very inspired this day. We began by calling forth to the Mahatma to take us to the planetary ascension seat in Shamballa under the direction of Sanat Kumara and the Buddha. The energy was very strong here; I had always very much liked this ascension seat. I highly recommend it to all lightworkers. The energy of the Buddha was strongly present due to his recent movement into the position of Planetary Logos. He spoke of his new position and of planet Earth becoming covered in a cloud of lower consciousness. He referred to this as the "astral hemisphere." It was not Sanat Kumara's job to break this up, however; Buddha said it was *his* job.

The Buddha has come now, along with the Christ, Lord Maitreya, to impress upon humanity the compassion that brings peace and self-sacrifice as surrender to peace. Buddha said he had just begun this process, then prophesied that we would be seeing an enormous shift in the years from 1995 to 2012. He asked us to have faith in this. This, he said, would come about because of the union of the Buddha and the Christ Maitreya, the two great brothers and leaders of our race.

Many of you may remember that they had teamed up together in the Eastern world in ancient days as Krishna and Arjuna. These beings are the two most advanced souls from our Earth chain. Sanat Kumara is overlighting the Buddha every step of the way in his job of overlighting the Earth and being the logos of two other planets. This all came about at Wesak 1995. There was some initial confusion on this point, because different channels were getting different information. (We have now checked this out very thoroughly, as Buddha again stated it in this meditation.) We are now receiving the triple impact of Lord Maitreya, Lord Buddha, Sanat Kumara—and really a fourth, whom Buddha did not mention here: Sai Baba, who is a universal avatar and spiritual regent from a different galaxy. The first three are connected to our Planetary Hierarchy and are fully realized galactic masters, with Sanat Kumara perhaps even beyond this.

Buddha asked us to be very watchful of this process. He spoke of the Wesak celebration, which I would coordinate, an event that would significantly help him in his great work. (I invite you to join us each year at the full moon in Taurus for these annual Wesak celebrations. These yearly events over the years from 1995 to the year 2000 will be the primary events that activate the waves of mass ascension on the planet.) Each year they will be hosted by Melchizedek, Lord Maitreya, Djwhal Khul and the Buddha. The Buddha personally invites you now.

As we entered, we also saw Sanat Kumara remove his ascension seat and replace it with Buddha's ascension seat. Then he stood behind the Buddha, signifying this new relationship. He spoke of all of us—including my readers—as being emissaries of his and of the Christ/Buddha union.

We were then guided by the Mahatma to continue our ascension-seat journey to the solar ascension seat in the core of Helios and Vesta. We began our communication with Helios and Vesta with a prayer that Helios and the Mahatma would help anchor and activate our solar body and chakras through 100 over the next year to year and a half. On behalf of the three of us I requested this divine dispensation and that they work with us during sleep and waking time, during our meditations, ascension walks, relaxing time, and when we watch television or participate in any other recreational activities without even having to ask.

I figured that Helios and Vesta were the perfect masters to ask for this kind of help, given that it was the solar body and solar chakras we were now trying to realize. Our chakra grid immediately began to light up with a series of crosshatched x's. Helios said he and his crew of core disciples were building a bridge to the next level. He said that this was the bridge to the solar chakras that make up the solar body. He then graciously agreed to help us in this prayer request. Vesta, who appeared as a beautiful woman, placed the solar sun in our field. While Helios worked on the grid of x's, Vesta went to the inner depth of our chakras to help the light come forward and connect. We experienced this as a downpouring of golden yellow light moving through all our chakras. It was a very rejuvenating experience.

Vesta also spoke about removing and cleansing the madness and lunacy affecting the Earth that Buddha spoke of as a dark field encasing it. She referred to it as lunacy, which is related to moon madness, the effect of the full moon on people. This affects humans if they are not totally centered in the light. The connection with the solar sun, she said, will help cleanse this madness from our field. I then asked Vesta if it was now possible to anchor and activate this solar sun permanently. She said it was, but as it was a process, it could not be done immediately.

Vesta said that moon madness has been one of the problems of many great channels on the planet. She said it comes directly from the craters of the Moon, and that the craters were actually a stronghold for the Dark Brotherhood. It is common knowledge that some of the more negative extraterrestrials have used the Moon as a base. She said that the Great White Brotherhood has its capital on Sirius in the Great White Lodge. The Dark Brotherhood capital is on Orion, which was news to me; I had never heard this before. Besides the effect of the Moon itself, the Dark Brotherhood would often send dark rays to the Earth from these craters, just as the White Brotherhood is constantly sending rays of light.

She also said that this process has a connection with Greek mythology, wherein Zeus is said to send thunderbolts, and with the Hebrew gods, who were not always loving and forgiving in temperament. It is also why NASA's Moon missions have had such a difficult time. The work the lightworkers do on the thirteen yearly full moon festivals is to transmute a lot of this energy and take advantage of the added amount of light that can come in during this time. This is nothing to be afraid of, for lightworkers en masse are taking their third initiation, merging with the soul, which acts as a protection. It is only a danger for those who walk around on automatic pilot and/or are on drugs and so on—people who are total victims. Lightworkers do not need to concern themselves with this, though it is interesting information.

Many lightworkers are very naive about the existence of the Dark Brotherhood. It is a separate government on the inner plane that is dedicated to serving the negative ego instead of God. It is hard to believe that souls could be so confused as to engage in such a thing, but they do. They are simply confused sons and daughters of God. The best thing to do is ignore them completely; never think about them, read about them or even focus on them. Act like they don't exist, and they won't be in your reality. Some people make the mistake of reading many books about them, which only attracts them.

The best thing to do is completely ignore them. If they ever come around, instantly call in Archangel Michael and ask for protection. They will disappear because they can't stand the light, and cannot exist in a lighted aura. Spend your life focusing on God and love, and this will become a meaningless issue. It is important only to know they exist, and that is all. Just forgive them, love them, stay strong and protected, and live in the light.

It is also important to understand that the thirteen full moons are the highest light emanations of the year and that Wesak, the full moon in May (Taurus), is the highest. I want to keep this full moon business in perspective. The thirteen full moons are in truth the true high holy days of the Earth because of the light frequency that comes forth at this time. Vesta suggested that the 1200 high-level initiates and ascended beings who attend the Mount Shasta celebration might, as part of our next program, do a combined light cleansing of the Moon. This would help remove this dark cloud that Buddha spoke of and would invite a truce and cease-fire with the Dark Brotherhood—offering our hands in friendship, so to speak. Helios said to remember that these are sons and daughters of God just as we are. They are not evil, just unconscious. There is no one who cannot be turned by love, forgiveness and friendship, as Gandhi and Mother Teresa have epitomized.

Visiting the Great White Lodge on Sirius

The next step in our cosmic ascension journey was to the Lord of Sirius and the Great White Lodge. The Lord of Sirius graciously welcomed us with open arms. I began the conversation with a prayer for his help in anchoring our solar, galactic and universal bodies and 200 chakras. As with Helios and Vesta, I asked for his help at night while we sleep and during our receptive waking hours. He graciously agreed. His eyes were filled with light as few masters we had ever seen. The Lord of Sirius then reminded us of our mushroom hats, or space helmets, as he also called them. He said these are gifts that must be used. He suggested focusing our light through this hat to the people we speak to or see who need our help. This hat will spin and connect with our third eye, emanating a healing light. Not all people will take this light in, but it is a gift given freely. This is one way they test our ability to remember to send light.

The Lord of Sirius then presented us with an incredibly wonderful gift—a scroll placed at the top of our spines and pushed (metaphysically) down the whole length of the spine. This scroll contains the knowledge we need to go forward and do the work. The Lord of Sirius said that we have been given this scroll because we have asked to excel on every level possible, to the highest place. This scroll contains sacred geometries. As we need this information, this scroll will unfold. We can access this scroll anytime we use the mushroom hat. The two together are very powerful. The knowledge and light were coming from the heart and head. The scroll began to imprint and imbed into every fiber of our being. This was one of the most powerful experiences we had ever had. The scroll was anchored into our pelvis.

I couldn't help but share then with the Lord of Sirius what a profound feeling of connection I felt with him and the Great White Lodge. He quickly chimed back to me, "It is truly your destiny, Joshua." No words could be truer. I am really looking forward to working in Djwhal Khul's ashram, which will be a wonderful training and opportunity to serve. However, the Great White Lodge feels like one of my true homes, a spiritual place that fits my total vibration in a perfect match. I look forward eagerly to this experience when the time is right.

Our Subsequent Dreams

Later that night when I went to bed, I dreamed that there was a beautiful statue of Quan Yin in the middle of my living room where the ascension column exists and where we meditate. In the dream my friend walked by the statue, and the lady master from Sirius began to speak to her from inside the statue. The Lord of Sirius, who was also inside it, began to talk to me. His words were like a cheerleader's at a football game. He chanted, "Balance, balance, balance." It was a wonderful dream.

This scroll was almost like a diploma of graduation for entering a new level. This was new information we could use in this new graduated level of service work. The Lord of Sirius then placed his hand on the top of our spines and recited a sacred mantra that fully integrated these scrolls. It turned out that the sacred mantra called forth the lady master from Sirius who, I think, is the Lord of Sirius' partner. We were all very pleased to make her acquaintance.

It turned out that my friend had met her in a dream in which all the high initiates from Sirius gathered after descending onto a mountain on Earth. My friends were in charge of one group and I was in charge of another. This lady master was the section leader of their group. Another master from the Great White Lodge was the leader of my section, the group of disciples and initiates who were in my charge. This lovely master has long black hair.

My connection seemed to be more with the Lord of Sirius, as indicated in my dream. The lady master from Sirius confirmed this a few moments later. We all then began to receive what can only be described as a suntan from inside out. It felt like a lighting and igniting that penetrated our bodies. Strangely enough, it felt like an atomic bomb setting off a positive chain reaction within us, allowing the knowledge placed within us to be expressed and used to its greatest extent. We had the sense of butterflies fluttering around us.

Somehow placing this scroll within us had allowed the Lord of Sirius and the lady master from Sirius to work from the inside out instead of from the top down, as is usual. She said that this was a wonderful tool and part of us now. There seemed to be a synergistic effect resulting from the scroll, the mushroom hat and the sacred mantra just spoken. The masters said that this energy we were experiencing would be poured into the group of 1200 initiates and ascended beings at Wesak. The lady master from Sirius said that the initiates in attendance would be given the opportunity to receive this scroll as we had this day if they chose.

These two masters from Sirius are the highest-level beings that humans can realistically aspire to. We are speaking here of galactic realization. These mushroom hats and scrolls, one could say, are the galactic technology that corresponds with a consciousness ready and willing to move to this level.

Our Journey to the Multiuniversal Ascension Seat

We then continued our journey with the Mahatma to the multiuniversal ascension seat under the guidance of the Mahatma and Melchizedek. This, of course, is the platinum ray. We skipped the golden chamber ascension seat only because we were so familiar with it and because this meditation was turning out to be a marathon. This was fine with us, but for the sake of efficiency and familiarity, we skipped it under guidance from the Mahatma. I asked Melchizedek whether there was a Lady Master Melchizedek, as is the case for the Great White Lodge and for Helios and Vesta on the solar level. He said no, that as the universal archetype, he was the perfect embodiment of the male and female in one androgynous body. He did say that he had an equal number of male and female universal initiates and disciples under his tutelage.

This ascension seat has an incredible calm. The effect of this multiuniversal ascension seat is "perfect resonance and attunement," said Melchizedek, such as the pearly gates as spoken of in the Bible. It has an incredible feeling of inner peace. As we sat there, we absorbed the energies, which seemed to have an enormously healing effect on our bodies. It was as if the seas and skies and time had stood still. Melchizedek said that we were in this place of no-time and no-space to absorb all that there is, all that has been and all that will be in preparation for the next step (which I took to mean the Source ascension seat). The three of us were on the inner plane holding each other and drinking in this divine nectar and energy. There was a timeless quality, like dreaming, where hours go by that have actually been only seconds.

We were guided by Melchizedek to stay a little longer than planned for, because it was having such a profound healing effect on us. Sitting there, we felt almost like we were levitating, not simply sitting in the ascension seat. Then all three of us were holding hands together on the inner plane, continuing our absorption. There seemed to be a crosshatching of light that joined us together in our new group body. I jokingly commented that I was in seventh heaven. This was closer to the truth than any of us realized. There also seemed to be a process of visiting many people on the inner plane and giving them gifts of this energy.

Our energies also seemed to be extended to large groups of children. The image was like the movie *Close Encounters*, when Richard Dreyfuss' character was entering the spaceship and the smaller extraterrestrials were gathering around him and taking his hands. These children seemed to be children of the Earth, but also a few high-initiate souls who were about to be born on the Earth.

Going to the Source Ascension Seat

We continued our cosmic ascension-seat journey to our final destination, calling forth the Mahatma to take us to the Source ascension seat at the 352nd level of the Mahatma and/or Godhead. Immediately a tremendous vibration resonated through our heads, then throughout our whole bodies. There seemed to be a process of penetrating this ascension seat layer by layer. We felt a holiness and sanctity as we seemed to travel higher and higher. It seemed we had to move up in stages as a protective measure because of the high voltages. The only reason we were allowed to do this was because we were doing it in our group vehicle (none of us would have been allowed to do this separately because of the damage it could cause to our etheric vehicles) and because we were still being insulated by the Mahatma and, I believe, Melchizedek.

We were, by the grace of God, being allowed to enter the holy of holies and to have our first true experience of God, not just the soul, monad, galactic masters, universal masters, multiuniversal masters and the Mahatma. This was an *actual* experience of the God ascension seat. There was a sense of a coating or wrapping or bubble around us so we would not get burned etherically.

There is some protection by the masters that goes on, but lightworkers should realize that if disciples and initiates continue to invoke cosmic energies and experiences beyond their range of spiritual development, they can be severely hurt. This is why I have given strict warnings about the timing and appropriateness of using these different cosmic energies and technologies. If you are not sure, ask the masters and your own mighty I Am Presence to protect you and give you only the experiences you are ready for.

(After this log entry, the masters gave a special dispensation to use the God ascension-seat meditation beginning with the 1996 Wesak celebration. Those who continue to use this meditation tape or share it with fellow lightworkers have nothing to be concerned about. The masters have put a personal cap on how much energy any individual will receive. This has been done so that the highest benefits can be made available from the ascension seat without danger. Let the meditation take you upward and do not force anything. Just be guided to flow easily and gently into the heights that the tapes take you, and you will be gifted with the highest energies you can comfortably receive.)

One example of this sort of danger comes from working with the kundalini. Many lightworkers have tried prematurely to force the awakening of the kundalini, severely damaging their etheric body. Sometimes it has taken many lifetimes to recover, but often setting them back five or ten years. (God has given us free choice and will intervene to a certain extent, but what you sow, you reap, and what you put out comes back to you.)

I share this experience and others out of love and respect for my brothers and sisters. I share them not out of ego, but just the opposite. If I were into my ego, I would hide them to keep for myself. I share them so all may be helped and served. In freely sharing these experiences, which in the past have never been revealed, I am trusting that you will use this information wisely and be patient, using them only when the timing is appropriate.

I wish to give you a cosmic map of your destiny. There are few books on the planet that deal with this level of information; that is why I am sharing it. Timing is everything. Forcing spiritual experiences you are not ready for will only create karma for yourself. Every person who reads my books is fully capable of completing seven levels of initiation rather easily if they use the tools and information. Everyone is also able to focus on cosmic ascension, but be patient and take it step by step. If you don't, you can damage yourself. Please heed this warning, for the masters have guided me to make this qualification in order to share this information with you.

There is a great responsibility I carry in releasing such information to the general public. That is why I must speak so strongly now about keeping the proper perspective toward these cosmic technologies. I thank you for your deep consideration of these cautions. I share this information honestly because to hold anything back from you would be to hold back on God and myself, all of which are one.

To focus on calling in cosmic energies when you haven't even completed your planetary ascension, let alone bridged your solar, galactic and universal levels, will invite gross imbalance. It is a misinterpretation and/or misunderstanding of the process in our work. This is why we have been guided to work with three masters simultaneously: Djwhal Khul, Lord Maitreya and Melchizedek. This three-tiered overlighting process makes sure we do not skip any levels. I suggest that you too set up your three-tiered master guidance system.

Even though we have completed the seven levels of initiation and the fifty-chakra anchoring and activation, nine-body anchoring and activation and 99 percent light quotient, we are still just beginning the process of bridging to the solar level. The big confusion among many lightworkers is, they think that by achieving planetary ascension and mastery they are at the top of creation at the 352nd level of the Mahatma. But in truth they are only one-tenth up a ten-inch ruler. This is because people have never been exposed to an in-depth understanding of what cosmic ascension is compared to planetary ascension.

As we continued to go higher in our Source ascension-seat journey, it kept getting lighter. On the periphery there was a dancing of light all around us. We were told by the Mahatma that we were in a process of reentry; a spaceship too has to come in at a certain trajectory or it will burn up. We were going through a similar process, but our reentry was in reverse, toward Source. Intense openings of everything, layer by layer, began to occur. I commented that we were truly in seventh heaven now, and my friend chimed in, "and beyond."

An enormous feeling of bliss began to pervade my being. I felt inspired to pray, thanking God from the bottom of our collective heart for all the bountiful blessings He had bestowed upon us. I also prayed for God's and the Mahatma's blessings on our service mission in all its ramifications, and for their blessing on our personal evolutionary goals. It was hard to put into words the gratitude I was feeling. It is hard to write about this experience, for I am not doing justice to it, writing about it a week later. All I can say is that this experience was probably the peak experience of my entire life. It felt like a completion of a very long cycle. I felt like I had come home. I was aware of how much work it had taken me to get here and how blessed I felt in all areas of my life. My cup had truly run over. It was an experience where words only detract. We spent a long time simply sitting in the silence. I felt I never wanted to leave.

I was also surprised and pleased to hear that we would be initiating people into this experience at Wesak. Can you imagine doing this with 1200 high-level initiates and ascended beings on Wesak, at the full moon in Mount Shasta, activating the first three waves of mass ascension? We all felt that was the deepest cleansing we had ever experienced. I felt profoundly altered by it. Even after the meditation was over, we sat in the energies for about a half hour and softly talked about our experience and feelings while the energy was winding down. I felt that I would never be the same. We were all also aware of the importance of the process of moving up the ascension seats as we were doing, which built up the energies.

Group Consciousness and the Ascension Buddy System

On the fourth day of our pow-wow we went for our usual early-morning ascension walk, filled with an awesome sense of the power and potentialities of working in a group body. When Melchizedek had first suggested the idea about a month before, I had thought of it on the etheric-body level, of a new group-body webbing being created. Since the three of us had never done this before (as have few in the history of the Earth), we had not known what to expect.

I had studied family systems in my training to become a marriage/family/child counselor, so the concept of a group organism was not foreign to me. This, of course, was taking it a step further, where a new identity was being formed, like three cells forming a new, larger cell. I don't think any of us realized the implications and magnitude of what we were doing. In our morning ascension walk and later in our breakfast discussion, we were all sensitive to not only the new etheric group matrix, but also the amazing increase in what I can only describe as our intelligence quotient. It was as if we had a larger brain, and the level of information that had been coming in the last four days was more awesome and advanced—and had come in more quickly—than ever before.

Then there was also the increase in the power of our spiritual battery. Permission to experience the Source ascension seat would never have been given if we had not been working in this group consciousness. The larger spiritual body that was created allowed us to have this experience without damaging our etheric bodies. The other experience was the sense of expansiveness. Something had really changed in the last four days. Our energy fields all felt much larger and more expansive.

Four days into our pow-wow I was overwhelmed by the effects on the physical, emotional, mental and spiritual levels. I had not previously considered the potential increase on these levels. I had considered it only on a rewiring and energetic level. The ultimate thought and feeling is that we were all completely sold on the process. Melchizedek told us quite clearly that what we were doing was an experiment. Billions and billions have, of course, formed group bonds, but few had actually formed a fully functioning group body. This was also an exercise in transcending negative-ego consciousness and mass consciousness. It goes against all mass programming to see oneself as a three-person body instead of residing in one's physical body alone.

I am not saying here that this is something everybody should do. Many people, of course, form what might be considered the closest bond, marriage. This is different, however, in that it is not a romantic or sexual process, but a spiritual, professional friendship and group-service vehicle. I realized that the lines of separation were falling away even in our work as the week went on.

In this state of consciousness there can be no competitiveness, no selfishness or self-centeredness. Realistically, we realized we are not perfect, and we all have little sensitivities of our inner child at times. The plan was to share these or keep them to a minimum as much as we could. I was profoundly aware, however, that I would never consider doing this experiment with anyone but these two wonderful ladies. For some strange reason it was just right. Djwhal Khul told us that it was because our monads were connected with his on the inner plane in a larger group pattern, and we all shared a very similar monadic pattern.

The fact that my friends were happily married in their private life made it even more perfect. I had recently ended my marriage and had been involved in relationships for the last seventeen years. I now felt ready to give myself to the celibate life so that all my energies could be given to planetary service. These factors created a nice balance in this trinity.

I highly recommend that my readers find ascension buddies to work with in your focus upon ascension activation and world service. Do come to the Wesak celebration each year in Mount Shasta, where we will all form another group body with 1200 people as we move toward the turn of the century. Can you imagine the power of 1200 high-level initiates and ascended beings for an entire weekend doing this work?

I remember a woman who called me when we had 350 people at the 1995 Wesak celebration. Before the event she was trying to decide whether to come. She asked a psychic friend of hers whether she should come to our event or go on a spiritual retreat and celebrate on her own. The psychic told her that the power of the energies of this event would be one hundred times more powerful. This is not because this woman was not advanced, because she was.

The same would be applied to myself. I can honestly say that being a part of the Wesak celebrations has been the most awesome spiritual experiences of my entire life, and nothing I have ever experienced by myself or even in working in small groups has ever come close to this power and these frequencies. That is because of the group consciousness that is created out of the love and egolessness of the people who attend. This creates a new, much larger battery, which allows an exponential increase in the magnitude of energies, healing and acceleration to take place.

Ascension-Activation Meditation

In one of our next sessions we did a focalized meditation using some of the things we had been learning. We began by calling forth the platinum ray and yod spectrum, the twelve bodies and 200 chakras. Then I called for a divine dispensation for the installation and activation of the soul braids on the monadic, group-soul, group-monadic, solar, galactic and universal levels. This deals with viewing the characteristics of the life pattern. When this was complete, I called for the installation and activation of the overlay (divine blueprint) on the monadic, group-soul, group-monadic, solar, galactic and universal levels. We called in Helios and Vesta for help in anchoring and activating the solar sun, solar body, solar chakras 50 through 100 and help in building the electrical bridging system to this level.

I then called forth Djwhal Khul to hook us up to the holographic screen room in his ashram and to clear, cleanse, balance and accelerate our solar activation. This was all done while we were in the Golden Chamber of Melchizedek with Djwhal Khul, Lord Maitreya and Melchizedek. Then I requested the full activation of our mayavarupa overlay on a permanent basis, after which I called to Melchizedek to anchor permanently the galactic sun and universal sun. I called forth the Lord of Arcturus and the Arcturian advanced technology to help on an ongoing basis with the solar body, solar chakra, solar sun and solar bridging work we were now doing. I then called for the anchoring of our multiuniversal ascension seat and Source ascension seat into our four-body system on a permanent basis, and into our homes and our ascension columns. The combined effect of all these activations pretty much knocked our socks off as we sat in silence for about twenty minutes.

Our Arcturian Starship Meditation

In our next session we were taken to the mothership of the Lord of Arcturus. We were greeted by the Lord of Arcturus and his partner, Lady Leda. They began to give us a tour of the ship when we came upon this very large (seven-foot) clamshell device. The Lord of Arcturus and Lady Leda referred to it as an Arcturian light chamber. As we all stood around it, they told us that because we had now completed our seven levels of initiation, had anchored and activated the nine bodies and fifty chakras and begun our cosmic ascension process, we were now ready to be exposed to this advanced Arcturian light technology.

What they said was quite interesting. They said up to this point we had been receiving the Arcturian energies from the mothership or through Djwhal Khul's ashram. We had now graduated, however, and were being offered the opportunity to receive energies directly from Arcturus through this Arcturian light chamber that looked like a clamshell.

As is my way, I immediately volunteered to climb in while the others watched at first. It felt wonderful. I felt my whole twelve-body system light up. My friend said that as she watched me inside this clamshell, she could see four new sacred letters being activated from the sixty-four-letter sacred grid of the DNA and RNA, which is the code that activates the twelve strands of DNA. We had talked about this that morning, and it was now being processed. The two then got in their clamshells with some kind of headphones, connecting us as one in our group body. The Lord of Arcturus said that this would give us a lot more strength and energy.

Then they did something that was really wild—they actually began to alter our heart and EKG reading. They began re-forming our heartbeat pattern with this laser connected to an EKG-type monitoring device. I asked why, and they said this would increase our longevity. An Arcturian doctor was present. He said we all had some limiting programs, which was pretty much standard procedure for growing up on Earth. They said they had cleared most of the cancers and/or the unwanted dark webs in the brain. The Arcturian doctor said we still had not strengthened the heart-mind action enough to tolerate the vibrational shifts and shocks that are needed for the complete physical-immortality program. This surgery on the heart was now doing this. Lady Leda said that this Arcturian light chamber and heart operation would eventually be available to everyone, but they must first go through the steps I have outlined in my books. So just keep working the program, and very shortly this will be available to you too if it is something you wish.

As I have said many times, levels can't be skipped. You can't go from junior high school to college, skipping high school. Lady Leda said that if people try prematurely, the energy field simply won't open, even though their minds or egos tell them they are having the experience. This is what she said, for whatever it's worth.

The Arcturian doctor said this was a permanent operation, and that if we ever had our hearts checked by an ordinary physician, the difference would be noticeable. Earth doctors might consider this an irregular heart rhythm, but it is really an advanced, ascended-master heart rhythm that extends the length of life. Really a trip!

We were all kind of blown away by this process. The doctor from Arcturus looked a lot like our doctor friend from the Great White Lodge, Dr. Lorphan. It turned out they knew each other well.

The ship's generator looked like a windmill, with balls at the end of rotating arms. They form a perfect balance of all energies and bring everything in the ship's field into harmony and regeneration. This is a million times more dynamic than any atomic generator we could think of, and it is not harmful in the slightest.

Lady Leda said we would receive the strengthening of this attunement. This Arcturian light chamber would automatically work on us for whatever we needed. It programmed *us*; we don't have to program *it*. She came up with a great idea, which she set in motion. She said that every night while we were sleeping we would be taken there for a period governed by the machine, determined by how much we needed. She said that we would also receive a treatment anytime the three of us came together in person or on the phone. She asked me then, as the spokesperson, to formulate this prayer request, which I did.

Lady Leda said that the generator produces neutron and proton substances of the highest molecular level in the universe. That feeds the etheric fields and molecular structures of the entire population of the Arcturian ship. By being connected now with the Arcturian light chamber, we too are plugged into this energy.

I also made one prayer request for the three of us, which was for the complete resurrection of our physical bodies and the complete realization of our mayavarupa bodies. Lady Leda chimed in that this was indeed part of the process. Lord Arcturus then very diplomatically emphasized the importance of the triune union first because of its importance to the divine plan and the spiritual leadership positions we had now been given.

The Lord of Arcturus spoke of this bonding or group process as a ring-pass-not that increased the strength and protection of all three of us. This protection is essential for those who have a service mission dealing with the mass consciousness, which the three of us obviously have. I think all three of us were grateful for the added protection that the work we had done this week was now affording us.

The Lord of Arcturus also said that the ring-pass-not was made of our new group body on the etheric (really all levels) and was now being connected to the Arcturian light chamber, which in a sense reinforced this field more strongly. He told us that nothing could stop our service mission now because of the ring-pass-not, the group bonding and the individual commitments the three of us had made to ourselves, to God and the masters and to humanity.

For some reason this reminded me of Sai Baba, who said in one of his books that nothing could stop his mission. This is not meant to be arrogant or to test fate, but reflects our complete commitment on all levels, with the blessing and help of all the different masters we work with. Our group body was now built and had a new Arcturian energy field around it. It is much like the energy field we saw surrounding Lord Arcturus' mothership. I was becoming clearer now that this was the ring-pass-not that the Lord of Arcturus was speaking of.

I was then inspired to make one more prayer request to have the Arcturian light chamber also be programmed to help us in our current personal evolutionary goals of anchoring and activating our solar, galactic and universal bodies, our 200 chakras, twelve strands of DNA and 40 percent cosmic light quotient. My friend then chimed in with an additional prayer for help on all levels with the Wesak celebrations for 1000 to 5000 people and with the writing of all the books. I then said, "I sense an Arcturian book in the near future." The whole Arcturian contingency chimed in, "Oh, yes!"

The Lord of Arcturus then reviewed all the different aspects of our service program and said they were all covered now. He said another interesting thing about the three of us. Having come onto the world spiritual scene in a major way, we were not carrying a lot of excess baggage. We have all had fame and reputations in the cities we live in, but not on a global or planetary level. With my published books and the Wesak celebrations attracting from 1000 to 5000 people from 1995 to 2000, even 2012, we were now coming onto the world spiritual scene, he said, with a pretty clear and clean image. Not having had a global reputation already, there would be no prejudgments.

The Lord of Arcturus was basically saying that we were now flowering and blooming in our highest-level work without having to fight our past. In a sense, the timing of our fame or worldly recognition could not be better. He said that this would make our work even more impactful than it already is. His exact words were that there is "no glamour, no ego, no history." He said everyone would be coming into the work with no preconceived notions, which was a wonderful advantage to us. People would come into the work completely open, which is wonderful for us, wonderful for them and wonderful for the masters. He said we have been allowed to grow and fully bloom at just the right time.

He also said that another reason we had been given our leadership position was because of our stability and consistency individually and as a group. He said this was rather a rare quality. I was still thinking about this issue of not having a lot of excess baggage or past history, which I found very interesting and positive the more I thought about it.

In concluding our visit to Lord Arcturus' starship, we made one last prayer request for the cleansing and integration of our 144 soul extensions on the monadic level, the 72 oversouls of our group soul's eighth level, and our 864 soul extensions on the ninth group-monadic level, which was new information we had received in our morning session. Then a final dispensation was requested for beginning the process of integrating and cleansing the solar soul-extension level along with activation of the solar body, solar sun, solar braid and solar chakras.

Lord of Arcturus and Lady Leda were pleased with our prayer requests and gave another resounding yes. Then we were whisked back down to Earth, for he said we had received our fill of Arcturian energy for the day. We thanked them for their wonderful help and felt very grateful for the incredible blessings that had been given us. After all these energies, the guidance, the information and new tools, our minds were whirling. We all felt an incredible love for these wonderful beings.

Concluding Dream and Meditation

On November 15, as I was concluding this book—which is my journey from the beginning to the completion of my planetary ascension—I had a dream. In the dream I was in Djwhal Khul's ashram, where he was explaining its leadership structure. He said we formed a triangle. I was at the top of the triangle and the others were at the other two corners. I was being given the main leadership position of the ashram as a spokesperson for the planetary ascension movement. My friends were definitely in a leadership position as a part of the triangle and group body, but in a supportive leadership role. Djwhal explained that there could only be one person in the main leadership role, or the ashram would not function properly. When I asked him why I was chosen for this position, he said very simply, because of my steadiness and stability.

I felt incredibly honored and humbled to be given such a vote of confidence and responsibility. Never in my wildest dreams had I expected to find myself the head of Djwhal Khul's ashram and a spokesperson for the planetary ascension movement. After digesting this for a number of days, I spoke to Djwhal and fully accepted the hierophant's hat and mantle of authority. I told him I would not let him down and that I would try to do as good a job as he had done. When I finally told him that I accepted this position with 100 percent commitment, he did something unexpected. He wiped his brow, which seemed to be a momentary sign of relief. Djwhal was now free to go upward and onward to the Great White Lodge on Sirius to continue his cosmic evolution in the year 2012. He could not have been allowed to go until he found someone to take his place. Upon seeing this show of emotion, I told him that he could rest easy, for on a scale of 1 to 100 percent, my commitment to this job assignment was an unchanging 10,000 percent.

I don't think I ever felt closer to Djwhal than I did then. I was filled with awe at what had transpired in my life in the past two or three years, and I also felt the awesome responsibility that was now on my shoulders. I told Djwhal that I felt that God had built me to do this particular work, which I feel in the deepest core of my being. There is nothing in the universe I would rather do than this. To have the opportunity to work in close association with Djwhal, Kuthumi, Lord Maitreya, the chohans of the seven rays, Lord Buddha (our new Planetary Logos), the Lord of Sirius and Melchizedek was truly a bestowal of grace and the ultimate answer to my prayer to serve.

Djwhal told me that his second-ray Synthesis Ashram was the only ashram that would be taken over by an incarnate master. I was truly honored. I also like the fact that his ashram is called the Synthesis Ashram, which has a unique function of integrating all seven ray vibrations. It was specifically created for this purpose. All of you who read my books know my eclectic and universalistic approach. It is perfectly fitting that my work is in the Synthesis Ashram, for I have an eternal bond of love and devotion to the chohans of all the rays as well as the many and varied spiritual masters, paths and religions. I also have a unique and profound connection with the

Mahatma, who is himself the Avatar of Synthesis!

Lord Metatron Meditation

I would like to share a meditation I had when we were talking with Lord Metatron. He installed what he called the platinum rod. The platinum energy has the highest frequency coming to Earth at this time, directly from the God Source at the 352nd level of the Godhead. Metatron also installed and hooked us up to the God crystals, which worked in unison with the platinum rod.

This allowed us to run the platinum energy through our four-body system twenty-four hours a day. In truth, it should really be called the twelve-body system now, which is the physical, emotional, mental and spiritual bodies, each one divided into three parts, which total twelve. This gift has had a wondrous effect on my life and has raised my frequency and attunement. The God crystals have resulted in not only raising my vibration, but have had a profound harmonizing and cleansing effect.

Lord Metatron has just told me that for those who would like to experience the installation of the platinum rod and God crystals, he will install it for all who come to the Wesak celebration no matter what year you attend. This experience will be heightened as your evolution progresses. This is a pact I have made with Metatron on your behalf by his grace. It is worth it to come to Wesak just for this, let alone all the other blessings and dispensations.

For those who aren't that familiar with Lord Metatron, it is my great honor to share with you the profundity of this most glorious being. Lord Metatron is, first of all, an archangel connected to the highest Sephira of the Tree of Life. Metatron is the creator of the electron and the outer light of the universe. In essence, he could be said to be like the right hand of God whose prime function is dealing with light.

It is Metatron's lighted hand that reaches down toward humanity, awaiting only the lifting of humanity's hand to reach out to him. Metatron can be especially helpful in building light quotient, light for healing, light for understanding, light to pierce through the darkness clouding one's life. He is also instrumental in anchoring the microtron and replacing the human electron with his superelectron. He was instrumental in bringing forth *The Keys of Enoch* and in standing at the top of the Tree of Life, in the Sephira of Kether, which has the ability to touch *all* the branches.

Lord Metatron wishes you to know in this moment that he is available to all disciples and initiates who call on him; he is not beyond reach. He embodies the essence of light in the universe; Melchizedek embodies the wisdom teachings of the universe; Lord Michael embodies the protection of the universe; the Mahatma embodies the universe; Sai Baba embodies the di-

242

vine love of the universe. Buddha embodies the compassion of the planet
and beyond; Djwhal Khul embodies the essence of planetary wisdom and
beyond; Lord Maitreya embodies unconditional love, wisdom and teaching
on a planetary level and beyond; and the Virgin Mary and Quan Yin embody the divine Mother, who in turn embodies unconditional love and compassion for the infinite universe.

I bring forth this information by Lord Metatron to share with my beloved readers that every planetary and cosmic master embodies and represents a specific quality and function in God's divine plan at the various levels of God's infinite universe. I myself, having just completed my planetary
ascension and begun my cosmic ascension at the tenth or solar level, have
the mission to embody the synthesis of all the rays and paths and to represent, as a spokesperson for the planetary ascension movement, all the planetary and cosmic masters even though my ascension lineage is the second-ray Djwhal Khul, Lord Maitreya and Melchizedek lineage.

In being given the leadership position to take over Djwhal Khul's inner-plane ashram in the year 2012 when he moves onto his path of cosmic
evolution on Sirius, I am taking over what is called the Synthesis Ashram.
This was specifically created by the Hierarchy as a unique ashram to represent all the rays. This is why I have written the *Easy-to-Read Encyclopedia
of the Spiritual Path*, which has been my humble attempt to synthesize all
pertinent spiritual knowledge of all the rays into one easy-to-read and practical set of books.

This is also why I have been guided to put on the Wesak celebration every year at the full moon of Taurus to gather all the disciples and initiates of
all the rays and spiritual paths for one massive weekend celebration of Lord
Buddha's birthday and his newly appointed position (as of Wesak 1995) of
Planetary Logos. He has replaced Sanat Kumara, who has moved to a
higher position, yet still overlights the Buddha in his work. My books embody synthesis. The Wesak Festival, which gathers from 1500 to eventually
as many as 50,000 initiates, embodies the ultimate in synthesis. Last,
serving as an anchor and focal point for the Mahatma (the Avatar of Synthesis who embodies all 352 levels of God) is the cosmic level of my mission of
synthesis. This is why I feel that having this assignment with the Mahatma
is so perfect for me. The Mahatma is the ultimate in synthesis, embodying
all levels.

It is a big job trying to represent everyone, but because of the way I was
built by God, it is the perfect thing for me. Being a second-ray soul and
monad, my path is similar to Djwhal Khul's, because the second ray is that
of spiritual education. So, in essence, my spiritual function is to embody a
synthesized wisdom on the planetary level and beyond. This is also why I
am attracted to Metatron, who, at the top of the Tree of Life, touches all the

branches and all the Sephiroth.

It also explains my connection to Sai Baba, for he, in his mission as the cosmic Christ, has attempted to unify all religions under his cosmic leadership. In *Golden Keys to Ascension and Healing: Revelations of Sai Baba and the Ascended Masters* I have attempted to synthesize with the Earth level Sai Baba's unification, as an Eastern avatar, with the inner-plane ascended masters. This unification has always existed on the inner plane, but it is my mission, through his grace, to make this known throughout the New Age community and beyond.

In closing, Lord Metatron states, "Live in the light that has filled the pages of this meditation and in all the pages preceding. Live in the light I Am and the light You Are, and never hesitate to call upon me when any shadows need to be cast out or darkness veils the truth. For I am here to help, as are we all of the cosmic planetary brotherhood. And so should you be each unto the other."

Afterword of 1996-1997

Wesak 1996

By the grace of God the Wesak celebration unfolded perfectly. It was like four days of unfolding perfection. We ended up having almost 1300 people—truly one of the events of the century. Everyone involved fulfilled their parts, and there were almost no mistakes, which is amazing for an event this large and multifaceted. I did five of my most powerful ascension meditations. My friends did a wonderful job in their roles. There was an enormous level of love and oneness that was achieved, which is amazing, considering how diverse and unique were the lightworkers who attended. This was definitely the peak experience of my life.

By the grace of God, the second I got on stage on the opening night to start the program, I felt in absolute command, and that continued for four straight days. I honestly believe that the lightworkers there received one of the most powerful sequences of planetary and cosmic activations ever given for such a large group. Combining such an advanced group on Wesak in Mount Shasta to activate the first three waves of mass ascension was enormously powerful.

The feedback we have gotten has been gratifying. It is really hard to put into words how powerful and life-transforming this event was. To meditate for three straight days with this high a level of initiates and ascended beings under these circumstances was phenomenal. The masters were incredibly pleased when it was over. It had surpassed even their highest expectations. I actually had to turn away over 400 to 500 people because there was not enough room in the auditorium.

Putting on this event with my dear spiritual brother and my secretary and personal assistant was the biggest spiritual assignment I had ever taken on. I had spent a year of my life putting this event together, and it was deeply fulfilling to see it come together so well. It was one of those rare peak experiences where everything is perfect. My earthly father and my stepmother were there, and they were transformed. It felt good to me to have them see me at my best, as well as an enormous number of the spiritual leaders from around the globe and tens of thousands of ascended masters, both planetary and cosmic, in attendance—and I am not exaggerating.

It was a true celebration of unity among all lightworkers and all ascended masters, all coming together in oneness under the banner of ascension. It was God's ashram coming together, where no one was excluded and all were included. This may have been the most profound feeling of all for me. I had advertised this event as one of the events of the century, and the masters told us when it was over that it had truly achieved this goal. The guest speakers were wonderful, adding flavor to the work I and my friends presented. Even the cosmic masters were present at this event, which made it yet more powerful.

The highlight of the event may have been when I took everyone on a meditation to God's ascension seat. This was one of the most profound experiences of my life, and an enormous number of people there told me the same thing. The permission to go to God's ascension seat was a special Wesak dispensation given by Melchizedek and the Mahatma. It was allowed only because of the 1300 high-level initiates who formed a group body. As I said in a previous chapter, no single individual on Earth is allowed to visit this seat because of the danger to the etheric body. The special circumstances of Wesak and this unique group allowed this special dispensation. As earlier stated, the recording of this meditation can be safely used. Both those initiated and the lightworkers who are guided to use this meditation are carefully watched over by the masters so that no one exceeds the ring-pass-not of their own energy capacity. We have received permission to do this once a year at Wesak, which is another motivation for you, my beloved readers, to consider attending in the future. In a group such as this, as in all meditations, the power is increased a hundredfold!

It is extremely fulfilling to go for something 100 percent, not holding back anything, and have it work out so perfectly. It was one of those experiences where if I died now, I would die a very happy man, knowing that I had accomplished something significant. I do not mean this to come across as egotistical; I am simply trying to share my feelings of fulfillment, happiness, joy and satisfaction with the outcome.

I feel transformed by the whole experience, as I feel everyone does who attended either physically or spiritually. I feel that I moved into my full leadership as a spokesperson for the planetary ascension movement and as head of Djwhal Khul, Lord Maitreya and Melchizedek's global ashram. The second most fulfilling thing was afterward, when we were told that as of this Wesak we had officially completed the first nine levels of planetary ascension and were now ready to enter the tenth level, which is the solar level, officially beginning cosmic ascension.

This Wesak, the masters said, was the capstone, the official completion, of planetary ascension. Sai Baba, Lord Melchizedek and Metatron entered our bodies, signifying our readiness for cosmic ascension activation. Metatron did this by installing within us the platinum rod (the rod of light that connects us with the God crystals at the 352nd level of the Godhead) and pouring down the platinum ray, the most advanced cosmic ray available to lightworkers on Earth, on a continual basis. We were allowed to receive this for fulfilling our spiritual assignments. This is an activation we will do again at the next Wesak, which I encourage all my readers to attend. The feeling of completing the first nine dimensions in terms of anchoring and activating all chakra bodies, light quotients and all the rest is quite fulfilling. I share this not to imply how great I am or we are, but to let you know that this is also available to you, my beloved readers, if you will follow the simple, practical steps outlined in my books.

All the meditations I have received I did at Wesak. I know for a fact that in the history of the Earth there have never been so many activations at one event. It will take years for the lightworkers to consciously understand what they received then. Actually, most will never consciously realize all they received—and that applies to me, too.

On the Monday following the event was a meeting with around seventy-five of the major spiritual leaders from around the globe. I was asked by Melchizedek to chair this meeting. It was designed to bring all the spiritual leaders together to help one another and transcend all negative-ego consciousness, separation and selfishness. I think everyone agreed this had been accomplished and a great precedent had been set for humanity. This will continue each year. The meeting was held spiritually in Shamballa under the leadership of Lord Buddha, and the masters were in attendance, overlighting the different earthly high-level initiates and ascended beings who attended. This meeting was a tremendous success, and I was very pleased about this, too.

The Wesak celebration was so successful that it was a foregone conclusion I would spend the next year of my life setting up the next one. The plan was to do the next two in 1997 and 1998 in Mount Shasta, again for 1400 people, then in the year 2000 do one for 9000 people. My ultimate goal, moving toward the year 2012, is to do one for 50,000 people in some outdoor stadium. Can you imagine doing these profound ascension-activation meditations for 50,000 people? Can you imagine the effect this would have on the planet? Doing it with 1300 high-level initiates and ascended beings had been stupendous. The masters have guided me to make the Wesak celebration three times bigger every two years so that there is a step-by-step progression.

The key to making this kind of an event work is to have an excellent team of people working with me, and by the grace of God, this is what has now developed. I would highly recommend that people come to this event each year, for it is a time for us all to come together in our larger group body and celebrate.

This is the first time in humanity's history that Wesak is being celebrated on such a large scale in such an inclusive, universalistic and eclectic event, where all are invited regardless of religion, mystery school, spiritual teacher, ashram or path. All are welcome in Melchizedek's and/or God's ashram, which is really what this event is all about. People came to this event from every country on the globe, which was very exciting. I had made it my personal promise to consciously invite *every* planetary and cosmic master in the infinite universe to attend, so when I said there were tens of thousands of inner-plane ascended masters helping and watching, I was serious. You can see why I was so grateful and fulfilled by such an event. For one weekend, all of creation was focused on this little speck of a planet.

All of creation was watching because all of creation was consciously invoked in my meditations. I did this in a methodical manner to make sure no one was missed. My goal was to have one massive love fest with initiates, ascended masters and spiritual leaders from around the globe and all the planetary and cosmic masters I could possibly invoke in the Planetary and Cosmic Hierarchy—and, by the grace of God, it worked! It is difficult to put into words the feelings and transformations that occurred, but having done my best, I am sure this has given you some sense of it. (I have the audio tapes of the event, which are available.) It was a four-day event I will always treasure. It is my hope and prayer that in the future we may be able to do as well or even better than this, but for now I am eternally grateful for what our team accomplished at Wesak 1996.

This event and the official completion of my planetary ascension is the fitting end of this book, for it began with the beginning of my sixth initiation and ascension and ends with the beginning of the tenth initiation in a group body, even though heretofore no one has been allowed to go beyond the seventh initiation until leaving the physical body.

I was just told that by completing my planetary ascension and consciously working on my cosmic ascension, my cosmic light quotient is 12 to 15 percent. I share this information to give you a sense of how, once you achieve the 99 percent light quotient on the planetary scale and begin to work consciously on the cosmic scale, your spiritual goal is the equivalent of a tenth-degree initiate. Ninety-nine percent is equivalent to 10 percent on the cosmic light-quotient scale.

One other interesting piece of information I received on the mechanics of evolution has to do with cleansing karma. All of you remember from *The Complete Ascension Manual* how one has to balance or cleanse 51 percent of one's soul karma to achieve ascension, or the beginning of the sixth initiation.

What I was told was that I had balanced and/or cleansed approximately 80 percent of my karma now as the equivalent of a tenth-degree initiate.

Upon further questioning, Melchizedek, the Mahatma and Metatron told me that 15 percent of this karma was physical and only 5 percent was on the mental and emotional levels. The spiritual level has no negative karma for anyone and returns only positive karma. This shows the importance of focusing on cleansing karma as well as building light quotient. The key to accelerating evolution is in the mechanics.

I hope my personal experience in this book will be useful to you in your similar journey. If this is the case, great joy wells up in my heart. Never forget that all are God, nothing exists but God, and I am nothing more than God talking to God, who is receiving guidance from God. It is the same being speaking to itself through different lenses and bodies. So when you are helped, I am helped; and when I am helped, you are helped. The truth of creation is, we all are the eternal Self, simply incarnated in infinite forms that transcend the illusions of matter. Namasté.

Sai Baba Meditation

The other spiritual experience I had immediately after the Wesak Festival and which also was one of the most touching and gratifying moments in my life, was when Sai Baba came to me in a meditation. He told me how pleased he was with the new book I had recently completed—*The Golden Keys to Ascension and Healing: Revelations of Sai Baba and the Ascended Masters*. He also told me how pleased he was at how I represented myself at the recently completed Wesak celebration. Then he told me that because of my past devotion to him and my books and Wesak Festivals, he was holding an eternal place in his ashram for me on the inner plane. This gracious and unexpected gift and compliment was the most meaningful of all the positive feedback we have received since this event.

The fact that this feedback came from Sai Baba, whom I revere and love so profoundly, obviously made it even more significant to me. In a later meditation he gave me an ever-expanding flower filled with the essence and aroma of the "heart of love itself," which I placed in my heart as a sacred bond of eternal devotion.

My beloved readers, as with the Mahatma, do call on Sai Baba for help in all ways and all things. Regardless of your religion, spiritual path, mystery school, spiritual teacher and/or ascended masters you work with, Sai Baba will always be there as a type of cosmic guru and teacher who has no need for you to change your spiritual path to receive his omnipotent, omnipresent and omniscient blessings as the Cosmic Christ on Earth, the highest physically incarnated being in the history of the Earth.

After you read *The Golden Keys to Ascension and Healing: Revelations of Sai Baba and the Ascended Masters* and Howard Murphet's two books on Sai Baba, I personally guarantee that you will never be the same! Sai Ram

Between 1996 and 1997 Wesak

The year after Wesak 1996 was amazing. The tremendous success of the Wesak Festival prompted an enormous number of phone calls and correspondence from around the globe. The masters guided me to officially end my partnership and core-group connection, telling me that it was time for each of us to stand in our own leadership and do our own thing, so to speak. They told me that this group-consciousness process had been an experiment and a very successful one, but the process was now complete. This was done in an extremely loving way, and I am still great friends with all parties involved. Although we are no longer professionally connected, we are still extremely supportive of one another. The truth is, we still work together under the umbrella of God's ashram. My personal destiny, as explained to me by Melchizedek, the Mahatma, Metatron and Djwhal Khul, is to eventually take over sole leadership of Djwhal Khul's inner-plane Synthesis Ashram when he moves on in his cosmic evolution. I currently hold this leadership position on Earth for him and I am in training with Djwhal, the three M's (Melchizedek, the Mahatma, Metatron) and the core twenty-one (the council of inner-plane masters I work with).

I am very grateful and appreciative for the two-year experience I had in this partnership. I grew tremendously, as I know they did. If I had to do it over again, I wouldn't change a thing. It was like a beautiful and wonderful marriage that was simply time to end. I didn't stay too long in this marriage, and I didn't leave too soon. I remained in the perfect tao, as they did, and I couldn't be more grateful and appreciative for the experience and the loving conclusion of the process. It lasted exactly as long as it was supposed to for all of us, and now a new destiny and adventure begins for us. I thank God, the masters and my partners for this two-year experience. This transformation led to a new process, which I will now briefly share with you, my beloved readers.

The Melchizedek Synthesis Light Academy & Ashram

One of the first major changes that took place was the guidance from the masters to change the name of the Synthesis Ashram to the Melchizedek Synthesis Light Ashram, and to establish for the first time the Melchizedek Synthesis Light Academy. The name of the ashram and academy speaks to Melchizedek (the Universal Logos) and synthesis, which refers to the Mahatma, also known as the Avatar of Synthesis. Light refers to Archangel Metatron, who is the creator of the electron and the creator of all outer light in our universe. On a galactic, solar and planetary level, the term "synthesis" refers to the ascended master Djwhal Khul, who is leader of the second-ray synthesis ashram on the inner planes in our Planetary Hierarchy.

"Synthesis" also refers to the core twenty-one, which is the loving term I use for the council of masters I work with when writing books, articles, doing Wesak and running the academy and ashram. These twenty-one masters are Melchizedek, the Mahatma, Metatron, the divine Mother, Sai Baba, Helios and Vesta, Lord Buddha, Lord Maitreya, Saint Germain, Quan Yin, Virgin Mary, Lakshmi, Djwhal Khul, El Morya, Kuthumi, Serapis Bey, Paul the Venetian, Hilarion, Sananda and Isis. "Synthesis" also refers to all the masters of the Planetary and Cosmic Hierarchy, so everyone is included. This, my beloved readers, is the true nature of my work—to bring forth synthesis on all levels. This can be seen in the encyclopedic nature of my thirty-volume series, the synthesis nature of all the lightworkers and inner-plane masters involved at the yearly Wesak Festival in Mount Shasta, and the synthesizing character of the academy and the ashram itself.

The Melchizedek Synthesis Light Academy is the newest process that the inner-plane masters have guided me to create. It is a multifaceted mobile teaching vehicle that sponsors the yearly Wesak celebrations in Mount Shasta and the thirty-volume series of books, fifteen of which are now complete at this writing. It also sponsors spiritual, psychological, and physical healing sessions available by phone and a correspondence course that the masters have asked me to create over the next two to three years to train spiritual counselors and teachers and ascension seekers in the work of fully realizing "integrated ascension," the title of the book I am currently working on (*Integrated Ascension: Revelation for the Next Millennium*). I am very excited about this entire process and the tremendous expansion of the Melchizedek Synthesis Light Academy & Ashram that is now taking place.

My Thirty-Volume Series

One amazing development after 1996 Wesak was the completion of eight new books beyond the five already published. These eight books are *Cosmic Ascension, Your Cosmic Map Home (Vol. 6); A Beginner's Guide to the Path of Ascension (Vol. 7); Golden Keys to Ascension and Healing: Revelations of Sai Baba and the Ascended Masters (Vol. 8); Manual for Planetary Leadership (Vol. 9); Your Ascension Mission: Embracing Your Puzzle Piece (Vol. 10);* this volume; *How to Teach Ascension Classes (Vol. 12); Ascension and Romantic Relationships (Vol. 13);* and *How to Clear the Negative Ego.* When the last-named book was in manuscript form I was able to finish *Integrated Ascension: Revelation for the Next Millennium.* By the time the last book is published, the others will be out. (I am still negotiating with a major publisher for the last two.) Meanwhile they are available by mail in manuscript form.

This year I will work on *The Divine Mother and the Lady Masters, Revelations of the Mahatma* and *The Divine Blueprint for the Golden Age.* My plan is to finish them this year. The series is a cocreation of myself and the Spiritual Hierarchy, in which we consolidate ancient and modern hierarchical teachings into one series. It has been one of the greatest joys of my life to write them. I have the titles already lined up for the next fifteen volumes. My goal is to complete three or four books a year. The only thing slowing this process is the time needed to complete the correspondence course for the Melchizedek Synthesis Light Academy. It is my sincere hope and prayer that you, my beloved readers, have found these books useful.

Taking My Eleventh Initiation

As mentioned earlier, I took my tenth initiation at Wesak 1996. After this Wesak I asked Archangel Metatron how long it would take to achieve my eleventh initiation. In the beginning of the year he told me it would probably take two to three years. This was because the previous nine initiations each dealt with anchoring and activating only seven chakras. As the tenth initiation was the beginning of cosmic ascension, it required the anchoring and activation of *fifty* chakras. (You can see how much vaster the cosmic initiations are compared to the planetary initiations.) The first nine initiations together involve anchoring and activating chakras 1 through 50. The movement from the tenth to the eleventh initiation required anchoring and activating chakras 50 to 100. It also required integrating and cleansing 10,000 soul extensions of one's monadic group, compared to integrating and cleansing 144 soul extensions for the first nine initiations.

As the year developed, such enormous expansions and developments on all levels were taking place that with the help of the cosmic and planetary masters I was able to take my eleventh initiation in *one year*—in other words, at the 1997 Wesak celebration! Much of the progress I made occurred on the inner plane, because most of the year I was completely immersed in my service work and did not really meditate much. My life became my meditation, and it was truly the grace of the masters that pushed me forward so quickly. For this reason I refer to working with the cosmic and planetary ascended masters as the rocketship to God. To anchor and activate 50 chakras and 10,000 soul extensions and the needed light quotient in this short period was truly amazing to me, and quite humbling. This initiation involved the integration and activation of the solar level and solar body, which is the tenth-level body. The eleventh-level body is the galactic, and the twelfth-level initiation and body deal with the universal level. My gratitude to the cosmic and planetary masters, especially Melchizedek, the Mahatma, Metatron and Djwhal Khul, is enormous.

My God Ascension-Seat Experience

After Wesak 1996 one day I was speaking with the three M's and asked if I could receive permission to go into the God ascension seat by myself. Previously this was allowed only at the Wesak celebration in Mount Shasta and on a couple of other occasions when it was done with the core group. I had been told in the past that the level of frequency of the God ascension seat was so high that no one on the planet except maybe Sai Baba was allowed to go there alone because of the danger to the etheric body. (Again, this should not be a concern for those who bought the tapes of my God Ascension Seat Meditation, for no one is allowed into the God ascension seat on his or her own. Those who are using the tape or this meditation are watched over by the masters, and there is a special cap placed on each person to prevent overstimulation and keep you just at the outer rim of the ascension seat.) You must remember that this is level 352. To my surprise, the three M's gave me permission to go by myself. I had spent so much time sitting in the various ascension seats throughout the cosmos at the time that I didn't look at this as a big deal. I didn't realize the profundity of what I was doing.

This may sound funny to my readers, but I used to enjoy sitting in the ascension seats while I watched television. I would go into a kind of hypnosis, blanking my mind, which was perfect for meditation. I asked the three M's about watching the television and they said it was a great idea. They wished more lightworkers would do it. In the past it allowed me to meditate for much longer periods of time without becoming distracted or uncomfortable after a longer meditation.

So I casually turned on the TV, plopped myself down on my comfortable chair and said, "Three M's, God ascension seat." I was so used to soul travel and bilocation that I instantly went into the heart and center of the God ascension seat when *Roseanne* began. The energy I felt was enormous, but this was such a common practice for me that it didn't seem to be a big deal. I got lost in watching two episodes of *Roseanne* when in truth I should have come out of the God ascension seat after about thirty minutes. I felt wonderful, but the extra thirty minutes at that level of frequency was far too much for even me to handle, and my liver got totally fried.

It took me about a week to ten days to recover. I didn't feel physically that bad; I was just subtly aware that my liver had been electrically overloaded and was not functioning normally. I asked the three M's and Djwhal what had happened, and they told me that because I had been given the keys to the kingdom, so to speak, as leader of the Synthesis Ashram, as a high priest spokesperson for the planetary ascension movement and as anchor and focal point for the Mahatma energy, I was basically allowed to go where I pleased. I was my own guard, so to speak. As is my style, I had gone right to the heart and center of the God ascension seat, which most lightworkers are not allowed to enter.

I learned an important lesson from this experience. I was not invulnerable; there was a level of energy that was too much for me to handle. It was a wonderful experience, and I was not sorry about it, but I learned to be more respectful of the power of some of the activations I was working with. Djwhal told me it had a very positive effect on my spiritual growth. It also had an incredibly cleansing effect on my liver, but it was a little quicker than I was ready to handle all at once.

The masters on the inner plane got a big kick out of it. They told me that where I had gone, most of them had never gone themselves. The funny thing is, all I did was say, "Three M's, God ascension seat" and watched *Roseanne!* I think this experience was one of the reasons I made such rapid spiritual progress that year. It wasn't the only reason, but it was one catalyzing event. I continue to find the experience very humorous, as do the masters I work with.

The other lesson I learned from it was how easy it is for me to meditate. Yogis strain and put themselves through all kinds of contortions to experience God at higher and higher levels. I said five quick words, plopped on the chair, watched *Roseanne*, and entered the heart of God. I share this as a lesson to all my beloved readers that *the experience of higher and higher levels of divinity does not have to be a major strain or require years of asceticism.* I am not saying that you will go to the same place I did. The many years of meditating, soul travel and bilocation at lower levels as well as the level of initiation and leadership responsibilities I have been given allowed me to have this experience. You, my beloved readers, can just as easily go to the Golden Chamber of Melchizedek, for example. Make the request and it is literally that simple.

Part of the lesson here for all lightworkers is that more or higher is not necessarily better. What is best is the amount of light or activations you are ready for and that is in the tao for you to work with. This reminds me of certain yogic practices that try to force the raising of kundalini. This is a practice that the inner-plane ascended masters do not recommend. Many lightworkers would like to go straight to the God ascension seat and skip the planetary, solar, galactic, universal and multiuniversal levels. I have spent many, many, many years working at these different levels, which has slowly but surely prepared me for this experience. Even though I was prepared and had been given the keys to the kingdom, the amount of time one spends has also to be considered. Being a master, I was given permission to do what I wanted. I am very respectful of that privilege now. The key lesson here being not to force the tao. If you go too slow, you will miss the wave when surfing; however, if you go too fast, you will get dumped by it. The key to life is to live in the tao. As Buddha said so eloquently, "Follow the middle path."

God Ascension-Seat Anchoring

One other activation that greatly accelerated my spiritual progress after 1996 Wesak was a request I made to the three M's for the anchoring of the God ascension seat into my home and ashram. The three M's told me that this would take about two to three months to accomplish, for it could not be done too quickly. However, once it was accomplished, my spiritual progress was greatly accelerated.

Health Activations

Another activation I worked with this year that greatly helped my physical health I stumbled upon in my work with the masters. This was the *cosmic viral and bacterial vacuum*. With all the acceleration, I would sometimes feel subclinical viral or bacterial energy in my field. I would immediately call to the three M's, Dr. Lorphan and the galactic healers to suck it out of my system like a vacuum. Beloved readers, it works! Try it; you'll like it. The masters also told me to call on the *platinum net* to run through my field, my house, the ashram. It instantly gets rid of all imbalanced energy.

Two other spiritual/physical health tools I was guided by the masters to use that were of enormous benefit were, first, the help from the *platinum angels*. Whenever my throat would get sore or irritated from talking so much on the phone with students, employees, friends, family and while working, I worked out a deal with the platinum angels to come into my throat twenty-four hours a day, seven days a week, 365 days a year, to heal it and keep any bacteria out if it got irritated or strained. The Lord of Arcturus, Dr. Lorphan, the three M's and the galactic healers have also been extremely helpful here.

This is just one example of how I have used spirit and the masters. In truth, I use them for all of my physical health requirements. In the past I used the masters on more of a spiritual and professional level. This year I really took advantage of their phenomenal healing abilities. For all your health needs, do call Dr. Lorphan, the director of the healing academy on Sirius, and his team of galactic healers. The work they do is unbelievable. I am literally getting healing treatments twenty-four hours a day or whenever I need or ask for them. He is offering his services to all sincere lightworkers. He and his team are the finest healers in the galaxy.

The other healing tool I have found extremely helpful was an idea given to me by the three M's. I place a *platinum screen* in all the doorways and archways of my home and ashram. Once put in place, every time I walk through a door or archway in my home or ashram, my entire twelve-body system is automatically cleared with a platinum net. Any imbalanced energy is immediately cleared from my energy fields and shoots up the platinum net back to Source and the energy is then made available to me for service work. Beloved readers, I share this to encourage you to ask that this be set up in your own home so that your field will be constantly and automatically cleared.

A Constant Energy Circulation by the Three M's

One other ascension activation that I feel had an enormously powerful effect is a request I made to the three M's to run their energy twenty-four hours a day, seven days a week, 365 days a year. This became my spiritual blood, so to speak, and the *platinum ray* became the main source of my energy. The platinum ray is the highest color frequency available to lightworkers on Earth. Once we go beyond the platinum energy, we move to Source energy itself, which is beyond color.

Beloved readers, lightworkers must understand that once you get tapped into working with the ascended masters, it is like riding a wave of energy. You are brought along in a group consciousness in the wave that is right for you. Pray to the ascended masters to accelerate your spiritual progress as fast as possible while keeping you within the tao of your process. One of the biggest lessons I have learned in the past couple of years is how much spiritual growth can take place on the inner plane without having to work so hard to achieve it. This is the grace of working with the cosmic and planetary ascended masters. "Ask and you shall receive; knock and the door shall be opened."

I have explored hundreds of new ascension activations this year. The best I used at the 1997 Wesak Festival. They are given in Appendix A.

A Series of God Experiences

There were three other God experiences that had an enormous impact and acceleration on my spiritual progress this year. They were so profound and so humbling that I have seriously debated whether they should even be shared. I am making the choice in this moment to share them because I have, in writing this book, decided to tell all. Sharing them almost feels sacrilegious, but I do so out of love for you, my readers, in order to give my full story.

During a two-week period sometime between the 1996 and 1997 Wesak celebrations, I was exploring not only the God ascension seat, but the personal presence of God the Creator. I asked at one point if I could actually talk to God. I figured that if I could talk to the Mahatma or Melchizedek or Metatron, why couldn't I talk to God? Upon making this request, the Mahatma said that this was not possible, but that he would be willing as a special grace to channel God for me.

This experience was beyond anything I can say in words. Through these conversations, in a two-week period I made certain prayer requests (which are not appropriate to get into here), and as a byproduct certain blessings were bestowed. One of these was anchoring as much of God's lightbody into my field as I could handle; another was the light rod of God touching my head. Finally, I requested the anchoring of God into my field on Earth. God graced me by placing into my field His energy, the size of a grain of sand.

Realize that God, the infinite Creator, is immeasurably vast. For example, Melchizedek, the Universal Logos, is in charge of our universe, which contains millions upon millions of galaxies and billions of solar systems and planets. This is just one universe, and there are infinite numbers of universes. Now, this is just the *physical* dimension. There are at least forty-eight dimensions that are much vaster and more infinite than the physical universe. So receiving on Earth a grain of sand of God is enormous. There is probably no one on Earth who anchors more than three percent of Melchizedek's energy, and Melchizedek embodies our entire universe. Our planet is only one of ten billion inhabited planets in our universe alone. With an infinite number of universes, receiving a grain of sand of God is extraordinarily significant.

This series of experiences had an enormous impact on me and, along with my God ascension-seat experience, was a powerful catalyst toward shortening Metatron's original estimate of two to three years to only one year for moving to my eleventh initiation.

I received one last God activation that I shared at the 1997 Wesak Festival: the anchoring of the God seed packets into my field while I slept at night. These inner-plane seed packets are enormously powerful and catalyzing. I also requested seed packets from the Mahatma, the Multiuniversal Logos, Melchizedek, Melchior, Helios and Vesta, and Lord Buddha. I would highly recommend that you, my friends, make a similar request. I share these things for your enjoyment and edification.

Two further God experiences I remember from this time period are requests I made to anchor God crystals from the 352nd level of the Godhead at night while I slept. Once this request was agreed to, I requested the anchoring of the Mahatma crystals, the Multiuniversal Logos crystals, the Melchizedek crystals, the Melchior crystals, the Helios and Vesta crystals and the Lord Buddha crystals from Shamballa. These beings, of course, are the logoi at each octave, moving from planetary to solar to galactic to universal to multiuniversal and Godhead level.

Once this activation was set up, I also requested the anchoring of God's heart into my twelve-body system. Once this was anchored and activated, the same request was made at each of these progressive levels mentioned above and from the different logoi at each level.

The culmination of all these God blessings basically resulted in a direct spiritual current from God permanently set in place. I specifically asked for this and was told by the Mahatma that it was so. In a later activation I requested this in a different way, and I called it forth again at the 1997 Wesak celebration in my Ultimate Cosmic Ray Meditation when I called forth the Ray of God. In this meditation I also called forth all the planetary rays and all the rays at each successive octave leading back to the Godhead, as was the case with the God seed packets and seed-crystal ascension activation described above. (The Ultimate Cosmic Ray Meditation appears in Appendix A.) I think you can see how this series profoundly accelerated my ascension and initiation process.

Melchizedek Anchoring

I had a dream earlier in the year where I was told that I was one of the twelve prophets of Melchizedek. This came when I was writing *Cosmic Ascension*. I've always felt a tremendous connection to Melchizedek, as the name of this book signifies. One of the anchorings I requested during this year was for the full anchoring of Melchizedek's energy within me on Earth. What he told me was that by Wesak 1997 I would embody three percent of his full energy as Universal Logos. He told me that each year thereafter I would embody one percent more. Given what a vast being he is, whose body is our entire universe, this seemed an enormous amount, and I was very grateful to Melchizedek for this blessing. You, my beloved readers, can ask for Melchizedek, the Mahatma, Metatron, the Divine Mother, Sai Baba, Archangel Michael or any master of your choice to anchor their energy within you in a progressively increasing manner. The wisdom I had was to ask, and to live a life dedicated to unconditional love and selfless service. If you do the same, all blessings will also be bestowed upon you at the level and potential you are able to receive and use them for the purpose of serving mankind and all the kingdoms of God.

Living on Light

One of the byproducts of running the level of frequency and energy I do and the strict dietary practices I have kept for many years is that more and more I'm living on light—or, as I like to say, I'm living on God and the three M's. I eat very little food. The three M's have told me that they still want me to eat a little food for certain grounding purposes, but the amount I live on would seem impossible to the third-dimensional mind. For me, it is the ideal diet, the perfect way to eat. I didn't force anything; it just happened. The masters do not recommend that people live totally on light except in very, very rare instances.

Cosmic Love Quotient and the Light Rods of God

There's an enormous amount of focus now among lightworkers upon increasing one's light or light quotient. One thing that has been conveyed to me by the masters is the equal importance of also increasing one's love quotient. I received a great deal of help from the three M's, the divine Mother, Sai Baba, Lord Maitreya and the Virgin Mary this year in increasing my love quotient. It is important for lightworkers to realize that there must be an equal balance of love, wisdom and power to fully realize God. Call for this in your meditations.

Another a series of activations I worked with this year was calling forth from the different logoi at the planetary, solar, galactic and universal levels the light rods of Lord Buddha, Helios and Vesta, Melchior and Melchizedek. These light rods had an enormously catalyzing and accelerating effect on my ascension process and in building my light quotient.

Huna Prayers

Many of you have read my book *Beyond Ascension*, in which I spoke of the value of creating Huna prayers for yourself. I believe it is one of the most powerful prayer processes available on Earth. It involves writing out a prayer to God and the ascended masters, saying it three times, then commanding the subconscious mind to take the prayer to God and all the masters with all the vital force and mana needed to manifest and demonstrate the prayer.

One of the most powerful ascension activations of the entire year that occurred on an almost daily basis was doing my Huna prayers in the different ashrams of the different masters around the cosmos. For example, each day I would go to the different ashrams of the different masters of the core twenty-one. This would be done through bilocation. Whatever Huna prayer I was working on, all the masters would gather upon my request in the ashram I had chosen. The entire cosmos soon became familiar with my prayers. It became a most wonderful gathering of masters on the inner plane, and I honestly feel that they even enjoyed the camaraderie.

Every day we would gather in a new place in the cosmos, which would be hosted by a different master that day. I would begin the process by asking them to join me in saying The Great Invocation that Lord Maitreya brought forth for the world, and then we would all do the Huna prayer together.

Once in a while I would add different prayers. For example, if we went to the Virgin Mary's ashram, we would do the rosary. This process became one of the most enjoyable parts of the day, and at the end I and my staff would spontaneously share any other personal prayers we had. I would do this for all the Huna prayers I had created, whatever the subject. So it was actually a combination of traditional, Huna and spontaneous prayers of all of us. It was also a meditation.

This illustrates what I tried to say earlier when I mentioned that my life and service work became my meditation. I don't rationally know how or why; I just know that doing this prayer process almost every day not only helped manifest all my goals and priorities on every level, but also greatly helped in my ascension activation.

Djwhal told me that the members of his ashram on the inner plane took on some of my Huna prayers as their own in an attempt to further the expansion of the Hierarchy's mission on Earth.

My beloved readers, I share this information, as guided by the masters, to encourage you to consider using such a method of prayer practice yourself. A detailed explanation of how to use the Huna prayer method is in *Beyond Ascension*.

An Exercise in Psychological Archetypal Personages

I had a number of visions, dreams and conversations with the masters during this year that related to my psychological archetypal pattern. My energy is unique, but certain archetypal themes and images were emerging that related to my particular essence and mission. My essence seemed to be made up archetypically of four masters, which may surprise my readers: the ascended master Djwhal Khul, Sananda, Moses, and Abraham Lincoln! I had a dream during the year in which I was telling someone that my name was Djwahl Khul. This is how much our energies had merged over time. In an experience about seven or eight years ago Vywamus told me in one of my first encounters with him that I looked like a younger version of Djwhal Khul, something about the intensity in my eyes. I want to make it clear here that I am speaking of psychological archetypes, not past lives.

I've always had a close connection to Sananda, and the name *Joshua* in the metaphysical dictionary is another name for Jesus. Sananda has told me that I look much like he did in his life as Jesus. He told me that if I would grow my hair a little longer and part it down the middle, the physical resemblance would be striking. I have an enormous attunement and affinity to *A Course in Miracles*, which he wrote. When I look in the mirror I see a great deal of Jewish prophet energy. Sananda has told me that my mission this lifetime is much like his was 2000 years ago, in terms of bringing in a new dispensation of teachings and in some of the choices I have made. I've had many dreams that showed me this connection, and I often call upon Sananda's teachings, both biblical and modern, and upon him personally for healing.

I remember attending a three-month channeling class many, many years ago, after which we did an exercise where we went around the room and the people in the class told you who you reminded them of. It just so happened that when starting this class I knew none of the people personally. Everyone in the class said I reminded them of Moses, majestically carrying his books. I've always admired Moses, although I've not called on him very much. The Mahatma told me he was connected to my monad somehow. One of my favorite movies of all time is *The Ten Commandments*. I love the scene where Moses goes to the top of the mountain and talks to the burning bush, then comes back down and is transformed. My past-life incarnations are definitely Judeo-Christian in essence, which I greatly love. Joshua was also a biblical figure who led the Jewish people to the promised land after Moses died. Interestingly, the biblical figure of Joshua was also a past life of Jesus. The synchronicity is quite eerie.

When I changed my name to Joshua at the age of twenty-seven (I am now forty-four in 1997), the director of the counseling center where I worked told me that I *looked* like a Joshua. Only the previous night, she said, she had been watching a movie about Jesus and thought to herself that I reminded her of him. I've had many dreams telling me I looked like Jesus. When Sai Baba materialized a lost medallion for me, which he told me would be a symbol of his and my connection, it wasn't a picture of him, but a picture of Jesus receiving the Holy Spirit. Sai Baba knew what he was doing.

I had a dream where I was shown that my archetypal essence was similar to that of Abraham Lincoln. Many people have told me that I look like Lincoln. I have a lot of first-ray energy in my field and a certain aura of leadership. I am very interested in politics and constantly watch the news and all the political talk shows. I would highly recommend that you read *Manual for Planetary Leadership*, in which I have given free expression to this aspect of myself. Some of the leadership that I've been given in Djwhal Khul's Synthesis Ashram, the Melchizedek Synthesis Light Ashram and the Melchizedek Synthesis Light Academy is related to this energy.

Leadership is quite natural to me, and the Wesak celebrations are my attempt to unite the entire spiritual movement and bring all the spiritual leaders from all paths together for one united celebration. Understanding these archetypal themes within my own consciousness and past-life structure has helped me to understand and manifest my mission more clearly. I encourage you to explore the archetypal personages that make up the core themes of your own soul, monadic essence and puzzle piece as a possible useful exercise.

Very early in my life, even as early as twenty-one, I knew my spiritual name was Joshua. As the 1996 Wesak program ended, the first person to approach me was a woman who said, "Did you have a past life as Moses and Abraham Lincoln?" I just smiled and politely said no; however, inwardly it did not surprise me in the slightest that this lady had picked up on this archetypal relationship.

Two New Ascension Seats

Two new incredibly powerful ascension seats I worked with this year were the ascension seats of the divine Mother and the divine Father at the left and right side of God. I have shared these ascension seats with you in my updated God Ascension Seat Meditation, which you will find in Appendix A.

The 1997 Wesak Ceremony

My beloved readers, I have also placed in this book the Wesak ceremony meditation given to me by the masters, which was performed at the 1997 Wesak celebration. The masters wish me to suggest that if you cannot come to the Wesak Festival in Mount Shasta each year, they would like you to set up a Wesak ceremony in your local area and use this meditation at the exact moment of the full moon, or at the exact moment you are celebrating the Wesak. This is a request put forth by the entire Cosmic and Planetary Hierarchy at this moment through me, for they would like the Wesak to be celebrated in every city around the globe. They suggest that you request them to be linked to this global event in Mount Shasta and to the actual Wesak ceremony in the Wesak Valley in the Himalayas, which are the two most powerful events on the planet at Wesak.

You are welcome to use any other meditations as well as a preliminary process to build the energies if you feel guided to do so. In *Cosmic Ascension* I give information on Wesak and the twelve major festivals. The Wesak is the high point each year of the incoming spiritual energies to the Earth. Please deeply consider the request. It does not matter if you celebrate the Wesak with two people or 200, but you are now being asked to step forward to set up an event in your home or a larger event if you feel guided to do so.

The masters of the Spiritual Hierarchy thank you for considering this act of service. The event could consist of reading together the chapter on the twelve major festivals, doing a preliminary ascension-activation meditation, then at the appropriate time doing the actual Wesak ceremony. (These meditations are available on tape, which can make the process quite simple. If you contact me, I can share with you the exact time of the rising full moon in Taurus, thus exactly when the Wesak ceremony begins in the Himalayas. I will give this to you in Pacific Standard Time, which can then be adjusted to your zone.) I would be honored if you would consider connecting your Wesak ceremony with the one I conduct on behalf of the Hierarchy in Mount Shasta. In this way we will all be spokes on a wheel and share the collective love, light and power of the Godhead for the purpose of spiritual rejuvenation and planetary world service.

Wesak 1997[1]

Wesak 1997 was another tremendous success. We again had 1200 high-level initiates and ascended beings in attendance in Mount Shasta. This year I changed the concept of Wesak slightly to make it a little more of a group-consciousness event. There were many guest speakers. channels and musicians. All presenters performed their roles beautifully, and a tremendous feeling of God consciousness and cohesion was created. As the director and main coordinator of this event, I began a year in advance, and with the help of my staff in Los Angeles, professionalized the event and organized every detail—and it showed. By the grace of God and the masters, the event was a unanimous success even beyond the previous year, which I didn't think was possible. (I am simply telling the honest truth of my own observations as well as the tremendous amount of feedback I have gotten.)

The masters told me that there were over 50,000 inner-plane ascended masters and angels in attendance, and over the entire weekend there were another 100,000 cosmic and planetary ascended masters and angels who dropped in, so to speak, for different aspects of the program. It was truly a watershed event. My sister had a dream a week before she came, where she was at Wesak and kept saying to herself that everything was so professional. She had never been to Wesak before, and when she experienced the actual celebration, it was exactly like her dream.

The masters were very pleased. To me it was an example of what can be done when all 352 levels of the Godhead are honored equally and everyone involved fulfills their puzzle piece without negative-ego interference. This Wesak truly went beyond my highest expectations, just as had the previous Wesak. The primary feeling I have about the 1997 celebration is that it fulfilled its highest seed potential. It is not often in life that this can be done. It had taken me an entire year to put this event together, working twelve hours a day, six days a week for the entire year. I had a staff of about twenty-five people helping me at the festival, who were brilliant. It was very fulfilling for me personally to spend an entire year of my life working on something and see it actualize its highest potential.

Our opening night I unveiled my newest meditation, Ultimate Cosmic Ray Meditation. This meditation goes through all the planetary, solar, galactic, universal and multiuniversal rays, culminating with the God Ray. On

---

[1] See Appendix A for these meditations.

Saturday night I did the God Ascension-Seat Meditation, which I did last year, but with much new material.

On Sunday evening for the first time I did the official Wesak ceremony, which was incredible. My earthly father, who was in attendance, came up to me after that meditation and told me it was the most beautiful he had ever experienced. Later that evening I did the Special Ascension Activation for Wesak (see Appendix A). On Monday, after the main event and celebration, I hosted a leadership meeting for around 125 of the leading spiritual teachers and leaders from around the globe. The Mount Shasta resort served a buffet lunch, and our meeting fostered great networking and mutual support for one another and the divine plan. On a spiritual level the meeting was held in a large conference room in Shamballa. Each person in physical attendance was overlighted by an ascended master of their choice, and we were all bilocated the entire day as the meeting progressed. Melchizedek asked me to chair the meeting, which I was happy to do. There was a great feeling of camaraderie, friendship, joy and laughter.

The synchronicity of the universe never ceases to amaze me. As it turned out, four o'clock on that Monday—the exact moment of the full moon in Taurus when the Wesak ceremony in the Himalayas occurred—was the exact time the leadership meeting ended. This was perfect, for it ended with a final meditation that took us to the sacred Wesak Valley in the Himalayas. As it turned out, after the meditation we stayed just a little bit longer, continuing till around five o'clock. I felt amazed and grateful for the perfection of the unfolding of the past four days. It was the same feeling I had had the previous year, except that this Wesak had a unique flavor and personality. I felt that everyone involved and the lightworkers in attendance had claimed the event as their own. This had been my secret goal all along. Even though I was the director and main coordinator and people came because of my reputation and books, I wanted everyone to see and experience the fact that Wesak is an event for everyone. It is an opportunity for all spiritual leaders and lightworkers to come together in oneness, love, unity and joy, to unify under the banner of ascension and the ascended masters.

The other insight into this event that made it totally unique was the synthesis it embodied. It was an event for all religions, all spiritual paths, all mystery schools, all gurus, all spiritual teachers, all ashrams, all rays, all cosmic and planetary ascended masters. To bring together such a diverse group of spiritual leaders and lightworkers and inner-plane cosmic and planetary ascended masters was truly amazing. To meditate together with 1200 high-level initiates and ascended beings and 150,000 inner-plane masters in Mount Shasta under the full moon of Taurus was truly amazing, as you might imagine. I invite all readers to seriously consider coming to Wesak in Mount Shasta next year. (Call me or write me for a free information packet.) It will be an experience you will never forget.

Wesak 1998 and 1999

As the director and main coordinator of this event for the 1998 Wesak, I already have much of the event planned out, and we should have 1400 high-level initiates and ascended beings in Mount Shasta again. I expect this event to be even better than the last two years.

The masters are already giving me guidance for the 1999 Wesak celebration, which will again be held at Mount Shasta to bring in the new millennium. This event should also be a humdinger, to say the least. I've been discussing with the masters the possibility of renting a gigantic circus tent that can hold as many as 3000 people to bring in the new millennium.

My Twelfth Initiation

The year after Wesak 1996 was such an enormously accelerated year spiritually (as you can see from the previous twenty pages) that my twelfth initiation took me only eight months. This was by the grace of Melchizedek, the Mahatma, Metatron, Djwhal Khul and the core twenty-one masters. They sped me forward and I totally committed myself to planetary leadership and world service. I was amazed that I could anchor and activate fifty chakras, integrate and cleanse 100,000 soul extensions in my monadic group and achieve the necessary light quotient. When I took the eleventh initiation my light quotient was approximately 22 percent on the cosmic light-quotient scale. (I remind my readers here that when you achieve the 99 percent light quotient on the planetary scale, you switch over to the cosmic light-quotient scale. Ninety-nine percent on the planetary light-quotient scale is about 10 percent on the cosmic light-quotient scale.)

Upon taking my twelfth initiation the three M's and Djwhal told me that I was up to around 29 or 30 percent. Each of the cosmic initiations ten through twelve needs an additional 8 to 10 points to achieve that initiation, as well as the anchoring and activation of fifty chakras for each initiation. The attainment of the twelfth initiation was the anchoring and activation of chakras 100 to 150. Ten points on the cosmic scale is an enormous amount of light to anchor in one year, let alone eight months. A lot of this work was done on the inner plane at night while I slept and at a higher spiritual level during my waking hours. The ascended masters, especially the cosmic masters such as Melchizedek, the Mahatma and Metatron, and others such as the divine Mother, Sai Baba, Archangel Michael and a great many others I'm not mentioning here have the ability to speed up or slow down a person's evolution. Frankly, I worked out a deal with the three M's and Djwhal and the core twenty-one to speed up my evolutionary process at the highest possible rate, and my commitment in return was to totally dedicate my life to God and them in directing the Melchizedek Synthesis Academy & Ashram, completing the thirty-volume book series, directing and coordinating the Wesak celebration each year for 1400 to 3000 lightworkers and completing the Melchizedek Synthesis Academy correspondence course. So it is truly by the grace of God and the masters go I.

One more thought on the light quotient is that for the planetary initiations one through nine, one needs approximately nine light-quotient points per initiation. These nine points on the cosmic scale are far vaster than the nine points needed for the planetary initiations.

The twelfth initiation also corresponds to the full anchoring and activation of the twelfth body, which is the universal body that is connected with the anchoring and activation of the zohar body and the anointed Christ overself body as described in *The Keys of Enoch*.

One more interesting piece of esoteric information that helped me understand the mechanics of the initiations was given by Melchizedek, the Mahatma, Metatron and Djwhal: As of my tenth initiation I had cleared approximately 77 percent of my karma; at my eleventh initiation I had cleared 87 percent, and at my twelfth initiation 96 percent of my karma had been cleared. In *The Complete Ascension Manual* I told you that to achieve your planetary ascension, the sixth initiation, you need to balance 51 percent of your karma. Looking at the mathematics of this process, one cleanses 7 to 8 karmic percentage points per initiation. (To those interested in more information on this process, I would recommend reading *Cosmic Ascension*.)

I personally find the mechanics of the process of spiritual evolution quite fascinating. It is through understanding the mechanics that I have been able to create the activations and prayer requests to accelerate evolution. Once you understand the mechanics of the process, it is a matter of asking for those things that accelerate the process. My beloved readers, the keys to accelerating spiritual evolution are, in my opinion, chakra anchorings, light-quotient-building, love-quotient-building, integrating and cleansing soul extensions, anchoring and activating the higher bodies, psychological clarity, commitment to service, commitment to spiritual leadership, Christ consciousness, transcendence of negative-ego consciousness, balancing the four bodies, overall synthesis and integration and unconditional love.

My beloved readers, focus on these things, and integrated ascension can be achieved. Your goal should not be ascension, but *integrated ascension*. There are a great many lightworkers on this planet who are achieving their higher initiations. However, it must be clearly understood that passing initiations has more to do with the amount of light or light quotient you are holding. It does not accurately reflect the true level of your God realization. What good is it to pass the seventh initiation if you are still run by the negative ego, inner child, subconscious mind, emotional body, lower-self desire, physical appetites and the mind?

This, my beloved friends, is more common than you realize. Light-workers on this planet are spiritually developing at an enormously fast rate; but, they are *not* equally developing psychologically. His holiness the Lord Sai Baba has said that the definition of God is that God equals man minus ego. Notice that he did not say God equals 99 percent light quotient. If our psychological lessons are not learned, they will totally corrupt and contaminate the spiritual level.

The single most important relationship in your life is not your relationship with God and the masters, but your relationship to yourself. Developing a right relationship to self is one of the most difficult lessons of the entire spiritual path. Increasing light quotient is easy, but developing a right relationship to self is not. It is a very complex and sophisticated process with a staggering number of pitfalls, traps and glamours. In my humble opinion, the single most important lesson of the spiritual path, bar none, is learning to control and transcend the negative ego and learning how to re-place the negative-ego thought system with the Christ consciousness thought system. If this isn't learned, if mastery over the subconscious mind and emotional body is not achieved and proper parenting of the inner child is not maintained, then corruption and contamination of all channeling, clairvoyance and spiritual teaching is guaranteed.

It is for this reason I strongly recommend that you do the ascension work I teach. But also spend as much or more time studying *Soul Psychology; Your Ascension Mission: Embracing Your Puzzle Piece; How to Clear the Negative Ego; Integrated Ascension: Revelation for the Next Millennium;* and *Ascension and Romantic Relationships.* To achieve true God realization and integrated ascension, one must become a master of all three levels: the spiritual, psychological and physical. I strongly urge you, my beloved readers, to be sure to "pay your rent to God" on each level. The psychological and physical/earthly levels are just as important as the spiritual. In truth, the psychological level is even more important than the spiritual, for that is the foundation of your symbolic house. How can you build a second floor if you don't have a properly built first floor?

I repeat again, a wrong relationship to self will corrupt and contaminate the spiritual level and will, if you are not careful, totally stop your initiation process in its tracks at the seventh initiation if this work is not done. Cosmic initiation and true liberation are not allowed to open up if these psychological lessons are not learned. Even after passing the seventh initiation and achieving liberation from the wheel of rebirth, if these psychological lessons are not learned you may be freed from the wheel of rebirth on a physical level, but not on the astral and mental level. You will have to reincarnate again on the astral or mental plane to work out your stuff if you don't do it now.

The tricky negative ego will tell you that you resolved all this stuff back in the spring of '72, but mastery of the psychological level takes constant work and vigilance. I cannot tell you how many spiritual leaders and teachers, channels, psychics, clairvoyants, students and friends I have seen fall who have taken their sixth, seventh, eighth and even ninth initiation because thay had not learned the basic psychological lessons. I do not say this as judgment, but as a point of spiritual observation and discernment. What I speak of here is of enormous concern to the Planetary and Cosmic Spiritual Hierarchy, and I write these things at their request, for a great many lightworkers are unfortunately falling into this pattern.

Lightworkers often tend to be much more interested in the ephemeral and the celestial and the ascended masters. There is nothing wrong with this as long as equal attention is given to the psychological level. If I may be so bold, the world doesn't need more channels; it needs more spiritual counselors who understand the spiritual level and can help other lightworkers integrate this properly into their psychological self, physical/earthly self and into right relationships with their brothers and sisters on Earth. Integration and balance is ever the key. As our Planetary Logos Lord Buddha said in his incarnation on Earth, "Moderation in all things, and follow the middle path." As Djwhal Khul has said, "Ponder on this."

The Completion of My Twelfth Initiation

The masters told me that I would be completing my twelfth initiation and beginning my thirteenth initiation sometime in 1998. By this time the pattern of taking these cosmic initiations seemed to be set, and the mathematical sequencing would fall right in line with what I have shared already: eight to ten more points on the cosmic light-quotient scale, fifty more chakras anchored and activated (chakras 150 to 200), full anchoring and activation of the twelfth body, the zohar body and the anointed Christ overself body, love quotient, integration and cleansing of one million soul extensions, increased karma cleansing, and full anchoring, activation and actualization of the twelve strands of DNA.

One more interesting synchronicity that I discussed with Melchizedek, which we both found meaningful, is that this book tells the story of the completion of my twelve initiations, but is also the twelfth book I have written. I also, synchronistically, took my twelfth initiation in my forty-fourth physical birth year. On a personal level this felt synchronistic and significant, providing what I felt was the perfect conclusion.

Most books on ascension seem to focus on achieving planetary ascension, which is the process of completing the sixth initiation and taking the beginning of the seventh. This book begins with the sixth initiation and moves toward completing the twelfth. This is uncharted territory, for these initiations have never been taken before on Earth until this present dispensation from 1995 to the year 2000, when the window for mass ascension on planet Earth opened up. To my knowledge, no easy-to-read, easy-to-understand and practical books have ever been written that explain initiations six through twelve. To get a full overview of this process, read *Cosmic Ascension* and *Integrated Ascension*. The present book gives a very personal autobiographical account of this process. *Cosmic Ascension* gives the theoretical framework and cosmic map for completing your twelve levels of initiation. *Integrated Ascension* gives the full spiritual, psychological and physical/earthly viewpoint of how to realize the twelve levels of initiation in an integrated manner, not just on the heavenly or spiritual plane.

Now that I am close to realizing this whole process, what I would say is, do not be afraid to call on the ascended masters for help, for they are truly the rocketship to God. Stay balanced in your approach. Concern yourself less with passing initiations as time goes on and more on immersing yourself in world service. Find your right puzzle piece in the divine plan and do not try to live someone else's. Fame and glamour are not important; what *is* important is serving God and your brothers and sisters in any way you can.

Enjoy your life and enjoy living on the Earth, for the material universe is one of God's heavens. Do not compete or compare with other lightworkers or spiritual leaders. Follow the beat of your own drummer and above all else, to thine own self be true. Ask and you shall receive, knock and the door shall be opened. Be patient, and do not be concerned with advanced ascended-master abilities, for they will come in God's time.

Always strive to be of the Christ consciousness in every moment, and be ever spiritually vigilant to keep negative-ego thinking out of your consciousness. And never forget that happiness is a state of mind and has nothing to do with anything outside of self. The most advanced ascended-master ability of all is unconditional love, and if you do only one spiritual practice this entire lifetime, let it be this and you will be on the mark.

It is my sincere hope and prayer that these humble words in this book serve as a catalyst and guiding light in the process of accelerating, achieving and fully realizing your twelve levels of initiation, your integrated ascension and your full God realization on Earth! Namasté.

A Final Note

By the grace of God and the inner-plane ascended masters, I completed my twelfth initiation at the time this book was ready for publication, which seemed like a fitting capstone to the personal journey and sharing I have had with you, my beloved readers. It seems a fitting conclusion.

Use the ideas, insights, training, tools, information and meditations to speed up your integrated ascension process to be of greater service on Earth to all sentient beings. My beloved friends, I invite you to write and/or call me if you would like more information on the Academy, manuscripts yet unpublished, audio and video tapes or the next Wesak celebration in Mount Shasta. For a free information packet, contact Dr. Joshua David Stone, Melchizedek Synthesis Light Academy & Ashram, 5252 Coldwater Canyon #112, Van Nuys, CA 91401, (818) 769-1181, fax (818) 766-1782, http://www.drjoshuadavidstone.com.

Epilogue from Melchizedek

I Am Melchizedek. I have opened this book, and thus mine shall be the final closing. Yet in truth the book of life is an ongoing process where there is no beginning, no end. Also, in truth we are one, so a smile ripples through the universe as I say I have at once introduced this book, written this book, read this book through many eyes and now close this book.

Know that the story unveiled has been the unique process of one of my aspects of self, even as you each are unique aspects of my self. Know also that there is only one path, loosely called the Path. The approaches to the path are as diverse and unique as each of you. Yet what a gift from one to another is the sharing of one's journey and the expansions of one's revelations!

Take these precious words as food for thought (thought via the higher mind). Know the food to be the substance of light, even as I Am the light and the food of my being is light. The author gives many a tool for use in the bridging of you (the awakening part of love and light) with me, the embodiment of love and light. Please use these tools, but in so doing know that it is your own unique puzzle piece that will be brought to light and not that of the author or anyone else. There are no two people meant to express God in exactly the same way.

Yet as all my children climb the "mountain cosmic" in a circle of joined hands (for in the inner and higher planes all are known to be so joined), learn what you can from the revelatory journey of one who speaks his path via the written word.

All words are but seed thoughts, and it is my prayer that you open to find which words are your seed thoughts of light. My gift to you is that I aid you in your process of unfoldment and ascension. Your gift to me is to seek out your own first, best destiny and follow the highest and brightest within yourselves.

Beyond the light of the word is the silence of the word. It is into that silence within that I would have you now proceed. Within each of you is the revelation of a Melchizedek initiate. Within each of you are the aspects of transcendence and individuality. I call you now to know me through both these aspects, for even as I embrace this universe, so too I transcend it. In that knowing does the divine paradox of truth stand naked and revealed. In that place where sound and light and love merge into one whole I will speak to you. I will speak each to each in your own voice so that I may be understood directly. I will speak each to each within the silence so that I may be known and realized and embraced by you directly, even as l embrace you. I ask you all to follow your own calling and to hear the voice of light speaking in tones recognizable to your own ears, intuitions, souls and monads.

I call you all, yet I am already there with you. I seek to bring you into the heights and depths of me, although you are already in and of me. For I seek your expansion and direct realization of me; I await you within yourselves. Such is the divine mystery and so too the hallowed pathway. Take into your hearts the oneness of our hearts. Take into your thought the blending of our lights and love. Take into your journey the knowledge that you are in truth expanding into the full realization that you are already home. Take into your cells the peace that, even as you are called to take the journey of initiations and expansions, comes from knowing you are never alone. For I Am—and therefore you are—Melchizedeks. We are one.

APPENDIX A

The 1997 Wesak Meditations

+ Ultimate Cosmic-Ray Meditation
+ God Ascension-Seat Meditation
+ The 1997 Wesak Ceremony
+ Special Ascension Activation
+ Final Wesak Meditation
+ Fifty-Point Cosmic Cleansing Meditation
+ Ascension-Activation Meditation in the
  Golden Chamber of Melchizedek

Ultimate Cosmic-Ray Meditation

Close your eyes. Let us begin by taking a deep breath. Exhale.

We call all the masters of the Planetary and Cosmic Hierarchy to help in this meditation.

We call forth a planetary and cosmic axiatonal alignment.

We call to Melchizedek, Mahatma and Metatron for the anchoring of the platinum net, to clear away any and all unwanted energies.

We call to Archangel Michael for the establishment of a dome of protection for the entire weekend.

We call forth the establishment of a pillar of light and a planetary and cosmic ascension column for the entire weekend.

We now begin the process of fully anchoring and activating the planetary and cosmic rays:

We begin by calling forth the ascended master El Morya, the chohan of the first ray, to fully anchor and activate the first ray, representing the will aspect of God, which is red in color.

Bathe in the positive effects of this red ray now. [Pause.]

We now call forth Master Kuthumi and the ascended master Djwhal Khul to fully anchor and activate the second ray of love/wisdom, which is blue in color.

Bathe in the positive effects of this blue ray now. [Pause.]

We now call forth Master Serapis Bey, who is the chohan of the third ray, to fully anchor and activate the third ray of active intelligence, which is yellow in color.

Bathe in the positive effects of this yellow ray now. [Pause.]

We now call forth Master Paul the Venetian, who is the chohan of the fourth ray, to fully anchor and activate the fourth ray of harmony, which is emerald green in color.

Bathe in the positive effects of this emerald green ray now. [Pause.]

We now call forth Master Hilarion, who is the chohan of the fifth ray, to fully anchor and activate the fifth ray of new-age science, which is orange in color.

Bathe in the positive effects of this orange ray now. [Pause.]

We now call forth Sananda, the chohan of the sixth ray, who in one of his past lives was known as the Master Jesus, to now fully anchor and activate the sixth ray of devotion, which is indigo in color.

Bathe in the positive effects of this indigo ray now. [Pause.]

We now call forth Saint Germain, the chohan of the seventh ray, who recently has taken the position in the Spiritual Government known as the Mahachohan. We now request from Saint Germain the full anchoring and activation of the seventh ray of ceremonial order and magic, which is violet in color.

Bathe now in the positive effects of this violet transmuting flame. [Pause.]

We now call forth the seven ray masters and the ascended master Djwhal Khul to clear all lower and/or negative attributes from these first seven rays and replace them with the higher, positive attributes of the Christ/Buddha archetype and imprint.

We now call forth the ascended master Lady Nada to now fully anchor and activate the eighth ray of higher cleansing, which is sea-foam green in color.

Bathe in the positive effects of this sea-foam green ray now. [Pause.]

We now call forth the Virgin Mary to fully anchor and activate the ninth ray of joy, attracting the lightbody, which is blue-green in color.

Bathe in the positive effects of this blue-green ray now. [Pause.]

We now call forth Allah Gobi, who holds the position in the Spiritual Government known as the Manu, which is a higher governmental position of the first ray. He has volunteered this evening to officially activate the tenth ray, which has to do with fully anchoring the lightbody, and this ray is pearlescent in color.

Bathe in the positive effects of this pearlescent ray now. [Pause.]

We now call forth Quan Yin, the bodhisattva of compassion, to fully anchor and activate the eleventh ray, which serves as a bridge to the new age and is pink/orange in color.

Bathe in the positive effects of this pink/orange ray now. [Pause.]

We now call forth the ascended master Pallas Athena to fully anchor and activate the twelfth ray, which embodies the full anchoring of the new age and the Christ Consciousness, which is gold in color.

Bathe in the positive effects of this gold ray now. [Pause.]

We now move from the planetary rays to the cosmic rays.

We call forth Lord Buddha, our new Planetary Logos, to fully anchor and activate the Shamballic ray of pure white light.

Bathe in the profundity and glory of this pure white light from Lord Buddha himself. [Pause.]

We call forth Helios and Vesta, our Solar Logos, to fully anchor and activate the cosmic solar ray from the solar core, which is copper-gold in color.

Bathe in the wonderful positive effects of this copper-gold cosmic ray now. [Pause.]

We now call forth Melchior, our Galactic Logos, to fully anchor and activate the galactic ray, which is silver-gold in color.

Bathe and soak in this exquisite silver-gold ray. [Pause.]

We now call forth Lord Melchizedek, our Universal Logos, for the full anchoring and activation of the universal ray, which is the purest and most refined golden vibration available to Earth.

Bathe and absorb into every cell of your being this golden radiation from Melchizedek. [Pause.]

We call forth Archangel Metatron to now fully anchor and activate the ten lost cosmic rays of the yod spectrum, which are all hues of platinum.

Bathe now and fully absorb these ten lost cosmic platinum hues. [Pause.]

We now call forth the Multiuniversal Logos to fully anchor and activate the pure core platinum ray itself.

Become like a sponge and soak in this pure core platinum ray. [Pause.]

We now call forth the Mahatma, who is a cosmic group-consciousness being who embodies all 352 levels of the Godhead, to fully anchor and activate the Mahatma Ray, which is a cosmic white light containing all colors of the spectrum.

Soak in this rainbow-colored cosmic white light, letting it into the core and *essence of your being. [Pause.]*

We now call forth the Cosmic Council of Twelve, who are the twelve cosmic beings that surround the Throne of Grace, to fully anchor and activate their twelve cosmic rays. These twelve cosmic rays are so refined in nature that they are translucent and beyond all color.

Let these exquisite rays and translucent vibrations soak into the core essence of your heart and soul. [Pause.]

Last, we call forth the presence of God and request an anchoring and activation of the clear light of the ray of God.

Let us enter the silence now. [Pause.]

Let us now come back into our bodies and into the auditorium, while continuing to absorb and enjoy these refined cosmic rays.

God Ascension-Seat Meditation

Close your eyes and take a deep breath. Exhale.

We call forth all the masters of the Planetary and Cosmic Hierarchy to help in this meditation.

We call forth a planetary and cosmic axiatonal alignment.

We call to our inner-plane spiritual hosts to completely balance the energies in this auditorium.

We call forth Melchizedek, the Mahatma and Metatron to anchor the platinum net to clear away all unwanted energies.

We call forth our inner-plane spiritual hosts to provide a group merkabah, like a gigantic boat, for everyone here.

We ask to be taken now in this merkabah to Shamballa to sit in the ascension seat of Lord Buddha, our Planetary Logos.

Feel and absorb the energies of this planetary ascension seat. [Pause.]

We call forth from Lord Buddha a special divine dispensation of ascension activation for this beloved group.

As a final blessing from Lord Buddha, we call forth and request a divine dispensation to experience the light rod of Lord Buddha, which will ignite our ascension realization even further. Let us receive this special blessing now. [Pause.]

We now call for our inner-plane spiritual hosts to move our gigantic group merkabah from the planetary to the solar level to visit Helios and Vesta and sit in their solar ascension seat.

Feel and sense the difference between the ascension seat in Shamballa and the ascension seat of Helios and Vesta in the solar core. [Pause.]

Feel and absorb these energies. [Pause.]

> We call forth from Helios and Vesta for the most accelerated ascension activation that is available to us at this time.

> We also now call forth a special divine dispensation to experience the light rod of Helios and Vesta, which will ignite and catalyze our ascension growth even further. Let us receive this special blessing now. [Pause.]

> We now call forth our inner-plane spiritual hosts and ask to be taken in our group merkabah to the galactic core and the ascension seat of Melchior, our Galactic Logos.

Feel the difference in frequency between the solar ascension seat and the galactic ascension seat you are now sitting in. [Pause.]

> We now call forth the merging of three other galactic ascension seats with the one we are currently sitting in.

> We call forth the ascension seats of the Lord of Sirius, Lenduce and the Lord of Arcturus to blend together so that we may experience the effects of combining these galactic ascension seats. [Pause.]

> We now call forth and request from Melchior, the Lord of Sirius, Lenduce and the Lord of Arcturus for the greatest possible ascension acceleration available to us at this time.

> We now call forth a special divine dispensation to experience the combined light rods of these four great and noble masters. Let us receive this unique and special blessing now. [Pause.]

> We now call forth our inner-plane spiritual hosts and ask to be taken in our group merkabah to the Golden Chamber of Melchizedek at the universal level, to sit in his ascension seat.

Notice again the difference in frequency and quality of energy between the galactic ascension seat and the universal ascension seat you are now sitting in. [Pause.]

> While at this universal level we also call forth a special divine dispensation from the archangels Michael/Faith, Jophiel/Christine, Chamuel/Charity, Gabriel/Hope, Raphael/Mother Mary, Uriel/Aurora, Zadkiel/Amethyst and the seven mighty elohim and their divine counterparts, requesting an ascension acceleration for each person individually and for the entire group body. We also request the combined help of these glorious beings for the entire weekend celebration.

> We now call forth from Lord Melchizedek for the greatest possi-

ble ascension acceleration available to us at this time.

We now call forth from Melchizedek for a special divine dispensation to experience the light rod of Melchizedek. Let us receive this very special blessing and grace now. [Pause.]

We now ask to be taken by Melchizedek in our group merkabah to the next level up, which is the multiuniversal level, to sit in the multiuniversal-level ascension seat, by the grace of the Mahatma and the Multiuniversal Logos.

Feel an even more refined frequency at this most rarified vibration. [Pause.]

We call to the Mahatma and the Multiuniversal Logos for a divine dispensation for the greatest possible ascension acceleration available to us at this time. [Pause.]

We now call to the Mahatma and the Multiuniversal Logos to now take the group merkabah up to the next level, which is the ascension seat of the divine mother at the left hand of God.

Feel the sublime energies of this ascension seat, which words fail to describe or comprehend. [Pause.]

We call forth to the divine Mother for a divine dispensation of the greatest possible ascension acceleration available to each one of us individually and collectively at this time.

Bathe in the divine cosmic love and acceleration of the divine Mother at this 352nd level of divinity. [Pause.]

We call forth to the divine Mother and ask that our group merkabah now be taken to the ascension seat of the divine Father at the right hand of God.

Bathe now in these most exquisite and sublime energies of the divine Father's ascension seat. [Pause.]

We call forth to the divine Father for a divine dispensation of the greatest possible ascension acceleration available to each of us individually and collectively at this time.

Absorb this divine Father acceleration into the very core and essence of your being. [Pause.]

As a special dispensation given once a year to those presence at Wesak, we call forth the divine Mother, the divine Father, the Mahatma, Melchizedek, Metatron and Lord Michael to take us in our group merkabah to the Throne of Grace itself, to sit in God's ascension seat.

Let us humbly receive this blessing now as we enter into the silence. [Pause.]

From the bottom of our hearts we thank the beloved presence of God for this most sanctified blessing and grace.

We now call forth the divine Mother, the divine Father, the Mahatma, Melchizedek, Metatron and Lord Michael, humbly requesting to be taken in our group merkabah back down through all the levels and dimensions of reality into our physical bodies in the auditorium at Mount Shasta.

The 1997 Wesak Ceremony

Close your eyes and take a deep breath. Exhale.

We again call forth the entire Planetary and Cosmic Hierarchy to help in this meditation.

We call forth the full opening now of all our chakras, including the ascension chakra, which sits at the back center of the head (where a ponytail would begin).

We will now soul-travel together to the Wesak Valley in the Himalayas to experience the Wesak ceremony conducted by the inner-plane ascended masters, which has been held every year at the Taurus full moon for eons.

Let us now prepare ourselves for this holy and sanctified experience with a moment of silence. [Pause.]

We now call forward our inner-plane spiritual hosts and ask for the re-creation of our group merkabah, like a gigantic boat, to take all present on both the inner and outer plane to the Wesak Valley in the Himalayas to experience the Wesak ceremony.

Feel yourself descending now into the Wesak Valley, joining all the other ascended masters, initiates and disciples already gathered there.

See and/or feel the presence of Lord Maitreya, the Planetary Christ; Saint Germain, the chohan of the seventh ray and new Mahachohan; and Allah Gobi, who holds the first-ray position in the Spiritual Hierarchy known as the Manu.

See these three masters standing in a triangular formation around a bowl of water that sits on a very large crystal. See or feel all the other masters of the Spiritual Hierarchy standing in a circle around these three.

Just before the moment of the rising of the full moon, which is now upon us on the inner plane, the expectancy and excitement begin to build as we all await the arrival of Lord Buddha.

As the Moon begins to rise, a stillness settles upon the gathered crowd, and all look toward the northeast.

Certain ritualistic movements are made and mantras sound forth under the guidance of the seven chohans of the seven rays.

A tiny speck can be seen in the sky in the far-distant northeast. This speck gradually grows larger and larger, and the form of the Buddha seated cross-legged grows near.

He is clad in a saffron-colored robe, bathed in light and color, with his hands extended in blessing.

While Lord Buddha hovers above the bowl of water, a great mantra is sounded by Lord Maitreya, one that is used only once a year at Wesak.

This invocation sets up an enormous vibration of spiritual current, marking the supreme moment that culminates a year's intensive spiritual effort of all initiates and masters present.

In this moment let us watch Lord Buddha as he hovers over this bowl of water, transmitting divine and cosmic energies into this water and through Lord Maitreya.

The energy is then sent forth by Lord Maitreya to the entire Spiritual Hierarchy and into all of us who form a part of this hierarchy on Earth.

Feel this massive downpouring of cosmic energies from the Planetary and Cosmic Hierarchy, flowing not only through us, but also flowing out into the world and into the very Earth herself.

As these energies continue to pour in, see the bowl of water that had sat on the large crystal being passed around the crowd.

See and feel yourself taking a sip of this holy, blessed and sanctified water.

See yourself now walking toward Lord Buddha, Lord Maitreya and Sanat Kumara, our previous Planetary Logos, who now overlights Buddha in his new position in the spiritual government.

Stand now before these three glorious masters and share with them on the inner plane what you feel your service work, mission and puzzle piece is in God's divine plan on Earth. [Pause.]

Take this time also to make any prayer requests to God and these three masters for help in manifesting your mission and for answering any personal prayer requests for self or others. [Pause.]

Take thirty seconds of silence to make these prayer requests. [Pause.]

Feel and visualize these prayers being answered, and thank Lord Buddha, Lord Maitreya and Sanat Kumara for their guidance and blessings. [Pause.]

Find yourself walking now in the Wesak Valley toward a less populated and very beautiful nature spot.

Sit down and allow yourself just to be, resonating with all that has taken place. [Pause.]

Take a moment now to feel the full joy and blessings of this moment and of the entire Wesak ceremony. Allow this feeling to become fully imbued into the core of your being. [Pause.]

Know that all of us and the entire Hierarchy of inner-plane ascended masters are one.

Now look toward the ceremonial circle and gather around the large crystal and bowl.

See or feel Lord Buddha begin to rise in the lotus posture, floating back to the northeast to the realm from which he came.

As Lord Buddha again becomes a small speck in the distance, see and feel the arrival of our inner-plane spiritual hosts with their gigantic group merkabah.

Feel yourself now joining this merkabah in total oneness, joy and love.

Feel the group merkabah floating now through space and time, now returning to Mount Shasta and this auditorium.

Before opening your eyes, let us take one last moment to send love to all our brothers and sisters here who have shared this journey and this entire Wesak celebration with us. Let us send and receive this love now. [Pause.]

Let us now call forth from the inner plane his holiness the Lord Sai Baba, the Cosmic Christ, to give his final blessing and benediction to close this Wesak ceremony by sprinkling his sacred vibhuti ash etherically upon all gathered in this auditorium.

Let us receive this final Wesak ceremony and celebration blessing now. [Pause.]

When you feel complete, open your eyes.

Special Ascension Activation

Close your eyes and take a deep breath. Exhale.

We call forth all the masters from the Planetary and Cosmic Hierarchy to help in this meditation.

We call forth a planetary and cosmic axiatonal alignment.

We call forth from Melchizedek, the Mahatma and Metatron to now anchor the platinum net to clear away all unwanted energies.

(The following major activations were especially created for this 1997 Wesak celebration.)

We call forth Lord Buddha, our Planetary Logos, and request the permanent anchoring and activation of all God crystals and seed packets from Shamballa.

We now move up to the solar level and call forth Helios and Vesta to anchor and activate all the God crystals and seed packets from the solar core.

We now move to the galactic level and call forth Melchior to anchor and activate all the God crystals and seed packets from the galactic core.

We now move up to the universal level, calling forth Melchizedek to anchor and activate all the God crystals and seed packets from the universal core.

We now move up again to the multiuniversal level, calling forth the Multiuniversal Logos to anchor and activate all the God crystals and seed packets from the multiuniversal core.

We now move to the 352nd level of the Godhead and call forth directly to God, the Cosmic Council of Twelve, and the Twenty-Four Elders that surround the Throne of Grace for the anchoring and activation of all the God crystals and seed packets from the heart of God.

As we continue to soak in and absorb the God crystals, seed packets and cosmic energies from Source, the Mahatma has asked me to make a special request to all of you gathered here physically and upon the inner plane, to take on a specific spiritual assignment.

This assignment as a group body is to be a planetary anchor and focus for his cosmic energies.

So in this moment I'm asking you all if you are willing to take on this spiritual assignment upon his request.

If so, inwardly give your consent and approval to the Mahatma within the core of your being.

For those who have now agreed, we will now take thirty seconds of silence while he runs his cosmic energy embodying all 352 levels of God through us. [Pause.]

We now call forth from the Mahatma for the opening of the 352 levels of the heart, in the sense of a holographic penetration of the Mahatma's entire being.

We now call forth from Melchizedek, Metatron, the Mahatma, archangels and the Elohim Councils for the anchoring and activation of all fire letters, key codes and sacred geometries to anchor and activate the master divine blueprint for each person present.

We now call forth to our inner-plane spiritual hosts this weekend for the anchoring and activation of the light grid of ascension for all monads of the 144,000 currently working on ascension.

We now call forth the beloved Master Kuthumi, the chohan of the second ray, who will now confirm the status of World Teacher to all who are in attendance at this time, if you choose to receive this blessing.

Visualize yourself now standing before Master Kuthumi, with your palms held open and turned upward. See Master Kuthumi first touching your heart, then your third eye and then your crown chakra.

Feel the spiritual current run through you as you now take on this mantle of responsibility.

Now call forth the divine Mother, Quan Yin, Vesta, Lakshmi, Lady of the Sun, Lady Liberty, Portia, Lady Nada, Pallas Athena, Lady of the Light, Lady Helena, Hilda, Alice Bailey, Isis, the Virgin Mary and all the lady masters of the Planetary and Cosmic Hierarchy.

We call forth from this great Sisterhood of Light for the full anchoring and activation of the divine feminine within, in order to resonate in perfect harmony with the divine masculne within.

We ask for a complete balancing of the male/female, yin/yang energies within each of us so that these energies may flow and manifest in perfect harmony and ease as God would have it be.

Visualize the divine Mother placing a lotus blossom composed of the love/wisdom and power of God within the center of each person's heart.

We also now request that the divine Mother and lady masters who are hosting this weekend become permanently anchored inside our hearts.

We now call forth Archangel Metatron and request a divine dispensation for the full anchoring and activation of the platinum rod for each person present who wishes to receive this grace and blessing.

We call forth the ascended master Djwhal Khul from the planetary Synthesis Ashram to now officially anchor and activate, with the help of the seven chohans, each person's divine puzzle piece so that each person may easily and effortlessly fulfill his or her divine mission and life's purpose.

We call forth El Morya, Kuthumi, Djwhal Khul, Serapis Bey, Paul the Venetian, Hilarion, Sananda, Saint Germain, Allah Gobi, Lord Maitreya, Lord Buddha and Vywamus for help in weaving each person's ascension fabric to take them to the next level of planetary and cosmic ascension realization.

We now call forth Melchizedek, the Mahatma, Metatron, Lord Michael, the archangels and the Elohim Councils for light-quotient building at the highest potential available to each person and to the entire group body.

We now call forth the divine Mother, Helios and Vesta, Quan Yin, Lord Maitreya and the Virgin Mary for love-quotient building at the highest potential available to each person and to the entire group body.

As the love quotient continues to flow in, this segment of the specialized ascension activations for Wesak 1997 is now concluded.

Final Wesak Meditation (Leadership Meeting)

We will conclude the leadership meeting with our final Wesak meditation. The timing of this meditation could not be more perfect, for at 4:00 p.m. Pacific time, the ceremony in the Wesak Valley is taking place. I have been asked by the masters to do one final Wesak meditation guiding us back to the Wesak Valley, which will be different from Sunday night's meditation in that there will be many more periods of silence for each person to have a personal experience.

Close your eyes and take a deep breath. Exhale.

While the actual Wesak ceremony is taking place in the Wesak Valley at this very moment, we now invoke the group merkabah to surround us and take us again to the Wesak Valley in the Himalayas.

As this is occurring, we ask that all of the activations done over the last three days be restimulated and reactivated. We are now fully radiant beings of God, charged with all the light, love, wisdom and power of the cosmos.

In our radiance of purity, the group merkabah lowers us upon the sacred rocks of the Wesak Valley, just as we visualized it last night.

At this very moment the full moon of Taurus is rising and we stand in our bodies of light with the Manu Allah Gobi, the Mahachohan, Lord Maitreya, Saint Germain and the masters of the seven rays, all planetary and cosmic masters, the bodhisattvas and all initiates who have gathered to be part of this most sacred event.

Feel the expectancy and excitement build as in the far distance Lord Buddha begins to make his appearance.

Feel the absolute, all-pervasive stillness and sanctity.

Let us sit in the silence for three to five minutes. [Pause.]

As the Buddha hovers above the sacred bowl of water and the Christ sounds the sacred mantra, remain perfectly still within, bathing in the vibration of the supreme spiritual current that is being released at this very moment.

Stay within your center, within your own silence. We will now take three minutes of silence. [Pause.]

This is a moment that is shared with the entire Spiritual Hierarchy, yet this is also a moment of utter quietude where self merges with God. Stay within the sacred silence of the moment, allowing it to unfold for you as your own mighty I Am Presence or monad would have it unfold.

Let us take two more minutes of silence. These moments are between you, your monad, the masters and God. [Pause.]

Just be with that as we sit in silence for five more minutes. [Pause.]

Remember the spiritual intention you made last night, and be with that intention, the service work you seek to do, and the areas where you seek to progress as we take another minute of silence. [Pause.]

Ask Lord Buddha and the masters to bless this intention, and ask that your way of service may be as easy and harmonious as possible.

Feel the light! Feel the love! Feel the power! [Pause thirty seconds.]

Be love—wisdom—power.

Rest in the beingness of your own divinity. Know that you are yourself the master. Be that master. Embrace the joy of it, and the love, light and peace of it.

Simply allow yourself to be.

Wesak is now. Let us meditate on the Wesak energies for five minutes. [Pause.]

Now watch as Lord Buddha recedes into the distance from whence he came. Peace overflows you as he seems to grow smaller and smaller, while the energies that he has invoked grow larger and larger within you.

The group merkabah surrounds us once again. Gently and easily, we are carried back into this room, to the chairs where we are sitting and into our bodies.

Feel all the wonderful and glorious energies enter your mental, emotional, etheric and physical bodies. Sit with this wondrous splendor for another moment.

Feel yourself grounded back into the physical body, and when you feel ready, gently open your eyes.

We thank Lord Buddha and all the beloved Wesak masters who have guided us on this holy journey.

The following two meditations I did not use at the 1997 Wesak, although I wrote them specifically for it. The first one is the Fifty-Point Cosmic Cleansing Meditation, a more refined version of the 18-Point Cosmic Cleansing Meditation I did the previous year. It is truly powerful.

The second meditation is the Ascension-Activation Meditation in the Golden Chamber of Melchizedek. This may be the most powerful meditation in my entire arsenal, for it is three of my best ascension-activation meditations distilled into one. In my books and at Wesak I always want to make sure all of you get your money's worth. I share these with you, my beloved readers, with all my love.

Fifty-Point Cosmic Cleansing Meditation

The meditation we are about to do is extremely deep. It will foster an enormous ascension acceleration, so I want you to completely relax, be like a sponge, and let the masters do their divine handiwork.

Close your eyes and take a deep breath. Exhale.

> *We call forth the entire Planetary and Cosmic Hierarchy for help in implementing this meditation for the entire group.*
>
> *We call forth a planetary and cosmic axiatonal alignment.*
>
> *We call forth Lord Michael to establish a golden dome of protection for all present.*
>
> *We call forth Vywamus and the archangels to bring forth their golden hands as a net to cleanse any and all negative energies in the field of each person and the collective group body.*
>
> *We call forth from Melchizedek, the Mahatma and Metatron for the anchoring of the platinum net to cleanse the energy fields of each person even more deeply.*
>
> *We now call forth to the Lord of Arcturus and the Arcturians for the anchoring of the prana wind clearing device individually and in our collective group body.*

See this prana-clearing device as a type of fan that is anchored into the solar plexus, blowing and clearing all unwanted energies out of the etheric body system.

Feel the prana-clearing device now being lifted out of your field by the Lord of Arcturus and the beloved Arcturians.

> *We now call forth Djwhal Khul, the seven chohans, Lord Maitreya, Allah Gobi, Lord Buddha and the cosmic masters to anchor the core-fear removal program.*

See this as a latticework of light anchored into the four-body system, highlighting any negative energies or blockages in your energy fields.

We begin by calling forth the removal of all fear programming and blocks from every person in this room in order to achieve ascension at the highest possible level.

See this fear programming as black roots intertwined in your energy fields, now being pulled out by the masters like a vacuum cleaner at your crown chakra.

Planetary and Cosmic Hierarchy, please now remove all separative thinking from the four-body system.

Please also now remove all judgmental programming from the four-body system.

Please remove all lack of forgiveness from the four-body system.

Feel these negative aspects again being pulled out of your energy fields through the crown chakra like unwanted weeds being removed from a beautiful garden.

Planetary and Cosmic Hierarchy, please remove all impatience and negative anger.

Please remove all negative selfishness, self-centeredness and narcissism.

Please remove any negative thought forms, negative feelings and emotions and or imbalanced archetypes from the four-body system.

Please remove all superiority and inferiority thinking created by the negative ego.

Please remove all aspects of guilt and shame consciousness created by the negative ego.

Please remove all negative-ego and fear-based programming in a generalized sense.

Please cleanse and remove all extraterrestrial implants and negative elementals.

We call forth the cleansing and removal of all unwanted astral entities.

We call to Melchizedek, the Mahatma and Metatron for the cosmic viral vacuum to remove and pull out any clinical or subclinical viruses currently existing in any of our energy fields.

Please also remove all negative bacteria with the cosmic bacterial vacuum program.

We call to the archangels and the elohim to remove all disease energy from the physical, etheric, astral and mental vehicles.

We call forth each person's personal inner-plane healing angels to now heal, repair and sew up any irritations, spots and/or leaks in the aura.

We call forth to Melchizedek, the Mahatma, Metatron, Archangel Michael and the archangels for the removal of all improper soul fragments.

We also ask for the retrieval in divine order of all the soul fragments from the universe that belong to us.

We call forth each person's etheric healing team, and now request that the etheric body be repaired and brought back to its perfect blueprint now.

We call forth the anchoring of each person's perfect divine monadic blueprint body and/or mayavarupa body, to be used from this moment forward to accelerate healing and spiritual growth on all levels the rest of this lifetime.

We call forth a complete cleansing and clearing of our genetic line and ancestral lineage.

We call forth the Lord of Arcturus to now bring forth the golden cylinder to remove and vacuum up all remaining negative energy in our collective energy fields.

We call forth a clearing and cleansing of all past and future lives.

We call forth now the integration and cleansing of our 144 soul extensions from our monad and mighty I Am Presence.

We now call forth a clearing and cleansing of all karma. We need to balance 51 percent of our karma to take the beginning phase of our planetary ascension, so we ask for the greatest possible cleansing of our karma now.

We call forth from Melchizedek, Mahatma and Metatron for the anchoring of a matchstick worth of the cosmic fire to very gently burn away all astral, mental and etheric dross and gray clouds from our fields.

We now request a complete clearing and cleansing of our entire monad and mighty I Am Presence itself.

We now call forth the greatest cleansing process this world has ever known from Melchizdeck, Mahatma, Metatron, Lord Michael, the archangels, the Elohim Councils and from God.

We now call forth the ultimate cosmic cleansing and clearing back to our original covenant with God, upon our original spiri-

tual creation.

We will take a few extra moments of silence to receive this blessing and grace. [Pause.]

> *We now call forth from all the cosmic and planetary masters gathered here a downpouring and light shower of core love and the Christ/Buddha/Melchizedek attributes to replace all that has been removed and cleansed by the grace of God and the Cosmic and Planetary Hierarchy.*

> *We call forth Archangel Sandalphon, Pan and the Earth Mother to help us now become properly integrated and grounded back into our physical bodies.*

> *We call forth our personal inner-plane healing angels to perfectly balance our chakras and four-body system.*

When you are ready, open your eyes and enjoy the tremendous sense of well-being and crystal clarity in your energy fields.

Ascension-Activation Meditation in the Golden Chamber of Melchizedek

This meditation is longer than most in order to set in place all the spiritual hookups needed to fully activate all present to their highest ascension potential.

Close your eyes and take a deep breath. Exhale.

> *We call all the masters of the Planetary and Cosmic Hierarchy to help in this meditation.*

> *We now call forth a planetary and cosmic axiatonal alignment.*

Allow yourself to completely relax, soaking in all the cosmic energies and ascension activations.

> *We now call forth to the seven chohans, Djwhal Khul, Lord Maitreya and Lord Buddha to provide a gigantic group merkabah for all present to be taken spiritually to the Golden Chamber of Melchizedek in the universal core.*

> *We call forth each person's 144 soul extensions from their monad and mighty I Am Presence to join us, if they choose, for this meditation.*

> *We call to the seven chohans for the opening of all chakras, the ascension chakra, and all petals and facets of all chakras.*

> *We call to Archangel Metatron for the permanent anchoring and activation of the microtron.*

We call to the Lord of Sirius for the anchoring and activation of the Scrolls of Wisdom and Knowledge from the Great White Lodge on Sirius that are appropriate for this group.

We also ask to be connected to the cosmic initiation that Vywamus has recently taken, for the purpose of accelerated ascension activation.

We call forth Sanat Kumara, Vywamus and Lenduce for help in establishing each person's planetary and cosmic antakarana back to each person's oversoul, monad and to God.

We call Melchizedek, Mahatma, Metatron, the Elohim Councils and the archangels for the permanent anchoring and activation of the planetary and cosmic Tree of Life.

We request the complete opening and activation of the seven cosmic seals and the ten Sephiroth, as well as the hidden Sephiroth of Daath.

We call forth from the Cosmic and Planetary Hierarchy the anchoring and activation of all fire letters, key codes and sacred geometries to help in this process.

We call to the archangels for the full anchoring and activation of our fifty chakras, which will take us through planetary ascension, and also request the anchoring and activation of our 330 chakras, taking us back to the Godhead.

We call for the permanent anchoring and activation of our twelve bodies, including the solar, galactic and universal bodies.

We call to Melchizedek, the Mahatma, Metatron, Archangel Michael and the Planetary Hierarchy for the anchoring and activation of the annointed Christ overself body, our zohar body, our overself body, our electromagnetic body, our gematrian body, our eka body, our epi-kinetic body, our higher Adam Kadmon body, and the Lord's mystical body as described in The Keys of Enoch.

We call forth the permanent anchoring and activation of the sixty-four keys of Enoch in all five sacred languages.

We call forth the illumination of the seventy-two areas of the mind, as described in The Keys of Enoch.

We call forth the decadelta light encodements and emanations from the ten superscripts of the divine mind.

We call forth to Metatron for the anchoring and activation of the seventy-six names of Metatron to permanently flow through us.

We call forth the removal of all veils of light and time.

We call forth Djwhal Khul, Lord Maitreya and Lord Buddha for the permanent anchoring of the greater flame of the monad and mighty I Am Presence into the lesser flame of the personality and soul incarnated on Earth.

We call to the mighty archangels for permanent anchoring and activation of the twelve heavenly houses and twelve cosmic stations.

We call to Lord Buddha, whose festival we celebrate this weekend, for the permanent anchoring and activation of the planetary sun and the planetary cosmic heart into the core of our being.

We call to Helios and Vesta for the permanent anchoring and activation of the solar sun and the solar cosmic heart into the core of our being.

We call to Melchior for the permanent anchoring and activation of the galactic sun and galactic cosmic heart into the core of our being.

We call to Melchizedek for the permanent anchoring and activation of the universal sun and universal cosmic heart into the core of our being.

We call to the Mahatma and the Multiuniversal Logos to now permamently anchor and activate the multiuniversal sun and multiuniversal cosmic heart into the core of our being.

We call to the Godhead for the permanent anchoring and activation of the ultimate Great Central Sun and God's own heart into the core of our being.

We call forth to the source of our cosmic day and Melchizedek for the anchoring of the forty-three christed universes.

We call forth to Melchizedek to initiate each person attending this celebration into the Order of Melchizedek.

Melchizedek, we ask you to bestow your rod of initiation, if it is each person's individual free choice to receive this blessing now, without an intermediary.

(Melchizedek told me that this next activation may be the single most powerful activation and blessing of this entire meditation.)

We call forth the entire Planetary and Cosmic Hierarchy, hereby collectively requesting a complete merging of the lightbodies of all the inner-plane masters present with this group body, both individually and collectively.

We call forth God, the Mahatma, Melchizedek, Metatron, Elohim Councils, Archangel Michael and the archangels to now anchor from the cosmic Treasury of Light, the light packets of information from the Tablets of Creation, the elohim scriptures, the Torah Or, the cosmic Ten Commandments, and the cosmic Book of Life.

We now call forth from the entire Planetary and Cosmic Hierarchy and all the inner-plane masters that each person has brought to this festival, for a combined light shower the likes of which this world has never known.

Let us close this meditation by repeating out loud together the famous mantra from The Keys of Enoch. *Please repeat after me:*

Kodoish, Kodoish, Kodoish, Adonai, 'Tsebayoth! Holy, Holy, Holy is the Lord God of Hosts!

We now call forth our inner-plane spiritual hosts and request to be taken together in our group merkabah back into our physical bodies in the auditorium in Mount Shasta.

APPENDIX B

New Meditations of 1998

Here are four brand-new meditations I created just before this book was ready for house publication. I include them here for your enjoyment and edification.

+ The Seven Levels of Initiation within
  the Great Pyramid
+ Cosmic Ascension Activations in the
  Temple of God
+ Updated Wesak Ceremony Meditation
+ Ascension-Activation Meditation in the
  Golden Chamber of Melchizedek

The Seven Levels of Initiation within the Great Pyramid

Let us now close our eyes.

We now call forth the Cosmic and Planetary Hierarchy to help in this meditation: Isis, Osiris, Thoth, Horus, Master Serapis Bey, and the Ptahs and the Melchizedeks of the Ancient Order of Melchizedek.

Isis now steps forward in splendid glory, shimmering in a sea of golden white light. She now lifts up her spiritual veils and embraces the entire group in a giant merkabah in the form of a twelve-pointed star.

Isis now carries us to Egypt, where we land at the foot of the Sphinx. Let us take careful note of the form of the Sphinx, seeing the perfect blend of the divine feminine and divine masculine.

Just as Isis blends with Osiris, allow the masculine and feminine energies of each one of you to also find the perfect balance within yourself.

As this preparatory process is completed, we travel now through the subterranean levels of the Sphinx into the Great Pyramid of Giza.

Feel now the intensity of the energies of antiquity as they stimulate and reawaken the ancient knowledge that abides within each one of us.

See here a lake of midnight-blue waters and several streams that run through this level.

Notice that the water reflects an underground moon, shimmering platinum-silver and gold upon the waters.

We are inwardly aware that these energies radiate the qualities of the divine

Mother herself.

While meditating in the stillness of the energies of the divine Mother, the divine Ptah, also known as Thoth/Hermes, appears in radiant splendor.

He lovingly takes us in hand and guides us into a chamber within the Great Pyramid, known as the Well of Life.

There Thoth asks us to gently lie down on a soft white mattress, covering us with golden white blankets after we lay our head upon a silk pillow.

Thoth then gently takes us in our soul body up the shaft of the Well of Life to the chamber of new birth, also known as the Queen's Chamber.

There we are met by Isis and Osiris. Isis blesses us with an outpouring of goddess love, gentleness, purity, tenderness, nurturing, compassion and mercy.

Osiris then steps forward and blesses us with divine strength, decisiveness, courage and spiritual discernment.

Feel these masculine and feminine energies merge now in perfect balance.

Isis and Osiris now lead us in our soul body to the King's Chamber of Initiation. We are now asked to lie down again, this time in our soul body, on a platinum mattress of light, with a platinum pillow and blanket.

As we look up, we see the top of the pyramid, with a gigantic capstone crystal shining divine light into the chamber. Surrounding us are Isis, Osiris, Thoth, Master Serapis and Horus. They collectively chant the Om mantra.

We are now telepathically told that we will be going through seven levels of initiatory testing, through a series of seven questions. A yes response to each question will allow us to pass this initiation and go to the next one.

Initiation and question 1: Do you choose to be the master of your physical body and lower appetites?

Initiation and question 2: Do you choose to be the master of your emotions and astral/desire body?

Initiation and question 3: Do you choose to be the master of your mind and negative ego?

Initiation and question 4: Do you choose to let go of all your attachments to people, places and things, keeping only preferences?

Initiation and queston 5: Do you choose to begin now the process of merging with your monad and/or mighty I Am Presence, and to be freed from all spiritual blindness?

Initiation and question 6: Do you choose to take on the responsibility and spiritual leadership that accompanies passing this ascension initiation?

Initiation and question 7: Do you choose to live on Earth as the mighty I Am Presence in a totally integrated and egoless manner and in service to all sentient beings?

As these seven initiations are passed, Thoth steps forward and performs a blessing over our head and intones the following statement:

"Thou art crowned in the Hall of Renunciation so that hereafter thou mayest wear a crown of life that fadeth not away."

Isis now steps forward and takes us by the hand in our soul body to the star Sirius, also known as the Great White Lodge. There we see a temple carved of crystal and diamond.

You are asked, "By whose name do you seek admission?"

Isis replies, "In the name of the Mighty Ones, the Sons and Daughters of Melchizedek the Just, the Grand Carpenters of the Universe of Worlds of Male and Female, by whom all things are made."

We walk with Isis up seven sacred steps to stand in the midst of the pure white light. As we stand in the light, Master Serapis Bey steps forward with the ascension flame from Luxor. He now sends a purifying current into our entire twelve-body system.

Osiris now steps forward, and with a wave of his hand fully anchors into the core of our being, our anointed Christ overself body and our zohar body of light. He also now anchors into our twelve-body system our thirty-six chakras and our 99 percent planetary light and love quotient.

Hermes/Thoth now places wings on our feet and guides us to Horus, where we find ourselves within his sacred left eye. Here the right side of our brain is totally activated. The higher emotional and intuitive qualities are cleansed of any hindrances or encumbrances.

We now find ourselves within the right eye of Horus. Here we drink in the essence of divine logic, the understanding of sacred geometries and the wisdom within the language of light.

Melchizedek, the Universal Logos, now steps forward out of the brilliant light with his rod of power. He touches us on our third eye and we are officially crowned Melchizedeks and full-fledged ascended masters.

We now find ourselves in a large auditorium, surrounded by the Egyptian contingency of masters, fellow Melchizedek priests and priestesses and the entire Planetary and Cosmic Hierarchy.

Lord Buddha steps forth, and with his rod of initiation anoints us on our crown chakra, welcoming us into the ranks of planetary service.

Lord Maitreya steps forward and places around our necks an ankh necklace made of gold with a radiant crystal in the center.

Sananda places around our shoulders a white robe, symbolic of the purity of spirit we have attained.

Horus now steps forward and places a sacred scarab in the palm of our hands, symbolic of divine protection.

The lord and lady masters of Sirius place upon our heads the hierophant's hat. This hat is symbolic of our status as priest and/or priestess in the Order of Melchizedek.

As this final gift is given, our ascension and resurrection as the fully integrated mighty I Am Presence on Earth is complete.

The congregation of masters rejoice as new fully realized ascended masters of the Great White Lodge and fellow Melchizedeks have joined their ranks. All the masters now bow to the mighty I Am Presence and the integrated Christs we have become.

For those who are riding the wave of cosmic ascension, which refers to initiations eight through twelve, allow these energies to now pour into and through you.

For those who are still working on taking your full ascension initiations, please know that this meditative experience has laid the foundation for enormous acceleration of your process.

Take a moment now to fully enjoy the spiritual magnitude of what you have received and been blessed with. [Pause]

Isis now steps forward and once again embraces and enfolds us in her divine merkabah.

We now find ourselves gliding back from Sirius to Egypt, then back to Mount Shasta and into the auditorium and our physical bodies.

As a final benediction and completion of this Egyptian meditation and of this Wesak weekend experience, his holiness the Lord Sai Baba now steps forward in etheric form into the auditorium. He is wearing his orange robe and radiating light like a magnificent sun.

For his final benediction and blessing, he showers the entire auditorium with his sacred vibhuti ash. This sacred ash carries in its essence the purest unconditional love.

Breathe and drink in this love. Allow this cosmic and universal love to fill every cell, molecule, atom and electron of your being. [Pause]

Send this love now to all of your brothers and sisters around the globe, and to all sentient beings.

Cosmic Ascension Activations in the Temple of God

Close your eyes and take a deep breath. Exhale.

We call forth all the masters of the Planetary and Cosmic Hierarchy to help in this meditation.

We call forward Melchizedek, the Mahatma, Metatron and Archangel Michael to bring forth a platinum net to remove any and all imbalanced energies.

We now call forth our inner-plane spiritual hosts to bring forth a gigantic interdimensional crystalline merkabah.

This merkabah is in the form of a dome-shaped mothership with windows covering the top of the dome. See yourself now entering this domed merkabah with everyone in attendance both on the inner and outer planes.

As everyone finds seats, the gigantic domed merkabah begins to rise and we look out the windows.

As we rise, we find ourselves moving through a sea of interdimensional color.

We first rise up through the red dimensional frequency.

Then up through the orange frequencies.

Now the yellow frequencies.

The emerald-green frequencies.

Now the blue frequencies.

The indigo spectrum.

Now we move into the violet frequencies, lifting higher and higher.

And now into the ultraviolet.

We move up higher still into the frequencies of white light as we begin to leave the planetary dimensions of reality.

Rising higher still, now into the solar dimensions of Helios and Vesta. We are immersed in the color spectrum of copper-gold.

We rise higher now into the galactic regions of Melchior, which are golden in color.

We continue to rise into the universal realms of Melchizedek, composed of the most rarefied and refined golden hues.

We rise even higher through the multiuniversal levels of platinum space.

Rising higher and higher, we now enter into the very heart of Father/Mother God at the 352nd level of divinity. The merkabah now lands within the pure colorless light of the Godhead.

The merkabah immediately disappears. We are now in the most glorious spiritual cathedral the mind and heart could possibly imagine. We have entered the Temple of God as a special dispensation of God and the Cosmic and Planetary Hierarchy for this Wesak. This temple is also known on the inner realms as the Temple of I Am That I Am.

See and feel with all your inner senses the sanctified place we now find ourselves in at this most blessed moment. [Pause.]

His holiness Lord Melchizedek, the Universal Logos, now steps forward in a radiance of golden white light. With his sacred rod of initiation in hand, he now brings it forward to touch each person's crown chakra. This immediately awakens and reactivates the key codes, fire letters and sacred geometries of the ancient Order of Melchizedek.

The Mahatma, also known as the Avatar of Synthesis, now steps forward in a magnificent auric field of rainbow-colored white light. He reaches into the very core of each person's cellular being and installs the Crystal of Synthesis that has never been anchored and activated on Earth before. This will activate and stabilize an aura of harmony and unity within each of you. This will also bring you into divine resonance with the All That Is.

Archangel Metatron now steps forward wearing a robe of electric platinum light. He now places within each person the God electron into the heart center. This crystal stimulates the removal of the veils hiding the hidden chambers of light.

Feel now a new awakening to truth arising within you.

Now stepping forward are the cosmic trinity of Melchizedek, the Mahatma and Metatron in unified magnificence. They now collectively bring forth their combined universal rod of light to increase ascension potential a thousandfold.

Archangel Michael now steps forward with his blue-flame sword. He now materializes an exact etheric duplicate in each person's right hand, a gift and symbol of his eternal protection and connection with you.

His holiness the Lord Sai Baba, the Cosmic Christ, now steps forward in his flaming orange robe. He now places within each person's heart a rose quartz crystal filled with his eternal energy and love. This sacred gift serves as a symbol of his eternal love connection with you.

His holiness the Lord of Sirius, from the Great White Lodge, steps forward in flowing robes of white light. He now presents to each person a golden key as a special dispensation for Wesak. This key holds the matrix that unlocks the secret chambers in Shamballa and the Great White Lodge.

Now steps forward Vywamus in a brilliant aura of yellow-gold light. He offers the gift of expansion of each person's spiritual and psychic inner senses for the purpose of world service.

Now stepping forward in a blaze of copper-gold are Helios and Vesta, our Solar Logos. They collectively ignite the solar essence within each person present. This gift and activation forms a permanent deep integration with the Great Central Sun.

Now stepping forward is the ascended master Djwhal Khul in a radiant field of electric-blue light. He brings forth the gift and blessing this evening of brain illumination. This profound gift is now serving to fully activate the seventy-two areas of the mind.

Stepping forward now is the beloved Lord Maitreya, the Planetary Christ. He comes clad in a robe of golden white light within an aura of pink, radiating from his heart chakra. He offers first the gift of an archetypal imprinting of his universal love into each person's chakra system. He now seals this sanctified blessing into each person's auric field with a wave of his hand.

To close this ascension-activation meditation, the seven chohans of the seven rays step forward one by one to make their personal offerings.

El Morya steps forward with the gift and activation of greater personal power for each person in daily life.

Beloved Master Kuthumi steps forward with the gift and activation of greater heart/mind integration.

Master Serapis Bey steps forward with the gift and activation of the quickening of the ascension process. He also offers a personal invitation to come to his ascension retreat in Luxor on the inner plane.

Master Hilarion steps forward with the gift and activation of a greater understanding of the science involved in the manifestation of the new age.

Beloved Sananda steps forward with the gift and activation of greater devotion and commitment to the higher spiritual principles and ideals for which you stand. He also installs in this moment a special encodement to activate the devotion to compassion.

Saint Germain steps forward with the gift and activation of a greater power, faith and strength in our daily life in using the violet flame.

Take a moment silently now to inwardly thank God and the cosmic and planetary masters for the gifts and blessings that have been bestowed this evening. [Pause.]

We find ourselves now magically sitting back in the dome-shaped crystalline merkabah. Feel it begin to descend, first through the platinum fields, then the golden dimensions, then copper-gold, then white light.

We are descending farther down now through the ultraviolet, violet, indigo, blue, green, yellow, orange and red color spectra.

Finally, feel yourself coming back into your physical body.

Now ground yourselves firmly back to the Earth and into this auditorium, carrying fully within yourselves all the gifts, love, activations and light just received.

When you are ready, open your eyes.

Updated Wesak Ceremony Meditation

The meditation we are now about to begin is the highlight of the Wesak celebration weekend.

Close your eyes and take a deep breath. Exhale.

We call forth the entire Planetary and Cosmic Hierarchy, including all the archangels, angels and elohim, to help in this

meditation.

We also call forth the anchoring and activation of our twelve higher bodies, including the zohar body and the anointed Christ overself body.

We call forth the full opening now of all our chakras, all the petals in all the chakras and all the facets of each individual chakra.

We are now going to soul-travel together to the Wesak Valley in the Himalayas. There we will experience the Wesak ceremony conducted by the inner-plane ascended masters, which has been celebrated for eons at the Taurus full moon.

Let us now prepare ourselves for this holy and sanctified experience with a moment of silence. [Pause.]

We now call forward our inner-plane spiritual hosts and ask for the re-creation of our group merkabah, like a gigantic tetrahedral light crystal.

We ask now to be taken to the Wesak Valley in the Himalayas to experience the annual Wesak ceremony.

As we travel now through time and space, feel your energies blending with all the other groups participating in Wesak around the globe this night.

Let us feel ourselves now descending into the Wesak Valley, joining all the other ascended masters, initiates and disciples.

See and/or feel the presence of Lord Maitreya, Saint Germain and Allah Gobi. See these three masters standing in a triangular formation around a bowl of water that sits atop a very large crystal.

See and feel the rest of the masters of the Spiritual Hierarchy standing in a circle around these three.

Just before the moment of the rising of the full moon, which is now upon us on the inner plane, the expectancy and excitement begins to build.

We all now await the arrival of Lord Buddha.

As the moment of the rising moon now takes place, a stillness settles upon the gathered crowd, and all look toward the northeast.

Certain ritualistic movements and mantras sound forth under the guidance of the seven chohans of the seven rays.

In the far-distant northeast, a tiny speck can be seen in the sky.

This speck gradually grows larger and larger, and we see the Buddha seated cross-legged. He is clad in a saffron-colored robe and is bathed in light and color, his hands extended in blessing.

While he hovers above the bowl of water, a great mantra is sounded forth by Lord Maitreya that is used only once a year at Wesak. It marks the supreme moment of intensive spiritual effort of all initiates and masters in attendance for the entire year.

This invocation sets up an enormous vibration of spiritual current.

In this moment let us watch Lord Buddha hovering over this bowl of water, transmitting his divine and cosmic energies into the water and through Lord Maitreya.

The energy is then sent forth by Lord Maitreya to the entire Spiritual Hierarchy and into all of us, who form a part of this hierarchy on Earth.

Feel this massive downpouring of cosmic energies from the Planetary and Cosmic Hierarchy now flowing through us.

As these energies move through us allow them now to flow out into the world and into the Earth herself.

As these energies continue to pour in, see the bowl of water that had sat on the large crystal being passed around the gathered crowd.

See and feel yourself taking a sip of this holy, blessed and sanctified water.

See yourself now walking toward Lord Buddha, Lord Maitreya and Sanat Kumara.

Stand now before these three glorious masters and share with them on the inner plane what you feel your service work, mission and puzzle piece is in God's divine plan on Earth.

Take this time also to make any prayer requests to God and these three masters for help in manifesting your mission.

Also make any personal prayer request on behalf of yourself or others.

Let us now take thirty seconds of silence to allow you to make these prayer requests. [Pause.]

Feel and visualize these prayers being answered, and thank Lord Buddha, Lord Maitreya and Sanat Kumara for their guidance and blessings.

You move away now from the crowd, almost gliding rather than walking.

You find yourself on a small mountain peak looking down on the gathered crowd. Appearing above you is Melchizedek, the Mahatma and Metatron.

Feel now these three cosmic masters touch your crown chakra with their individual and combined cosmic light rods. Feel a downpouring of cosmic current directly from the heart of God.

Feel your entire twelve-body system now become illuminated with the light, love and power of God.

Remain still now for one minute of silence to be given the highest potential voltage your twelve-body system can receive at this time. [Pause.]

This is a sanctified gift and blessing from Lord Melchizedek, the Mahatma and Archangel Metatron, specifically for this Wesak ceremony.

Take one final moment now to fully absorb the energies of this most powerful and blessed moment.

Now integrate into the core of your being the totality of all the Wesak energies set in motion by Lord Buddha and this sanctified gathering of planetary and cosmic beings.

Breathe these collective energies into every cell and molecule of your twelve-body system.

Find yourself once again standing within the ceremonial circle and gathering around the large crystal and bowl.

See and feel Lord Buddha begin to rise in the lotus posture, floating back to the northeast to the realm from whence he came.

As Lord Buddha again becomes a small speck in the distance, see and feel the arrival of our inner-plane spiritual hosts with their gigantic tetrahedral light-crystal merkabah.

Feel yourself now joining this merkabah in total oneness, joy and love.

Feel again the tremendous illumination of energies in your auric field, which has been vastly expanded by participating in this experience.

Feel an enormous upwelling of love and unity for all your brothers and sisters who have shared this experience with you.

Feel the group merkabah floating through space and time and once again returning us to Mount Shasta and into this auditorium.

I now call forth from the inner plane the divine Mother, the lady masters and all the Goddess energies of the cosmos to give forth their final blessings and benediction to close this Wesak ceremony.

They bring forth now a light shower of core love in the form of a downpouring of pink, magenta and violet rose petals. See and feel these rose petals showering not only everyone in this auditorium, but all sentient beings on Earth.

See these petals now being absorbed into the very core heart of the Earth herself.

Let us receive this final Wesak ceremony blessing now.

When you feel complete, you may open your eyes.

Ascension-Activation Meditation in the Golden Chamber of Melchizedek

Close your eyes and take a deep breath. Exhale.

We call all the masters of the Planetary and Cosmic Hierarchy to help in this meditation.

We call Melchizedek, Mahatma and Metatron to bring forth a platinum net to remove any and all imbalanced energies.

We now call forth to the seven chohans, Djwhal Khul, Lord Maitreya and Lord Buddha to provide a gigantic group merkabah for all in attendance.

We ask now to be taken spiritually to the Golden Chamber of Melchizedek in the universal core.

We call forth each person's 144 soul extensions from their monad and/or mighty I Am Presence to join us for this meditation if they choose.

We call to the seven chohans for the opening of all chakras, the ascension chakra, and all petals, chambers and facets of all chakras.

We call to Archangel Metatron for the permanent anchoring and activation of the microtron.

We call to the Lord of Sirius for the anchoring and activation of the appropriate scrolls of wisdom and knowledge from the Great White Lodge on Sirius.

We call forth Sanat Kumara, Vywamus and Lenduce for help in establishing each person's planetary and cosmic antakarana back to each person's oversoul, monad and to God.

We call Melchizedek, Mahatma, Metatron, the Elohim Councils and the archangels for the permanent anchoring and activation of the planetary and cosmic Tree of Life.

We request the complete opening and activation of the seven cosmic seals and the ten Sephiroth as well as the hidden Sephiroth of Daath within this cosmic Tree of Life.

We call to the archangels for the full anchoring and activation of our fifty chakras, which takes us through planetary ascension.

We request as well the anchoring and activation of our 330 chakras, helping us move in the direction of realizing God on Earth.

We call for the permanent anchoring and activation of our twelve bodies, including the solar, galactic and universal bodies.

We call forth the permanent anchoring and activation of the sixty-four keys of Enoch in all five sacred languages.

We call forth the anchoring and activation of the yod spectrum and the ten lost cosmic rays.

We call forth the decadelta light encodements and emanations from the ten superscripts of the divine mind.

We call forth from Melchizedek, Mahatma, Metatron and Archangel Michael for the highest possible building of our light quotient at this time.

We call forth to Metatron for the anchoring and activation of the seventy-six names of Metatron to permanently flow through us.

We call forth to the divine Mother, Sai Baba, the Virgin Mary, Quan Yin, Isis, Lord Maitreya and Sananda for the highest possible anchoring of love quotient.

We call forth the removal of all veils of light and time

We call forth the highest possible integration and cleansing of soul extensions from our monad and our higher group monadic consciousness that is available to us at this time.

We call forth the anchoring and activation of the garment of Shaddai, also known as the lightbody of Metatron.

We call to the mighty archangels for permanent anchoring and activation of the twelve heavenly houses and twelve cosmic stations.

We call forth the anchoring and activation of the star codes of Melchizedek.

We call forth the anchoring and activations of the light encodements of the Mahatma.

We call forth the anchoring and activation of Melchizedek's transmitting system into our chakras and ask that they be tuned up to each person's highest potential.

We now call forth a cleansing and clearing of all our karma.

We now call forth a cleansing and clearing of our monad.

We now call forth a cleansing and clearing back to our original covenant with God.

We call to Melchizedek, the Mahatma and Metatron for the permanent anchoring and activation of the ultimate Great Central Sun and God's own heart into the core of our being.

We call forth to the source of our cosmic day and Melchizedek for the anchoring and activation of the forty-three christed universes.

We call forth to Melchizedek, the Universal Logos, to initiate each person present into the Order of Melchizedek, if it is each person's free choice to receive this blessing now.

We call forth the entire Planetary and Cosmic Hierarchy and hereby request a complete merging of their lightbodies with this group body for all those who would like to receive this blessing now.

We call to Melchizedek, the Mahatma, Metatron, Archangel Michael and the Planetary Hierarchy for the anchoring and activation of the anointed Christ overself body, our zohar body, our overself body, our electromagnetic body, our gematrian body, our eka body, our epi-kenetic body, our higher Adam Kadmon body and the Lord's mystical body as described in The Keys of Enoch.

We call forth Djwhal Khul, Lord Maitreya and Lord Buddha for the permanent anchoring of the greater flame of the monad and mighty I Am Presence into the lesser flame of the personality and soul incarnated on Earth.

We call forth God, the Mahatma, Melchizedek, Metatron, Elohim Councils and the archangels to now anchor from the cosmic Treasury of Light the light packets of information from the Tablets of Creation, the elohim scriptures, the Torah Or, the cosmic Ten Commandments and the cosmic Book of Life.

We now call forth from the entire Planetary and Cosmic Hierarchy and all the inner-plane masters that each person has brought to this festival for a combined light and love shower the likes of which this world has never been before known.

We now call forth a baptism of the Holy Spirit.

We now call forth our inner-plane spiritual hosts and request to be taken together in our group merkabah back down the dimensions of reality into our earthly physical bodies.

Feel this taking place now, bringing with you all the glorious light and love you have received in this meditation.

When you feel comfortable and ready, you can open your eyes.

A Special Thanks to My Readers

. . . for sharing my journaling process through the path of initiations. It is in the sharing of one person's process that the process of others can become a little less burdensome, for you learn you are not alone, nor do you need to reinvent certain insights that a fellow traveler on the path has already found of great value. It is in that spirit that I have shared my personal log with you, and in the same spirit I encourage you to be open with one another. The path of initiation is a group journey. I thank you again for partaking of my personal journey with me. Namasté.

Dr. Joshua David Stone

the ENCYCLOPEDIA of the SPIRITUAL PATH

*Dr. Stone has a PhD in Transpersonal Psychology and is a licensed marriage,
family and child counselor in Los Angeles, California. On a spiritual level,
he anchors the Melchizedek Synthesis Light Academy & Ashram.*

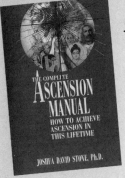

✦ THE COMPLETE ASCENSION MANUAL

How to Achieve Ascension in This Lifetime

BOOK I of a fourteen volume series,
THE EASY-TO-READ ENCYCLOPEDIA OF THE SPIRITUAL PATH.

For those who have the intention but lack the lifetime it would take
to study the entire history of spirituality, this extraordinary compendium is a great gift. Stone has gleaned the essentials from vast
research as well as intuitive information and woven them into a sim-

• The monad, soul and personality ple and engrossing exploration of self-realization.

• God and the cosmic Hierarchy

• Ascension, the sixth initation

It is both practical and enlightening, a guidebook through the past
and how-to manual for ascension.

• Twenty ascension techniques to
build your Light quotient

• Mantras, names of God and
words of power

Created to be read as an overview of the spiritual path, this book
explores the world's great religions, Great Masters, spiritual psychology and the Ascended Masters' teachings with specific steps to accelerate our process of ascension.

• 147 Golden Keys to achieving
ascension in this lifetime

SOFTCOVER 297P.

ISBN 0-929385-55-1

✦ ASCENSION AND ROMANTIC RELATIONSHIPS
with REV. JANNA SHELLEY PARKER

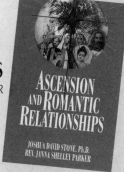

BOOK XIII of a fourteen volume series,
THE EASY-TO-READ ENCYCLOPEDIA OF THE SPIRITUAL
PATH.

Inspired by Djwhal Khul, Dr. Joshua David Stone has written a
unique book about relationships from the perspective of the
soul and monad rather than just the personality. This presents
a broader picture of the problems and common traps of romantic relationships and offers much deeper and spiritually sound
guidance and advice. Drawing on his experience as a psy-
chotherapist and licensed marriage, family and child counselor,
Dr. Stone has written an excellent manual for initiates, disciples
and ascended beings.

SOFTCOVER 184P.

ISBN 1-891824-16-3

• Finding Your Mate
• Bonding Patterns
• Unconditional Love and
  Commitment
• Competition and the Path of
  Ascension
• Our Sexual Selves
• The Differing Elevator Syndrome
• In Search of Your Soulmate: The
  Deeper Meaning
• Spiritual Parenting
• The True Meaning of Marriage
• God, the Consummate Union
• Living the Spiritual Life Together
• The Golden Keys to Effective
  Romantic Relationships

DR. JOSHUA DAVID STONE

Dr. Stone has a PhD in Transpersonal Psychology and is a licensed marriage, family and child counselor in Los Angeles, California. On a spiritual level, he anchors the Melchizedek Synthesis Light Academy & Ashram.

THE ENCYCLOPEDIA OF THE SPIRITUAL PATH

The Encyclopedia of the Spiritual Path consists of thirteen books and an index in this ongoing series on the subject of ascension, self-realization and a further deepening of the ascended-master teachings.

These books collectively explore the deepest levels and understanding of ascension through the personal, planetary and cosmic levels, offering the reader tools to work with that span the spectrum of all the bodies and ultimately bring them into the subtle realms of cosmic ascension.

These tools are practical gems for the purification, healing, cleansing, acceleration and ascension process that cover the individual incarnated soul and extend into the vast monadic and cosmic realms.

 # ASCENSION COMPLETE INDEX

Complete Ascension Index
Book XIV of the multi-volume series,
THE EASY-TO-READ ENCYCLOPEDIA OF THE SPIRITUAL PATH

The Encyclopedia of the Spiritual Path consists of thirteen books and an index in this ongoing series on the subject of ascension, self-realization and a further deepening of the ascended-master teachings.

These books collectively explore the deepest levels and understanding of ascension through the personal, planetary and cosmic levels, offering the reader tools to work with that span the spectrum of all of the bodies and ultimately bring them into the subtle realms of cosmic ascension.

These tools are practical gems for the purification, healing, cleansing, acceleration and ascension process that covers the individual incarnated soul and extends into the vast monadic and cosmic realms.

Books in the Ascension Series by Dr. Joshua David Stone:
THE COMPLETE ASCENSION MANUAL - How to Achieve Ascension in This Lifetime
SOUL PSYCHOLOGY - Keys to Ascension
BEYOND ASCENSION - How to Complete the Seven Levels of Initiation
COSMIC ASCENSION - Your Cosmic Map Home
A BEGINNER'S GUIDE TO THE PATH OF ASCENSION
GOLDEN KEYS TO ASCENSION AND HEALING - Revelations of Sai Baba and the Ascended Masters
MANUAL FOR PLANETARY LEADERSHIP
YOUR ASCENSION MISSION - Embracing your Puzzle Piece
REVELATIONS OF A MELCHIZEDEK INITIATE
HOW TO TEACH ASCENSION CLASSES
ASCENSION AND ROMANTIC RELATIONSHIPS

ISBN 1-891824-30-9
Softcover 233p.

EASY ORDER
24 HOURS
A DAY

Order ONLINE!
www.light
technology.com

Order by Mail
Send To:
Light Technology Publishing
PO Box 3540
Flagstaff, AZ 86003

Order by Phone
800-450-0985
(928) 526-1345

Order by Fax
800-393-7017
(928) 714-1132

Visit our online bookstore: www.lighttechnology.com

THE EXPLORER

THE SERIES Humans—creators in training—have a purpose and destiny so heartwarmingly, profoundly glorious that it is almost unbelievable from our present dimensional perspective. Humans are great lightbeings from beyond this creation, gaining experience in dense physicality. This truth about the great human genetic experiment of the Explorer Race and the mechanics of creation is being revealed for the first time by Zoosh and his friends through superchannel Robert Shapiro. These books read like adventure stories as we follow the clues from this creation that we live in out to the Council of Creators and beyond.

❶ THE EXPLORER RACE

You individuals reading this are truly a result of the genetic experiment on Earth. You are beings who uphold the principles of the Explorer Race. The information in this book is designed to show you who you are and give you an evolutionary understanding of your past that will help you now. The key to empowerment in these days is to not know everything about your past but to know what will help you now.

Your souls have been here for a while on Earth and have been trained in Earthlike conditions. This education has been designed so that you would have the ability to explore all levels of responsibility—results, effects and consequences—and take on more responsibilities.

Your number one function right now is your status of Creator apprentice, which you have achieved through years and lifetimes of sweat. You are constantly being given responsibilities by the Creator that would normally be things that Creator would do. The responsibility and the destiny of the Explorer Race is not only to explore, but to create.

574p $25.00 ISBN 0-929385-38-1

❷ ETs and the EXPLORER RACE

In this book, Robert channels Joopah, a Zeta Reticulan now in the ninth dimension, who continues the story of the great experiment—the Explorer Race—from the perspective of his civilization. The Zetas would have been humanity's future selves had not humanity re-created the past and changed the future.

237p $14.95 ISBN 0-929385-79-9

❸ EXPLORER RACE: ORIGINS and the NEXT 50 YEARS

This volume has so much information about who we are and where we came from—the source of male and female beings, the war of the sexes, the beginning of the linear mind, feelings, the origin of souls—it is a treasure trove. In addition, there is a section that relates to our near future—how the rise of global corporations and politics affects our future, how to use benevolent magic as a force of creation and how we will go out to the stars and affect other civilizations. Astounding information.

339p $14.95 ISBN 0-929385-95-0

❹ EXPLORER RACE: CREATORS and FRIENDS the MECHANICS of CREATION

Now that you have a greater understanding of who you are in the larger sense, it is necessary to remind you of where you came from, the true magnificence of your being, to have some of your true peers talk to you. You must understand that you are creators in training, and yet you were once a portion of Creator. One could certainly say, without being magnanimous, that you are still a portion of Creator, yet you are training for the individual responsibility of being a creator, to give your Creator a coffee break.

This book will give you peer consultation. it will allow you to understand the vaster qualities and help you remember the nature of the desires that drive any creator, the responsibilities to which that creator must answer, the reaction a creator must have to consequences and the ultimate reward of any creator. This book will help you appreciate all of the above and more.

435p $19.95 ISBN 1-891824-01-5

❺ EXPLORER RACE: PARTICLE PERSONALITIES

All around you in every moment you are surrounded by the most magical and mystical beings. They are too small for you to see as single individuals, but in groups you know them as the physical matter of your daily life. Particles who might be considered either atoms or portions of atoms consciously view the vast spectrum of reality, yet also have a sense of personal memory like your own linear memory. These particles remember where they have been and what they have done in their infinitely long lives. Some of the particles we hear from are Gold, Mountain Lion, Liquid Light, Uranium, the Great Pyramid's Capstone, This Orb's Boundary, Ice and Ninth-Dimensional Fire.

237p $14.95 ISBN 0-929385-97-7

❻ EXPLORER RACE and BEYOND

With a better idea of how creation works, we go back to the Creator's advisors and receive deeper and more profound explanations of the roots of the Explorer Race. The liquid Domain and the Double Diamond portal share lessons given to the roots on their way to meet the Creator of this Universe and finally the roots speak of their origins and their incomprehensibly long journey here.

360p $14.95 ISBN 1-891824-06-6

RACE SERIES

CHANNELED THROUGH ROBERT SHAPIRO

Superchannel Robert Shapiro can communicate with any personality anywhere and anywhen. He has been a professional channel for over twenty years and channels with an exceptionally clear and profound connection.

❼ EXPLORER RACE: The COVNCIL of CREATORS

The thirteen core members of the Council of Creators discuss their adventures in coming to awareness of themselves and their journeys on the way to the Council on this level. They discuss the advice and oversight they offer to all creators, including the creator of this local universe. These beings are wise, witty and joyous, and their stories of Love's Creation creates an expansion of our concepts as we realize that we live in an expanded, multiple-level reality.

237p $14.95 ISBN 1-891824-13-9

❽ EXPLORER RACE and ISIS

This is an amazing book. It has priestess training, Shamanic training, Isis' adventures with Explorer Race beings—before Earth and on Earth—and an incredibly expanded explanation of the dynamics of the Explorer Race. Isis is the prototypal loving, nurturing, guiding feminine being, the focus of feminine energy. She has the ability to expand limited thinking without making people with limited beliefs feel uncomfortable. She is a fantastic storyteller and all of her stories are teaching stories. If you care about who you are, why you are here, where you are going and what life is all about—pick up this book. You won't lay it down until you are through, and then you will want more.

317p $14.95 ISBN 1-891824-11-2

❾ EXPLORER RACE and JESUS

The core personality of that being known on the Earth as Jesus, along with his students and friends, describes with clarity and love his life and teaching 2000 years ago. He states that his teaching is for all people of all races in all countries. Jesus announces here for the first time that he and two others, Buddha and Mohammed, will return to Earth from their place of being in the near future. And a fourth being, a child already born now on Earth, will become a teacher and prepare humanity for their return. So heartwarming and interesting, you won't want to put it down.

354p $16.95 ISBN 1-891824-14-7

EXPLORER RACE: EARTH HISTORY AND LOST CIVILIZATIONS

Earth's recorded history goes back only a few thousand years, its archaeological history a few thousand more. Now this book opens up the past as if a light was ❿ turned on in the darkness, and we see the incredible panorama of brave souls coming from other planets to settle on different parts of Earth. We watch the origins of tribal groups and the rise and fall of civilizations, and we can begin to understand the source of the wondrous diversity of plants, animals and humans that we enjoy here on beautiful Mother Earth

310p $14.95 ISBN 1-891824-20-1

⑪ EXPLORER RACE: ET VISITORS SPEAK

Even as you are searching the sky for extraterrestrials and their spaceships, ETs are here on planet Earth—they are stranded, visiting, exploring, studying the culture, healing the Earth of trauma brought on by irresponsible mining, or researching the history of Christianity over the last 2000 years. Some are in human guise, some are in spirit form, some look like what we call animals as they come from the species' home planet and interact with those of their fellow beings that we have labeled cats or cows or elephants. Some are brilliant cosmic mathematicians with a sense of humor presently living here as penguins; some are fledgling diplomats training for future postings on Earth when we have ET embassies here. In this book, these fascinating beings share their thoughts, origins and purposes for being here.

350p $14.95 ISBN 1-891824-28-7

⑫ EXPLORER RACE: Techniques for GENERATING SAFETY

Wouldn't you like to generate safety—so you could go wherever you need to go, do whatever you need to do—in a benevolent, safe and loving way for yourself? Learn safety as a radiated environment that will allow you to gently take the step into the new time line, into a benevolent future and away from a negative past.

$9.95 ISBN 1-891824-26-0

The Origin ... The Purpose ... The Future of Humanity

SPEAKS OF MANY TRUTHS AND ZOOSH THROUGH ROBERT SHAPIRO

SHAMANIC SECRETS for MATERIAL MASTERY

Learn to communicate with the planet

This book explores the heart and soul connection between humans and Mother Earth. Through that intimacy, miracles of healing and expanded awareness can flourish.

To heal the planet and be healed as well, we can lovingly extend our energy selves out to the mountains and rivers and intimately bond with the Earth. Gestures and vision can activate our hearts to return us to a healthy, caring relationship with the land we live on.

The character and essence of some of Earth's most powerful features is explored and understood, with exercises given to connect us with those places. As we project our love and healing energy there, we help the Earth to heal from man's destruction of the planet and its atmosphere. Dozens of photographs, maps and drawings assist the process in 25 chapters, which cover the Earth's more critical locations.

$19⁹⁵ SOFTCOVER 498P.
ISBN 1-891824-12-0

Chapter Titles:

- Approaching Material Mastery through Your Physicality
- Three Rivers: The Rhine, the Amazon and the Rio Grande
- Three Lakes: Pyramid Lake, Lake Titicaca and Lake Baikal
- Mountains: Earth's Antennas, Related to the Human Bone Structure
  - Three Mountains: The Cydonia Pyramid, Mount Rushmore and Mount Aspen
  - Mountains in Turkey, Japan and California
  - Eurasia and Man's Skeletal Structure
  - Greenland, the Land of Mystery
  - Africa and North America
  - South and Central America and Australia

- Shamanic Interaction with Natural Life
- Africa and the Caspian and Black Seas
- Mauna Loa, Mount McKinley and Shiprock
- The Gobi Desert
- Old Faithful, Cayman Islands, Blue Mountains and Grandfather Mountain
- Meteor Crater, Angel Falls and Other Unique Locations on the Planet

PART II, THE FOUNDATION OF ONENESS

- The Explorer Race as a Part of Mother Earth's Body
- Spiritual Beings in a Physical World
- Earth Now Releasing Human Resistance to Physical Life
- Healing Prisoners, Teaching Students
- The Shaman's Key: Feeling and the Five Senses
- How to Walk, How To Eat
- Breathing: Something Natural We Overlook
- How to Ask and Let Go, and How to Sleep
- Singing Our Songs
- Some Final Thoughts

SHAMANIC SECRETS for PHYSICAL MASTERY

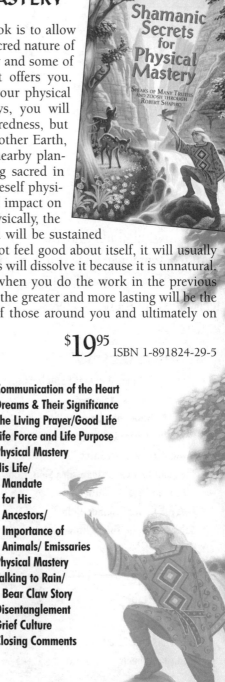

COMING SOON

The purpose of this book is to allow you to understand the sacred nature of your own physical body and some of the magnificent gifts it offers you. When you work with your physical body in these new ways, you will discover not only its sacredness, but how it is compatible with Mother Earth, the animals, the plants, even the nearby planets, all of which you now recognize as being sacred in nature. It is important to feel the value of oneself physically before one can have any lasting physical impact on the world. The less you think of yourself physically, the less likely your physical impact on the world will be sustained by Mother Earth. If a physical energy does not feel good about itself, it will usually be resolved; other physical or spiritual energies will dissolve it because it is unnatural. The better you feel about your physical self when you do the work in the previous book as well as this one and the one to follow, the greater and more lasting will be the benevolent effect on your life, on the lives of those around you and ultimately on your planet and universe. SOFTCOVER 600P.

$19⁹⁵ ISBN 1-891824-29-5

Chapter Titles:

- Cellular Clearing of Traumas, Unresolved Events
- Cellular Memory
- Identifying Your Body's Fear Message
- The Heart Heat Exercise
- Learn Hand Gestures
  - —Remove Self-Doubt
  - —Release Pain or Hate
  - —Clear the Adrenals or Kidneys
  - —Resolve Sexual Dysfunction
- Learning the Card Technique for Clarifying Body Message
- Seeing Life as a Gift
- Relationship of the Soul to Personality
- The New Generation of Children
- The Creator and Religions
- Food, Love & Addictions

- Communication of the Heart
- Dreams & Their Significance
- The Living Prayer/Good Life
- Life Force and Life Purpose
- Physical Mastery
- His Life/ Mandate for His Ancestors/ Importance of Animals/ Emissaries
- Physical Mastery
- Talking to Rain/ Bear Claw Story
- Disentanglement
- Grief Culture
- Closing Comments

Book 10 of the EXPLORER RACE

EARTH HISTORY AND LOST CIVILIZATIONS

by Robert Shapiro/Zoosh

Zoosh reveals that our planet Earth did not originate in this solar system, but the water planet we live on was brought here from Sirius 65 million years ago. Anomalous archaeological finds and the various ET cultures who founded what we now call lost civilizations are explained with such storytelling skill by Speaks of Many Truths that you feel you were there. $14.95 Softcover

NEW RELEASE

ISBN 1-891824-20-1

Chapter Titles:

- Lost Civilizations of Planet Earth in Sirius
- Ancient Artifacts Explained
- Ancient Visitors and Immortal Personalities
- Before and After Earth Was Moved to This Solar System from Sirius
- The Long Journey of Jehovah's Ship, from Orion to Sirius to Earth
- Jehovah Creates Human Beings
- Beings from the Future Academy
- Sumer
- Nazca Lines
- Easter Island
- Laetoli Footprints
- Egypt and Cats
- Three More Civilizations
- Medicine Wheels

- Stonehenge
- Carnac in Brittany
- Egypt
- China
- Tibet and Japan
- Siberia
- Natural Foods/Sacrament of Foods
- SSG's Time-Traveling Interference in Israel Imperils Middle East: How to Resolve It

ROBERT SHAPIRO

ZOOSH AND OTHERS THROUGH ROBERT SHAPIRO

Superchannel Robert Shapiro can communicate with any personality anywhere and anywhen. He has been a professional channel for over twenty-five years and channels with an exceptionally clear and profound connection.

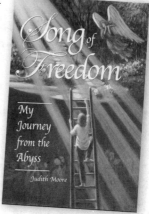

THE ENCYCLOPEDIA OF THE SPIRITUAL PATH

The Encyclopedia of the Spiritual Path consists of thirteen books and an index in this ongoing series on the subject of **ascension**, **self-realization** and a further deepening of the ascended-master teachings.

These books collectively explore the **deepest levels** and understanding of ascension through the personal, planetary and cosmic levels, offering the reader tools to work with that span the spectrum of all the bodies and ultimately bring them into the subtle realms of cosmic ascension.

These tools are practical gems for the **purification, healing, cleansing, acceleration** and **ascension process** that cover the individual incarnated soul and extend into the vast monadic and cosmic realms.

DR. JOSHUA DAVID STONE

Dr. Stone has a Ph.D. in Transpersonal Psychology and is a licensed marriage, family and child counselor in Los Angeles, California. On a spiritual level, he anchors the Melchizedek Synthesis Light Academy & Ashram.

1 THE COMPLETE ASCENSION MANUAL

How to Achieve Ascension in This Lifetime
A synthesis of the past and guidance for ascension. An extraordinary compendium of practical techniques and spiritual history. Compiled from research and channeled information.
SOFTCOVER 297P.   ISBN 0-929385-55-1

2 SOUL PSYCHOLOGY

Keys to Ascension
Modern psychology deals exclusively with personality, ignoring the dimensions of spirit and soul. This book provides groundbreaking theories and techniques for healing and self-realization.
SOFTCOVER 256P.   ISBN 0-929385-56-X

3 BEYOND ASCENSION

How to Complete the Seven Levels of Initiation
Brings forth new channeled material that demystifies the 7 levelsof initiation and how to attain them. It contains new information on how to open and anchor our 36 chakras.
SOFTCOVER 280P.   ISBN 0-929385-73-X

4 HIDDEN MYSTERIES

ETs, Ancient Mystery Schools and Ascension
Explores the unknown and suppressed aspects of Earth's past; reveals new information on the ET movement and secret teachings of the ancient mystery schools.
SOFTCOVER 330P.   ISBN 0-929385-57-8

5 THE ASCENDED MASTERS LIGHT THE WAY

Beacons of Ascension
The lives and teachings of 40 of the world's greatest saints and spiritual beacons provide a blueprint for total self-realization. Guidance from masters.
SOFTCOVER 258P.   ISBN 0-929385-58-6

6 COSMIC ASCENSION

Your Cosmic Map Home
Almost all the books on the planet on the subject of ascension are written about planetary ascension. Now, because of the extraordinary times in which we live, cosmic ascension is available here on Earth! Learn about self-realization, evolvement of nations and more.
SOFTCOVER 263P.   ISBN 0-929385-99-3

7 A BEGINNER'S GUIDE TO THE PATH OF ASCENSION

with REV. JANNA SHELLY PARKER

This volume covers the basics of ascension clearly and completely, from the spiritual hierarchy to the angels and star beings.
SOFTCOVER 166P.   ISBN 1-891824-02-3

8 GOLDEN KEYS TO ASCENSION AND HEALING

Revelations of Sai Baba and the Ascended Masters
This book represents the wisdom of the ascended masters condensed into concise keys that serve as a spiritual guide. These 420 golden keys present the multitude of insights Dr. Stone has gleaned from his own background and his path to God-realization.
SOFTCOVER 205P.   ISBN 1-891824-03-1

9 MANUAL FOR PLANETARY LEADERSHIP

Here at last is an indispensible book that has been urgently needed in these uncertain times, laying out the guidelines for leadership in the world and in one's life. It serves as a reference manual for moral and spiritual living.
SOFTCOVER 283P.   ISBN 1-891824-05-8

10 YOUR ASCENSION MISSION

Embracing Your Puzzle Piece
with REV. JANNA SHELLEY PARKER
This book shows how each person's puzzle piece is just as vital and necessary as any other. Includes all aspects of living the fullest expression of your individuality.
SOFTCOVER 249P.   ISBN 1-891824-09-0

11 REVELATIONS OF A MELCHIZEDEK INITIATE

Dr. Stone's spiritual autobiography, beginning with his ascension initiation and progression into the 12th initiation. Filled with insights, tools and information.
SOFTCOVER 306P.   ISBN 1-891824-10-4

12 HOW TO TEACH ASCENSION CLASSES

This book serves as an ideal foundation for teaching ascension classes and presenting workshops. It covers an entire one- to two-year program of classes.
SOFTCOVER 135P.   ISBN 1-891824-15-5

13 ASCENSION AND ROMANTIC RELATIONSHIPS

with REV. JANNA SHELLEY PARKER
Inspired by Djwhal Khul, Dr. Stone has written a unique book about relationships from the perspective of the soul and monad rather than just the personality. This presents a broad picture of the problems and common traps of romantic relationships and offers much deep advice.
SOFTCOVER 184P.   ISBN 1-891824-16-3

14 ASCENSION COMPLETE INDEX

Ascension Names and Ascended Master Terms Glossary plus a complete index of all thirteen books.   ISBN 1-891824-18-X

LIGHT TECHNOLOGY PUBLISHING
P.O. Box 3540 • Flagstaff, AZ 86003

(800) 450-0985 or (520) 526-1345 • FAX (800) 393-7017 or (520) 714-1132   *. . . or use our online bookstore at www.lighttechnology.com*

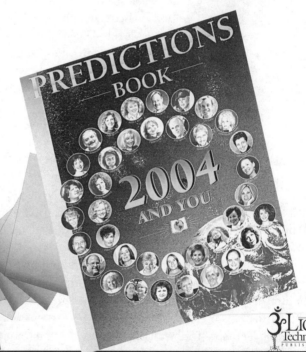